—— Empire of Sacrifice ——

Empire of Sacrifice

The Religious Origins of American Violence

Jon Pahl

NEW YORK UNIVERSITY PRESS

New York and London

NEW YORK UNIVERSITY PRESS
New York and London
www.nyupress.org

Library of Congress Cataloging-in-Publication Data

Pahl, Jon, 1958–
Empire of sacrifice : the religious origins of American violence /
Jon Pahl.
p. cm.
Includes bibliographical references (p.   ) and index.
ISBN-13: 978-0-8147-6762-7 (cl : alk. paper)
ISBN-10: 0-8147-6762-1 (cl : alk. paper)
1. Christianity and culture—United States. 2. Violence—Religious aspects—Christianity.
3. Violence—United States. 4. Sacrifice—Social aspects—United States. 5. United States—
Church history. I. Title.
BR517.P34   2009
261.8—dc22   2009030331

New York University Press books are printed on acid-free paper,
and their binding materials are chosen for strength and durability.
We strive to use environmentally responsible suppliers and materials
to the greatest extent possible in publishing our books.

Manufactured in the United States of America
10 9 8 7 6 5 4 3 2 1

Contents

Tables and Figures

Preface and Acknowledgments

This book is an experiment. It took shape over decades, well before current events and academic fashion made the study of religion and violence popular. All my previous books have touched on the ways that people of faith in the United States sometimes became entangled with violence, and this work pulls together my theoretical and empirical reflections across a range of case studies drawn from various fields. Most of the ideas in these chapters first appeared in classrooms. Since the mid-1990s I have occasionally taught a course entitled Religion and Violence in America, initially at Valparaiso University, later at the Lutheran Theological Seminary at Philadelphia, and most recently at Princeton University. Over those years, my lecture or discussion notes gradually became these chapters, and eventually the chapters became this book. Therefore, while this book is an experiment, it also is well tested in a variety of laboratories, and I know that these materials work in the classroom. It has become my habit to share drafts of my chapters with students, which gives them the benefit of my most current thinking and gives me the benefit of one less lecture to prepare.

Some of these chapters are fuller versions of talks I gave at academic conferences. Parts of a few chapters have been published in abbreviated forms in a variety of mostly obscure, and widely scattered, publications. And a few of the chapters have already been used in other classrooms around the country, by scholars who asked for a printed version of my arguments.

I am grateful to the many scholarly readers of these chapters, and if I have forgotten a student or colleague, I can only beg forgiveness and blame the turtlelike pace of my scholarly production and a less than elephantine memory.

This book is different from the lecture notes or conference papers that preceded it, in that these materials have been tossed around in a variety of conversations and I have been pushed to think through the interrelationships of the topics, both theoretically and empirically. Linking the case studies is thus a sustained effort to clarify how and why Americans—by whom I mean primarily citizens of the United States—tend to be both religious and violent. I use what might seem to be an "old school" model of American studies, in that I seek a consistent thread, historical trajectory, or core to American culture that might explain these tendencies. In fact, though, I have no illusions that this core actually exists. As I point out in the introduction, I am postmodern enough to know that "essentialist" hypotheses say as much about the subject who writes about them as about the object imagined. Although I might appear to be engaged in finding what one early reader called a "historical wholly mammoth," or a "master narrative" from Puritan Boston to the Baghdad adventures of George W. Bush, at the same time I am consciously testing the limits of disciplines, methods, and the use of evidence—thinking outside the typical historical boxes, so to speak—to see what kind of creatures Americans might have been. I am quite aware that mammoths exist now only as fossils, but that does not mean we cannot talk about their place in history. If the patterns I tease out of the historical record do not constitute a "master narrative" or some Frankenstein-like appearance of the American living-dead, it does seem to me that they can plausibly describe some discernible trajectories in the historical evidence. Still, I do not imagine this work being the definitive word on anything. Instead, it is a series of exploratory pieces. Their value, as I conceive of them, is to provoke inquiry, enliven debate, and discover new areas for research by scholars more congenially suited to the archives than I am.

All this is said by way of confession. I explore more fully in the introduction and chapter 1 how I think scholars (and citizens) would benefit from rethinking some rather crucial categories, notably "religion" and "violence," in American history. In the few remaining pages of this preface, I hope to discharge some of the debts I owe to those many readers who have subtly and unmistakably shaped these chapters over the years. To each, I am grateful for the ways they pushed me to think critically and, especially, to consider the interrelationships of "religion," "violence," and "America." I know I have failed to realize the clarity that some of these readers had hoped for me. But I hope that whatever provocations I offer are clear enough to produce more results from specialists working in the various areas where I trespass, perhaps cavalierly, here.

My first debt to discharge goes to the Colloquium on Violence and Religion, or COVR. COVR exists to explore, criticize, and develop the "mimetic theory" of the relationship between religions and violence as first defined by René Girard. I joined COVR shortly after it was formed in 1990 and have attended many of the group's annual meetings, which are held at various sites in Europe and the United States. I have found the group a congenial place for discussion, and the feedback I have received on my various applications and critiques of Girardian theory has been invaluable. I especially appreciated my conversations with COVR members Ann Astell, Lisa Bellan-Boyer, Paul Bellan-Boyer, Daniel Cojocaru, Diana Culbertson, Nadia Delicata, Sandor Goodhart, Michael Harden, Cheryl Kirk-Duggan, Paul Neuchterlein, Len Praeg, Vern Redekop, Tom Ryba, Julia Shinnick, and Thee Smith. René Girard himself has been consistently kind and encouraging to me, and while I occasionally take issue with elements of his theory or take mimetic analysis in directions he might not sanction, I gratefully acknowledge the persuasiveness of his diagnosis of many of the causes and contours of religious violence, including those in American history.

The first group of students on whom I inflicted (directly or indirectly) Girard's theory, along with smatterings of Augustine, Heidegger, Kant, Sallie McFague, Jarsolav Pelikan, and more, were undergraduates in the Christ College Honors Program at Valparaiso University in the mid 1990s. Some of these students, astonishingly and to my delight, I still keep in touch with, notably Jennifer Beste, who earned her doctorate in theology and ethics from Yale University; Martin Lohrmann, who now is studying for his own doctorate in Reformation history here in Philadelphia; Rob Saler, who is working on a PhD at the University of Chicago; and Mike Kessler, who is now on the faculty at Georgetown University. Others I have lost touch with but remember fondly for their feedback and critiques: Aaron Gin, Sarah Hamlin, Heather Jensen, Paul Koch, Jeremy Lakin, Kerrie Morgan, Erin O'Connell, Mandy Pencek, and Amy Rogge.

Since moving to Philadelphia, I have been fortunate to work with students at the Lutheran Theological Seminary who have brought to their studies with me a willingness to inquire and a passion for social justice. Among my student conversation partners on topics of religion and violence in Philadelphia are Chris Bishop, Delores Brown, Rev. Donald Burems, Heeralal Cheedie, Ann Colley, Tim Cook, Virginia Cover, Moses Dennis, Andy Evenson, Lois Fernando, Peggy Frischmann, Korey Grice, Lura Groen, Peggy Hayes, Cheryl Hensil, Brenda Jack, Dianne A. Johnson, Sandy Jones, Ed Kay, Travis Kern, Jennifer Kingstorf, Sarah Lang, John Lewis Sr., Gloria Meeks, Danielle Miller, Ernie Mossl, Jim Neal, Tricia Neale, Deb Payson, the late Scott Reeder, Andrew Ruggles, Patrick Seyler, A'Shellarien Smith, Greg Shreaves, Beth Stroud, Josh Wilson, and Bud Zehmer. The recent addition of a PhD program at the Seminary has given me the occasion to share chapter drafts from my works in progress with Derek Cooper, Rebecca Howell, Luka Ilic, Matthew

Laubenstein, Martin Lohrmann, Cosmos Moenga, Jonathan Riches, and Lee Zandstra. I also have enjoyed good conversations on these topics with three PhD students at Temple University, where I have also done some teaching, namely, Bradley Copeland, Matthew Hunter, and David Krueger. Several of my colleagues in religion at Temple—Rebecca Alpert, Laura Levitt, Leonard Swidler, and David Watt—have been reliable sources of critical and engaged conversation. To all these students and colleagues: Thanks.

Finally, among my debts to discharge in the category of students-inflicted-with my prose, the most recent batch were the eight intrepid Princeton students who studied with me in the spring of 2007. My conversations with this group were among the most productive in my teaching career, and I am thankful to each of them for their careful and detailed feedback on the chapters: Kris Berr, Rachel Crane, Jon Fernandez, Tom Lank, Tim O'Neill, Gillian Pressman, Madeleine Walsh, and Zach Zimmerman.

In the fall of 2006, I was fortunate to have a fellowship in the Center for the Study of Religion at Princeton University, directed by Bob Wuthnow, where I was a participant in Leigh Schmidt's Friday Religion and Culture seminar. I am grateful to both Bob and Leigh for their warm collegiality and for putting me in touch with the remarkably good-natured and smart other fellowship holders who provided me with more feedback and encouragement than they could possibly have known: Angela Ards, Ian Barber, Gretchen Boger, Craig Caldwell, Karoline Cook, Rebecca Davis, Erin Forbes, Healan Gaston, Kathryn Holscher, Eduard Iricinschi, Jason Josephson, Kevin Kalish, Oliver Krueger, Alan Petigny, Melissa Proctor, Asuka Sango, Uriel Simonsohn, and Stuart Young. Throughout 2007 I was a participant in a graduate seminar in American religious history, also led by Leigh Schmidt, at which I shared chapter 4 with the group. Participants included Laura Bennett, Gretchen Boger, Darren Dochuck, Ryan Harper, Matt Hedstrom, Elizabeth Jemison, Nicole Kirk, Melani McAlister, and Anthony Petro. Among other colleagues at Princeton with whom I have shared critical conversations about religion and violence, I am particularly grateful to Wallace Best, Erik Gregory, Marie Griffith, Jeffrey Stout, and (especially) Judith Weisenfeld. I also am grateful for the careful readings of two anonymous scholars from New York University Press and to my editor there, Jennifer Hammer, whose words of praise and sharp critiques pushed me to clarify many crucial passages.

Two other scholarly societies have been important to this work. The American Academy of Religion has been a great source of collegial support for me, with friends and conversation partners such as Betty DeBerg, Rick DeMaris, Mark Granquist, John Lyden, Bob Orsi, Jim Wellman, and Mark Wallace making attendance at meetings a joy. Many of them read various versions of these chapters and made them better. As the cochair of the AAR Religions, Social Conflict, and Peace Group, I'm regularly kept up-to-date with, and have to make difficult choices about, the best current research in the field. My cochair, Marla Selvidge, has been a steady collaborator, and I look forward to continuing to work with her in shaping the field of religion, peace, and conflict studies. The other scholarly society where I have found a congenial home is the Society for the History of Childhood and Youth (SHCY), whose members have been most helpful as readers of chapter 3, although my conversations with them have sharpened all my work. Among my most frequent interlocutors at SHCY, to whom I owe thanks, are Jim Block, Paula Fass, Mona Gleason, Michael Grossberg, Kristi Lindenmeyer, Laura Lovett, Jim Marten, John Pettegrew, Patrick Ryan, and Michael Zuckerman.

Finally, to my colleagues in my "day job" at the Lutheran Theological Seminary at Philadelphia (LTSP), I can only say thank you for putting up with me. It is truly a delight to work with colleagues whose regard is shared. Fred Borsch, Pamela Cooper-White, Katie Day, Wilda Gafney, Erik Heen, John Hoffmeyer, Phil Krey, Karl Krueger, Margaret Krych, Dirk Lange, Charles Leonard, Robin Mattison, Melinda Quivik, Paul Rajashekar, Stephen Ray, Nelson Rivera, Bob Robinson, Eloise Scott, Rich Stewart, and Tim Wengert have made this book stronger in many ways, not only by their close readings of several chapters, but also by their constant encouragement and collegial goodwill. I feel fortunate to be in the company of so many fine scholars and people. The LTSP's faculty secretary, Carrie Schwab, carefully put together the bibliography and saved me many embarrassing mistakes. I hope this work reflects the collective strengths of so many wonderful conversation partners. The weaknesses, of course, are my own.

As mentioned, some of these ideas previously appeared in different forms. An early and much abridged version of chapter 3 originally appeared as "Spectacles of Sacrifice: The Cinema of Adolescence and Youth Violence in American Culture," in *Visible Violence: Sichtbare und verschleierte Gewalt im Film*, ed. Gerhard Larcher (Munster: Lit Verlag, 1998), 169–186. An abbreviated early version of chapter 5 appeared as "Founding an Empire of Sacrifice: Innocent Domination and the Quaker Martyrs of Boston, 1659–1661," in *Belief and Bloodshed: Religion and Violence across Time and Tradition*, ed. James K. Wellman Jr. (Lanham, MD: Rowman & Littlefield, 2007), 97–114. I am grateful to Oxford University Press for permission to reprint the woodcuts from John Bunyan, *The Pilgrim's Progress* (New York: Oxford University

Press, 2003), 96, 263. The original woodcut of "Faithful" was published in the fifth edition of part I of the work, during Bunyan's lifetime, and the woodcut of "Gyant Dispair," in the first edition of part II, published in 1684, but Oxford used nineteenth-century facsimiles, available in George Offor, *The Works of John Bunyan*, 3 vols. (Glasgow: Blackie and Son, 1860–62), vol. 3, 79–84, as cited by W. R. Owens, "Note on the Text," xliii. The provocative cover art "Untitled (Abu Ghraib)" was graciously donated by Bill Concannon, www.aargon-neon.com, of Crockett, California.

Introduction

Blessed Brutalities

Through some kind of diffusion or infection, the character of sanctity and inviolability—of belonging to another world, one might say—has spread from a few major prohibitions on to every other cultural regulation, law and ordinance. But on these the halo often looks far from becoming: not only do they invalidate one another by giving contrary decisions at different times and places, but apart from this they show every sign of human inadequacy. It is easy to recognize in them things that can only be the product of short-sighted apprehensiveness or an expression of selfishly narrow interests or a conclusion based on insufficient premises. The criticism which we cannot fail to level at them also diminishes to an unwelcome extent our respect for other, more justifiable cultural demands. Since it is an awkward task to separate what God Himself has demanded from what can be traced to the authority of an all-powerful parliament or a high judiciary, it would be an undoubted advantage if we were to leave God out altogether and honestly admit the purely human origin of all regulations and precepts of civilization.
—Sigmund Freud, *The Future of an Illusion*, 1927

It is a truism that industrial capitalism since the nineteenth-century has been increasingly destructive of forms of social life, that its markets have dislocated persons and things throughout the world, that the pollution of its factories and transport systems had disastrous effects on the natural environment and global climate that all humans inhabit. And yet industrial capitalism is the volatile condition in which Western liberties have been constructed, defended, and gifted to the world. The violent freedoms of industrial capitalism can be said to have constituted political life as the space of an earthly permanence that can compensate for the death of the past—at the cost of a fatal threat to the future. For the modern sovereign state has an absolute right to defend itself, a defense that may—as the Inter-

national Court of Justice has held—legitimately involve the use of nuclear weapons. Suicidal war with incalculable global consequences exists in the liberal world as a legitimate possibility.
—Talal Asad, *On Suicide Bombing*

This book concerns a single problem: "America" has become an empire, and that empire is not innocent, even though many citizens of the United States seem to imagine that their nation has some sort of divine right to dominate that does not implicate Americans in anything that might deserve blame.[1] I am bothered by this logic, which ascribes innocence to all things American, not because I am particularly alienated but because it seems to me not to be true. For instance, how could almost three out of four U.S. citizens in 2003 be persuaded to support sending young men and women off to die in battle for the ultimately unsubstantiated suspicion that Iraq *might* harbor a weapon of mass destruction, when the United States already possesses an unmatched arsenal of such lethal firepower?[2] Such hubris, pride, or sheer chutzpah—what I call *innocent domination*—is the historical tangle that I try to unravel a bit in this book. As Freud might have put it, many Americans have seemed willing to put a halo on American history and policies. To me, that halo appears more than a little unbecoming. My basic argument here is that American history is riddled with patterns of religious violence. Americans are, by all accounts and especially their own, "the most religious people on the planet." Yet America is also obviously, brutally, violent, as our history from the public executions of Puritan Boston to the human tortures of Abu Ghraib suggests.[3] To me, as a religious person, a scholar of religion, and a citizen of the United States, it is this problem of the conjunction of religion and violence in American history that obsesses me.

Most of this book was written during the so-called global war on terror, even though the terrorist attacks of September 11, 2001, and the U.S. retaliation in Afghanistan and Iraq took place nearly a decade after I started this book. The scholarly context that led me to pull together the essays into a single volume and a single argument is the fact that since 9/11, dozens of books published by academics across the United States have explored "religion and terrorism," "global religious violence," "killing in the name of God," how "religion becomes evil," and so forth.[4] What was most interesting to me is that these books almost universally located "religious violence" *outside* the United States. Consequently, many scholars of religion and many citizens in America seemed shocked at the recent "resurgence" of "conservative" religion, the "new religious Right," "fundamentalism," "theocracy," "American fascism," "Amerikkka," or whatever one wants to call it, in U.S. politics.[5] Those works on religious violence focusing on America have tended to fixate on one doctrine as root, cause, and consequence—millennialism—or the idea that America's future is aligned with God's future.[6] *Millennialism* is a Christian notion that maps out the end of time. According to millennialists, America has a particularly important role to play in end-time dramas. God will use America to bring blessing to the world or will punish America for its sins. Obviously, there is ample potential in such a doctrine for violence, but in fact there is much more going on in American religious violence than a theological doctrine about the future can explain, and there is in fact very little new about the "new religious right."[7] Indeed, in order to develop my thesis a bit more fully, my central historical argument is that violence in America has almost always been grounded in a complex set of religious discourses and practices in many communities and institutions. These shifting yet discernible patterns of discourse and practices—things like dualism, ecstatic asceticism, and, above all, sacrifice—produced what I call an American "empire of sacrifice," or instances of "blessed brutalities." In essence, Americans have found ways to consider blessed some rather brutal attitudes and behaviors, such as age-based domination, racism, gender discrimination, and land grabbing, in patterns that are identifiably religious and yet cannot be explained simply as the working out of the logic of Christian millennialism.[8]

I am hardly the first to see American religious history as riddled with violence. For instance, the epigraph from Talal Asad at the opening of this introduction points to a clear-headed refusal to accept any easy distinction between "religious" and "secular" practices that sanitizes the history of liberal democracies, which is also a crucial contribution I try to advance here for the liberal democracy that is the United States. Similarly, social historian Jon Butler and literary historian Tracy Fessenden each have, in very different ways, located less-than-innocent features in the American religious past.[9] Building on these beginnings, each chapter in this book highlights a distinctive trajectory in the history of religious violence that led to the emergence of an American "empire of sacrifice."[10] Exactly what I mean by sacrifice will become clearer shortly, but for now it may be enough to say that as used here, *sacrifice* refers less to the voluntary commitment of people to give up something for the common good, which is often admirable, than to systemic exclusions, prejudices, or biases—that is, ritualized incantations or performances—that substitute violence against scapegoats or victims for actual solutions to social problems. Such forms of sacrifice are rarely admirable, yet they are remarkably common in American history. When I speak of an American empire of sacrifice, I am suggesting that systemic market forces, military operations, national identity, and political rhetorics produced hybrid religions—American "civil religions" or "cultural religions," for the lack of better terms—which have borrowed from Christianity (and other traditions) to prop up their fragile power. These hybrids have depended on religious discourses and practices, often in secular guise, to place sacrifices on altars constructed of social conventions concerning age, race, and gender. Such processes have focused on imagining, communicating, and enforcing an "American" identity in history. In this manifestation of America, citizens have sacrificed both their own and enemy others while simultaneously imagining that they were innocent in doing so. Again, these durable patterns cannot be explained simply as the working out in politics of a doctrine of millennialism, manifest destiny, or America as a chosen, redeemer nation. All the dying, killing, and suffering has more complicated roots than that and has less to do with doctrines like millennialism than it does with practices and the cultural work carried out by various systems of sacrifice.

I call this cultural work *innocent domination*, by which I mean patterns or systems of domination, hegemony, or power over others that are largely absent of malice on the part of the perpetrators. This absence of malice is not necessarily simple bad faith; it might be due to cultural contingencies such as the long history of the sexual subordination of women or a sincere belief that one is "doing the right thing" for the nation. Besides drawing on the work of Asad, Butler, and Fessenden, my work also builds most directly on the insights of two other scholars. The first is Catherine Albanese, whose text *America: Religions and Religion* I used for ten years to introduce students to the field of American religious history. From Albanese (who, like me, studied with Martin E. Marty at the University of Chicago), I learned to push Marty's attention to the public dimensions of religion beyond denominations and their institutions and to explore explicitly religious innovation and hybrid "relocations" across discourses and practices. For instance, in her textbook Albanese discusses not only various streams of tradition such as Protestantism, Catholicism, Judaism, and Native American spiritualities in America but also such hybrids as American "civil religion" and "cultural religion." Under the latter, in particular, Albanese isolates both "dominance" and "innocence" as key features in the American experience. Both, she notes, are facets of what she regards as a broader phenomenon of "millennialism," or an assumption of being chosen for a particular historical destiny:

We have identified the controlling theme that runs through much of American culture as millennialism. With a long history among us, millennialism has repeatedly appeared in one of two forms. Sometimes it has been the dominating millennialism that takes its cue from visions of a final battle when good will triumphs over evil. At other times it has been the innocent millennialism that seeks to make utopias in an uncorrupted landscape. Both kinds of millennialism . . . direct [Americans] in the course of their lives, interpreting the meaning of things, offering occasions for ritual, and providing ways to seek empowerment for daily life. With millennialism as the unifying center, dominance and innocence have been two sides of the same cultural coin. Those who dominate and win try to find ways to prove their innocence. Those who stress innocence discover that the world will not go away and that the same struggles for power beset utopia as trouble any human venture.[11]

The following cases all explore Albanese's contention that in America, dominance and innocence have been "two sides of the same cultural coin." But the center, I contend, is not merely millennialism, utopianism, or the hope for salvation, as Albanese suggests. Americans have been more practical and pragmatic than that. Instead, at the center of American religious history is sacrifice, as both rhetoric and practice. Sacrifice—the religious exclusions and substitutions through which power has been concentrated and legitimized—has been a key factor in producing American identity.[12] And sacrifice has established cultural patterns resulting in a particularly virulent penchant for violence, both symbolic and material, while also cloaking that violence in religious innocence. A sacrifice can be holy in ways that simple killing is not. Religions sanctify dominance, or render it innocent, less through millennialism than through sacrifice.

A second immediate scholarly source for this notion of "innocent domination" is a monograph by historian Richard T. Hughes. According to Hughes, Americans have developed several "myths" that have implicitly shaped both everyday living and national policy and practice throughout the centuries of national development. Among them is what he calls "the myth of the innocent nation," which Hughes locates as the peculiarly dominant myth of the twentieth century: "A profound sense of innocence characterized the American experience for much of the twentieth-century. . . . In the mainstream of American life, most had no doubt about the ultimate meaning of their nation: America stood for good against evil, right against wrong, democracy against tyranny, and virtue against vice."[13]

Unlike Albanese, Hughes does not explicitly connect this myth to an American millennial desire for dominance, but he makes clear that this myth has produced consequences that have not been salutary:

> Any exploration of the history of the myth of innocence almost invariably reveals that it finally transforms itself into its opposite. Indeed, it typically encourages those who march under its banner to repress those they regard as corrupted or defiled. Paradoxically, then, the innocent become guilty along with the rest of the human race.[14]

In fact, I believe that the historical record indicates less a "transformation" of "innocence" into "repression" than a symbiotic relationship between innocence and dominance in one unified, albeit paradoxical, worldview. In short, an assertion of national innocence may have emerged along with the existence of national dominance and serves as its necessary complement. The historical process to be investigated is how religion and politics together promoted not innocence alone, or its transformation into repression, but a mutual process of innocent domination or a historical set of circumstances through which "force" became "pure," brutalities became blessed, or sacrifice built an empire. These initial forays, I admit, are only preliminary case studies for what needs to be much fuller, more careful, and more focused work in the archives and microhistories by historians better suited and more able to undertake such studies than I.

I contend that forms of sacrifice—patterns of exclusion, elimination, and domination, if not actual killing—have been repeated in American history as if they were incantations or ritual processes, which in fact they are. Even though scholars do not agree on what constitutes a "sacrifice" or how sacrifice relates to the broader category of "religions," recent work might help us identify better at least four key elements of sacrifice.[15] Sacrificial acts are a combination of a victim or object to be offered; the substitution (including metaphor or synecdoche) of a victim or object for a larger group; giving up (e.g., burning), expelling, or killing the victim or object; and catharsis, which includes the identification with the victim or object and the association of some emotion or attribute that serves as motive or rationale for the gift, expulsion, or killing. Traditionally, of course, catharsis refers to purification (usually removing guilt). More accurately, however, sacrifices compress or channel fears and desires—including the desires to dominate, associate, and flee—in ways that displace, purify, and legitimize desires through symbols or symbolic action. These processes are not noted for their rationality.

Although sacrifices may be intentional acts or discrete ritual performances, they may also be largely unconscious *systems* of substitution that symbolically channel fears and desires. Most notably, violence is sanctified through sacrifice. Such trust in symbols both stabilizes the social order and promotes the transformation of societies, albeit within bounds. Sacrifice includes both creative and destructive elements. Especially in archaic societies, sacrifices can unleash generosity and gift giving, and they can create social solidarity.[16]

In America, I contend, sacrificial patterns have had truly terrifying effects in the lives of individuals and groups and have led to massive quantities of unnecessary suffering, death and destruction. Some commentators (mainly those exercised by "Islamofascism") also increasingly appear to juxtapose such patterns of American "innocent domination" to "religious violence," which is precisely the historical (and rhetorical) sleight of hand I hope to present in this book for critical analysis.[17] American history as I tell it here appears to be particularly ruthless and bloody and contains lots of domination and little (other than asserted or assumed) innocence. Indeed, American history has been marked by the tendency of politicians (and citizens) to invoke blessings on their preferred brutalities. This predilection is behind their wonder at "why they hate us." If you are sure of your own innocence, you will find it hard to believe that others see you as being in alliance with the Great Satan. Religion's ambivalent legacy in American history has thus both produced and obscured violence. In the future, I would like to trace the history and significance of religious peacemaking in America; how once freed from the need to justify domination as innocent, religions might in fact contribute to creating a more just, reasonable, and peaceful world. In fact, they have already begun to do so.[18]

This book is a postmodern history, or as one reader told me: "This is your Quentin Tarantino, *Pulp Fiction* book." I took that as a compliment. I use strange, even anachronistic evidence like 1990s Hollywood films to explain how I understand events that happened centuries ago. And I arrange that evidence in an inverse chronology running from the recent past to what I take to be the iconic founding of "America" in Puritan Boston. Moreover, I foreground in the narrative my own normative judgments, not as assumptions that I have to bracket as a purportedly objective historian, but as intuitions about the historical record worth exploring and, if need be, modifying, in light of the record. Alongside my historical argument, in other words, is an explicit normative claim. This claim is that we can, and must, differentiate reasonably (and contingently) among *types of religion:* those that legitimize or produce systemic violence and those that can help prevent it. Doing so is not easy and requires rethinking some rather crucial categories, not the least of which is "religion" itself. The problem of religious violence is shared both within and across all major "world religions," all of which are now also represented in the United States. That is, there is no pure tradition, and surely Christians—the primary tradition with which I identify—cannot imagine their own history as the gradual progress of peacemaking in contrast to, say, Muslim violence. This is even less the case with Protestantism, which, as I will suggest, can with no stretch of the evidence be held responsible for an original American form of blessed brutality, dating back to the Puritans. All in all, it will not do, as Northwestern University scholar Robert Orsi insisted, to smuggle into religious studies any simple distinction between "good" religion and "bad" religion, in a subtle (or not so subtle) effort to justify one's own tradition.[19]

Nevertheless, contradicting Orsi, some such distinction between more and less violent patterns of religious discourses and practices will invariably be made, not just by scholars, but even more by citizens. It thus is part of a scholar's public responsibility to make clear where the fault lines of religion and violence are, guided by his or her loyalties to some inescapably parochial traditions and by testing (verifying, falsifying, modifying) those loyalties against the contingencies of the historical record itself. Fortunately, many historians, anthropologists, theologians, and other scholars have been busy in recent years describing exactly these patterns, as we shall see in chapter 1, while at the same time practitioners of religions have also been mining the deep meanings and practices of many historic religious traditions for their potential contributions to peacemaking. I cannot develop those latter trajectories here. But such individuals who represent traditions nonviolently have often been visionaries—within, outside, and across traditions—who have articulated ways to make religious nonviolence or religious peacemaking normative. These visionaries have organized protests or led social movements to critique and transform nation-states or other collectives when they perpetrated injustices or tyranny. All this is to say that this postmodern history shares a normative horizon with these visionaries and movements, namely, the hope for a less violent America and a less violent world overall. But just as there is nothing inevitable about the link between religion and violence, neither is there anything inevitable about the prospects of religious peacemaking.

One last question is whether America is an "empire."[20] Suffice it to say that although I do not want to quibble about semantics—about whether "hegemony," say, might be a more accurate term to describe America's role in the world—I also understand that the use of the term *empire* in my book title is, for some, a loaded, perhaps illegitimate, choice.[21] In fact, the term has been used in relationship to American policy and practice for several decades, and the debate about its applicability extends at least as far back as the Spanish-American War and the founding of the Anti-Imperialist League.[22] I admit that the scholarly literature's application of this term to the United States has grown dramatically since 2001, with much of it polemically either for or against such usage.[23] Readers can no doubt discern where I stand on that debate, although the epilogue might also give pause, insofar as I envision something like U.S. power (properly understood) being used to promote religious peacemaking as a social good. If this is not, exactly, a Pax Americana, it is likely to be misconstrued as such. And in fact I am persuaded by the arguments of political scientists Michael Hardt and Antonio Negri that whatever form of "empire" currently exists actually transcends (while also building on) the old model of imperial/colonial domination by nation-states and therefore will require resistance to or transformation from new models of organization by "the multitudes."[24] Whether the latter can be enlisted to participate in pluralist and interfaith agencies beyond tribal identities remains to be seen. But I use the term *empire* to refer, historically, to the centralization of material resources around "American" nationalism and its corporate extensions and also to the way that "sacrifice" has produced these centralizations by obscuring the operation of interests and the exclusions, displacements, or violence involved in their execution as a policy.[25]

I develop this argument in five chapters. In chapter 1, "Rethinking Violence and Religion in America," I define some key terms and develop a theoretical approach to the problem of religion and violence. "Violence," I suggest, exists as illegitimate physical aggression and also in systemic forms that produce unnecessary suffering just as surely as a gunshot, and with broader effects. Similarly, I redefine "religion" so as to shift scholarly attention away from simple institutional definitions and toward the complex compressions of experience and displacement of desire into various projections of transcendent authority marking what we call "religion." Too often, simple institutional definitions (and the mark of "affiliation" that goes with it) have obscured the complex interactions between religious systems and other forms of cultural authority, mainly politics and economics. Finally, building on the views of the leading theorists of religion and violence—René Girard, Scott Appleby, Mark Juergensmeyer, and Regina Schwartz, among others—I cite things to look for as markers of "religious violence" in American history. Finding them might not be surprising to readers, but where, and how, might be.

In chapters 2 through 5, I explore case studies, arranged in inverse chronological order, of ways in which religious discourses and practices interacted with various forms of violence throughout American history. In chapter 2, "Sacrificing Youth: From *Reefer Madness* to *Hostel*," I trace the way in which religious violence has emerged in relationship to constructs of age in American history, especially in the representations of youth in recent American films. After a brief introduction setting the films in the context of larger institutions created to lionize and problematize, or honor and punish, young people in America, I analyze five films, from *Reefer Madness* in 1936 to *Hostel* in 2005. In these films, youth are represented as "abject objects" in ways that match their actual displacement through national policies of a "war on drugs," on the one hand, and actual war making, on the other. The "sacrifices" depicted in film mirrored—if they did not produce—the actual violence done to young people in American culture. Imagined categories (or identities) of "age," increasingly reinforced by niche marketing, served as a first site of religious violence in American history.

In chapter 3, "Sacrificing Race: 'The Slaveholding Religion' from Jarena Lee to Spike Lee," I examine how the category of "whiteness" served as a religious construct to produce the practice of chattel slavery in early America and continues to undergird more durable forms of racial discrimination and bias. Many scholars have noted that whiteness is an empirical and historical fiction, but few have recognized its religious significance. Furthermore, the role of religion in the practice of slavery has often been recognized, but never with the clarity and consistency first expressed by Frederick Douglass, for whom the practice itself became the foundation for what he called a "religion of slaveholding." African American cultural criticism like Douglass's, which recognizes the religious origins of racism and its significance in the birth of a nation and culture, is a consistent feature from the thought of the early nineteenth-century religious leader Jarena Lee to the more recent work of filmmaker Spike Lee. Throughout, the assertions of innocence associated with the U.S. nation and American culture, via the construct of "whiteness," have failed to ring true to these thinkers and have consistently been challenged.

In chapter 4, "Sacrificing Gender: From 'Republican Mothers' to Defense of Marriage Acts," I turn to the way that violence around the category of gender has frequently found its roots in religion in American history. This should come as no surprise, but in fact the way male and female identity and heterosexual norms have depended on displacements of desire onto constructions of asserted innocence, purity, and transcendence mark these processes as an intrinsic component of religion. From the earliest conceptions of patriarchal power in America, in which women were excluded by law from participating in the "human, contingent, and temporal," until today, when women continue to be excluded from full participation in American culture along with others who do not match the heterosexual male norm (gays, lesbians, bisexuals, and transgendered individuals), the way that displacements through metaphor and ritual have operated to sanction violence along the lines of gender has not been carefully studied in American history. With the help of a significant early document, the 1815 memoir of Abigail Abbot Bailey, as well as Margaret Atwood's novel *The Handmaid's Tale* (released as a Hollywood film in 1992), we can begin to determine how closely the displacements of religion have been connected with violence along the lines of gender and sexual difference in American history.

In chapter 5, "Sacrificing Humans: An Empire of Sacrifice from Mary Dyer to *Dead Man Walking*," I conclude my examination of religious violence in American history with a case study of the Puritans. This case highlights the intersections of religion with nation-building, race, and gender in an example from early America, the execution of four Quakers on the Boston Common between 1659 and 1661. By closely reading the discourse and ritual processes evident in these executions, we can see again how overlapping constructions of authority by state and church established some basic terms around which religious violence has operated in American history from almost the first years that Europeans established settlements. Mary Dyer was executed, I believe, to solve a "crisis of differentiation." She manifested a form of "ecstatic asceticism" that produced a mirror reaction by the established power and led to her execution in what can be described as an act of "performative violence." She was, in short, sacrificed to produce cultural power for the Puritans. In this single event, we can identify a trajectory that set America on its course as an empire of sacrifice, in patterns that the filmmaker Tim Robbins carefully reiterated and critiqued in his 1996 film *Dead Man Walking*.

The brief epilogue, "Innocent Domination in the 'Global War on Terror,'" wraps up the threads of my argument by extending the colonial ritual in which Mary Dyer was a crucial participant to a recent international, or imperial, context. In the epilogue, I also explore an emerging subplot in American religious history in which diverse traditions, shorn of their need to prop up empires or nations, might work nonviolently to produce what I call "A Coming Religious Peace." The development of that subplot will be, I hope, in good *Pulp Fiction* fashion, a sequel to this volume.

Rethinking Violence and
Religion in America

Every physician will admit that by the correct diagnosis of a malady more than half the fight against it is won; also, that if a correct diagnosis has not been made, all skill and all care and attention will be of little avail. The same is true with regard to religion.

—Søren Kierkegaard, *The Present Moment*, 1846
(*Diagnosis*, no. 4, 1)

Once the bureaucrats sink their pens into the lives of Indians, the paper starts flying, a blizzard of legal forms, a waste of ink by the gallon, a correspondence to which there is no end or reason. That's when I began to see what we were becoming, and the years have borne me out: a tribe of file cabinets and triplicates, a tribe of single-space documents, directives, policy. A tribe of pressed trees. A tribe of chicken-scratch that can be scattered by a wind, diminished to ashes by one struck match.

—Nanapush, in *Tracks*, by Louise Erdrich, 1988

Sacrifices . . . made possible . . . [a] nation, even when these sacrifices were not understood as such by the victims.

—Benedict Anderson, *Imagined Communities*, 1991

The genesis of this book, although I did not know it at the time, was a conversation at a Wednesday luncheon in Swift Hall of the Divinity School at the University of Chicago in the early fall of 1988.[1] I had just returned from South Dakota where I had attended a powwow in Oglala. The temperature had been 104 degrees Fahrenheit under a blazing, cloudless sky, yet the dancers and drummers had not missed a beat as they wove the sacred hoop in a circle of movement and sound. As I was about to launch into an extended ode of admiration for this ancient form of devotion, a table mate at the luncheon interrupted me with what I took, at the time, to be a rude question: "But what does it mean?" I paused briefly and then launched into explaining about the hoop as a symbol of unbroken Lakota identity and a sign of the perseverance of a people. I might even have quoted Black Elk. But the question came back to me again in a slightly different form: "But what does it mean *to you*—as a Lutheran? Or as an American religious historian? Or as a white man?" I was taken aback. I had no answers to her questions, and the conversation soon moved on. This book is my attempt to answer why I was unable—as a Lutheran or a historian or a white male—to articulate what I was doing that day in Oglala, watching the dancers go around and around in the heat to the constant rhythm of a drum.

Put more prosaically, any account of American religious violence has to begin with the First Peoples of North America. The violence done to the Lenape, Pequots, Menominee, Cherokee, Lakota, and so many other groups had (and has) explicit roots in religion.[2] Yet many historians, anthropologists, sociologists, and others continue to misdiagnose that malady. Such misdiagnoses produce pages of chicken scratch that exacerbate the suffering, turning living traditions into pressed trees. In other words, I have become convinced that what stymied my ability to answer my inquisitor at lunch two decades ago was not so much the result of my lived experience of Lutheranism or Christianity, although aspects of both traditions contributed to my incomprehension. Instead, as my interlocutor hinted, the greatest barriers to understanding what I was doing in Oglala came from my presumed identities as a historian and a white male. I innocently assumed that I could understand "as a scholar" what was going on in a Lakota dance, when in fact I was an outsider to the rite, with little or no comprehension of the history that led to the dancing, why the dancing continued, or even what it felt like to dance wearing full regalia in 104-degree heat. The research for this book has led me to recognize anew my arrogant naïveté and to see how this conjunction of arrogance and a presumed innocence replicated processes by which native lands were taken from the First Peoples of North America. In short, in my spectator consumption of a "native American" powwow and then in bragging about it, I participated in what I have come to call *innocent domination*. My blinders were religious. But those blinders were not only my participation in Lutheran or Christian circles, which in some ways might have helped me understand what was happening (given that some of the dancers were, in all likelihood, Christians). Instead, my primary blinders were of race, gender, class, and nation. What led me to be unable to answer what a Lakota dance meant to me was my identity (then still aspirational as an earnest PhD student) to be an "American scholar" and the attendant religious assumptions. As my fellow Lutheran Kierkegaard might have put it, I had misdiagnosed the root of my malady.

Understanding myself as an "American" meant that I had inherited or assumed particular ways of thinking about violence, religion, and their relationship that made it easy for me to attend a powwow without really thinking about what I was doing there. In this chapter, I try to unravel some of those assumptions, to remove some blinders, and to rethink violence, religion, and their relationships in American history. I do so as a historian, a white male, and a Lutheran Christian who has come to realize that all these constructions have given me access to privilege. Such privilege has been anything but universal, however. What follows is my attempt to begin discerning how so many white, male, Christians in America, joined by many others, have repeatedly failed to see how their actions have produced suffering and violence in the world. At the same time, it is also my hope that my insights might help turn readers away from such patterns of innocent domination, to which, I believe, all humans are attracted. I hope that we might build a more collaborative, just, and peaceful future. That I express this hope on paper made from pressed trees is only one of the many layers of irony: at some level, until we meet face to face, we all are simply going around in circles. But I do hope that out of this circling, some readers might realize that while my words might be nothing more than chicken scratch, they are a gift we can offer to motivate one another to attend to and care for the living trees in our midst and to forge sustainable and sustaining relationships with the diverse and beautifully different people we come to meet: Lakota, Lutheran, and beyond.

Rethinking "Violence"

The word *violence* as used in this book refers not only to acts of individual physical aggression but also to social and linguistic systems of exclusion and collective coercion, degradation, or destruction of property, persons, and the environment.[3] Violence is any harm to or destruction of life, whether intended by individuals or enacted by systems of language, policy, and practice. By defining violence in this way, I intend to identify with what can be called a "maximalist" approach to the topic. This approach contrasts with a "minimalist" approach that would limit the term *violence* to acts of individual, illegitimate, or illegal physical aggression, although sometimes minimalists also include *conflict* in their purview.[4] Systems of exclusion, coercion,

TABLE 1. *The Violence Iceberg*

CRIMINAL VIOLENCE
practices of vandalism, rape, murder, etc.
INSTITUTIONAL CONTROL
institutions such as prisons, military, legal system, etc.
SYSTEMIC/SOCIAL/COMMUNITY VIOLENCE
community-based inequities in housing, healthcare, education, etc.
CULTURAL, RELIGIOUS, OR VERBAL VIOLENCE
discourses and images of domination and revenge

and so forth emerge from a collective consent of some kind, minimalists argue, and might therefore be called "unjust," but to label them *violence* is to blur terms.[5] My reasons for preferring the broader, if blurrier, definition will become apparent in due course, but my main reason is consequentialist: people die just as surely from unjust systems as they do from a gunshot or interpersonal conflict. In fact, they die more slowly and with greater suffering. To exclude these systems from the opprobrium associated with the word *violence*, therefore, is to release the agents responsible for these systems from accountability, which may be, of course, exactly why many people want to limit the term.

In my teaching, I often explain what I mean to include under the term *violence* by referring to the metaphor of "the violence iceberg,"[6] which is shown in table 1. As this metaphor of an iceberg suggests, each "layer" of violence builds on the previous one, and the layers interweave and interact, in what I am willing to argue is a causal connection. Discourses—words and symbols—are the crucial forms of violence and also the foundation on which other acts and practices are built.

More specifically, I believe that violence almost invariably begins at the bottom of the iceberg. That is, violence begins with, or is implicated in, words or other gestures of communication or what can be loosely called *culture*. At the "bottom" of the iceberg rest those ways in which human beings decide on the terms that make violence plausible against the world, another, or one's self. Any act of aggression, especially if it is enacted collectively, must involve some signs or symbols that motivate or at least initiate the action. To locate the origin of aggression in this way is to include in the scope of its study such phenomena as myth and ritual as well as other aspects of culture like art, literature, music, and manifold forms of communication. People must somehow persuade themselves that this aggression is worth enacting, and this internal process is manifest in such cultural products as languages, religions, and other such phenomena noted primarily for their conceptual and practical complexity.

This foundational layer of complexity is only the beginning. Individuals also gather together in communities, societies, or social groups, and these groups empower individuals to act on one another, or to act en masse, in often informal patterns of practice that might turn violent or produce destructive consequences. Classes, guilds, families, nations, and so forth all enact interests to exclude some, include others, and distribute resources in more or less equitable ways. Informal practices can also become policies, and policies regarding education, health care, housing, and any number of other matters of social survival can produce consequences that result in coercion, degradation, harm to and destruction of life: that is, in violence. Not all policies are just. Some policies protect the interests of a few at the expense of the many. This is why politics is so often a blood sport. Power can be hoarded and used, legally, to violate others.

Consequently, among the social groupings that humans have constructed are those that use formal institutional (or bureaucratic) structures to respond to human aggression and then themselves legitimize coercion to control or contain violence. Among these institutions are the military services, prisons, legal systems, and states—understood in the broad sense as agencies of civilization that may, or may not, be coextensive with a nation.[7] These forms of violence may be extensions of the kind of exclusions that emerge from "below" in various social groupings and policies, in which case they are unjust and serve primarily to rationalize violence itself. Any police state, or arbitrary use of police power is a good example. But laws can also emerge from the consent of the governed and respond to illegitimate acts of aggression to protect collective interests and control the unchecked spread of violence. In such cases, the coercion is an unfortunate accompaniment of living in a world of competing interests, in which some people will not always use nonviolent means to reach their goals. In such cases, violence is warranted and just. Violence here is the legitimized control through institutional means of individuals or groups that do not consent to live together peaceably by the rule of law, through means that ascertain and formalize the consent of the governed. To be clear, I am not a pacifist. In some cases, violence, as a last resort, can be justified. But I do think such cases are rare, even though they have been far too frequent in the history of human cultures. Nonetheless, in some cases, duly authorized states or governments, acting in response to an initial act of aggression, have good reasons to respond with counteraggression.

Accordingly, it is at the "top of the iceberg" that we discover the most overt form of violence and the only form usually recognized as such in popular culture, namely, acts of criminal aggression such as vandalism, murder, and rape. Everyone recognizes these practices as violent, and they often are the paradigm against which other forms are measured and in relation to which "solutions" to violence are recommended. The reasons that solutions tend to address the tip, rather than the foundation, of the iceberg are not difficult to understand. Individual acts of physical aggression seem to be subject to the simplest solutions. Needless to say, they may not always be, but just as I cannot defend that claim here, neither can I, in this brief historical work, defend either the iceberg metaphor or its specifics. Suffice it to say that I believe the model has both plausibility and significant explanatory power. Violence cuts across language, culture, society, and individual behavior in ways that implicate all of them. The effectiveness of this approach to studying violence in American history will, I trust, be apparent in the following case studies, in which the connections between discourse and practice will be made explicit.

Rethinking "Religion"

If *violence* is difficult to define, *religion* is no less so. Many previous sui generis definitions have fallen into disrepute, particularly following the critique of anthropologist Talal Asad, who found the notion of "religion" inherently biased in favor of the privatized, sanitized, and hegemonic Protestantism of the Euro-American West.[8] Asad's critique has been joined by those of several other scholars, notably Russell McCutcheon and Tomoko Masuzawa, who find "religion" complicit in various forms of Western imperialism.[9] I grant these thinkers their points, but I also agree with the University of Chicago historian of religions Bruce Lincoln that a relatively nonbiased way to talk about "religion"—always provisional, evolving, and contingent on particular circumstances and settings—is not only possible but necessary. To refuse to define *religion* is to allow the term to be defined by journalists and politicians who bring to the table agendas other than critical understanding. Religions are, no doubt, varying sites of knowledge and practice with widely divergent goals, contours, and boundaries. Yet to fail to offer an alternative critical meaning of the term to those who continue to use the term uncritically is to abdicate the scholar's public responsibility. Mere critique is too

TABLE 2. *Bruce Lincoln's Four Elements of "Religion"*

1. **Discourse:** "A discourse whose concerns transcend the human, temporal, and contingent, and that claims for itself a similarly transcendent status."
2. **Practices:** "A set of practices whose goal is to produce a proper world and/or proper human subjects, as defined by a religious discourse to which these practices are connected."
3. **Community:** "A community whose members construct their identity with reference to a religious discourse and its attendant practices."
4. **Institution:** "An institution that regulates religious discourse, practices and community, reproducing them over time and modifying them as necessary, while asserting their eternal validity and transcendent value."

easy. Fortunately, Lincoln takes up the challenge of identifying some terms that might be useful for comparing cultures and understanding different religions. I think he does so in a way that sets the stage for a definition that can be both accurate and useful in diagnosing some of the links between religion and violence (see table 2).

This way of identifying elements of religion does not clarify either what religions are (their substance) or what religions do (their functions). Nonetheless, some moves toward both substance and function are implicit in Lincoln's four elements, in ways that perhaps can lead to a working hypothesis about what "religion" means.

In this book, I will develop Lincoln's definition of "religion" using a linguistic-cultural approach that can be summarized in the following three assertions. First, I contend that religions are relational networks of discourse patterns, embodied practices, and social structures through which people construct, consolidate, regulate, and defend cultural power around projections of transcendent authority.[10] Second, these projections compress or condense collective desire[11] and displace historical and material contingencies into demonstrably continuous forms, whose most visible manifestations are the enduring institutions that regulate discourse and practices and police the community's boundaries.[12] Third, from this foundation of what religions are, I will operate as if the primary function of religions is to eliminate things. That is, I believe religions exist as the cultural equivalent of ecological and biological systems of elimination. Just as rains and rivers eliminate ecological waste, and digestive systems operate biologically, so religions exist to limit cultural options for people. Religions channel the materials of everyday life—time, space, and desire—while focusing human longing on particular objects and particular behaviors. More succinctly, religions eliminate desire. Most provocatively, religions waste time and space. This is not, as one earlier reader of this argument put it, to say that religions are "shit." Again, religions exist as the cultural equivalent of environmental and biological systems of elimination. And just as most people are grateful for a gentle rain, flowing rivers, and a functioning liver, or for vacations on which they can "waste" time, so too this approach to the function of religions can reveal that religions are not only culturally valuable but perhaps even necessary. The ultimate suggestion of this linguistic-cultural approach to religions is that at their limits, or in their fullest development, *religions exist to eliminate violence.*

I am well aware that none of these assertions is self-evident and that this last assertion in particular—that religions exist to eliminate violence—seems almost laughable in light of the long history of rivalries and conflicts engendered by religions. I also am aware that the way I propose to understand "religion" is hardly the way the term is used by politicians, journalists, or, for that matter, most scholars, although in fact my definition builds directly on Lincoln's and is continuous with several other scholarly definitions. I am aware as well that by proposing a novel definition like this, I am joining a very lively debate. My goal here is not, however, to advance a grandiose unified theory of religion; that would require a much longer book, or several. Instead, my goal is to sketch out a linguistic-cultural approach to religion for heuristic purposes, to help untangle some of the unfortunate ways that instead of eliminating violence, religions have been the causes of violence in American history. Next I will try, briefly, to explain what I mean by these three assertions.

Religions are relational networks made up of people who use discourses like myths, and practices like rites of initiation, to build cultural power. Religions are preeminently concerned with cultural power, as opposed, say, to military power. This should be obvious. The elements of religions are the elements of cultures: words, practices, groups, and institutions. Moreover, the peculiar power of religions arises less from force than from persuasion. This does not mean, of course, that a religious devotee will not use a weapon if one is offered to him or her; history is full of examples like that. But the primary elements of religious traditions are found in language and other embodied practices such as chanting, dancing, reading, and reciting. Furthermore, the distinctive discourse codes of religions, as opposed to other avenues to cultural power such as art, economics, and politics, are projections of transcendent authority. Throughout history, especially in the West, religions have been defined in association with "God" or "gods" or perhaps with "the Sacred," as a nod to those traditions without a deity or deities. In fact, however, what distinguishes religions from other forms of cultural power is their adherents' assertion that some reliable avenue of authority, or some way to realize desire by focusing or limiting it, transcends the temporal and contingent, transcends human fallibility and transience. Religions claim for themselves a peculiar reliability. This avenue of authority provides a vehicle for human being and becoming that promises to end suffering, promote justice, create solidarity—or any number of possible outcomes. Needless to say, for any scholar in the humanities and social sciences, the first task in the critical study of a religion is to locate the sources of transcendent authority claims within the temporal and contingent.[13]

These projections of transcendent authority that define the appearance of religions within the flow of history can be theistic or nontheistic, but they involve in various ways efforts to deal culturally, rather than through sheer force, with the messiness of living. Religions assert something "more" than messiness, suffering, or chaos as the principal characteristic of life. That is, religious adherents assert that there is some authority or power to which people have access—grace, Enlightenment, God, nirvana—beyond the ordinary contingency, fragility, and misery of existence. These projections of transcendent authority operate in two steps. First, they compress collective desire, most visibly into discrete language units like words, symbols, metaphors, images, doctrines, stories, and texts.[14] Such compressions or condensations of experience emerge through imitation as learned projects, with roots in material needs and fruits in language. Second, these compressions or condensations take on a life of their own. That is, they are projected outside history and the processes of material needs in which they originated. People displace the contingent origins of religions and ascribe to them power beyond the ordinary power of other cultural agencies. This is why religions have cultural power that art, or even politics, do not have, for either good or ill. In short, religions become vehicles of authority that purportedly transcend fallible time and space. And when a symbol or practice gains association with transcendence—when it proves effective for an adherent in compressing desire and gaining cultural power or when it helps people deal with the messiness and suffering of living—then it coalesces with other symbols into a system or network. If this network of condensation and displacement proves itself over time, it might give rise to a community or institution that consolidates, regulates, and defends the patterns of discourse and network of practices. When this network of discourse, practice, community, and institution associated with transcendence extends across generations in demonstrable continuities, then historians like me might call it a *religion*. It is, to be sure, only a subtle shift when a symbol replaces a thing, but that crucial displacement is the foundation of religion and why my approach is best described as linguistic-cultural.

If this is what religions are from a linguistic-cultural perspective: relational networks of condensation and displacement that lead to cultural power through projections of transcendent authority, what religions *do* is eliminate things. Literally, again, religions substitute a symbol for a thing, and that displacement is at the root of religious processes. More prosaically, religions reduce the chaos of unmediated experience to discernible patterns. As linguistic compressions, religious systems inevitably are meager compared with the vast (if not infinite) fields of desire, experience, or intention in which they originate. Religions reduce complexity and focus attention, narrowing the availability of objects in the material world. Taken together, the prohibitions, prescriptions, and rules found across religious traditions, not to mention their crystallizations in discrete texts, places, or times, tend to contradict one another. For example, the Tanakh, New Testament, Qur'an, Dhammapada, and Bhagavad Gita do not point to the same avenues of authority, much less to the same communities and institutions, at least not without some serious interpretive sleight of hand. One also would have a serious scheduling problem simultaneously celebrating the sacred times of Judaism, Christianity, Islam, Buddhism, and Hinduism, as one could do nothing else but attend to rituals! These and other religious traditions do, however, limit the attention of religious devotees by prescribing a reliable path to the particular ends associated with their communities and cultures of origin. These paths—these vehicles of cultural power—are associated with an aura of transcendence. In religions, the "chaos" of unmediated experience, or the contingencies of living in the relativities of time and place, are compressed into manageable relations by means of which desire is focused and directed, if not overcome.

Again, if religions function to eliminate things, then at some level religions are simply a waste of time and space. This makes sense to anyone who has sat through a boring ritual or wondered at the purpose of the opulence of many religious shrines. But for insiders, such preferences for this action and not that action, or this image and not that image, all make sense in an effort to fulfill desire by channeling or compressing it in order to make human existence meaningful in the flux of time and space. Religious systems rule out some options and mandate others, but their ultimate purpose is to gain cultural power for their adherents, to realize their desires by eliminating some options.

This paradoxical feature of how religions function to realize or overcome desire by eliminating things is easy to see in practice. For instance, in this book we will pay special attention to sacrifice. Sacrifice, as defined in the introduction, is, among other things, a process of elimination. In sacrifice, an adherent burns, offers, gives up, expels, kills, or otherwise eliminates some object for some purpose or identifies with those who do these things. In sacrifice, adherents often emphasize the purpose of the action: there is a reason for the offering. Indeed, in many rituals and not only in sacrifice, there is a reason for each step in a process that is often carefully circumscribed. Sacrifices and other religious practices are always means to some end. Yet to outside observers, these reasons or ends often seem less obvious than the sheer fact of elimination or exclusion; something is given up, left out, or left behind. This basic function of religions to exclude and eliminate is precisely what I want to expose to critical study, since this function is so often implicated in violence. Exclusions may constitute communities, but they also create enemies. Sacrifice is a particularly evident form of how religions function to eliminate things, but it is hardly the only one. Prohibitions, laws, prayers, doctrines, and disciplinary procedures of all sorts illustrate in fragmentary ways the processes by which cultural power is achieved through condensed projections of transcendent authority that displace their material origins by eliminating things. If religions do function as the cultural equivalent of ecological and biological systems of elimination, then the ultimate challenge religions face is to eliminate human rivalry, conflict, and violence. Thus transcendence finally may translate into the desire to eliminate rivals.

This linguistic-cultural approach to "religion" may be further clarified by relating it to several other prominent definitions, two "classical" and one more recent. According to the historian of religions Mircea Eliade, religions are manifestations of the sacred in human experience—*hierophanies* is the technical term—which can appear almost anywhere and anytime. When they do appear, *hierophanies* produce sacred spaces and sacred times that are distinct from ordinary, or profane, space or time. Profane time is homogenous, undifferentiated. Sacred space or time is distinct and more real, more actual, and more powerful than an ordinary place or event. In the realm of the sacred, one finds an orientation and discovers practices: myths and rituals that can be repeated endlessly to perpetuate or remind participants of the sense of orientation or meaning they have gained by association with "the Sacred."

Notice that Eliade's definition has two essential steps and one crucial function. First, Eliade posits an "experience" that is compressed or selected from among many others. Sacred space is distinct from profane space. Second, Eliade describes the recognition by the participants in, or the recorders of, the experience that this phenomenon is "more" than ordinary. It is, in short, a displacement of whatever material desires or contingent causes produced the experience onto a transcendent agent ("the Sacred") that "manifests itself" in the event or act. Finally, these compressions and displacements distinguish "sacred" from "profane," ultimately to eliminate the profane and to allow adherents to live in a "sacred" cosmos.

Eliade has rightly been criticized by scholars like Jonathan Z. Smith for naively or ideologically accepting accounts of *hierophanies* as if they actually took place (rather than were imagined or produced by struggles over power or land or other such material realities).[15] Even though these critiques undoubtedly are accurate historically, they miss Eliade's point. It is that religion as a phenomenon is about the compression of experience (or events) into discrete displacements of whatever material causes might have produced the phenomenon, in order to gain a sense of orientation or meaning amid the chaos of life. These compressions and displacements became "sacred" systems that then took on lives of their own as religions. That is, Eliade's work can be adjusted to take into account historicist critiques. In fact, more than any other previous historian, Eliade launched the disciplines of comparative religions and religious studies by grounding religion as a human phenomenon. For Eliade, religions were systems of compressed material relations (his work is filled with natural features such as waters, rocks, and trees) into symbolic displacements (myths and rituals) that attempted to express the human encounter with "the Sacred." One need not, in short, accept Eliade's reified notion of "the Sacred," or his mystical conception of sacred space and time as hierophanies, in order to appreciate that he offers insight into the way religions operate to condense and displace human events into relations of language and practices that are as accurately called "myth" and "ritual" as anything else and that do some real work for people by eliminating some options and focusing attention on others.[16]

Similarly, the once widely cited functionalist definition of anthropologist Clifford Geertz has recently been criticized as an overly "interior" or "Protestant" or "Western" way to locate the dynamic cultural processes associated with religion.[17] According to Geertz, a religion is "a system of symbols which acts to establish powerful and pervasive moods and motivations in [people] by formulating conceptions of a general order of existence and clothing these conceptions with such an aura of factuality that the moods and motivations seem uniquely realistic." This is, no doubt, too psychologically interiorized. To say that religions only motivate, without accounting for their origin in social and cultural practices, is to say too little. But Geertz's basic point, that religions are systems of symbols that produce real effects in the world, communicates both the condensing and the displacing features of religious processes. The remainder of his definition points to the ways that systems of symbols can assume lives of their own with profound consequences across human communities. Once shorn of the unnecessarily psychologized language of moods and motives, Geertz's central insight into the ways that condensations of experience and displacements of material desires organize human communities and institutions can be recognized as a crucial contribution to the understanding of human behavior. Although Geertz does not extensively discuss the eliminative aspects of religion, his turn toward a functionalist definition is crucial.

Finally, and more recently, the religion scholar Thomas Tweed has suggested that religions can be understood as "confluences of organic-cultural flows that intensify joy and confront suffering by drawing on human and suprahuman forces to make homes and cross boundaries."[18] As Tweed admits, this definition is "hardly transparent." In fact, it unnecessarily romanticizes religion by locating its function first in emotion, as in "intensifying joy." This repeats Geertz's mistake. Tweed also mystifies religions by granting passes, so to speak, to the existence of "suprahuman forces," whatever those might be historically. Yet at the core of Tweed's definition is a two-step process that he describes, more prosaically, as "dwelling" and "crossing." That is, religions compress the materials of living (producing "confluences of organic cultural flows") in ways that allow people to feel at home in an often chaotic world. At the same time, religions displace the fragilities of contingent existence into discourses and practices concerned with finding ways to transcend symbolically the recognizable limits of the world (to "cross boundaries"). I do not mean merely to conflate my definition with Tweed's, for his has an integrity of its own, especially in its attention to geographical or place metaphors. But it is striking that we both see a two-step process in religions—what I call compression and displacement and what he calls "dwelling" and "crossing"— as ways that people actually seek to live in the world. Tweed also does not discuss the eliminative function of religions or, more specifically, religious violence.[19]

Needless to say, no single approach to defining "religion" will satisfy all readers or encompass all forms of the phenomenon, and it is not my aim to defend such a definition. Instead, my aim is more modest and diagnostic. I am offering one piece of a much larger puzzle in an effort to contribute to the efforts of many other scholars to untangle the ways in which religions have caused violence. I do hope, however, that my approach to religion has the advantage of recognizing how much the term is the product of the scholar's study while also pointing to the behaviors and cultural practices to which the term points. Finally, religions always assume a particular form. People practice as "Buddhists," "Hindus" or "Jews," not as adherents of "religion-in-general." But as cultural systems, the elements of religions are susceptible to sharing. And as vehicles of cultural power, religions contain other aspects of culture, such as art, politics, and economics. As cultural systems, hybrid forms of religions emerge, such as the forms we shall describe as *civil religions* or *cultural religions*. These terms, like *religion* itself, should be understood as heuristic and diagnostic, as efforts to understand the crucial dynamics of the American nation and American markets, respectively.

Although a linguistic-cultural approach to religion insists that religions draw on the ordinary stuff of culture—language, symbols, and other cultural practices—not "everything" is religious. Anything might be put to service in a religious system; nothing is beyond the religious imagination. Finally, though, religions have specific dynamics and functions within cultures. Most of life has nothing to do with religion. Eating, sleeping, making love, making art, buying and selling, ruling, and being ruled have nothing to do with religion unless a human being makes one of those ordinary processes a component of a relational network of other cultural elements through which people gain power around projections of transcendent authority in ways that eliminate things. If historians in the past have attended primarily to religious institutions, there is good reason for that. Enduring institutions—agencies of Hindus, Buddhists, Christians, Jews, Muslims, and so forth—provide the most visible continuities of what scholars call "religions." But the core dynamics, the nuclear processes, are found in discourses and practices and how they shape communities, violently or otherwise.

Until very recently, or at least until the dawn of "modernity" in roughly the seventeenth century, religious traditions accomplished with relative efficiency their task of channeling desire through systems of symbols. Religions usually were able to keep the peace in their communities because they operated within limited geographic and cultural zones where their claims to consent were largely unquestioned. Projections of transcendent authority were not recognized as projections; they were simply "the truth." But this geographical and cultural isolation allowed the buildup of resources associated with particular communities that could then be allied with increasingly sophisticated weaponry as the modern era dawned. As modernity proceeded, these weapons were used by hybrid imagined communities, notably nation-states whose agents then used religious discourses and practices to justify their claims to authority under a cloak of transcendence, with often violent, if not genocidal, results.[20] In the postmodern period, nation-states have been largely been subservient to global market–based processes that similarly have enlisted religious agents, discourses, and practices in the interest of controlling resources.[21] Selective agents of traditional religions have reacted to these developments with understandable fury, in movements often labeled *funda-mentalist*, but have also sought to ally themselves with whichever political agents promised them greater security and fulfillment.[22] Indeed, nowhere have these processes of religious blending and diffusion, and the violence they can spawn, been clearer than in the history of the United States.[23] To paraphrase the epigraph to this chapter from Benedict Anderson, my argument is that religion made possible the American empire, even if this religion was not understood as such by its victims or its adherents.

Rethinking "Religious Violence" in America

The condensations and displacements that have characterized religion throughout American history have occurred in three sectors: the voluntary, the public, and the cultural. These three sectors correspond to the existence today of sects (or denominations), the nation, and markets. For simplicity, the presence of *religious* operations in each sector can be summarized as traditional religion, civil religion, and cultural religion. Note that these three labels are, like the term *religion* itself, heuristic constructs to help analyze the complex ways in which authority operates. They are necessary to overcome the fictional dichotomies of "religion" and "politics" or "church" and "state" that obscure the functional interaction between the constructions of cultural power that have given American history its distinctive dynamic and produced the hybrids that have led to an empire of sacrifice or to repeated episodes of blessed brutalities.

To understand the role of religion in the emergence of American empire, we need to look beyond any simple opposition or interaction between "church" and "state" and see instead how the construction and corrosion of power and authority have operated across sectors of society, especially around apparently "secular" categories in which the displacements of religious logic have most effectively operated under assertions of innocence, purity, or transcendence. Those categories through which the material origins of desire have most consistently been compressed and displaced in America are age, race, and gender, as expressed in the culture in various identities associated with collectives like the nation or, now, an empire.

This argument develops into an approach to understanding religious violence that builds directly on elements drawn from several key thinkers. The first is René Girard, who over the past two decades has undoubtedly been the leading (albeit not transcendent) authority on questions of religion and violence.[24] According to Girard, whose work touches on literary criticism, anthropology, and philosophy of the social sciences, violence is contagious, a product of imitation. Following Freud (and, before Freud, Augustine), Girard suggests that the desires of others that we imitate include the desire to dominate others. "Rivalry does not arise because of the fortuitous convergence of two desires on a single object," Girard contends. "Rather, *the subject desires the object because the rival desires it.*[25] Once mutual desires converge, conflict follows the erasure of difference. "It is not the differences [between people and cultures] but the loss of them that gives rise to violence and chaos. This loss forces [human beings] into a perpetual confrontation, one that strips them of all their distinctive characteristics—in short, of their 'identities.'"[26] Mutual desire can engulf societies in perpetual conflict, constituting a recurring pattern of attack and reprisal, which Girard calls "reciprocal violence," or a "crisis of differentiation." With its increased possibility of intercultural encounter, modernity has produced such a global "crisis of differentiation."

From this analysis of a "crisis" and its resolution through "sacrifice," Girard locates both the origin and the significance of "religion." "The sole purpose of religion," he contends, "is to prevent the recurrence of reciprocal violence."[27] But hidden in this "preventive" cultural mechanism is violence itself, the justification of the expulsion, murder, or sacrifice of a scapegoat. "Religion shelters us from violence," Girard writes, "just as violence seeks shelter in religion."[28] For the "illegitimate" violence of unchecked rivalry, attack, and vengeance, religion substitutes a "legitimate" violence, as enacted in the practices of ritual and encoded in the discourse of myth. In religion, according to Girard, a "vicious cycle of reciprocal violence, wholly destructive in nature, is replaced by the vicious circle of ritual violence, creative and protective in nature."[29]

TABLE 3. *Rene Girard's "Mimetic Model" of Violence and the Sacred*

1. **Mimetic Desire/Acquisitive Mimesis:** A subject (individual or group) imitates a rival's desire for an object
2. **Crisis of Differentiation/Rivalry:** Conflict for the object is threatened, or occurs
3. **The Scapegoat/Legitimation of Violence:** A scapegoat is identified whose elimination can resolve rivalry without fear of reprisal or escalating vengeance
4. **Sacrifice/Enactment of Violence:** The scapegoat is expelled or killed; the object's possession clarified
5. **Restoration of Order:** Unanimity (temporarily) prevails
6. **Repetition, Masking, and Prevention through Religion:** Myth, ritual, prohibition, and (eventually) apotheosis of the victim ("the Sacred") create a cycle of desire, enactment, and restoration that sanctions "legitimate" violence, but rules out unchecked rivalry

This vicious circle that constitutes the relation between violence and the sacred can be mapped, according to Girardian theory, as shown in table 3. My debt to Girard is great, as my own thinking has been profoundly informed by his work. But Girard never addresses violence and religion in American culture and consequently does not recognize the hybrid forms of religious violence as they have emerged in civil and cultural religions. Even so, I will continue to build on and draw from his theory, particularly his notion of the centrality of "sacrifice" as a means both to end violence and to enact it.[30]

A second source for my discerning patterns of religious violence is R. Scott Appleby, the executive director of the Kroc Institute for International Peace Studies at the University of Notre Dame. According to Appleby, religious violence emerges from what he calls "weak" or "extremist" religions, by which he means traditions that have been compromised by accommodation to political agencies. Weak religions, whose chief examples are the movements around the globe loosely called *fundamentalisms*, share some features, as shown in table 4.

For the time being, the salience of each of these characteristics can only be suggestive. I will draw especially on Appleby's emphasis on dualism, which has been confirmed by many scholars of religion as a key catalyst for violence, and his emphasis on "ecstatic asceticism." Needless to say, I will also

TABLE 4. *Scott Appleby's "Marks of 'Extremist Religion'"*

1. **Reactive to External Factors:** often under circumstances of political suppression, manifesting an "innovative traditionalism" that combines tradition with elements of secular modernity (especially technology and mobility)
2. **Selective Retrieval of Elements within a Tradition:** often the result of "illiteracy" regarding "second order" or comparative reflection
3. **Male Charismatic Leaders/Young Followers:** often manifesting "totalism" of dress, diet, and discipline
4. **Dualism/Exclusivism:** cognitive patterns of "us" versus "them" in discourse, with strict boundaries to group belonging
5. **Exceptionalism:** Extraordinary times call for abrogation of central religious teachings or prohibitions against killing, or for use of unusual measures
6. **Ecstatic Asceticism:** Dominant ideology of "reward through sacrifice"

try to avoid those flaws in his thinking that have been pointed out by critics and will try to avoid his inability (or refusal) to address religious violence as a problem in American culture and history.[31]

A third source for my thinking about religious violence in American history is Mark Juergensmeyer. Like Girard and Appleby, Juergensmeyer has developed a series of characteristics of "religious violence," by which he means mainly terrorism. These characteristics can be summarized as a discrete logic, as in table 5. What I find distinctive about Juergensmeyer's logic in the context of American history is its attention to the "performative" aspects of religious violence and to the goal of "empowerment" that resides underneath enactments of religious violence. But like Girard and Appleby, Juergensmeyer has generally not applied his insights to American cases.[32]

Two other steps are necessary to sketch the rethinking of religious violence in American history. The first follows Regina Schwartz's *The Curse of Cain: The Violent Legacy of Monotheism* to locate religious violence in a social construction she variously labels "collective identity" or a principle of "sovereign power legitimated by transcendence."[33] Schwartz, a professor of English at Northwestern University, reduces, unnecessarily and inaccurately, the roots of identity-based religious violence to biblical monotheism. In fact, the context her words suggest is much broader:

A principle of scarcity . . . pervades most thinking about identity. When everything is in short supply, it must all be competed for—land, prosperity, power, favor, even identity itself. . . . [When] scarcity is encoded in the Bible in a principle of Oneness (one land, one people, one nation) and in monotheistic thinking (one Deity), it becomes a demand of exclusive allegiance that threatens with the violence of exclusion. When that thinking is translated into secular formations about peoples, "one nation under God" becomes less comforting than threatening.[34]

It is this identity based on an assumption of the scarcity of power, and therefore the need to control or possess it, that Schwartz sees as a trigger for violence, whether expressed in a biblical text or as a ground for national identity.

This latter prospect is particularly salient for our purposes, namely, that religious violence, or violence inherent in the process of forging identity, can flow from nation-states. "We secularists," Schwartz writes, "have confidently, and I believe mistakenly," supposed

that a sharp division has been achieved between the premodern sacred worldview and the modern secular one. But sacred categories of thought have not just disappeared. They have lingered into the modern world where they are transformed into secular ones. As Carl Schmitt, a political theo-

TABLE 5. *Mark Juergensmeyer's "Logic of Religious Violence"*

---

1. **A Theater of Terror:** terrorist acts are often examples of "performance violence," given "credibility by their social context," where violence functions symbolically to "reach an audience" and make a point whose political utility may not be immediately apparent
2. **Cosmic War:** religious images of divine struggle are put to service in worldly political battles
3. **Sacrificial Victims:** religious violence in the context of cosmic war is "justified" by appeal to "martyrdom," or the notion of a "heroic, transforming death"
4. **"Satanization":** enemies are "invented," and invested with "cosmic" significance, allowing their dehumanization
5. **Empowering Marginal Men:** religious violence is often a way "radical patriarchalism" asserts itself in acts of "symbolic empowerment"

---

rist who became an important ideologue to the Nazis, well understood, "All significant concepts of the modern theory of the state are secularized theological concepts not only because of their historical development— in which they were transferred from theology to the theory of the state, whereby, for example, the omnipotent God became the omnipotent law-giver—but also because of their systematic structure."[35]

Nationalism, like religion, has depended for its existence on a "legitima-tion by transcendence." "Nations are the will of God. National borders are the will of God. National expansions and colonization are the will of God. Every nation is the one nation under God."[36] Schwartz also briefly turns her attention to the United States. "In the United States, symbols of nationalism are wedded to invocations of the deity from the dollar bill to the pledge to the flag."[37] It is almost unnecessary to add that these invocations are offered with the utmost innocence, with only "patriotic" motives, surely nothing so vola-tile as "religion." The transcendent nation depends on an innocent people.

Once this mythic process is under way, it tends to mushroom. Schwartz turns again to the Nazi ideologue, Schmitt, to clarify her point:

Once sovereign power is legitimated by transcendence, it is elusive (and unlike human sovereignty) inviolate. There is no check upon the will of a nation-God. Carl Schmitt understood this: "The concept of sovereignty in the theory of the state . . . and the theory of the 'sole supremacy of the state' make the state an abstract person so to speak . . . with a monopoly of power 'mystically produced.'" Mystically produced and miraculously inviolate, the sovereignty of the divinely legitimated nation is, unlike its human counterpart, ultimately unimpeachable.[38]

To say that a nation is "inviolate" and "unimpeachable" is another way to say that it represents itself as innocent. Although this is a religious claim, it appears not to be religious, because references to the divine (or to some other object of transcendence) are displaced unto the nation, which is, obviously, contingent, temporal, and humanly created. In effect, then, politics becomes religion without the historical baggage. As Schwartz puts it, "In national-ism, the religious is secularized, and the national sanctified."[39] To summa-rize, under the supposed "separation" of church and state, the displacement characteristic of traditional religion has been transferred to the state in what amounts to a double displacement into a sort of meta-religion or (as I have suggested) a civil religion. It is precisely this process we see repeatedly at work in American history, behind some cases of extreme violence that match some of the marks of religious violence identified by leading theorists.

If Schwartz helps us move beyond the assumption of innocence associated with nation-states to recognize how civil religions arise, my own last book might help explain why market processes must be subject to a similar critique under the construct of cultural religion. The title of my book is *Shopping Malls and Other Sacred Spaces: Putting God in Place*. In it, I argue that ordinary, apparently secular places like shopping malls, Walt Disney World, and the suburban home operate as "sacred places" in the lives of many Americans. This argument is not, as it is here, based on a definition of religion as a system of compression and displacement. Instead, I built on the work of a number of previous thinkers about the interface between economics and religion to contend that market processes—commodification, shopping, domestic sanitation, and even lawn care—can have a religious meaning depending on how such objects and behaviors are presented by the producers (notably in advertising) and how they are appropriated by the consumers.[40]

For instance, consider shopping malls, particularly the Mall of America, just outside Minneapolis in Bloomington, Minnesota. Like most malls, the architectural features of the Mall of America are reminiscent of classic religious shrines, especially in the vestiges of Christian symbolism appropriate to the hegemonic sway of Christianity in American culture. Thus, most malls, including the Mall of America, contain water, light, trees, and bodies to disorient (displace) and then reorient (condense) the visitors' experience of the place, which is then exaggerated as "more" than an ordinary event, even "innocent." Similarly, advertising communicates that a visit to the mall is a visit to a "special" place, where one can be "devoted" to shopping and can discover "love" in many and various ways. Of course, such religious rhetoric obscures that one's primary purpose for going to a mall is to acquire a commodity. But this enchantment of commodities and the disorientation and reorientation of visitors, I believe, are intended (but obscured) parts of the experience of the place, making it in effect a "sacred" place in American culture. As geographer Jon Goss explained, "The modern megamall is a dreamhouse of the collectivity, where fantasies of authentic life are displaced onto commodities. . . . The shopping mall brings together the archetypes of the 'good world' with the world of goods, presenting the world of commodities apparently innocent of the commodification of the world."[41] In short, the mall is a sacred place in what might be called a "religion of the market," or what we are calling here more generally, American "cultural religion." That there is violence associated with malls can be confirmed by anyone who has had to shop in one during the winter holidays in the United States, although recent mall bombings and shootings have punctuated the usual banality of violence in mall operations with overt conflict.[42]

The mall is only one of many examples of how the line between markets and religion has been crossed in American history through the formation of what might be called "cultural religions." Even so, scholars have barely begun to explore the interface between religions and markets, despite some historians' helpful forays into this interdisciplinary thicket.[43] Even less well understood is the way that religion, markets, and violence intersect. My principal purpose in this first chapter has been to invite readers to rethink how the domains for "violence" and "religion" and their interactions need to expand. Violence is not only criminal violence, for it also can have social and cultural (systemic) forms. Religion is not only an institutional phenomenon associated with traditional sects or denominations, as it can also acquire hybrid forms as civil or cultural religions. Religious violence results, then, as people condense and displace material desires into transcendent authority across institutional sites, particularly in relation to collective identities and practices in association with nations and markets.

Sacrificing Youth

From Reefer Madness *to* Hostel

The smooth functioning of . . . society . . . [is] in no way impaired
by the fact that . . . that same "society" puts to death or (but fail-
ing to help someone in distress accounts for only a minor difference) allows to die of hunger and disease tens of millions of
children . . . without any moral or legal tribunal ever being considered competent to judge such a sacrifice, the sacrifice of others to avoid being sacrificed oneself. Not only is it true that such
a society participates in this incalculable sacrifice, it actually
organizes it. The smooth functioning of its economic, political,
and legal affairs, the smooth functioning of its moral discourse
and good conscience presupposes the permanent operation of
this sacrifice.
  —Jacques Derrida, *The Gift of Death*

Growing up is always hard to do. Lately it has not become any
easier.
  —Harvey J. Graff, *Conflicting Paths: Growing Up in America*

Agents of both modern secular and sacred communities have ben-
efited from relegating "religion" to its appearance in traditional denominations or private practices.[1] Secular agents have selectively exploited for their
own interests the symbolic power of appeals to transcendence without necessarily embracing the ethical limits and ideological baggage (e.g., "superstition") associated with historic traditions.[2] Conversely, agents of historic
religious traditions have cooperated with the institutions of politics and markets by differentiating the operations of these "realms" from those of religion,
thereby gaining access to material power and ensuring their own "salvation,"
or at least the peacefulness of their consciences. Such cooperation across the
spiritual and secular sectors of society, however, has been obscured by what

the sociologist Edward Shils called the "anti-traditional tradition" of modernity.[3] This peculiar phenomenon makes it seem as if religious innovations or hybrids, or what some scholars have called civil or cultural religions, are not properly "religious" or, in other words, not properly passé.

Nevertheless, during the twentieth century, young people in the United States have been rather intensively indoctrinated into a powerful religious hybrid that communicates scandal over acts of individual aggression or moral transgression while ignoring, if not legitimizing, the symbolic sacrifice and systemic violation of significant numbers of children and youth.[4] This religious operation has been most overt in its civil dimensions when the United States has engaged in large-scale military actions (six times between 1945 and 1988 and nine from 1989 to 2008), in which violence engaging young people in war has been cloaked overtly in the euphemism of "sacrifice."[5] But religious features also crop up repeatedly in youth-serving cultural institutions like schools and the criminal justice system in which young people become projects, problems, or "at-risk" abject objects whose being "saved" depends on the intervention of a secular authority.[6] Such authoritative agencies often originated in traditional religious communities, with the YMCA perhaps the best studied of them, but during the twentieth century, most of their religious functions went underground.[7]

Furthermore, these redeemer institutions have not always fulfilled their roles with the characteristic charity that one might expect. They sought, often explicitly, to honor youth by putting them on a pedestal. But equally often, young people found these agencies to be degrading and resentment-driven efforts at control and containment.[8] Indeed, when young people, as they are sometimes wont to do, resisted their indoctrination or precociously expressed desires to take control of their own destinies, the very institutions that existed to "protect" youth quickly turned them into scapegoats to be sacrificed for the very failures that their resistance or precocious willfulness exposed.[9] Indeed, this religious system represented young people simultaneously and interchangeably as knife-wielding priests or bloodthirsty monsters, as victims whose blood atones and as the mob whose guilt is expiated through the ritual process. Among the most visible (in many senses) sites where these intergenerational religious dynamics have been evident is the film industry.[10] In other words, an American empire of sacrifice has been both created and communicated through film, especially through some blessed brutalities that constitute a subset of what film historian David Considine named "the cinema of adolescence."[11]

Genres in film are notoriously difficult to define.[12] But from *Reefer Madness* in 1936 through *Rebel without a Cause* in 1955, to *Halloween* in 1978, *Scream* in 1996, and *Hostel* in 2005, consistent but flexible stereotypes have emerged to depict a certain segment of youth in America as abject objects suitable for "innocent" sacrifice.[13] By depicting youth as containers of contagious desire who are deservedly disciplined and punished as vulnerable (and often virginal) victims or as ruthless monsters who perpetrate "evil," these films have communicated to young people over the past seventy years a consistent message: that it is their duty to endure and/or enact violence.[14] These films understandably encode this message in the symbolic safety of the ritual setting of the theater and are attractive to youth in direct proportion to how well they (supposedly) scandalize adult sensibilities.[15] Every viewer of these films can take pleasure, as film scholar Isabel Cristina Pinedo pointed out, in surviving the adrenaline-producing "tests" that watching them provides.[16] The sacrifices in these films appear to be innocent because they are "only entertainment" or "just a movie."[17] This violence therefore is not only justified, but it is also virtuous, or at least consistently profitable.

To categorize these films as mere entertainment, however, masks how this theatricalized terror coincides with the way that young people have been enlisted in all kinds of violence across American culture in recent decades and how adults have denied responsibility as the creators of this violence, as the epigraph to this chapter from Derrida indicates. For once removed from the sacred confines of the theater, the devotion of young Americans to causes of conquest and domination, honor and vengeance, was marshaled during the twentieth century for missions that have not always resulted in happy Hollywood endings. From wars to prisons, young people have populated policies and institutions whose practices are built on their bodies. Indeed, this empire of sacrifice, evident in the cinema of adolescence, bears a remarkable similarity to patterns of religious logic that underlie other forms of religious violence, particularly acts of terrorism. In sum, the blessed brutalities of an American empire of sacrifice would appear to exercise the maximum toll on the young, those with the fewest material resources at their disposal to resist them. In short, age has been the principal category through which violence has been religiously produced in America, albeit without the explicit sanction of traditional religious leaders and sometimes despite their apparently vigorous protests.[18]

If religions are systems or relations of condensation and displacement that communicate transcendent authority, then one of the chief religious categories in American culture around which violence has operated is the construction of age. It is a truism that the category of adolescence arose among religious communities in the late nineteenth and early twentieth century to mark youth as occupying a "liminal" space.[19] The reasons for this social construction of a life stage are many, and while historians of childhood generally acknowledge that "adolescence" has religious origins, it is less clear from many studies that the religious functions of this category endure, albeit in paths different from those traced by the YMCA.[20] Beholden to a wooden assumption of secularization, many historians of youth have missed the ongoing religious valorization, if not anxiety, attached to the coming-of-age process in America.[21] Critical to this process is the socialization of youth to accept violence as a part of culture, to see brutalities as blessed, and to welcome domination as innocent. This religious process was foreshadowed, if not foreordained, in popular films of the cinema of adolescence between 1936 and 2007.[22]

Spectacles of Sacrifice in the Cinema of Adolescence

In *Teenagers and Teenpics: The Juvenilization of American Movies in the 1950s*, the film historian Thomas Doherty documents how "the teenpic [developed as] a version of the exploitation film."[23] Beginning in the 1930s, filmmakers realized that they could make money by producing films that subtly exploited titillating imagery and controversial issues so long as they were presented in a moralistic framework that would get them past the censors. *Reefer Madness* (1936) is perhaps the best known of the genre today, although in its time it was not the most successful. Originally financed by a church group under the title *Tell Your Children*, the project was purchased shortly after its completion by the exploitation producer Dwain Esper. Esper gave it the sensational new title *Reefer Madness* and added a variety of salacious shots. After a brief run, the movie was all but forgotten until its resurrection in the 1970s as a cult classic, rivaled as an audience favorite only by *The Rocky Horror Picture Show*.[24]

No such market lag beset *Rebel without a Cause*. This classic teenpic, released in 1955, exploited images of turbulent or "juvenile delinquent" adolescents, the various roles played by James Dean, Sal Mineo, and Natalie Wood.[25] Following *Rebel*, the importance of teen actors and teen audiences to box office success was well established. Nevertheless, John Carpenter's *Halloween*, filmed in 1978 for around $300,000, broke all kinds of profit margins by generating more than $60 million in revenue. In *Halloween*, furthermore, Carpenter subsumed the moralistic context for the earlier films' violence under frank emotional appeal. He admitted in an interview that the film was "true crass exploitation. . . . Fuck everybody. I don't care if this is something I shouldn't be doing. I really like it."[26] So did many others. The film spawned thirteen sequels, as well as a host of imitators and their sequels, such as *Friday the 13th* (1980), *Prom Night* (1980), *Graduation Day* (1981), and *Hell Night* (1981). More recently, the *Scream* trilogy (1996–2002) revitalized the genre, according to some critics, or at least renewed its market appeal to another generation of adolescents.[27] With *Hostel* (2005, sequel 2007), sadism took center stage as the director, Eli Roth, vividly depicted the market-driven torture of American youth with axes, scissors, wire cutters, scalpels, chainsaws, and more.[28]

On the most basic level, these films are linked together because they depict young characters confronted by or implicated in violence, whose dilemma and its resolution the audience is invited to invest in and identify with. More significant are the formulaic roles that young people play in these films: they are innocent and vulnerable, and/or guilty and worthy of punishment, if they are not in fact psychotic killers themselves. The films also tend to depict an "absent presence" that must, finally, come to the rescue of the youth and resolve the violent crisis.[29] Traditional religious institutions, of course, never appear in these films. Although the cinema of adolescence appears to be remarkably secular, the way the films depict youth at risk, sacrifice a few, and then save the others gives them a rather overtly religious logic. As film scholar Barbara Creed observed, building on philosopher Julia Kristeva's work on abjection, "Human sacrifice as a religious abomination is constructed as the abject in virtually all horror films."[30] More bluntly, suggests the historian of cinema Tim Shary, in these films teens are "sadistically brutalized" on screen and then are "expected to enjoy such a negative representation of themselves with masochistic abandon."[31] It is as if these films discover (when in fact they create) an excess of youthful desire, transgressive and troubling, and then represent such desires on the screen in order to contain them. Film critic and professor Stephen Prince put it well when writing about horror films generally:

> [This] may be regarded as a compulsive symbolic exchange in which members of a social order, of a class or a subgroup, nervously affirm the importance of their cultural inheritance. Emphasis is placed on a culture's rituals, beliefs, and customs, its means of imposing a system of punctuation on the world, important because this system is easily lost and because it is crucial to the task of maintaining existing definitions of the human.[32]

In short, these films articulate and visualize religious displacement. They waste desire, but in cinematic form, in order to lead to transcendent authority or to reinforce an aura of transcendence in association with several apparently "secular" institutions.

Reefer Madness (1936) presents a logic of sacrifice in didactic form. The protagonists of the film are "Bill" and "Mary," two pure youth who excel as students and athletes. Over the course of the movie, Bill and Mary become involved with a group of teens who gather at the apartment of Jack and Mae, the surrogate "bad parents" of the genre, to smoke marijuana. The effects of the weed are, shall we say, dramatic. *Ecstasy* is not quite the right term to describe the excessive enthusiasm the actors display "under the influence," but it comes close. In any event, pure Bill is seduced by a weed-addled older woman, and even purer Mary is subjected to sexual advances by another weed-possessed youth, named Ralph. In an effort to protect Mary's virtue, Bill scuffles with her assailant. An adult, "Jack," intervenes, bringing a pistol onto the scene. The gun goes off, and Mary dies. But Bill is so high that he believes he is guilty of the crime. A criminal trial ensues, in which the judge declares that the perpetrators of this violence must be judged or the community will be "contaminated." Consequently, Ralph is sentenced to life in an asylum for the criminally insane. Mae commits suicide. Eventually, Bill learns the facts behind Mary's death and is spared jail, but only after the intervention of the police. The film then ends as it began—with an address to a group of concerned parents about the "menace of marijuana" by a school official, who announces that he intends to "lay the foundation for a national policy." That policy is founded on the spectacles of the sacrifice of youth, whose roles as scapegoats are intended to establish the unanimity (and purity) of the community around the need to control teenagers' desire through the "innocent" and noble institutions of education and police power.[33]

In *Rebel without a Cause* (1955), two scenes especially give evidence of the emerging iconography of sacrifice.[34] The first is the film's most famous sequence, the "chickie run" in which two young men, Buzz and Jim—the latter played by James Dean—race two stolen cars toward a cliff. The ritual elements in the scene are obvious. Jim and Buzz are competing for status among a group of teenagers and for the affection of Judy, played by Natalie Wood. They are mimetic doubles, or rivals, a common phenomenon in myth and ritual. The two young men agree to race in order to prove their manhood. To refuse the test would make one a "chicken," a bit of discourse that in a few years came to characterize the entire female gender. When Buzz inadvertently dies in the race, a rite of passage now assumes the salience of a sacrifice. Buzz's death, which is hardly mourned and quickly forgotten, becomes the apotheosis of James Dean's own ascent to manhood.[35]

The second scene of sacrifice is even more overt.[36] In it, yet another vulnerable youth, now bearing the not insignificant name of Plato, is the victim. He is gunned down by the police on the steps of a secular temple, the Griffith Observatory in Los Angeles. Screenwriter Stewart Stern explained in an interview his purpose for creating the tableau:

> The setting of the planetarium . . . I liked very much. . . . It was like a Greek temple, like the Theater Dionysus, and the way the steps came down from its great doors reminded me of the skene that used to stand in front of the back wall of the ancient Greek theaters—where they did the sacrifices. . . . So it seemed like an amazing place to round out the story of Rebel. I felt that the story should begin there and that some crucial, concluding event should take place there as, well, maybe a sacrifice of some kind.[37]

What critic Thomas Doherty describes as Plato's "sacrificial snuff-out" occurs as the counterpoint to Jim's own attainment of masculine virtue.[38] Plato's sacrifice was inevitable in the parameters of Hollywood gender conventions; in fact, the homoerotic attraction between Mineo's and Dean's characters was clear enough in the script to draw a warning from Hollywood censors.[39] Manhood needed reinforcement, and thus immediately after the sacrifice, Jim and his father, whose own Oedipal conflicts move the story along, are reconciled. The father promises to his son that he will "try and be as strong as you want me to be" and then wraps his arm around his wife in a patriarchal and protective embrace. This all happens, of course, under the approving gaze of the police gathered around the planetarium, who have just gunned down a youth. An equation of manhood with the willingness to endure, or undertake, violence is all but explicit.[40] Jim has proved that he is no chicken. Naturally, he gets the girl. These ritual sacrifices compress a vision of a young man willing to endure violence as a normative expectation, if not a transcendent duty, in cold war America.

By *Halloween* (1978), the violence that young people endure is personal, graphic, frequent, and overtly gender laden, if not misogynist.[41] Four victims fall, three of whom are women. The first establishes the sacrificial motif: the killing is carried out with a knife and is depicted as a consequence of sin, in the interest of preserving purity. The viewer follows the killer through a first-person camera angle. The viewer/killer then observes a young couple kissing on a couch and going upstairs to a bedroom. The viewer/killer dons a Halloween mask, through the eyes of which the camera follows the action into a kitchen, where a large knife is taken from a drawer. After the young man of the couple bolts down the stairs and out the door, adjusting his clothing, the viewer/killer ascends to find the young woman in the bedroom, naked, seated at a nightstand brushing her hair in front of a mirror. The viewer sees her through the killer's eyes, as a knife flashes on the screen while the sound-track represents repeated gashing noises of steel penetrating flesh.[42] The young woman is sacrificed as a bad babysitter.

Three other killings follow in the ninety minutes of the film, and the function of all of them as sacrifice becomes explicit in the last murder. In it, the two victims are Annie and Lynda, friends of the protagonist or virginal "final girl," Laurie (played by Jamie Lee Curtis).[43] Lynda, like the first victim, dies a postcoital death. Annie, who also is sexually promiscuous, is then gruesomely displayed on the bed, as if on an altar, in an unmistakable framing.[44] Once again, of course, no one mourns these victims. All of them were bad babysitters who deserved to die for their assumption of adult desire without the attendant responsibility. Accordingly, Jamie Lee Curtis's survival is ensured because she is a virgin, and even then, her being saved depends on the intervention of a psychiatrist, an expert in the matter of "evil," as he claims in the film, who arrives at a crucial moment with a gun that stops the killer in his tracks. In the wake of the sexual revolution, teen desire made an easy target for scapegoating. A transcendent (or at least uncritical) nostalgia for (fading) sexual purity, ironically communicated through exploitative images of its opposite, was the basic religious message.

Such spectacles of sacrifice had progressed (if that is the word for it) to the point of postmodern self-referentiality by the time Scream appeared in 1996. Both the actors and the participants knew they were "only" taking part in a ritual for the purpose of entertainment. Scream screenwriter Kevin Williamson and director Wes Craven (a graduate of the evangelical Wheaton College in Illinois) wrote the knowing agency of the audience into the spectacles of sacrifice. Over the years, audience observers had noted that youth occasionally had cheered at the slaughters depicted on the screen in some horror films and had ironically asserted the pleasure they took in the graphically violent and sexually laden images with shouts like "we want boobs."[45] In Scream, consequently, it was precisely the agency of the "final girl," played by Neve Campbell, that saved her. Campbell's character was, furthermore, no longer a virgin, which rendered moot the salvation-through-purity motif in Halloween. Indeed, the only way that Campbell was able to survive the eight "sacrifices" in the narrative of the film was through her own willingness to embrace violence. But this internal logic in fact validated the most obvious "absent presence" in the film: the film itself.[46]

Throughout *Scream*, the various characters "survive" in more or less direct proportion to their abilities to manipulate the cinematic conventions of the horror genre. "To successfully survive a horror movie," one character, Randy, points out during the film, "you have to abide by the rules. You can never have sex: The minute you do, you're as good as gone. Sex equals death. Never drink or do drugs: It's an extension of the first. And never, ever say, 'I'll be right back.'"[47] Randy, of course, dies. Enslaved to the rules, he does not recognize that the survivors make the rules, just as filmmakers make horror movies. The violence is a game, or a ritual, between the filmmakers and the viewers in which the only "sacred" thing, or locus of transcendent, saving authority, is the film itself and whatever an audience member makes of it. The only victims, so the film asserts, are the ones on the screen, and we know, of course, that they are only actors. The sacrifices are merely spectacles—depicted as vividly as possible to heighten the scandal to adult sensibilities—but of which knowing young viewers are fully aware that it all is a ruse.[48]

Craven was thus quick to silence any ideological critics of his genre. "There's a tremendous temptation in this country to get up and pontificate," he told one reviewer. "It really is thought control coming from an overblown sense of righteousness."[49] It is impossible that someone so familiar with the conventions of the exploitation genre as Craven could possibly be as blind to the history of pontificating associated with the genre as this statement makes him appear to be. Exploitation films that triggered desires and fears almost always had some moral point or "deeper" meaning, and Craven's intent—at least in one expression—was no different, as we shall see. But for the moment, the point is that in a deep irony, by pontificating against pontificating, Craven seems tempted to offer an overblown, even "tremendous" if not self-righteous, defense of his own ritual product. The transcendent aura of the film *auteur* trumped the moralism of religious traditionalists.

By the time of *Hostel* (2005), irony had given way to what one critic called "torture porn."[50] Countless young people are seduced, chased, manacled, tortured, and killed in the ninety-minute movie, and other young people's bodies (they already are "dead") are literally hacked into pieces and fed into a furnace on the screen. The plot features three young men who are backpacking in Europe. Two are Americans, "Josh" and "Paxton," and one is an Icelander, "Oli." The film begins in Amsterdam, where the young men are looking for, and finding, a good time, which they define primarily as sex, drugs, and rock and roll. Eventually, the youth learn about a hostel in Bratislava, Slovakia, where young women are supposed to be particularly eager to meet Americans. The trio hops the next train. They find the hostel (which was actually a former monastery near Prague). They also find the women, but the women are being paid to seduce backpackers and then deliver them to a business enterprise, "Elite Hunting." Elite Hunting is run by shady-looking Eastern Europeans who provide young victims for businessmen. The businessmen pay for the "pleasure" of torturing and killing these unfortunate youths. Oli disappears first—his dead body makes a brief appearance later. Josh falls next—after having holes drilled in his body with an electric drill and his Achilles tendons severed with a scalpel. Paxton is left alone, after passing out in a bar, to discover the torture chamber in an abandoned factory that has been rigged up like a prison. He is led there by one of the young woman who first seduced him and his friends. Pax ("peace") survives his ordeal, but not until he loses two fingers from one of his hands and narrowly escapes a sadistic German torturer who has paid to kill Pax with a chainsaw. In the process of escaping, Pax also learns that American youth earn a premium price on this sordid black market. As the film closes, Pax exacts vengeance on all of those who led him to the hostel. He kills the young man who told him about the hostel and the two women who seduced him and Josh. And he kills the client who killed Josh, by stuffing the middle-aged man's head in a toilet bowl and then slitting his throat. The scene of violent vengeance is a fitting conclusion for a film filled with blood, vomit, and other theatrical bodily fluids.

To be fair, this film could be read as a clever critique of American policies and practices. At one point, Paxton, who has just had sex, quotes President George W. Bush's famous (and slightly premature) line about the Iraq War: "Mission Accomplished!" More generally, the film might be a critique of actual "hunting" operations in America in which people pay to kill animals carefully controlled and released for their "pleasure" (former Vice President Dick Cheney was apparently quite a fan). Most obviously, the film both exploits and critiques the relationship between markets and violence; the "clients" who pay Elite Hunting for the privilege of torturing youth are universally depicted as twisted and sick (even though the audience also, of course, vicariously "enjoys" their peculiar fetishes). But the critiques in the film are, at best, oblique. In fact, the trailer suggests that the movie's intended audience is precisely the (potential) torturer in every viewer. "There is a place," it begins, "where all your darkest, sickest fantasies are possible; where you can experience anything you desire; where you can torture, punish, or kill for a price." As a spectacle of sacrifice, the film creates a place—namely, the screen—where those fantasies do "come true." The film compresses desires and fears and displaces them into ritualized scenes of torture, punishment, and killing. As Peter Hutchings summarized it, such scenes "suggest that horror perhaps deploys religious ideas more commonly than is sometimes supposed and not necessarily in the context of surmounted belief."[51] Not surprisingly, then, the United States Council of Catholic Bishops condemned this religious competitor as "morally bankrupt" and "nauseatingly vile."[52] The film earned Lionsgate Studios roughly $40 million.

From *Reefer Madness* to *Hostel*, young people have consistently (if flexibly) been depicted in American cinema as abject objects suitable for sacrifice. Any accurate analysis of these films has to begin with the pleasure they produce in some viewers and with the attraction they have held for young people over the decades.[53] Needless to say, we cannot conduct a thorough audience-response analysis here, but let us look at least three possibilities. On one level, then, the films have probably provided youth with a symbolic affirmation of their own power as agents. These are "coping strategies," in the words of Mary Beth Oliver and Meghan Sanders.[54] These films depict (and, to a degree, allow young people to distance themselves from or put boundaries around) the escalating violence of a culture in which youth have been increasingly controlled through schools, patrolled by curfew laws and cruising police, and continuously invited (if not coerced) to participate in military institutions and ventures.[55] Young people can work out some of their fears through watching these films, usually the concern that they might not find a path to replace their parents in the "adult" culture of violence that is the United States. As these films depict it, the choice is bleak, but at least there is a choice to kill rather than to be killed, to be the torturer rather than the tortured. That the viewers survive this "choice" when some of the actors do not, is a rush and might give viewers hope that they will be among the survivors in a violent America, even if they have to use force to do so.[56] For sensation seekers of all ages, the films are an adrenaline-boosting experience. They compress desire and channel or displace it into the ninety minutes or so of cultural product. They are avenues to cultural power.

On another level, though, these films might fulfill the classical function of tragedy and other forms of theatricalized sacrifice. They might serve to purify the community of its violence and steel young people for the difficult work of engaging in the long symbolic struggles necessary to contain arbitrary power with the humane forces of word and image. Directors and producers thus become postmodern priests and shamans. They tell terrifying stories to young people through flickering images that initiate youth into the path of realistic adulthood. These films thus fulfill functions of "rites of passage." They offer tests through which youth can demonstrate their willingness to be incorporated into the communities, practices, and institutions that will help perpetuate the culture of middle-class America.[57] These films are ritual processes in the American cultural religion. They are ways that young people might eliminate violence by facing violence, ritually represented on a screen in ways that enlist youthful identification with the survivors of violence. They are American catharses.

Finally, we must examine what might be called the shifting projections of transcendence in the films to see how the violence in them might serve a third, perhaps less salutary, function. Put bluntly: who (or what) "saves" these young people?[58] In the films' narratives, the transcendent, saving authorities vary over time and include youthful purity, good parents, police power, and even psychology. Accordingly, through these films youth might learn proper gender roles and sexual norms, respect for police authority, ways to get along with peers and parents, and so forth. But the truly enduring continuity in these films is the self-contained (if not self-righteous) conviction of the cultural power of film itself.[59] Writing specifically about horror films, Barbara Creed again explains, but with significance for teenpics generally:

> The central ideological project of the popular horror film [is] purification of the abject through a "descent into the foundations of the symbolic construct." As a form of modern defilement rite, the horror film works to separate out the symbolic order from all that threatens its stability. . . . Viewing the horror film signifies a desire not only for perverse pleasure (confronting sickening, horrific images, being filled with terror/desire for the undifferentiated) but also a desire, having taken pleasure in perversity, to throw up, throw out, eject the abject (from the safety of the spectator's seat).[60]

In short, horror films are systems of displacement; ways to waste time. They compress and displace terror onto an image whose sacrifice can "save," or at least temporarily entertain, participants. These films function religiously, even though traditional religions are all but completely absent from their plots. They define boundaries by representing their defilement and eliminate options by depicting the terror of a world without limits on violence.

Creed argues further that in most horror films, the feminine is the abject object. There is ample justification for this claim, especially in *Halloween*, although as the genre has developed, Creed's argument appears to have perhaps a bit too much exclusionary anima, as men get hacked to death, too. Even more broadly, the abject object in the cinema of adolescence is youth itself. These films are thus invitations to "grow up," which in America means accepting the "innocent" violence of "sacrifice" from time to time. By confronting youth with the defilement of death, murder, and sacrifice, the films seek to push youth beyond "abjection," defined by philosopher Georges Bataille as "the inability to assume with sufficient strength the imperative act of excluding abject things (and that act establishes the foundation of collective existence)."[61]

At stake in these films is nothing less than the American way that has repeatedly fostered millennial or redemptive violence, the occasional need to expel some impurity or conquer some enemy, to demonstrate one's own self-righteous status as a chosen one.[62] The films accurately depict the escalation of violence in twentieth-century America and wrap that violence in the transcendent aura of innocent entertainment. All the young viewers of these films are thus invited to invest in maintaining the symbolic order that operates according to a religious logic in which sacrifice and violence are both warranted and unquestioned. Little wonder that Craven felt compelled to defend his project by pontificating against pontificating. Thought control is effective, after all, only when it is unrecognized as such. When the symbolic order itself becomes the object of righteous defense, in ways that legitimize the marketed operation of violence under an illusion of purity or innocence, then the truly "American," if not imperial, and the truly "religious," if hardly sacred, quality of these films may have been realized.[63] They produce domination "innocently." Their brutalities are blessed.

That these films about youth function "religiously" should not be surprising. After all, "youth" is a construction with demonstrably religious origins in the YMCA and similar agencies. Films calling for youth to sacrifice in fact date back to the very origins of cinema.[64] The conventions by which films featuring the sacrifices of youth do "religious" work are thus well established, even if they have been obscured through evidently "secular" forms. To be sure, there are nuances in this construction of "youth" and diverse ways in which we might interpret these films, according to race, gender, and class. These films are not universally attractive to all youth, and their meanings no doubt differ for different people. But I highlight age here apart from race, gender, and class only for heuristic purposes: to clarify the religious operations at work across the more typical social constructions around which American violence has often circulated. Age can be, and has been in America, a marker for violence. Among a particular segment of American young people, mainly white middle-class males, the trajectories in this brief history of the cinema of adolescent abjection would seem ripe to prepare them to endure, as well as to enact, violence. Many historians of horror films have noted that during its development, the genre shifted from films depicting "relative security about social authority" to films depicting "relative insecurity about social authority."[65] The subset of films we have profiled here seems to confirm this conclusion. Even more, that this construction of youth as abject objects suitable for sacrifice happens to coincide with the patterns that scholars have noted in other forms of "religious violence," or in all-too-real forms of terror, is surely worth noting.

A Theater of Terror, or Innocent Martyrs to the "Beast in the Boudoir"

As I have argued and if certain representations of youth in American cinema since 1936 can be read as examples of "religious violence," it should not be surprising that these compressions and displacements can also be shown to coincide with patterns of religious violence identified by scholars whose subjects of study are variously labeled religious "extremists," "fundamentalists," and "terrorists." We could trace any number of these patterns, apart from the single most crucial theme of "sacrifice," but I will concentrate on three that will appear repeatedly in my case studies. The first follows René Girard to see sacrifice as an attempt to resolve a "crisis of differentiation."

According to Girard, whose theory is outlined in chapter 1, a rival desires the same object as her model, producing "doubling" or a crisis of differentiation that must be resolved through the sacrifice, elimination, or violation of a scapegoat. The second pattern develops a notion from Mark Juergensmeyer, whose ideas also are described in chapter 1, that finds evidence of religious violence in ritual or performative empowerment, in which displays of violence empower "marginal men" who have access primarily to symbolic means of accomplishing their aims. Violence is enacted as a "theater of terror." Finally, following Scott Appleby, also introduced in chapter 1, we can see how the spectacles of sacrifice that feature and are marketed to youth provide them with an experience of "transcendence through suffering," or what he calls "ecstatic asceticism." In these experiences of ecstatic asceticism, a violent act "lifts" (which is the literal meaning of transcendence) the participant beyond the mundane through an act of violence that identifies the agent with a greater cause (e.g., an institution or tradition). Needless to say, all three of these ways to understand the films as religious violence highlight how the films function as displacements. They offer youth as substitutes for any viewer, particularly other American adolescents, and depict the sacrifice of youth to affect some experience of transcendence, or at least survival, for the viewer. Later in this chapter I examine the crucial questions of whether these films reflect, or shape, the social realities of young people and whether they assert, or critique, the innocence and purity of the adult institutions that ostensibly exist to "serve" youth.

That all five of these films highlight a crisis of differentiation is obvious. The films' central terror is whether the young people will survive, that is, reach the adult status they desire, just as, one can imagine, such uncertainty about identity might be a central terror among the young people who are the most frequent patrons of these movies. The way that adult desire is marked in the films does change over time. In *Reefer Madness*, adult desire is overtly marked by academic and athletic success. Bill and Mary are "good" kids who are only reluctantly seduced by the pleasures of pot smoking and sex. In *Rebel*, gender differentiation is the cause of the crisis. James Dean's Oedipal conflict with his feminized father frames the structure of the film. At one point, the father appears onscreen wearing an apron, which provokes a violent and disgusted reaction from his son, who must compensate with his own manly strength for his father's weakness.[66] By *Halloween*, parents are largely absent. Desire, now unleashed by the sexual revolution, is indiscriminately focused on physical pleasure. Nevertheless, the film's narrative does not make clear why the killer kills. He is simply described as "evil," even though he consistently targets youthful sexual experimentation. Thus even the "good girl," played by Jamie Lee Curtis, is shown knitting in the film, a cinematic staple for masturbation. She also is accused by her friend, Annie, of "thinking about those things," by which Annie means, of course, thinking about sex.[67] The "good girl's" vulnerability is thereby secured. In both *Scream* and *Hostel*, the crisis is less about sex than about violence itself. The "final girl" in *Scream* has sexual relations within the plot, which both heightens her vulnerability and suggests that the crisis of differentiation is not between those who are sexually pure and those who are not, but simply between those who will survive and those who will not. *Hostel* uses the market as the cause of the crisis among these youth: men pay to torture young people, much as young people pay to see these films. But precocious male sexual desire (and other profanity, with which the film is replete) also serves to justify their sacrifice. Throughout the later films, violence generally has an uncertain origin. The crisis of differentiation is shown as continuous and ongoing, thus justifying (of course) sequels, not to mention a continuing escalation of violence. That is, when youth themselves are the abject, there will never be an end to suitable scapegoats. As Girard explained, cultures seek scapegoats from among the "marginal," those whose sacrifice can appear "innocent," restore unanimity to the society, and release aggression in a paroxysm of pleasure.[68] Thus for the benefit of the whole culture, filmmakers enact the rituals of defilement that keep the symbolic order in place.[69]

It is this pleasure in finding suitable victims from among their own kind, in punishing vice and resolving the crisis of differentiation, that may draw young people to these films and give them much of their symbolic power. Mark Juergensmeyer claims that the crucial element of much religious violence is its ability to "empower marginal men" symbolically. Referring to acts of terrorism, using words that could easily apply to any of these films (but especially the later ones), he writes: "Such instances of exaggerated violence are constructed events: they are mind-numbing, mesmerizing theater. At center stage are the acts themselves—stunning, abnormal, and outrageous murders carried out in a way that graphically displays the awful power of violence—set within grand scenarios of conflict and proclamation."[70]

Here, *Scream* is undoubtedly the best example. In the opening sequence of the film, the actress Drew Barrymore is stalked by a phone caller who claims to be able to "see" her through the glass windows of her suburban home. Eventually, Barrymore is told to turn on the porch lights, so she is able to see her "boyfriend" tied to a chair and "disemboweled." Within minutes, she is "disemboweled" herself and hung from a tree like a deer. In the film's "Director's Commentary," which includes a voice-over discussion by the director, Craven, and the screenwriter, Kevin Williamson, the two note that these scenes were heavily censored by the Motion Picture Association of America. They were "too intense," as Craven scornfully reiterates the association's argument, after which he explains that he had to shorten the shots of Barrymore's "entrails" by 50 percent. He defends these graphic depictions by contending that he was trying to expose "the dark side of humanity." The scenes of disembowelment therefore should have remained uncut because "audiences respond to truth in films."[71]

These little tidbits of pontificating are highly illustrative in light of our earlier discussion of the origins of the cinema of adolescence in exploitation films. They suggest, of course, that the filmmaker intended to convey more than merely "entertainment" through these images. For all exploitation filmmakers, there is a (self) justification involved. Indeed, Craven's object was something as noble as "truth." Juergensmeyer can again help us draw out the significance of such a statement: "Creations of terror are done . . . to make a symbolic statement. . . . They are intended to refer to something beyond their immediate target: a grander conquest, for instance, or a struggle more awesome than meets the eye."[72] The violence enacted by terrorists is all too real, since it is enacted on the bodies of innocent victims, but it also carries a symbolic significance that extends beyond the immediate victims to make a larger point. In the cinema of adolescence, the violence is staged, but it also has symbolic significance beyond its immediate context. The violence in *Reefer Madness* was intended to shock parents into awareness of the "danger" of marijuana. *Rebel without a Cause* killed off two youths to warn parents to be vigilant to the dangers of juvenile delinquency. *Halloween* was a morality play that exploitatively targeted teenagers' sexual desire. *Scream* sought to depict the "truth" of the "dark side of humanity," in contrast to the control of censors. And *Hostel* suggested that the market unleashes unfettered, even "sick," desires.

The cinema of adolescence thus shares with acts of terrorism what Juergensmeyer calls "performative violence." By this phrase, Juergensmeyer is implying that acts of terrorism

are dramas designed to have an impact on the several audiences that they affect. Those who witness the violence, even at a distance . . . are therefore a part of what occurs. Moreover, like other forms of public ritual, the symbolic significance of such events is multifaceted; they mean different things to different observers.[73]

To compare the cinema of adolescence to terrorism does not mean that acts of violence on film are identical to acts of terror. I do not want to downplay the consequences of "real" violence, as opposed to "reel" violence. I simply want to point out that both cinematic violence and terrorist acts are *constructed* events. Juergensmeyer also points out that acts of terror are vehicles to empower "marginal men." Terrorists are often, he observes, agents with a grievance against established power and without political means to enact their aims. They thus resort to acts of performative violence in an effort to call attention to their causes. A similar logic may be at work in the cinema of adolescence, for both directors and viewers, one might suppose. By staging (and viewing) spectacles of sacrifice in a theater of terror, "marginal men" acquire a sense of power despite limits imposed by censors (and other scandalized representatives of authority), whose condemnation ironically confirms the "truth" of the images they create or view. To be sure, the objects of the two groups of marginal agents are different. Juergensmeyer maintains that terrorists accomplish their symbolic aims by "revealing the vulnerability of a nation's most stable and powerful entities," usually the government's ability to secure peace.[74] In contrast, the spectacles of sacrifice in the cinema of adolescence reveal the vulnerability of a nation's future and may have served to steel each new generation through graphic, symbolic depictions of the escalating violence that they have had to endure.[75]

Finally, such violence is cloaked in an aura of innocence, or perhaps of wounded pride, which justifies it. Here the work of theorist R. Scott Appleby is most relevant. Appleby notes that even though terrorist violence seems "irrational" to outside observers, in fact it follows a logic that is well established in the history of religions.

> [The] ability of religion to inspire ecstasy—literally, to lift the believer psychologically out of a mundane environment—stands behind the distinctive logic of religious violence. As unpredictable and illogical as this violence may seem to outsiders, it falls within a pattern of asceticism leading to the ecstasy of self-sacrifice that runs as a continuous thread through most religions.[76]

Considerable attention has been paid to the way that Islam has motivated "suicide bombers," or martyrs for the faith. Far less attention, though, has been given to the ways that American young people have been conditioned to accept various forms of "sacrifice" for a particular goal.

All these films in the cinema of adolescence offer young people "tests" of their ability to endure depictions or enactments of violence while simultaneously trying to steer them toward "acceptable" forms of transcendence. Watching these films thus provides experiences of "transcendence through suffering," as Appleby puts it, in which young people are invited to enter into horrific scenes of abuse and violation in order to demonstrate their willingness to endure such acts in the interest of some nobler, even transcendent, cause. These films are literally projections of transcendent authority; they project on a screen the contagion of violence and invite audiences to identify with those who survive it and with the means by which they do so. Again, the teleological purpose of these acts, or the vehicle of transcendent authority with which viewers are invited to identify, changes over time from police, to parents, to psychology, to the symbolic process itself. But the logic of displacement is identical: one must "endure" these films, even proclaim one's pleasure in them, in order to demonstrate to one's peers (and to the anonymous eyes of the market) one's ability to endure violence in the interest of some greater cause. The cinema of adolescence depicts repeated sacrifices of youth, their self-sacrifice, in a way that lifts believers/viewers beyond the mundane environment of everyday living in the United States and into an ecstatic identification with the survivors in the film.[77] These films represent, if they do not produce, an empire of sacrifice, with young people as both victims and survivors, if not saviors.

Hostel is the best example of this mimetic doubling or mirror imaging of the victim-perpetrator as manifest in youth. Pax (again, the name means peace) is, in the opening scenes of the film, almost as lust driven and crude as the Icelander, Oli. Pax thus is the American likely to die, according to the conventions of the genre. But it is relatively innocent Josh who is tortured and killed on screen (Oli's death is not shown). Josh is a reluctant participant in debauchery. In one scene, he actually refuses the ministrations of a naked hooker whose services have been paid for on his behalf. But Josh dies first, and it is Pax who needs to use his wits to escape the torture chamber. He does so and then exacts vengeance on his oppressors in ways that directly mirror their treatment of him. A scene at the end of the film in which he traps the middle-aged man who killed Josh in a bathroom perfectly reflects this mirroring in vengeance, He follows the man into the bathroom at a train station. After securing their solitude (by flipping the sign for the bathroom from "open" to "closed"), he takes the stall next to his assailant/prey. He then passes a business card for "Elite Hunting" under the stall's divider. When the man reaches for the card, "Pax" grabs his hand and slices off the two fingers that match the two Pax himself lost minutes earlier (in film time) in the torture chamber. Then as the man writhes in pain, "Pax" enters his stall and nearly drowns him in the toilet bowl before slitting the man's throat and leaving him dead, head down in the toilet. At one level, the point could not be clearer: the man's desires were perverse. He tortured youth until their bodily fluids were released; now he dies with his head in a receptacle for bodily waste. Youth thus turn the tables on the market and its middle-aged perverts: "Pax," like every youth who sees the film and survives it, prevails. They thus can feel free, we might conclude, to pursue their own perverse desires, as the trailer for the film explicitly suggests.

This is only a movie, of course. The most profound religious meaning of *Hostel*, as the culmination of a long trajectory of spectacles of sacrifice, is that these films have served as rites of passage in the American cultural religion to test the willingness of young people to claim for themselves an identity among the tribe of American imperial agents.[78] The chosen weapons in the quiver of this tribe of imperial warriors have not been bullets alone but also the products of popular culture. Films not only communicate, they create the identity of "America" in increasingly globalizing markets.[79] The identity created in the cinema of adolescent abjection is nothing less than an innocent empire, backed by the world's most extensive military force and cache of weapons of mass destruction but communicated through persuasive, even mesmerizing, myths depicted on a large screen in ways that mask or obscure both their religious operations and their imperial context. Convincing the agents of such colonial enterprises that their conquest is anything but innocent is precisely the problem. Both filmmakers and critics generally persist in locating "religion" in the domain of private life, or in institutions like "churches," and in ways that exempt the state and the markets from any involvement with something as irrational or primitive as "faith," and surely not "religious violence."[80]

It should be apparent by now that the violence in these films deserves the name "religious" if anything does. These depictions of violence are as "primitive" as anything one can find in the literatures or practices of ancient societies, and they serve equally primitive functions, even if they are presented with remarkably sophisticated technology. These films compress and displace desire, wasting it in "reel" time in ways that prepare participants to accept the truncation of desire or its channeling into "suitable" paths in real time. Such a conclusion reinforces, yet again, the need for scholars and other cultural critics to consider the flexibility of constructions of authority across social sectors of "private" and "public," "religious" and "secular."

For instance, according to psychoanalyst and film critic Harvey Roy Greenberg, horror films depict reality at their most terrifying when they show what he calls "the beast in the boudoir." This phrase, which Greenberg uses to refer primarily to King Kong in an essay with the ironic title "You Can't Marry that Girl—You're a Gorilla," refers also to the more general phenomenon in horror films of the "monstrous penetration of the bedroom."[81] Such penetration also is a standard feature in the cinema of adolescence, from the seduction of Bill in *Reefer Madness* to the seduction of the leading girl Neve Campbell by the deranged Skeet Ulrich in *Scream* to the young men's obsessive quest to "score" in *Hostel*. All these films take the camera into the bedroom, or at least into scenes of adolescent desire, and voyeuristically invite the viewer to identify with this desire. Such desire, however, also is inevitably punished, often with scary music, dramatic gore, and "realistic" sound effects. Such films not only represent, they become "the beast in the boudoir." They expand surveillance into the most intimate features of private life to serve a public (or perhaps mob) interest that borders on frenzy or panic. As itself a "beast in the boudoir," film suggests a "presence" that is the opposite of the absence elicited by the sacrifice of youth.

Surviving these films is, again, the point. A viewer is, experientially, resurrected by enduring a terrifying identification with the death of a victim and then walking out of the theater alive. In short, the film kills, and the film "saves," desire. These films condense the fear of death into a cinematic spectacle that displaces that fear onto various actors in traumatic circumstances, and then these films "save" the spectator by releasing her into the bright light of the "real world" after the show is over. The actual sacrifice is minimal, merely a few dollars, in exchange for a few hours of "entertainment." But the spectacles of sacrifice are brutal: primitive, perverse, bloody, and violent. As solely "entertainment," the brutalities are blessed by the gods of Hollywood, by the participation of "stars," and increasingly by scholars, if not by traditional sources of transcendent authority.[82]

As I tried to make clear at the beginning of this chapter, the media are hardly alone in assuming this role of punishing redeemer in American culture. Our focus on these five films is, again, heuristic, a case study of broader processes with more profound (and entangled) institutional implications. For instance, films operate with the tacit approval of the state. Directors and producers must adjust to meet the expectations, most immediately, of the Motion Picture Association of America (MPAA), or risk a rating that will kill the market potential of their product. The MPAA is a voluntary agency, but it also has to answer to viewers and their legislators in Congress, who established the Federal Communications Commission in 1934 to "regulate interstate and international communications." Similarly, directors and producers must tailor their products directly to the market. They have to reach an audience that is willing to provide the demand to sustain the product they supply. To do so, the film industry surveys, gathers statistics, and studies audience behavior in ways akin to those of the most careful politician.

The identity of the "beast in the boudoir" is a peculiar religious hybrid hiding somewhere between the nation-state and markets that apparently finds youthful desire problematic. Desire is titillatingly depicted but must also be surveyed, contained, and squashed by some excess of authority that operates to displace or sublimate it onto suitably innocent or pure pathways. To this beast of nation- and market-imposed "purity," youth's devotion must be cultivated in some form of a common faith and through some common practices and institutions to make the beast appear innocent, when in fact it is a voracious emperor demanding sacrifice.[83] Films are only exemplary (or symptomatic, as the epigraph from Derrida tries to make clear) of this process by which young people suffer for adult irresponsibility and violence. Films are hardly at the root of the problem. In reality, the agencies are manifold through which the consent of young people to very real practices of sacrifice, and not only spectacles, has been secured in recent American policies and practices. Do these films reflect, or shape, the social realities of young people, and do they reinforce, or critique, the innocence and purity—the transcendent authority—of adult institutions?

Beyond Hollywood's Happy Endings

Film historians Mark Jancovich and Cyndy Hendershot were among the first to ground an analysis of horror films in a particular context. Jancovich argued that horror films represented "rational fears" in an age of nuclear anxiety, and in *I Was a Cold War Monster: Horror Films, Eroticism and the Cold War Imagination*, Hendershot argues that the abjection depicted on the screen in many films from the 1950s and 1960s mirrored cold war fears, fantasies, and fascinations.[84] The same can be said about the spectacles of sacrifice in the cinema of adolescence. Two trajectories in recent U.S. history show how the religious logic of sacrificing youth has played out in national life. The first is in the so-called war on drugs. The second is in the rhetoric surrounding actual recent U.S. military campaigns, especially how the conflict in Vietnam will be remembered. In both examples, young people have been "sacrificed" in ways that have been all too real. In the first example, young people across American culture, but mostly young black males, have been punished and contained for acting on their desire to get high by means of a policy that is directly out of *Reefer Madness*. In the second example, a misguided war in which youth were drafted and sent to die for what proved to be both a futile and unnecessary cause has been gussied up through a rhetoric of "sacrifice," despite various efforts to mute or diffuse such appeals to the "heroic" or "romantic" memorializing of Vietnam.

Sociologist Mike Males documented how young people have become the primary targets of campaigns to prevent drug use, as well as the primary targets of police action and criminal prosecution for the possession and distribution of illegal drugs.[85] Young people who experiment with drugs do so for a variety of reasons, but foremost among them, according to most researchers, is an experience of "sensation seeking" or a quest to be "lifted . . . out of a mundane environment," to use Appleby's language.[86] Drugs get people "high," a metaphor whose spatial significance in a culture historically devoted to a sky god should not be missed. This spiritual desire is severely punished, however, when it is sought through chemical means by young people, even though as Males shows, the age of abusers and addicts has increasingly grown upward over the decades since the 1960s.[87] Youth, as Males explains, serve as a "scapegoat generation" for problems widely shared in adult populations, and young people become the victims of stereotypes that subject them to arbitrary testing, surveillance, and jail in numbers that defy any strategic explanation.[88] The "war" on drugs thus serves symbolic purposes that are perhaps very similar to those of the cinema of adolescence and that surely took root in that cinema as far back as 1936. In this cultural construct, manifest in both popular culture and policy, youthful desire—whether for sex or for other forms of sensation—deserves to be punished. Youthful desire makes young people worthy of sacrifice through incarceration. Youthful desire is a threat to the innocence of the symbolic order that depends for its operation on willing, if sometimes unwitting, compliance.

As is well known, one consequence of the "war" on drugs has been the dramatic expansion of the U.S. prison system. Currently, the United States has a higher per capita prison rate than any other nation on earth, including Russia and the former Soviet republics. In 2007, approximately 738 of every 100,000 U.S. citizens were in prison. This rate compares with the Canadian rate, for instance, of 107 per 100,000 or the British rate of 148 per 100,000, which is still the highest among the European Union's member nations.[89] What is one to make of this rush to discipline and punish?[90] In a provocative religious analysis, theologian Mark Lewis Taylor contends that the prison system functions not only as a material and economic system to reward particular communities and social groups but also as "theater," to provide "spectacles that have a negative impact" on target populations in the United States. More specifically, the spectacles of increasing imprisonment (think of the "perp walks" that are now regular features of television news) serve in ways akin to a "sacrifice" of marginal members of society and constitute "an intimidating display for exercising control throughout the wider society." This "sacrifice," Taylor contends, "helps maintain a public order that . . . is increasingly dominated by an elite class in the United States." Far from being an "innocent" bit of titillation, *Reefer Madness* has laid a symbolic foundation for what Taylor calls "Gulag America."[91]

Domestic imprisonment is one way that spectacles of sacrifice coincide with public policy in the United States, and imperial militarism is another. Every U.S. war in the past fifty years has been justified by a religious rhetoric of "sacrifice." The Vietnam War and the way it has been remembered can provide a good example.[92] The original design for the official Vietnam Veterans Memorial on the Mall in Washington, D.C., was a simple granite wall designed by Maya Ying Lin. But financier H. Ross Perot, who had put up some of the money for the competition that Lin's design won, protested along with some veterans' groups that "the wall" was not "heroic" enough. As a compromise, the "three men" statue designed by sculptor Frederick G. Hart was added to the memorial. Hart describes his intent in creating the statue:

> The [three soldiers] wear the uniforms and carry the weapons of warriors. They are young. The contrast between the innocence of their youth and the weapons of war underscores the poignancy of their sacrifice. There is about them the physical contact and sense of unity that bespeaks the bonds of love and sacrifice that is the nature of men at war. . . . Their strength and their vulnerability are both evident.[93]

This rhetoric is, of course, banal, and most pilgrims to the memorial hardly notice the statue. But an effort was under way to revive a "heroic" interpretation of a war that even one of its chief architects, former Secretary of Defense Robert McNamara, came to recognize was a "tragedy."[94] In this effort to sanitize memory, the rhetoric of "sacrifice" was a chief feature.

"Sacrifice" also became, not surprisingly, a theme in the effort to build a "Vietnam Women's Memorial" on the Mall. The statue, designed by sculptor Glenna Goodacre, was dedicated in 1993 after a long controversy. The official National Park Service webpage for the memorial suggests that the statue of three women coming to the aid of a soldier "recalls the courage and sacrifice of all women who served."[95] The visual imagery of the sculpture is even more overt, as it depicts a wounded (or dead) young male soldier laying across the lap of a female soldier, presumably a nurse. It is, in short, a pietà, a depiction of the dead Christ cradled by his loving and grieving mother. Here, an American soldier displaces Christ as a "sacrifice" to save the nation or at least to demonstrate a commitment to some kind of transcendent cause that would justify remembering war in this way.

In an earlier essay, published in 1996, I contended that this memorial could serve to diffuse the process of scapegoating that led to the deaths of 58,000 soldiers, whose average age was about nineteen.[96] Competing targets of blame and of devotion, I suggested, made the wall a democratic and pluralistic sacred place whose meaning could not be contained in any one version. I believe this is still true, but efforts have clearly increased to control the meanings of the memorial and to subsume the diverse experiences of the veterans under the category of "sacrifice."[97] In November 2003, for instance, President George W. Bush signed legislation to build a "visitors' center" at the memorial that will "educate future generations about patriotism and sacrifice." A cosponsor of the House bill, Congressman Jim Gibbons (R-NV), who is himself a Vietnam veteran, contended that "the sacrifices made by the soldiers and their families during the Vietnam War must never be forgotten. The Visitor Center will give every American generation the opportunity to gain a better understanding and greater respect for the sacrifices our soldiers made during this war."[98] Lest the context of this statement and its rhetoric of sacrifice be missed, Congressman Gibbons explained, "As our servicemen and women are engaged in a war against a brutal tyrant and an oppressive regime in Iraq, there is no better time to recognize the efforts and sacrifices of our veterans."[99] Here American brutality is projected outward, which in effect renders it blessed. In contrast to the tyrant Saddam Hussein, *suspected* of harboring weapons of mass destruction, the United States, holder of caches of known and verified weapons of mass destruction, appears innocent. Any "sacrifices" are both justified and necessary.

It may be true that the death of a soldier on a battlefield is, indeed, a "sacrifice," and I do not at all want to belittle the difficulties faced by military families and the grief that the loss of a loved one can bring. But this use of a religious term to refer to national policy ought to give us pause.[100] At one level, the euphemism of "sacrifice" for death in war is so conventional as to be banal. But as the philosopher Hannah Arendt long ago showed, it is precisely this banality that renders violence plausible to the human conscience.[101] Calling the death of a soldier in war a "sacrifice" makes *war* a religious phenomenon. This is the ultimate displacement: a desire for life becomes a demand for death. The human longing to live gives way to a lust for blood. But this lust must be normalized, tempered, made palatable by displacing it onto "suitable" agents who might become victims. Often in American history, the young have fit that bill. A subtle blurring of national policy with religious discourse and practice implicates youth in a system that demands their docile complicity, punishment, and even death in causes decided by the adults who run the nation and, increasingly, do so with a primary interest to secure the "free" flow of commodities across international markets and into corporate profits.[102]

Again, have the films in the cinema of adolescent abjection reflected or shaped the social realities of youth, including U.S. policies and practices, and have they served to reinforce or critique youth-serving institutions? To answer this in a way that I do not intend to be glib, U.S. policies and practices have come to reflect the worldview of *Reefer Madness*, and the social realities of young people have increasingly mirrored those in *Hostel*. Over the last few decades, young people in America have faced a trajectory of escalating violence. This trajectory has been represented accurately in the cinema of adolescence, in a way that reveals an increasingly critical attitude toward youth-serving institutions.[103] Adults are largely represented in these films as having failed in their promises to keep young people safe from harm. In this fashion, the films function as religion in a very particular sense, as spectacles of sacrifice that both reflect and seek to shape social realities.

Scream, in particular, in its emphasis on the "knowing" participation of youth in the conventions of film and on the role of youth to create their own rules, can be seen as an attempt to surface the problem of violence for imaginative solution and rational redress. As the scholar of religion John Lyden, perhaps the most articulate advocate of this view of the religious function of these films, would say, there is a "carnivalesque" facet to the participation of young people in these films that allows "catharsis through offering opportunities to participate vicariously in redemptive suffering . . . [in which] normally forbidden behavior is permitted as a means of questioning as well as reinforcing societal norms."[104] In other words, these films "allow young people to temporarily step outside of acceptable norms of behavior so that they might return to their prescribed roles refreshed and perhaps willing to accept them for the sake of structure."[105]

But what if the structure that young people are asked to "accept" or shape is itself violent? Here the appeal to catharsis—which of course means "purity"—is belied by the way that religions collaborate with not only ritualized but also real violence. That is, the displacement is ineffective if the suffering is not redemptive but merely produces more suffering. This is also a trajectory of these films: according to *Scream* and *Hostel*, no institution or community can be trusted to assist youth in their quest for survival, much less redemption. Such a trajectory suggests what ethicist Jeffrey Stout has called the modern "flight from authority."[106] There is no transcendence, no purity, no innocence in *Scream* or *Hostel* apart from the play of the story itself and apart from (and within) the story in which authority equals force. Violence itself is the transcendent projection. The filmmaker's job is merely to represent this "reality" so that youth can "grow up."[107] These films are religious in seeking to define boundaries and transgress them, but they are not religious enough to turn the displacements they reveal onto violence itself. They are, rather, weakly or vestigially religious. The peace they represent is nothing more than vengeance. They hold on to a shell of sacrificial substance without any enduring community to sustain meaning or enact the practices of a tradition, aside from those of the market itself, as the absence of traditional religions in the films surely shows. Their innocence, and even "scandal," is a sham, the flip side of the shame of abjection that perpetuates the status quo.

To clarify this final point, I find particularly helpful the analysis of historian Margaret Miles. Miles points out that "Hollywood film conventions reiterate a narrow range of desires." For all its vaunted "liberalism," the film industry is, in fact, quite conservative. Films must sell, and to sell they must "repetitiously designate what is desirable." This repetition serves not to engage the agency of viewers but to "constrain the collective imagination and impoverish the public symbolic repertoire."[108] More pointedly, this means that the films in the cinema of adolescent abjection may have functioned to fuel an escalation of violence in American culture. They have conveyed to young people the message that violence (even if only "ritually" enacted on the screen) is the only answer to violence. "Screen violence," Miles concludes, "functions to habituate Americans to actual violence . . . [and] anesthetize against empathy with the victim's pain."[109] Vices become habits as violence becomes normal, and seeing violence repeatedly transforms it from aberration to norm. To put it bluntly, the visible violation of youth on the screen has normalized the "sacrifice" of young people. They languish in prisons from the "war" on drugs, and they lay buried in the ground after wars from World War II to the "global war on terror."

What is truly terrifying is the presumed innocence with which all this violence has been unleashed on young people. Whether on the screen or in policies, American youth have been represented as scapegoats (and saviors) for a threatened, unstable, yet dominant culture. They have had to learn violence, and the spectacles of sacrifice in the cinema of adolescence have helped them do so. Cinematic scenes of innocent domination helped produce policies of innocent domination, and those scenes on the screen also could bring into question the very same policies. That is, after all, our thesis: religions can produce violence, but they also might bring peace. To turn toward the peacemaking potential of both films and traditional religions, we might then ask: What would a religiously nonviolent film look like? That is, can we imagine, or identify, films that have not reiterated a narrow range of desires, that have not restricted the symbolic repertoire to an equation of authority with force, but that have engaged the compressing and displacing functions of religion toward displacing violence? Have there been films in which the desires of youth are not ambivalently represented and in which the structural violence of American culture is not only not denied or ignored but is actively critiqued? Have there been films in which religious authority does not produce or thrive on complicity with violence but in which religious agents are depicted as seeking to distance viewers from participating in the sacrifice of scapegoats? Finally, have there been films that affirm historic religious traditions as capable of fostering authentic, life-giving, nonviolent, even loving relationships? By the end of the next chapter, after a long sojourn into the religious underpinnings of the brutal violence of American slavery, the prospect of representing traditional religions in their capacity to produce peace will appear in a perhaps surprising way when we take up Spike Lee's *Malcolm X.*

Sacrificing Race

"The Slaveholding Religion"
from Jarena Lee to Spike Lee

I know what the world has done to my brother and how narrowly he has survived it. And I know, which is much worse, and this is the crime of which I accuse my country and my countrymen, and for which neither I nor time nor history will ever forgive them, that they have destroyed and are destroying hundreds of thousands of lives and do not know it and do not want to know it. One can be, indeed one must strive to become, tough and philosophical concerning destruction and death, for this is what most of mankind has been best at since we have heard of man. (But remember: *most* of mankind is not *all* of mankind.) But it is not permissible that the authors of devastation should also be innocent. It is the innocence which constitutes the crime.

—James Baldwin, *The Fire Next Time*

[White] freedom has no meaning . . . without the specter of enslavement, the anodyne to individualism; the yardstick of absolute power over the life of another; the signed, marked, informing, and mutating presence of a black slave. . . . Whiteness, alone, is mute, meaningless, unfathomable, pointless, frozen, veiled, curtained, dreaded, senseless, implacable.

—Toni Morrison, *Playing in the Dark*

Aside from Nietzsche's insightful but mostly misdirected rantings, the history of slavery as a *religious* phenomenon has not yet been told.[1] That does not mean that there have not been many fine historical studies of religion and slavery in the Atlantic world.[2] But as with other scholarly examinations of faith traditions in the American academy, a tendency to reify religion into its institutional form has led observers to miss the dynamic interactions among forms of cultural authority across institutions and eras.[3] Historians are increasingly recognizing the complex origins and legacies of slavery in Atlantic cultures.[4] This recognition of the cultural complexity of slavery creates an opening to rethink the ways in which slavery was not only legitimized by religion but also acquired some of the contours of a faith tradition itself.[5] Such rethinking can, at the least, help clarify how religious discourses and practices, and especially constructions of "whiteness," produced what Orlando Patterson called the "social death" of millions of Africans in slavery or what Jon Butler labeled a "spiritual holocaust." As Butler's provocative phrase suggests, delving into the history of slavery is more than of just antiquarian interest.[6] As Curtis J. Evans explained, "We write to complicate simple narratives of national innocence."[7]

The central logic of "the slaveholding religion," to use Frederick Douglass's terms, sought to reduce slaves to their instrumental roles, their function as scapegoats or sacrifices whose bodies were vehicles of economic progress.[8] People who were red, black, yellow or who were not quite "white" enough, that is, not quite "American" or propertied or male, were displaced and their labor compressed to make way for the profits of a few.[9] Slavery naturally was conventionally represented not as religious but as secular. Slavery was simply a relationship between capital and labor. This neat distinction between sacred and secular matters, which was surely a distinction-without-a-difference as far as slaves were concerned, allowed slaveholders to operate under an assumed innocence or at least moral neutrality that shielded them from reproach or critique until the system was well established in the Atlantic world.

It took the sacrificial bloodbath of the Civil War to end slavery in the United States. As historians Harry Stout and Drew Gilpin Faust showed, the war actually drew more tightly the conjunction between religion and violence of displacements of death on the altar of the transcendent nation.[10] If Americans thus took refuge in religious innocence to shield themselves from secular violence, they also mobilized religious rhetorics and practices of sacrifice to bless their own brutalities. Indeed, the innocent domination of sacrifice actually united the U.S. North and South in the late nineteenth and early twentieth century. As Faust observed, "At war's end . . . shared suffering would override persisting differences about the meanings of race, citizenship, and nationhood to establish sacrifice and its memorialization as the ground on which North and South would ultimately reunite. . . . Death created the modern American union."[11]

This unity around death, which religiously meant unity around sacrifice, received confirmation and endorsement in D. W. Griffith's classic 1915 film

The Birth of a Nation. In that film, the nation was united as "white." That "whiteness" meant "Christian," and even Protestant, went without saying. But in fact it was the nation and the willingness of its citizens to sacrifice and be sacrificed that set the parameters of identity and determined how violence would be directed "innocently." After all, African Americans have been joined by many other groups—some of them quite clearly Christian and some even Protestant—in being invited or driven to "sacrifice" for "innocent" national (or global/economic) purposes of one kind or another.[12] Such sacrifices effaced individual agency and rendered members of many groups—Native Americans, Irish, Japanese, Latinos, and even Germans—as ideally silent and ostensibly obedient participants in plots rendered by various "masters," on the one hand, or as scapegoat targets on whom violence could be innocently vented and identity secured, on the other. As we saw in the previous chapter, age was one durable platform for enactments of religious violence. But race matters, too, as an enduring marker of innocent domination in America.[13]

As Nietzsche perceived, Christianity contributed to the economic and political core of slavery to reduce people to their instrumental capacity to perform and produce. But slavery was hardly coextensive with Christianity, whose contours were ambivalent enough to include both antislavery and proslavery voices.[14] Indeed, the Christian ambivalence toward slavery appears in the very earliest texts of the tradition, in the writings of Paul and the parables of Jesus.[15] These documents, whose cultural authority even increased during the nineteenth and twentieth centuries, subtly inscribed a view of human individuals that could reduce human beings to the instrumental purpose for which they might exist or the end for which they were created.[16] On the one hand, this was a liberating truth. Being "one" in Christ equalized humanity before God and universalized a process of human being and becoming that included potentially all individuals in its scope.[17] On the other hand, this "universalizing" tendency was articulated within a cultural context of slaveholding. The metaphor of enslavement to God could be torn from its theological setting and applied to economic life, thereby potentially including all in a material scope of unrelenting domination. From a partial system, in which only a few were violated and forced to obey, slavery to God spread metaphorically throughout the political and economic order. Obedience became a universal demand. Such missionary success, if that is what it was, gradually enabled "whites" to happily usurp for themselves the God role, with hardly anybody but the slaves objecting.[18] "Whiteness" was the projection of transcendent authority around which the religion of slaveholding revolved.

This totalizing system reached its apex in the peculiar institution of chattel slavery in the United States, as a symbolic hierarchy that elevated "white" over "black."[19] This system that elevated "white" over "black" followed the splintering of Christendom in the wake of the Protestant Reformation. It took shape from various sources, including Spanish and Caribbean influences, but in the American South especially, the justifications for slavery came to depend on a peculiar misapplication of the Augustinian-Protestant dialectic of the "Two Kingdoms" or "Two Cities." As Max Weber rightly perceived, Protestantism extended the Augustinian disenchantment (or bifurcation) of space, which in turn heightened anxiety about one's place.[20] Worldly asceticism or, more accurately, a propensity for "disciplined commercial life" was the outcome.[21]

No form of commercial life was more disciplined than slavery as practiced in America. In the United States, a religion of slavery transferred, projected, inscribed and imposed Protestant anxieties onto the body of the slave. Slavery displaced a human body from its integrity as an individual site of agency and as a site of human being and becoming. Slavery then opened or circulated that body on demand and made it available for the benefit of slaveholding priests and priestesses, who were able to cloak themselves with the purity and innocence of "whiteness."[22] By the time the Civil War had begun, slavery was more than a system of economic salvation in the South; it was something to kill and die for: a religion.[23]

In Frederick Douglass's *Narrative*, the operation of this religion is articulated with a perspective unparalleled in any source before (or since).[24] Douglass explicitly identified a "slaveholding religion." He also differentiated this new religion from Christianity and called on his readers to acknowledge the difference between the two faith traditions and to act like the Christians they claimed to be. He thus drove a wedge between a pure "Christianity" (which he claimed as his own) and the "slaveholding religion." Douglass also very clearly described the contours of this "slaveholding religion." Its discourse was marked by the displacement of transcendence into the curse (in several forms). Its practices included torture of the body (mainly ritualized public whipping). Its mythic community (or sacred place) was the domestic economy or household (usually the plantation). Its institutional form, ironically, was the nation.[25] Douglass made clear, more in his speeches than in the *Narrative,* that slavery continued only with the support of the U.S. government: the United States was a "white" nation, a slaveholding nation. Its civil religion (Douglass did not use these terms, but we can) was a religion of slaveholding. The nation was the tacit (and sometimes not so tacit) institutional patron of the slaveholding religion.[26] Douglass inverted the usual values in the Augustinian-Protestant dialectic by privileging the "city of humanity" (or the nation) as the agent of the "coming of the Lord." God was no longer a slaveholder but a liberator. In his efforts to abolish slavery, Frederick Douglass called on the nation to be more Christian rather than less, when Christianity meant something other than a slaveholding religion.

The way that Douglass rhetorically differentiated between "Christianity" proper and the "slaveholding religion" became apparent over the course of his long life and in comparison with other early African American public intellectuals. As he explained in a letter to his pastor written shortly before he died, Douglass's personal faith was in fact less beholden to orthodox Christianity than it was to the "noble" humanist practices of reading, writing, and speaking.[27] Such practices, so long denied to slaves, Douglass claimed for himself from within the slave system as both an act of resistance to it and a path of liberation. He was joined on this stony path by many other African Americans who also adapted Christianity to their own purposes. The means they used to do so were many and the examples plentiful. But both the *Life and Religious Experience of Jarena Lee*, and the *Narrative of Sojourner Truth* can stand with Douglass's *Narrative* to show how nineteenth-century African American individuals spoke, wrote, and acted to expose the violence of this religion of slavery, to transgress against it, and to assert their presence as embodied agents with an irreducible value beyond all efforts to turn them into instruments of economic progress.[28] Like Douglass, they turned Christianity away from the slaveholding religion and its sacrifices and toward something more life affirming.

In exposing the violence of the slaveholding religion, and even more in overcoming it, Douglass, Lee, and Truth saw little choice but to lean on the nation and its markets as the institutional loci of their hopes. In a context in which church and state were ostensibly separate and in which the churches were trying to sort out their own complicity in slavery, the nation and its representatives (including the military) became agents of redemption. But this turn to the nation quickly proved a mixed blessing for African Americans, as did the (highly selective) opening of wage labor and markets. The institutions of the nation and markets continued to expand the instrumental ideal and continued to impose on most African Americans a regime of silent obedience, punishing their refusals to accommodate it or their efforts to resist it. During Reconstruction and through the era of Jim Crow laws, African Americans were offered "separate but equal" facilities that were anything but equal and were given glimpses of a promised land of freedom that, for most, continued to be elusive. The North had won the military battles, but the South had won the culture war.[29] The religion of slaveholding had diffused across the nation's political economy, even as the institution of slavery ended. *The Birth of a Nation* confirmed the durability of this religion of slaveholding in both its plot and its record-breaking profits. In other words, religious violence along the lines of race surfaced throughout the twentieth century in the fringe groups who made racial identity their explicit marker. Religious violence also was evident in disciplinary practices and economic policies that spread across the nation, with all the innocence and privilege associated with the transcendent, and largely unquestioned, symbol of "whiteness."[30]

Not surprisingly, into that milieu again came a version of religious activism not beholden to slaveholding and its sacrifices but turned toward life affirmation beyond the dualisms of innocent domination. Building on the legacies of Douglass, Lee, and Truth, this strain of religion was affirmed in early race movies, notably in reaction to *The Birth of a Nation*. This nonviolent strain of religion also grew into the burgeoning civil rights movement, as evident especially in the theological writings and influence of Howard Thurman. A particularly surprising variant of this religious impulse became manifest in the films of Spike Lee, especially in his depiction of *Malcolm X*. Lee's *X* restated the ongoing religious challenge faced by the African American community and beyond. His recommendation, built on the tragedy of Malcolm's lost future, that African Americans assert their voice in society by any means necessary highlighted once again the need to resist the systemic reduction of human beings to an instrumental role, inscribed in a dichotomy between "whiteness" and "all others." Such a dichotomy was in many ways the founding compression and displacement in the "birth" of the nation. It continues to be a key discourse in an unofficially established religion in the United States, or as President Barack Obama recently described it, America's "original sin."[31] Little wonder, then, that African Americans have so consistently held up the hope of a rebirth for the nation centered not on violence but on the power of words and rites, community organizing, and institution building. Such a way to "remake America," to again quote America's forty-fourth president, would be based not on innocent domination or some orderly mystical or romantic ideal but on the difficult labor and joy of participation in all of the improvisational messiness that goes with democracy.[32]

From Christian Ambivalence to a Total System of Bodily Discipline

Christianity developed in a slaveholding society; the earliest Christians were both slaveholders and slaves. The significance of this fact, however, has not often affected writings on the history of Christianity. Indeed, many translations of the Bible avoid the literal English equivalent of the Greek *doulos*, "slave," and substitute instead the milder "servant."[33] There are many reasons for this substitution, some of them quite justifiable, but the consequences of suppressing the existence of slavery in the worldview of the first Christians may be significant. As Jennifer A. Glancy asked, "What effects did the institution of slavery have on the emerging structures and ideology of the early churches, even in those areas of communal and individual life that may not immediately appear to be associated with the practices of slavery or the persons of slaves?"[34] To recognize the existence of slavery in the earliest Christian texts is to complicate the way that power works in these texts and to question how these texts might continue to inscribe inequities.

Glancy's answer to her own question, developed through a careful study of the institution of slavery across classical cultures, is that slavery cast "various, multiform, and frequently indistinct" shadows within Christianity. Most important, there was

> an ancient equivalence between slaves and bodies. On a basic semantic level, the term *soma*, body, can function as a synonym for "slave," particularly when the slave is figured as object rather than subject. I have argued more broadly that the history of [biblical] interpretation underemphasizes the somatic dimensions of slavery, including the sexual availability of the slave body and the vulnerability of the slave body to corporal abuse. In contrast, the connection between slaves and bodies is often explicit in ancient sources. [35]

More specifically, the connection between slaves and the abuse of the body is a recurrent theme in early Christian writings, particularly in the letters of Paul and the gospel parables of Jesus.

To be sure, the apostle Paul "universalized" the "freedom" he experienced as a Jewish convert to Christianity,[36] most famously in Galatians 3:26–28:

> In Christ Jesus, you are all children of God through faith. As many of you as were baptized into Christ have clothed yourselves with Christ. There is no longer Jew or Greek, there is no longer slave or free, there is no longer male and female; for all of you are one in Christ Jesus.

This baptismal formula has served as a vision of liberation for many individuals and communities. Adoption by God invites an individual into a relationship with a transcendent power that can overcome conventional dualisms. In this context, however, Glancy contends that even this passage in Paul actually reinscribes a hierarchical view of human beings that subordinates the body (child) to the spirit (God) and that perpetuates the imbalance of power presupposed in slavery. Even more, for Paul, being a "child of God" was, finally, a metaphor and thus had nothing to say about the material arrangements of slavery. Indeed, as many passages from his other letters show, Paul assumed the continuing existence of slavery among Christians, even as he offered the "freedom" of the gospel to all.[37]

His Letter to the Romans is where Paul's ambivalence is clearest. In it, Paul invokes slavery as a double metaphor for the spiritual life. He uses an institution well known to his readers to explain the nature of "freedom" in Christ. "Do you not know," Paul exhorts his audience, "that if you present yourselves to anyone as obedient slaves, you are slaves of the one whom you obey, either of sin, which leads to death, or of obedience, which leads to righteousness?"(6:16). Jesus freed people from sin, Paul asserted, but the "freedom" gained thereby was in fact "slavery" to righteousness. Needless to say, a slave to righteousness might also be a slave of an earthly master. Far from questioning the institution of slavery, therefore, Paul used it to describe the character of the Christian life: one is either a slave to sin or a slave to God: "With my mind I am a slave to the law of God, but with my flesh I am a slave to the law of sin" (7:25).

As this passage demonstrates, the link between slavery and a vulnerable body was generally implicit in Paul's theology. In the parables of Jesus, compiled in the gospels some years after Paul's work, such a link between slavery and physical violence is explicit. As Glancy put it: "In the parables of Jesus, the bodies of slaves are vulnerable to abuse."[38] She documents how across the gospels, but especially in Matthew, the slave body is repeatedly the site of violence and corporal discipline. Slaves in Matthew "are seized (18:28, 23:35; 22:6), imprisoned (18:30), handed over to torturers (18:34), consigned to a place of 'weeping and gnashing of teeth' (24:51, 25:30), killed (21:35), and stoned (21:35)."[39] Perhaps the most chilling example is the parable in Matthew 18:23–35, in which God is depicted as a slaveholding king. One of this king's slaves, so the parable goes, owes the king ten thousand talents (or 150 years' worth of wages). The king threatens to sell the slave, together with his wife, children, and possessions. The slave pleads for mercy, and the king relents and forgives the slave's debt. But the slave then turns on another slave, demanding payment for a debt of his own. Word gets back to the king, who summons the slave and, "in anger, hand[s] him over to be tortured."

Using a third-party to punish or discipline slaves was standard operating procedure in both classical slavery and nineteenth-century America, as Frederick Douglass himself discovered when he was delivered for a year to "Mr. Covey," to be "broken." Jesus' parable in Matthew, however, extends the violence of the master–slave relation to the very nature of the divine-human interaction: "So," Jesus threatens his audience at the conclusion of the parable, "my heavenly Father will also do to every one of you, if you do not forgive your brother or sister from your heart." Here, those who advocate for Jesus as a moral teacher with a message of nonviolence face a rather severe interpretive challenge.[40] To be sure, Jesus' threat is set in the context of an admonition to forgive. But Glancy's point also stands: the parable "assumes and participates in the normalcy of such terror in slaves' lives."[41]

More broadly, Glancy claims that the uses of slavery as a metaphor in Christianity "promote[d] the view that the moral purpose of the slave is to advance the interests of the slaveholder."[42] A slave, obviously, was to be an instrument of the master's purposes. When early Christians used a metaphor of slavery or assumed the vulnerability of slave bodies to violence, they subtly accepted or reinscribed a hierarchical power relation between the commands of a master and the body of a slave. Even more, Glancy suggests, such a hierarchy served to manifest a generalized interest in "controlling bodies." Masters sought to control, instrumentalize, or use slave bodies as scapegoats or surrogates for their own exercises of power. Indeed, the logic was the same whether this control was internalized or externally imposed, that is, whether the controlling power was the will of God or the will of an earthly master: just as slave bodies were to serve their masters' purposes, so were Christians to offer their bodies for the service of the church. In time, of course, this logic of displacement would produce the systems of monasticism and ecclesiastical asceticism that dominated the medieval world. Glancy's work ends well before that time and even before the appearance of Augustine. But the trajectory is clear: by the time that Protestant thinkers like Luther and Calvin "rediscovered" the scriptures and St. Augustine's doctrine of the two cities, the stage was set to transfer the universal allegiance of Christian slaves from their spiritual masters to temporal ones, from the church to nations and markets. The "secularization" that made the monastery into the plantation proceeded through the Protestant Reformation.

That process was a long time in coming, but it was implicit in the most famous of Luther's Reformation treatises, *Christian Liberty*.[43] The thesis puts it well: "A Christian is a perfectly free lord of all, subject to none; a Christian is a perfectly dutiful slave of all, subject to all." This paradox has often been repeated and seldom understood. By it, Luther meant to free human beings from all systems of constraint on their agency, or their "faith," as he termed it, while also engaging human beings in the challenges of caring for one another and building a just society. To explicate this difficult balance between freedom and responsibility, Luther adapted from Paul an unfortunate dichotomy that located "faith" in what he called the "inner man" and located the site of duty and service in the "outer man." By this, Luther did not mean to identify slavery with the body and freedom with the soul, a fact evident in that he also used the metaphors of "old" and "new" to describe the distinction between the "enslaved" sinner and the "free" Christian. Indeed, Luther's intent was to unify the human individual as both sinner and saint before God and to engage people across vocations as Christians in service to their neighbors (as opposed to the system in which monks and priests were spiritually "higher" than average Christians). Yet Luther's dialectic quickly became a dualism. In time, as the nation-state developed, Luther's "inner man" became "religious"—identified with the church—and the "outer man" became a secular citizen—identified with the state. This dualism thereby produced the ostensible "separation" of state and church that both obscured and protected the flourishing of a religion of slaveholding.

How this doctrine of the separation of state and church produced a religion of slaveholding can be exemplified in a brief examination of an argument written in 1857 by the Reverend George D. Armstrong, pastor of the Presbyterian Church in Norfolk, Virginia.[44] According to Armstrong, quoting the synod of South Carolina in 1848, "The Church is the kingdom of the Lord Jesus Christ. Its officers are his servants, bound to execute his will. Its doctrines are his teachings, which he as a prophet has given from God. Its discipline is his law, which he as a king has ordained."[45]

This definition and its language of a kingdom, servants, and discipline would seem to provide a rather direct foundation for a religion in which God was a slaveholder and slaves had a duty to obey. But this was not the application Armstrong developed. To do so might have implicated all humanity along with Africans under slavery's curse. Instead, Armstrong argued that "the power of the Church . . . is only ministerial and declarative. The Bible, and the Bible alone, is her rule of faith and practice. . . . Beyond the Bible she can never rightfully go."[46] Given this apparent curtailing of religion's role, the question then became for Armstrong, "What do Christ and his Apostles . . . teach respecting slavery?" His answer:

They teach that slave-holding is not a *sin* in the sight of God, and is not to be accounted an "*offence*" by his Church. .... [T]he whole subject shall be left to be regulated by the State, as other civil institutions are, under the wholesome influence of God's providence, and his gospel truth faithfully exhibited by the Church.[47]

This was a distinction without a difference, since both church and state were "under . . . God's providence." But it allowed Armstrong to assert that the institution of slavery was religiously innocent. Slavery was "not a *sin*," but only a civil arrangement of "the relations of capital and labor."[48] That this is a religious claim is easy to miss but crucial to understand. Armstrong's work was entitled, after all, *The Christian Doctrine of Slavery*. His sharpest distinction between the two kingdoms is in the following:

God has assigned to the Church and the State each its separate province. To the Church God has intrusted all the interests of man which more immediately concern the life to come; his Gospel, and this she is to preach to every creature; and the supervision of the manners of his people, her members, and these she is to regulate by his law, and so train them for his heavenly kingdom. To the State God has intrusted all the interests of man which more immediately concern this present life—all questions respecting capital and labor, civil rights and political franchises, the protection of the weak, the forcible repression of crime, and the general administration of justice between man and man.[49]

This is the culmination of Christian ambivalence toward slavery as transformed by the Protestant ethic. Religion concerned only with the "inner man" had nothing to do with slavery, and slavery as a matter in the political economy had nothing to do with religion. But this dichotomy ignores that by definition, a Christian slave in the United States had to serve two masters. God ordained the church, and God ordained the state, but in the life of a slave, both demanded obedience. Conversely, for slaveholders, the "inner" or spiritual discipline of salvation was accompanied by an "external" or civil freedom to discipline and enslave the bodies of others for economic purposes. This turned Luther's paradox on its head, but self-interest made the logic seem the same.

Armstrong identifies himself, or the party with which he allies his interests, in various ways, but all of them imply that as a slaveholder he is, of course, "white." This means that as a slaveholder, he is thereby not engaged in sin, since he is simply arranging capital and labor, and he is positively benevolent as an agent of grace under the providence of a transcendent God. The very first sentence of Armstrong's work states his aim: "The hope of doing something toward bringing God's people, North and South, to 'see eye to eye' on the much vexed question of Slavery, this little book has been written."[50] But here "God's people" do not include slaves, although Armstrong is adamant that he does "firmly believe in the doctrine of the 'unity of the human race.'" This firm belief, however, wobbles eventually into yet another dichotomy: "Even if the physiologist could find no trace of this unity [of the human race] in the body: the body is not all of man, black or white. He has a soul also."[51] Humans are united by soul, but their bodies are either black or white. Indeed, Armstrong simply asserts that "the negro cannot mingle with the Anglo-Saxon."[52]

While the souls of all humans are equally "marked" by sin, according to Armstrong, some "nations" carry the wages of sin more heavily than others. Thus, "the African race in our own country is . . . degraded," Armstrong writes.[53] "The African slave," he reiterates, is "deeply degraded; the debasing effects of sin may at first sight, seem to have almost obliterated his humanity."[54] In fact, any "American laborer is far in advance of the African, as but a few generations removed, as the latter is, from the most degraded, debasing barbarism."[55] Underneath this logic is not only a shifting range of dichotomies—civilization versus barbarism, Anglo-Saxon versus Negroes, white versus black, American versus African—but also a theory of collective identity: nations as religions. For Armstrong, "American" religion overcomes sin. African religions are "heathenism." Slavery as Armstrong imagined it thus becomes part of a pilgrim's progress, from the "national sin" of African heathenism to "national slavery, at once a punishment for sin and a gracious provision for saving from utter extinction."[56] Amazingly, according to Armstrong, slavery saved.

This saving was accomplished, of course, by white folks, North and South, who were "God's people," agents of God's benevolent providence through the practice of American slavery. Armstrong projected the authority of the slaveholder onto the transcendence of the saving God. "In the history of nations," Armstrong admitted in one revealing passage,

> it would be difficult to find an instance in which a people have made more rapid progress upward and onward than the African race has made under the operation of American slavery. That they have not yet as a people, attained a point at which they are capable of safe self-government, is, we

believe, conceded by every one personally acquainted with them. . . . That it may take generations yet, to accomplish the gracious purposes of God in inflicting slavery upon them is very possible. . . . Nothing is more certain than that God's plan has operated well thus far.[57]

Civil arrangements between capital and labor were now "God's plan." That this plan was "inflicted" on Africans, Armstrong simply admits. But it was clearly working well for him and others who were, self-evidently, "God's" people. The transcendent authority of whiteness was how God was incarnate in the religion of slaveholding.

It was this logic or rhetoric, this "innocent" claim that race-based slavery was doing God's work and doing it well, that Frederick Douglass's *Narrative* questioned, just as James Baldwin's apocalyptic jeremiad and Toni Morrison's dense denunciation of "white freedom" a century later would do.[58] In his own experience, Douglass asserted, the boundaries between church and state, religion and nation, were not quite so clear as Armstrong claimed. Douglass had experienced in his own youthful body the condensed exploitation of his labor that slavery mandated. He had experienced in his flesh the "gracious" inflicting that displaced his freedom to justify the parasitism of his masters. But through his narrative—through the very performance of the black body speaking and writing, redirecting pain and suffering, desiring and gaining a freedom that would not be parasitical—Douglass reveals how "whiteness" alone, like that of Armstrong's other dichotomies, was, without its subjugated other, mute, meaningless, unfathomable, pointless, frozen, veiled, curtained, dreaded, senseless, and implacable. In short, Douglass uncovers how whiteness operated to undergird the functioning religion "of the land" of the United States, a system that wasted time and space: "the slaveholding religion." For Douglass, liberation from that system came through Christianity, a Christianity centered not on a slaveholding king but on a "peaceable Christ" and the practices of reading, writing, and speaking.

"A Severe Cross": Frederick Douglass and a "Religion of Slaveholding"

At the formal conclusion of his *Narrative*, before beginning the lengthy appendix that articulates most clearly his thoughts on the topic of "religion," Frederick Douglass describes how he came to be an abolitionist.[59] Shortly after escaping to freedom in 1838, he was given a copy of William Lloyd Garrison's antislavery newspaper, the *Liberator*, to which he eventually subscribed. Douglass declared that reading the *Liberator* gave him "a pretty correct idea of the principles, measures and spirit of the anti-slavery reform" (74). But not until three years later did Douglass first speak at an antislavery meeting. The way he explains how he came to do so reveals two key sources of his abolitionist thinking, only one of which Douglass highlights:

> While attending an anti-slavery convention at Nantucket, on the 11th of August, 1841, I felt strongly moved to speak, and was at the time much urged to do so by Mr. William C. Coffin, a gentleman who had heard me speak in the colored people's meeting at New Bedford. It was a severe cross, but I took it up reluctantly. The truth was, I felt myself a slave, and the idea of speaking to white people weighed me down. I spoke but a few minutes, when I felt a degree of freedom, and said what I desired with considerable ease. From that time until now, I have been engaged in pleading the cause of my brethren. (74–75)

What this passage does not say is that Douglass had been licensed to preach in the African Methodist Episcopal Zion Church in 1839.[60] So by the time he "took up" his "severe cross," he had already gained "a degree of freedom" by speaking to "the colored meeting" (75). But for readers of the *Narrative*, Douglass observed that speaking to white folks seemed to him at first a "severe cross." Why?

Throughout the *Narrative*, Douglass draws a key rhetorical distinction between what he calls "Christianity" proper and "the slaveholding religion."[61] He claims the former as his own faith, nurtured in churches filled with African Americans, and the latter as the faith of "this land." He thereby implicates his white (and overwhelmingly "Christian") audience in idolatry while seeking to engage them instead with an alternative faith in which slaveholding would have no part.[62] Douglass's reference to the "cross," then, was hardly accidental. Through it, Douglass identifies both himself and all slaves with Christ. The irony is that Douglass actually finds the yoke of Christ easy and the burden light. Compared with the bondage, discipline, and silence imposed on his body by slavery, the task of speaking as an abolitionist allowed him to "say what he desired" and to plead the cause of his brothers and sisters. Throughout the *Narrative*, Douglass implicitly claims for "Christianity" the practices of reading, speaking, and writing that stand as signs of freedom, in contrast to the silent obedience imposed on African American bodies in a religion of slaveholding.[63]

Douglass's narrative divides the contours of this religion into four parts, most clearly in the appendix, in one of the sharpest contrasts Douglass draws between Christianity and the "slaveholding religion":

> What I have said respecting and against religion I mean strictly to apply to the *slaveholding religion* of this land, and with no possible reference to Christianity proper. . . . I love the pure, peaceable, and impartial Christianity of Christ: I therefore hate the *corrupt*, slaveholding, *women-whipping, cradle-plundering, partial and hypocritical* Christianity of this land. Indeed, I can see no reason, but the most deceitful one, for calling the religion of this land Christianity. (75, italics added)

This distinction between a "slaveholding religion" and "Christianity" is not only a rhetorical device for Douglass.[64] By identifying this religion with "corruption," "women-whipping," and "cradle-plundering" and by identifying it as "partial and hypocritical," Douglass catalogs four characteristics of an actual system of condensation and displacement, that is, a functioning religion.

First, Douglass maintains that the slaveholding religion is "corrupt." This corruption is evident, he points out, in the way slaveholders use language. More specifically, slaveholders corrupt discourse into cursing, in at least two senses. The first type of curse surfaces in the earliest mention of religion in Douglass's *Narrative*. While discussing his birth, he tells the reader that his "father was a white man" (12). One of the most common arguments used to justify slavery was that it was the outcome of the "curse of Ham," described in Genesis 9. In that story, Noah curses with slavery the offspring of his son, Ham, traditionally understood as being dark skinned.[65] Staying with our typical example, Rev. George Armstrong therefore cites and interprets Genesis 9 under the heading "The Scriptural theory respecting the origin of Slavery." This theory, Armstrong contends, sees slavery as "the effect of sin, i.e., disobedience to God's laws, upon both individuals and nations." All people sin and thus fall under the "slavery" of physical wants and needs. But some people can be so sinful as to fall under a "second degree of slavery," to despotic governments. Finally, some "nations" can become so "degraded" that "personal slavery" becomes their lot. Indeed, of this "third degree" of slavery, Armstrong concludes, "we have a striking illustration in the case of the African race in our own country."[66]

Douglass undermines this threat by pointing out that his own genesis ironically contradicts a logic like Armstrong's. As the son of an African American woman and a white father, to which race did Douglass truly belong? Douglass also points out that "every year brings a multitude of this class of [mixed blood] slaves." He then cleverly draws out the logic:

> If their increase will do no other good, it will do away the force of the argument, that God cursed Ham, and therefore American slavery is right. If the lineal descendants of Ham are alone to be scripturally enslaved, it is certain that slavery at the south must soon become unscriptural. (14)

Douglass does not stop at the logical critique of this curse. He also argues that the moral behavior of masters, presumably including his own father, also belied the curse. All children born of slave women remained slaves, no matter who their father was. By thus denying their own paternity, slavery conveniently worked to "administer to [slaveholders'] lusts, and make a gratification of their wicked desires profitable as well as pleasurable" (13). He thus exposed slaveholders' appeal to the curse of Ham as corrupt. Slaveholders were cradle robbers.

Douglass also exposes the corruption of discourse in the slaveholding religion in a more overt way, by highlighting the prevalence among slaveholders of profanity, "cursing" proper.[67] Douglass repeatedly notes that physical violence against a slave was often accompanied by the corruption of language into cursing.[68] Indeed, the first example of physical violence recorded in the *Narrative* intentionally links violent words with violent actions (for the significance of this link, see the discussion of defining "violence" in chapter 1). The story involves an overseer named Plummer, whom Douglass describes as "a miserable drunkard, a profane swearer, and a savage monster." As if the presence of the first two behaviors alone were not sufficient to earn Plummer the third title (at least to the "refined" ears of his cultivated Christian audiences), Douglass adds that Plummer "always went armed with a cowskin [whip] and a heavy cudgel" (14).

The second incident of violence that Douglass records in the *Narrative* also refers to the language of the violent. "Captain Anthony," Douglass's first owner, is now the perpetrator. He is about to whip Douglass's Aunt Hester for disobeying one of his orders:

> Before he commenced whipping Aunt Hester, he took her into the kitchen, and stripped her from neck to waist. . . . He then told her to cross her hands, calling her at the same time a d——d b——h. After crossing her hands, he tied them with a strong rope, and led her to a stool under a large

hook in the joist, put in for the purpose. . . . He then said to her, "Now, you d——d b——h, I'll learn you how to disobey my orders!" (15)

That this particular epithet has religious significance should not take much deciphering: to be damned was the worst fate that might befall a Christian. The language of the curse was a sign of the violence and corruption of slavery as a religion. The way that slaveholders displaced the grace of speaking into the damnation of cursing was thus the first sign of this system's corruption.

Throughout his depictions of violence against slaves, Douglass oscillates between the discourse and the practices of the perpetrators. It is as if he wants his audience to see that the corruption of language is itself a practice of violence, as if words become curses as a sign of the religion's corruption. Accordingly, in one final example, Douglass observes that Mr. Severe, yet a third overseer,

> was a profane swearer. It was enough to chill the blood and stiffen the hair of an ordinary man to hear him talk. Scarce a sentence escaped him but that was commenced or concluded by some horrid oath. The field was the place to witness his cruelty and profanity. His presence made it both the field of blood and of blasphemy. From the rising till the going down of the sun, he was cursing, raving, cutting, and slashing among the slaves. (17)

In Christian cultures, language is the very medium of divine-human interaction, a means of transcendence.[69] By contrast, it must indicate the presence of a corrupt religion, or a debased transcendence, when a discourse as one sided as a curse appears. Finally, Douglass crafts his own language in the *Narrative* to be elegant, poetic, and refined, in a word, to be revelatory of a "true" transcendence or a transcendent truth.

This is why it was critical for Douglass to confirm that the *Narrative* was "written by himself," as the title asserts. Such an assertion sharpens the contrast between Douglass's own "Christian" use of language and the use of curses in the slaveholding religion. In one of his earliest speeches, Douglass defines slavery as "the granting of that power by which one man exercises and enforces a right of property in the body and soul of another. The condition of the slave is simply that of the brute beast."[70] In the *Narrative*, this reduction of the slave to property is signaled by the mandate of the slave to remain silent. "To all . . . complaints, no matter how unjust, the slave must answer never a word" (21). The curse was constructed on the assumption that the scapegoat would keep silent, (non)verbally accepting a role as sacrificial instrument. Douglass's *Narrative* explicitly challenges that assumption and contrasts the discourse of the curse in the slaveholding religion with his own Christian truth. As the literary scholar Ann Kibbey states, "The linguistic virtuosity of the slave who survived slavery must have been impressive. The incentive to acquire a linguistic capability far beyond what was minimally necessary to labor in the fields was considerable, if only because the penalty for linguistic mistakes was incredibly high."[71]

Indeed, the curse was backed up by the second element in the slaveholding religion: coercion and torture. Douglass uses the short-hand term "women-whipping" for this peculiar form of religious ritual, although he refers to the abuse of both female bodies and male slaves, including himself.[72] Douglass describes various incidents of whipping in the *Narrative*, and through his narration, many of them clearly take on the qualities of religious rituals. In regard to the whipping of his Aunt Hester, Douglass depicts with almost liturgical precision each step leading up to the punishment. The overseer punished Hester for "disobedience," which meant, Douglass suggests, that her body was not available to the overseer when he "desired her presence" (15). But this depiction of the relationship between the perpetrator and the victim of violence hardly encompasses everything about this episode. The reason for the religion of slavery was to reduce the slave body to the purposes of the master. Whipping, Douglass tries to explain to his audiences, was not only a violent act against an individual body but also a ritual of punishment to remind all slaves of the hierarchy of white over black. The value of whipping was as much symbolic or performative as material. Whipping was an exercise of power that produced compliance by the body of the slave being whipped, as well as (ideally) by the entire "congregation" of slaves, to which the overseer or slaveholder was the priest who held the sacred object of power: the whip. That the purpose of the whipping was ostensibly "secular" or economic, to render the slave willing to engage in labor that the slaveholder could not, or would not, undertake, does not at all lessen its symbolic or ritual functions.[73]

This is the economic context for the ritual of whipping that frames another scene in which Douglass explains how religion could intertwine with the practice of punishment. The perpetrator in this scene is his master, Thomas Auld, whom Douglass describes simply as "mean" (39). At one point, however, Auld "experienced religion," and Douglass briefly held out hope that his conversion would lead him to treat his slaves more humanely or even to emancipate them. Instead, though, "it made him more cruel and hateful in all his ways. . . . Prior to his conversion, he relied upon his own depravity to shield and sustain him in his savage barbarity; but after his conversion, he found religious sanction and support for his slaveholding cruelty"(40). Auld "prayed morning, noon, and night," and he even prayed while he whipped his slaves. Douglass depicts how Auld whipped a young woman named "Henny" who had suffered burns to her hands that made her unable to work and hence made her an economic liability. Despite, or rather because of, her physical inability to work, "she was a constant offence" to Auld. "I have seen him," Douglass recounted:

> tie [her] up . . . and whip her with a heavy cowskin upon her naked shoulders, causing the warm red blood to drip; and, in justification of the bloody deed, he would quote this passage of Scripture—"He that knoweth his master's will, and doeth it not, shall be beaten with many stripes." Master would keep this lacerated young woman tied up in this horrid situation four or five hours at a time. I have known him to tie her up early in the morning, and whip her before breakfast, leave her, go to his store, return at dinner, and whip her again. (41)

Douglass here uses the same narrative structure of the passage of time to describe Henny's whippings that he used to describe Auld's prayers. Through this parallelism, Douglass suggests that Auld's practice of whipping as an effort to harness "power" for his own purposes was identical to his practice of prayer.[74]

An important discourse in the religion of slavery was the curse, and an important practice within it was ritualized punishment. The third feature of this religion was the mythology of a sweet patriarchal slaveholding family; a mythology that was belied by the material relationships in the slaveholding community that Douglass abbreviated as "cradle-plundering." One example of this feature of the religion of slavery is slave masters' adulterous desires and practices. The patriarchs were not good parents to all their children. In fact, Douglass tells his readers that the presence of mulattos could be a source of "constant offence" to the mistress of any plantation and that these mistresses tended to be "never better pleased than when she sees [such slaves] under the lash" (13). In the first pages of his narrative, Douglass punctures the mythology of the patriarchal plantation and implicates both masters and mistresses in violence.

Douglass's exposé of the mythology of the idyllic slaveholding community extended beyond unmasking the consequences of adultery in households. The process by which slaveholders became devotees of the violent religion of slaveholding was subtle. Even a family that closely fit the slaveholding ideal—the household of Hugh and Sophia Auld—could descend into the abuses of power that followed from the "cradle-plundering" character of the religion of slavery. Douglass was sent to live with the Aulds in Baltimore when he was between seven and eight. Upon his arrival, Douglass saw in the face of Sophia Auld "what I had never seen before . . . a white face beaming with the most kindly emotions" (27). Douglass describes this vision of whiteness in explicitly religious language: "I wish I could describe the rapture that flashed through my soul as I beheld [her face]. It was a new and strange sight to me, brightening up my pathway with the light of happiness. . . . Her face was made of heavenly smiles, and her voice of tranquil music" (27–29). This beatific vision was confirmed in practice for Douglass when Sophia Auld began to teach him "the A, B, C," and he even learned to spell a few words.

But this angel had another side. Upon learning that his wife was giving Douglass reading lessons, Hugh Auld intervened. The patriarch

> at once forbade Mrs. Auld to instruct me further, telling her, among other things, that it was unlawful, as well as unsafe, to teach a slave to read. To use his own words, further, he said, "If you give a nigger an inch, he will take an ell. A nigger should know nothing but to obey his master—to do as he is told to do. Learning would *spoil* the best nigger in the world. Now," said he, "if you teach that nigger (speaking of myself) how to read, there would be no keeping him." (29)

This event—apparently Douglass overheard the conversation—he depicts as a turning point in his life: "I now understood . . . the white man's power to enslave the black man. . . . From that moment, I understood the pathway from slavery to freedom" (29). He characterized this moment, again using religious language, as a "new and special revelation" (29). He had discovered the source of the projected transcendent authority in the religion of slaveholding. The slaveholder's cultural power was reduced to the compressions and displacements of reading and writing.

Douglass's pathway to freedom continued to be blocked by the patriarchal family, just as the family itself continued to be spoiled by the system. As Douglass describes it, the Auld family quickly descended under the influence of slavery into a mirror image of the illiterate beast they sought to make out of Douglass. Douglass recalls Sophia Auld's transformation in especially dramatic terms. Slavery "effected a disastrous change in her" (38). Indeed, Mrs. Auld succumbed to "the fatal poison of irresponsible power. . . . That cheerful eye, under the influence of slavery, soon became red with rage; that voice, made all of sweet accord, changed to one of harsh and horrid discord; and that angelic face gave place to that of a demon" (31). Again, Douglass's use of religious language here is not coincidental. He intends it as rhetorical, to be sure, as a way to show his readers the disastrous effects of slavery. But he also intends it as a faithful description of the sway of slavery over a family, as a way to depict how a desire to turn a human being into an instrument turned all humans into instruments of "irresponsible power." Under the religion of slavery, a woman had been transformed from a face of "heavenly smiles" to the face of "a demon." Such was the power of this religion that did not appear to be a religion; this spirituality infected with its subtle "poison" countless domestic economies of patriarchal households and plantations in America.[75]

Finally, Douglass held responsible America—the nation itself, and not only its southern states—as the institutional patron of this religion. The slave-holding religion was "the religion of this land," as Douglass asserted (77). As William L. Andrews, the editor of Douglass's narrative, has suggested, Douglass's work can be read as an "American jeremiad." Andrews differentiates this genre from what he calls a "black jeremiad" by pointing to the former's nationalist context. A "black jeremiad," Andrews contends, "was preoccupied with America's impending doom because of its racial injustices." In contrast, "the American jeremiad foretold America's future hopefully, sustained by the conviction of the nation's divinely appointed mission."[76] This may put it a bit too clearly, but the suggestion is helpful. The status of the nation is ambiguous, not central, to the *Narrative*, and if there is to be a redemptive role for America, it must first include all its human residents in an authentic religion. Nevertheless, Andrews is correct that Douglass's outlook for the nation is ultimately hopeful. Douglass wanted to see a "pure" religion practiced, if not established, in contrast to the current "religion of the land," which is "partial and hypocritical."

That Douglass thought this partial religion had national sway cannot be questioned. In both the *Narrative* and his speeches from around the same time period, Douglas makes clear that the slaveholding religion went beyond a denominational or regional phenomenon. He even sometimes contrasts "pure" Christianity with "the hypocritical Christianity of this land" (e.g., 75) or to the practices of "professed Christians in America" (e.g., 77) and to "the religion of the south" (78). But the last, Douglass adds, "is, by communion and fellowship, the religion of the north" (78). More often, however, Douglass simply identifies "the slaveholding religion" as "the religion of this land." The import of this national identification for Douglass, though only implied in the *Narrative*, became more explicit in several speeches he delivered after 1845.

In May 1846, for instance, in a speech he gave in London, Douglass maintained that "slavery is not only a matter belonging to the states south of the line, but is an American institution—a United States institution."[77] As his political analysis developed, this complicity of the North with slavery became a more prominent theme in his rhetoric. In a speech delivered in Syracuse, New York, in September 1847, for instance, Douglass indicts "the Constitution" as "radically and essentially slaveholding. . . . The language of the Constitution is you shall be a slave or die."[78] He eventually developed a remarkably nuanced way to indict the nation and yet hold out hope for it. By 1852, in his famous speech in Rochester, New York, "What to the Slave Is the Fourth of July?" Douglass conceives of the Constitution as a "temple" of the nation in which slavery *ought* to have no part:

> Fellow-citizens! There is no matter in respect to which, the people of the North have allowed themselves to be so ruinously imposed upon, as that of the pro-slavery character of the Constitution. In that instrument I hold there is neither warrant, license, nor sanction of the hateful thing; but, interpreted as it *ought* to be interpreted, the Constitution is a GLORIOUS LIBERTY DOCUMENT. Read its preamble, consider its purposes. Is slavery among them? Is it at the gateway? Or is it in the temple? It is neither.[79]

Here Douglass appears to pull back from his earlier indictment of the nation, even though the entire point of his address was to show that the slave was "not included" in the Fourth of July. The holy day of "your nation," as Douglass put it, in which citizens celebrated the "blessings" of liberty, would be partial and incomplete as long as slavery endured. The "religion of this land" was "partial, and hypocritical."

Among Frederick Douglass's most important contributions to the antislavery debate was identifying the religious contours of slavery as a system. This contribution was, furthermore, remarkably thorough. It showed that the slaveholding religion had a distinctive discourse—the curse—in which transcendence was corrupted into a one-sided and vulgar condemnation. It also showed that the slaveholding religion had its sacred practices or rituals—like whipping—by which power was exerted on a body and displayed as a reminder to all who witnessed it. It showed that the religion of slavery had a mythic community—the patriarchal household—in which slaves were to be silent instruments of whatever roles their masters or mistresses assigned them. Finally, Douglass showed that the religion of slavery had a temple—the institutions of the nation—whose laws and perhaps its Constitution, made this religion the hegemonic, if not established, faith in the land.[80] It was a long struggle, that lasted until well after Frederick Douglass's life had ended, before the laws of the United States, much less the practices of its citizens, lived up to his hopes for a peaceable religion across the land. We can better understand how that trajectory developed by looking both backward, to the religious experiences of Jarena Lee, and forward, to the cultural criticism and religious hopes depicted by Spike Lee.

From Jarena Lee to Spike Lee: The (Re)birth of a Nation?

The principal site over which the religion of slavery sought to exercise power was the African American body, especially the female body. Slave women not only were reduced to performing labor as instruments in the political economy of slavery; they also had their "labor" captured when they gave birth to children. Douglass points out how slave masters thus objectified and commodified the female body when he describes Mr. Covey's practices:

> Mr. Covey was a poor man; he was just commencing in life; he was only able to buy one slave; and, shocking as is the fact, he bought her, as he said, for *a breeder*. This woman was named Caroline. . . . She was about twenty years old. . . . After buying her, he hired a married man of Mr. Samuel Harrison, to live with him one year; and him he used to fasten up with her every night! The result was that, at the end of the year, the miserable woman gave birth to twins. . . . The children were regarded as being quite an addition to his wealth. (45)

It also is significant that Douglass considered Covey to be the only one of his masters who succeeded in "breaking" *him*, transforming a "man into a brute." The religion of slavery worked on both male and female bodies.

Douglass also found ways to resist this transformation and to be "reborn" (he also uses the metaphor of "resurrection") as a human being. In fact, this process of resistance and assertion of bodily integrity in the midst of slavery must have been more or less continuous. Two other texts from Douglass's era help shed light on how this worked and thereby reveal both the bodily anxieties and obsessions in the religion of slavery and the way that African American women in particular were aware of these strictures, resisted them, and negotiated a way out from under them.

The first text is *The Life and Religious Experience of Jarena Lee*, first published in 1836, and the other is the *Narrative of Sojourner Truth*, first printed in 1850. These two texts chronologically bracket Douglass's *Narrative* and thereby explain the matrix from which his antislavery critique emerged and a trajectory toward which his assertion of the integrity of the human body and its "Christian" practices of reading, writing, and speaking—was heading. Lee and Truth, in short, embodied and expressed what Douglass only gradually came to embrace: the need to link the emancipation of slaves with the emancipation and participation in American culture of women, not as instruments, but as human beings.[81] That Lee, like Douglass, found Christianity to be a vehicle of liberation is significant.

Jarena Lee was born in 1783, probably to free African Americans living in Cape May, New Jersey. For most of her childhood, she worked as a residential "servant maid" for a white family about sixty miles from her home, but after a severe bout of illness, she moved to Philadelphia to live and work in the home of a Catholic family. As she matured, Lee developed a strong interest in religion and eventually negotiated her way to become an itinerant preacher. Although she did not directly experience the strictures of slavery, she surely knew the limits imposed on women's speaking and acting in both religious communities and civil society. Her memoirs, in fact, talk about the many efforts to contain and silence her, which she used as challenges by inverting the "religious" conventions associated with "the slaveholding religion" that Douglass later cataloged, analyzed, and critiqued.

For instance, Lee describes her conversion in ways that highlight how religion could exclude her, on the one hand, and how she could embody power through religion, on the other.[82] Shortly after arriving in Philadelphia, Lee began to attend a Methodist church, led by an Englishman by the name of Pilmore. She lasted about three months. Her story of what led her to leave is telling: "It appeared that there was a wall between me and a communion with that people, which was higher than I could possibly see over, and seemed to make this impression upon my mind, *this is not the people for you.*"[83] Using a spatial metaphor, Lee describes how a "wall" prevented her from "seeing" how to "commune" with white Christians. Rather than being activated, her senses were impeded by participating in this place. The wall was not one she had built: it was imposed on her to contain her, to keep her from "communion."

Lee couched her conversion proper in terms that foregrounded the role of the body as the site of her freedom. On the same day that she decided to leave the English Methodists, Lee was invited by the head cook of the house she lived in to join her at the afternoon service of the congregation that eventually became Bethel African Methodist Episcopal Church. That day, while listening to the preaching of Richard Allen, Lee decided that "this is the people to which my heart unites." Her conversion occurred within three weeks, "at the very outset of the sermon." Lee's narrative, again, develops metaphors rich in association:

> The text was barely pronounced . . . when there appeared to *my* view, in the centre of the heart *one* sin; and this was *malice*, against one particular individual, who had strove deeply to injure me, which I resented. At this discover I said, *Lord* I forgive *every* creature. That instant, it appeared to me, as if a garment, which had entirely enveloped my whole person, even to my fingers ends, split at the crown of my head, and was stripped away from me, passing like a shadow, from my sight—when the glory of God seemed to cover me in its stead.
>
> That moment, though hundreds were present, I did leap to my feet, and declare that god, for Christ's sake, had pardoned the sins of my soul. Great was the ecstasy of my mind, for I felt that not only the sin of malice was pardoned, but all other sins were swept away together. That day was the first when my heart had believed. . . . [And] for a few moments I had power to exhort sinners.[84]

This remarkable description inverts the usual instrumental reduction or stripping of an African American woman's body in the religion of slaveholding, into a narrative of purification and pardon. Unashamed of losing one "garment" and confident she was clothed in another transcendent fabric, Lee "did leap" to her feet, "declare," and find "power." Like the rebirth of baptism as Paul described it, although now in a material setting in which the metaphor took on flesh, Lee's conversion demonstrated the truth that "in Christ" there is no male or female, no slave or free person. Lee's rebirth was confirmed by Rev. Richard Allen, who declared that "another witness of the power of Christ" had been manifest in Lee's conversion.

It took Lee years, overcoming many obstacles, including some set in her way by Rev. Allen, to transform her experience of "the power to exhort sinners" from a momentary ecstasy to a recognized public calling. Indeed, she had to raise the money to publish her memoirs—the first prose work published by an African American woman in the United States, according to some accounts—on her own. But she was as convinced as Frederick Douglass was of the importance of what literary scholar Katherine Clay Bassard calls "writing as (religious) ritual." Lee's experience of finding power through a ritual of writing, which was such a sharp contrast to the illiteracy imposed by the religion of slaveholding, predated Douglass's. They both were convinced that the mastery of language—the extension of the body—was the turning point in being able to understand, and thereby overcome, the power of the slaveholding religion. But Lee's text was not only written; initially, it was spoken. Furthermore, her text was lived and took place in the context of a Christian community that was dramatically different from the sweet patriarchy of the slaveholding religion or from the silencing instrumentalism of the nation, where women's place was in the home. As Brassard points out, Lee's text explicitly strips away "the taint of sin associated with blackness" and, one might add, with female embodiment, and asserts a "representation of the glorified black female body," in which "the ideology of obedience to white superiors is 'swept away.'"[85] In her life and work, Jarena Lee embodied realities that no construct of "whiteness" could displace.

In the *Narrative of Sojourner Truth*, what we might call an embodied or "placed" (as opposed to displaced) subjectivity that both Douglass and Lee demonstrated appears in sharp relief. Isabella Van Wagner, later known as Sojourner Truth, had been born a slave in about 1797 in upstate New York. She had been freed when the state of New York declared emancipation in 1827. Around the same time, she was converted to Christianity, more specifically, Pentecostalism. As a consequence of her conversion, she, like Lee, became an itinerant minister and also a regular speaker at antislavery meetings. As an ex-slave who had not had access to education, Truth remained unable to read or write throughout her life. Nevertheless, a key, and frequently anthologized, incident in her *Narrative* reveals how Truth also used her body and rituals of speaking and performance to challenge the conventional representation of the displaced African American female body in the religion of slavery.[86]

The incident took place in 1858, and the *Narrative* records it through eyewitness correspondence that had been published in a Boston antislavery newspaper: "The border ruffian Democracy of Indiana appears to be jealous and suspicious of every anti-slavery movement. A rumor was immediately circulated [upon Truth's arrival in the State] that Sojourner was an imposter; that she was, indeed, a man disguised in women's clothing." As with Lee's narrative, the body and its clothing become a central site of negotiation between an African American woman and a community. In Truth's case, however, the circumstances are far more reminiscent of the usual representation of the African American female body in the religion of slavery. Her body is a source of scandal and confusion, of "jealousy" and desire.

At her third speech in Indiana, a local physician stood up to interrupt and repeat the rumor. He then "demanded that Sojourner submit her breast to the inspection of some of the ladies present." The correspondent reports that the meeting descended into "confusion and uproar," with some of the crowd "ashamed and indignant" at the physician's request but other members of the crowd insistent. During the tumult, Truth, like Lee, stood up. She asked the crowd why they suspected her, and the physician replied that her voice was "the voice of a man." He then called for a vote of the assembly regarding his request, to which "a boisterous 'Aye,' was the result." The narrative continues:

> Sojourner told them that her breasts had suckled many a white babe, to the exclusion of her own offspring; that some of those white babies had grown to man's estate; that, although they had sucked her colored breasts, they were, in her estimation, far more manly than they (her persecutors) appeared to be; and she quietly asked them, as she disrobed her bosom, if they, too, wished to suck! In vindication of her truthfulness, she told them that she would show her breast to the whole congregation; that it was not to her shame that she uncovered her breast before them, but to their shame.[87]

The potential meanings of this narrative are many. It is, at least, a brilliant assertion of bodily integrity as an act of nonviolent resistance to violence. Put differently, by including this act in the story of her life, Sojourner Truth inverted the usual values of honor and shame associated with the presence of the African American female body in the religion of slaveholding. By asserting her own bodily presence and denying the polite containment of her body that the medical doctor had sought to impose on her (as a new "priest" in the Northern version of the religion of slavery), Truth "clothed" herself in dignity even while exposing a "private" part of her body that, under slavery, had been turned into a commodity. Truth put into practice an incarnated Christianity that did not displace bodies into a system of violence. Instead, she reveled in revealing the compression of life-giving presence in the material reality of her breast. Her nonviolent resistance to the attempt to oppress her turned the tables on her oppressors. She used her body, her words, and even her subtle sense of humor to shame her oppressors and to demonstrate her own humanity.[88]

Both Lee and Truth offer examples that confirm Douglass's critique of the religion of slaveholding and considerably extend the reach of that critique. By demonstrating how women, as well as men, found liberation in the practices of speaking and writing and in Christianity, Lee and Truth confirm that Douglass's vision of a peaceable religion beyond its slaveholding parameters was an actual and not a utopian or romantic project. Some of the ambiguities associated with Douglass's turn to the nation and its markets as agents of redemption remain in these two narratives. Lee turned to the African American churches for support, and according to her biographer, the historian Nell Irvin Painter, Truth depended for subsistence on her ability to sell copies of her book and photographs of herself. "As embodied" in her story and photographs, Truth's persona "proved remunerative," but this was the exception rather than the rule, for many years after Emancipation, Painter concludes. Truth's "husband had died in an Ulster [New York] poorhouse before the Civil War, and her daughters died destitute in Battle Creek [Michigan] in the late nineteenth and early twentieth centuries. They lacked marketable personas and a supply of commodities with which to memorialize them."[89] Trust in the market proved a fragile foundation for many freed African American working men and women.

How the market and nation took over as institutional agents of the hierarchy and exclusions once associated with what Douglass called the slaveholding religion can be demonstrated in a brief reading of D. W. Griffith's 1915 *The Birth of a Nation*, the first blockbuster film in the history of cinema.[90] In a 1930 interview, Griffith himself asserted that the film was about "great sacrifices, suffering, and death."[91] As is well known, the basic plot of the three-hour long film was based on Thomas Dixon's novels *The Clansman* and *The Leopard's Spots*. Part 1 of the film documents the "senseless sacrifice" of the Civil War, including epic battle scenes and intimate close-ups of the dead and dying that dramatize, even sanctify, these sacrifices. Part 2 shows how, using vigilante justice, the Ku Klux Klan saved the South from chaos during Reconstruction. Throughout the film, the North is represented by the Stoneman family, and the South, by the Camerons. By the end of the film, the Southerner Ben Cameron (also known as "the Little General" for his role in the Confederate Army) marries the Northerner Elsie Stoneman (played by Lillian Gish), and Phil Stoneman, a Union soldier, falls in love with and marries Elsie Cameron. Births can be expected. These happy "white" unions are the result, however, of two other explicit scenes of sacrifice that together reveal the basic shift from a Christian to a national or racial religion that Griffith's film documented as well as promoted.

The first sacrifice is the death of Flora Cameron. Flora is the younger sister of Ben and Elsie and came of age during the Civil War. During Reconstruction, she is pursued by "Gus," a black veteran (who is played, as are all the major African American roles in the film, by a white actor in blackface). Gus proclaims to Flora that he is "a Captain now—and I want to marry." Flora is appalled, slaps Gus, and a long chase scene through a woods ensues. Eventually, Flora leaps to her death off a cliff. Ben finds her and holds her dying body in his arms in an unmistakable pietà. He slowly removes a Confederate flag that was wrapped around her waist as she mouths the name of "Gus" to her brother. Ben then hunts down Gus and, after another long chase, captures him. The Klan assembles in the woods. "The Trial" reads the title board. It takes about ten seconds. "Guilty," reads the verdict on the next board. Gus is then lynched, and his body is dumped on the steps of the house of the mulatto lieutenant governor of South Carolina, Griffith's compressed symbol of the terror of miscegenation.[92]

Griffith explicitly identifies as a sacrifice only one of these cinematic deaths of Flora and of Gus: guess which one? Shortly after Gus's lynching, Ben Cameron again rallies the Klan in the woods. This time he is there for another ritual purpose. He holds up the Confederate flag from Flora's waist and dips it into a basin of water, baptizing it while wearing his white robe inscribed with two red crosses on the chest. He then holds the baptized, blood-soaked flag aloft, and a title card draws out the significance: "Brethren, this flag bears the red stain of the life of a Southern woman, a priceless sacrifice on the altar of an outraged civilization." Ben then takes a burning cross from a Klansman standing behind him and holds it and the flag aloft. Flora's "sacrifice" has been avenged by the lynching of Gus; "civilization" has been restored. A hybrid religion, based in death, has been the means. The transcendent authority of whites as represented by the religious vigilantes of the Ku Klux Klan will prevail against all rivals.

During *The Birth of a Nation*, disunity and rivalry between North and South is overcome by the cinematic sacrifice (but which is not described as a sacrifice) of the scapegoat Gus. Griffith selected Gus to represent African American male desire and offered him to audiences to trigger their fears and to serve as a compressed substitute/rival for their own desires. He then kills off Gus in an act of vigilante justice. Whites graduate from sacrificed to sacrificers, with the Klan as the ritual's experts. This ritual expertise based on the brutal elimination of a black man opens up, Griffith suggests, the prospect of a lasting peace. Whites will be happily married (to each other). The film's final scene is a positively rapturous vision of this peace, with a nod to its Christian origins. Ben Cameron and Elsie Stoneman sit together on a bluff, high above the sea. Ben turns toward Elsie, with the vastness of the sea and sky in front of them, and the title card reads: "Dare we dream of a golden day when the bestial War shall rule no more. But instead—the gentle Prince in the Hall of Brotherly Love in the City of Peace." This millennial hope is then given traditional sanction as a huge diaphanous image of Christ appears in the background of a large crowd of dancing and processing people. But that this is less a Christian than a national peace Griffith makes plain: "Liberty and Union, one and inseparable, now and forever," the title card asserts. It is not Christ who unites, but the white, supremacist nation, built around death, sacrifice, and vigilante "justice." "THE BIRTH OF A NATION or 'The Clansman.' THE END" is the final title card. As Richard C. Salter pointed out, *The Birth of a Nation* is an American myth, a cinematic ode to American civil religion.[93]

What is remarkable about this film, made less than a century ago, is not only how blatant its racism (and religious violence) was, but how popular it was. *The Birth of a Nation* made D. W. Griffith rich. Audiences flocked to it across the country, paying premium fees previously associated only with live theater performances. Albert H. T. Banzhaf, Griffith's lawyer, estimated that by 1922, five million Americans, or one out of every eighteen adults in the country, had viewed it.[94] This popularity was despite intense criticism from the NAACP (founded in 1909). But that criticism eventually resulted in several films that responded directly to Griffith's racism. Princeton University historian of American religions Judith Weisenfeld carefully recovered these films' plots and mapped some of their trajectories. The first such film was *The Birth of a Race*, released in 1919. Directed by John W. Noble, but apparently with some support from Booker T. Washington's personal secretary Emmett J. Scott, the film's alternative title was *The Story of a Great Peace*. In a direct challenge to Griffith's white-supremacist vision of national peace, the "race" described in this film is neither black nor white but an "American" race. Weisenfeld helpfully identifies this worldview as a "Christian universalist position." Indeed, much of the film tracks the story of the Schmidts, a German American family, and their divided loyalties during World War I. But the point of the film is established in early scenes depicting a biblical epic of human equality, from Genesis through the crucifixion of Christ: "In the beginning," one title card reads, "God created the world to be a place of peace." This vision of peace was built around "God's thought in Creation—Equality." Jesus preached to followers of all races, teaching them "equality instead of slavery." Because of his "heretical" commitment to human equality, Jesus was crucified. The next scenes of the film move to America, where the "gospel" takes root in the Declaration of Independence and the Emancipation

Proclamation. After this historical prologue, the plot turns to the members of the Schmidt family who, after several difficult decisions, prove their patriotism during wartime.[95]

Many Americans joined President Woodrow Wilson (and writer H. G. Wells) to imagine World War I as the "war to end all wars." Consequently, for the filmmakers of *The Birth of a Race* to ground "A Great Peace" in warfare did not seem to be a contradiction. Weisenfeld concludes:

> [The film] emphasizes that for American men, black and white, to participate in the war is to act on behalf of the restoration of peace and freedom. Moreover, just as we have learned that neither Christianity nor American democratic principles recognize race, the film also tells us that the American fighting force will not: "Side by side—brothers-in-arms—fighting for the Cause of Mankind, no man says to the other—'What is thy creed?'" And we see two men, one black and one white, farming the same field. The scene dissolves and suddenly they are both in uniform and march off to war together.[96]

Contrary to Griffith's national unity around a dichotomy of white over black, *The Birth of a Race* imagines an American nation with room for blacks, whites, and even Germans.

A second film that Weisenfeld studied, Oscar Micheaux's *Within Our Gates* (1919), reveals an even more complex alternative to Griffith's dualism. The protagonist of *Within Our Gates* is an African American woman, Sylvia Landry, a teacher in a school for black children in the South. Because the school is struggling for money, Sylvia resolves to go North to raise the needed funds. While there, intrigue interferes with her efforts, and in one scene, an unscrupulous southern black preacher, "Old Ned," is shown flattering his flock with promises of heaven for them and damnation for whites. "Old Ned" makes these moves all while depending on the patronage of whites and hampering black economic and social empowerment. Micheaux's is anything but a romantic view of the power of black religion, and his perspective on violence is unflinching. Near the end of the film, in its most vivid and powerful scenes, Sylvia's past—which was part of the intrigue impeding her efforts to raise funds—is revealed. Her innocent family had been lynched, and she had nearly been raped, with both incidents depicted dramatically through Micheaux's camera. In the context of the story, these events are now actually held against Sylvia's honor, as if they were her fault. Weisenfeld again beautifully summarizes:

By including this lynching scene, Micheaux inverts and rights the logic of sexual assault and violence as presented in *The Birth of a Nation*. In Griffith's world, lynching is the justified response to the excessive and uncontrolled sexuality of black men. Micheaux argues, in a most graphic manner, that whites have been the real perpetrators of sexual and other violence in the postwar South.[97]

Sylvia is rescued from being a scapegoat when a prominent African American physician from Boston, Dr. Vivian, proposes to marry her. The funds for the school—and then some—are raised. So the film simultaneously critiques Griffith's religion of white innocent domination and some elements in black religion as complicit in the religion of slaveholding and lifts up a female protagonist. Sylvia was a survivor of assaults on her family, her body, and her honor, and she saved a school where African Americans could learn the self-determination that her own life story so vividly demonstrated.

Amy Kaplan, a professor of English at the University of Pennsylvania, reads Micheaux's film in continuity with Griffith's film and in support of American empire. She is correct that in the final scene, Dr. Vivian encourages Sylvia to be "proud" of her country and to recognize that African Americans were "never immigrants" but nevertheless served with honor in the military. This is similar to the point in *The Birth of a Race*, and it harks back to Frederick Douglass's faith in the nation. But Kaplan goes too far in suggesting that "African Americans . . . can only prove their national identity as imperial citizens by their participation in wars abroad."[98] This misses U.S. communities' utopian idealism regarding World War I and, even more, the way that Micheaux inverted the violence of Griffith's racism. Even the fact that Micheaux hired black actors and featured an African American female protagonist indicates how different his film was from D. W. Griffith's. To be sure, Micheaux does affirm the rights of African Americans to participate in the domestic pleasures of marriage and in the foreign successes of burgeoning military might, and Kaplan is correct to connect both to imperial designs. But even more, Micheaux vividly demonstrates African American men and women struggling to participate in all the possibilities and problems of a democratic society: to promote education, to gain economic stability, to survive trauma, to forge families, and to find a religion that does not replicate violence.

As is well known, efforts like Oscar Micheaux's to assert African American self-determination and to invert racist narratives eventually bore fruit in the civil rights movement. Elsewhere I have told the stories of African

American congregations and youth ministries before, during, and after the civil rights movement.[99] And it is important to remember that the conflicted, violence-laden story of this movement is susceptible to a romantic retelling that removes the conflict and difficulty from it and turns the assassination of Martin Luther King Jr.—to take just one tragic moment—into yet another sacrifice.[100]

Perhaps a brief foray into the life and thought of Howard Thurman, one of the lesser-known figures from the early years of the civil rights movement, can show why the critique of the religious origins of American racial violence remains important and forms a continuity from Jarena Lee to Spike Lee.[101] First is Howard Thurman's visit to Mohandas Gandhi in 1935. Initially underwhelmed by Gandhi's gift of a piece of homespun cotton at their initial meeting, Thurman listened as Gandhi explained how cotton united African Americans and Indians and how this simple cloth represented freedom. Gradually, Thurman reports a veil being lifted from his eyes—as in Jarena Lee's conversion—and he began to realize, along with Gandhi, that stolen labor was a religious problem, requiring a religious solution. After his visit with Gandhi, he returned to the United States as an advocate of Christian nonviolence, eventually becoming a mentor to Martin Luther King Jr. and an activist and author in his own right.[102]

In perhaps his most famous text, *Jesus and the Disinherited*, Thurman drives to the core problem, the construction of white identity:

> The religion of Jesus says to the disinherited: "Love your enemy. Take the initiative in seeking ways by which you can have the experience of a common sharing of mutual worth and value. It may be hazardous, but you must do it." For the Negro it means he must see the individual white man in the context of a common humanity. The fact that a particular individual is white, and therefore may be regarded in some over-all sense as the racial enemy, must be faced; and opportunity must be provided, found, or created for freeing such an individual from his "white necessity." From this point on, the relationship becomes like any other primary one.[103]

In other words, liberation had to be extended to the oppressor as well as the oppressed. This expansive vision of Christian nonviolence changed both African American destiny and America itself. As Curtis J. Evans stated, "King's religiously infused vision of the good society . . . testified to a specific contribution of religious faith and moral vision that blacks in particular had made to the nation."[104] That is, if the slaveholding religion sought to reduce human beings to an instrumental role in the political economy, then the emphasis on Christian nonviolence by leaders like Thurman and King directly contradicted and challenged these *religious* foundations. Nonviolence became the opposite of the religious violence that demanded sacrifice. Christian nonviolence displaced violence. It sacrificed sacrifice. Instead of demands for more sacrifice, the civil rights movement offered a counterassertion of fragile power and human dignity, with people standing in solidarity across constructions of race, nation, and religion.

Nonetheless, in the late twentieth century, a backlash and renewed racism resurfaced across the United States in ways seeking to perpetuate and advance white privilege and economic power often, ironically, in the name of Christianity. In that context, the films of Spike Lee both resurfaced Frederick Douglass's critique of the religion of slaveholding and again held up the possibility of respect for human difference and the possibility of solidarity (if not intimacy) across difference. From *She's Gotta Have It*, his first commercial success in 1986, to *He Got Game* in 1998, to *Bamboozled* in 2000, Lee directed much of his considerable cinematic attention to the way human beings, and especially African Americans, are coerced or bamboozled into playing roles in others' dramas. Of course, Lee is not unaware that this is precisely what actors do: act.[105] They are instruments. But here the instrumentalism is intentional, voluntary, and contingent. Filmmakers stage performances for subjective as well as objective profit. Films are rituals in which both production and consumption are voluntary. Lee's films both expose unintentional or involuntary instrumentalism—what I call the "religion of slaveholding" or "innocent domination"—and show that resistance is possible and that alternatives to this religion can be imagined and put into practice. Among his films, *Malcolm X* (1992) is undoubtedly Lee's most sustained and didactic meditation on these themes.

In many ways, *Malcolm X* reiterates how Frederick Douglass, Jarena Lee, Sojourner Truth, Oscar Micheaux, and Howard Thurman all asserted their bodily integrity by speaking, writing, and acting in ways that contradicted the attempts to impose silence on African Americans through corrupt rituals of bodily discipline such as the curse, whipping, lynching, and other overt forms of violence. But Lee also moves beyond these strategies, and not only because of the medium in which he works. His predecessors depended on nation, church, and markets, respectively, to ground their self-determination and to overturn the rituals of bodily discipline that contained their voices. But Lee, through his poignant depiction of Malcolm's life and death, counsels all those threatened with reduction to instrumental roles to assert their dignity and self-determination "through any means necessary." In fact, though, the means that Lee recommends through his representation of Malcolm's life are in fact quite clearly delineated and perhaps surprising.

The film does not hesitate to show the ways that Malcolm both embraced violent crime in his early life and was subjected to violent rituals of bodily discipline throughout his life: from the lye-based "conk" that he used to straighten his hair in an opening scene, to his treatment at the hands of white prison guards in the middle of the film, and to his final staged execution by members of the Nation of Islam near the end.[106] Throughout, Lee juxtaposes these scenes of violation with scenes revealing Malcolm's dignity and desire for self-determination. Thus, at the end of the film, after seeing Malcolm's body riddled by bullets, we hear Ozzie Davis recite his eulogy while seeing video footage of the historic Malcolm X (*not* Denzel Washington playing the role): "Malcolm was our manhood, our living black manhood. That was his meaning to his people and in honoring him we honor the best in ourselves." Such juxtapositions invert the tragedy of Malcolm's loss with the integrity of his commitment to African American (and especially African American male) self-determination.

Precisely because that manhood has just been executed on screen, before an audience that will not be of one race or creed, Lee also depicts Malcolm as a role model for a racially and religiously pluralistic society in which the dignity of difference might gain acceptance.[107] Throughout his years as a Muslim, Malcolm moved increasingly toward orthodox Islam and away from the separatism of the Nation of Islam. The key scene is Malcolm's participation in the hajj, which he described as follows:

While I was in Mecca making the pilgrimage, I spoke about the brotherhood that existed at all levels among all people, all colors who had accepted the religion of Islam. I pointed out that what it had done, Islam, for those people despite their complexion differences, that it would probably do America well to study the religion of Islam and perhaps it could drive some of the racism from this society. Muslims look upon themselves as human beings, as part of the human family and therefore look upon all other segments of the human family as part of that same family. Today my friends are black, brown, red, yellow and white.

This does not in the least mute Malcolm's (or Lee's) commitment to African American self-determination.[108] But it does open the way toward collaboration and solidarity across racial lines on causes that accord with the interests of

African Americans. This opening revives the universalist vision of *The Birth of a Race* and the hope of Howard Thurman, albeit now on a Muslim platform.

That Lee's film was a commercial success, when *The Birth of a Race* was a failure, indicates how far the United States has come toward a pluralistic society in which racial integration is not a code for economic enslavement.[109] But Lee never lets viewers forget how much labor remains. Like Frederick Douglass, Lee's *X* indicts the nation by calling it to accountability, or perhaps even a rebirth. Thus, in the opening scene, before the title or any credits roll, grainy video footage from the beating of African American Rodney King by a gang of Los Angeles police officers in 1991 is accompanied by a voice-over in which Denzel Washington intones the words of Malcolm X: "We haven't seen any American dream; we've experienced the American nightmare!" This rhetorical inversion is then joined by a fade to a burning American flag, which is quickly reduced to a red-white-and-blue X.[110] Underneath this destruction of a national icon remains the fundamental hope that Lee shares with his predecessors, that the nation may eventually live up to its rhetoric and fulfill its destiny in a new shape and through a new vision of its imaginative construction.[111]

Lee caught flak for this introduction to the film from a number of reviewers, many of whom also did not like the film's conclusion (*National Review*'s John Simon, for instance, called the introductory and concluding scenes "agit-prop").[112] The final scene of the film takes place in a Harlem classroom, after Malcolm's murder and funeral. Clothing suggests the present (1992). Several children stand up and declare: "I'm Malcolm X." This is, at first blush, an odd conclusion to a tragedy. Yet it is consistent with the vision of society that Malcolm was moving toward and that (perhaps) Lee perceived as the greatest potential legacy of Africans in America. By identifying a new generation of African American children with Malcolm X, Lee turns tragedy into a celebration of ancestor-identification in a pan-Africanist, if not panhumanist, affirmation. Malcolm, along with the nation and its ideals, is symbolically reborn. This vision also transcends nationalism, and in the final frames, South African Nobel laureate Nelson Mandela appears on the screen and states: "As Brother Malcolm said, 'We declare our right on this earth to be a man, to be a human being, to be respected as a human being, in this society, on this earth, in this day, which we intend to bring into existence by any means necessary.'" Here the effectiveness of African struggle is made plain, as in the nonviolent revolution against apartheid, and implicitly in the nonviolent revolution with which Malcolm can, in the end, be identified.[113] This is an African American humanism, broad enough to embrace Muslims, Christians, and those with no definite faith other than a commitment to being a human, that is the red thread of nonviolent reading, writing, speaking, and filmmaking that stretches from Jarena Lee to Spike Lee and beyond.[114]

Two final scenes, one from very early in the film and one at its turning point demonstrate what Lee has in mind and also the limits to the means of human self-determination and liberation he recommends.[115] The first scene is the second in the film and is a flashback of the KKK attacking the wood frame house Malcolm lived in as a child on the Omaha prairie. In a voice-over, Malcolm says: "When my mother was pregnant with me, she told me later, a party of Klansmen on horseback surrounded our house in Omaha." A shot shows the Klan on horses in front of the house. "They brandished guns, and shouted for my father to come out. My mother went to the door where they could see her pregnant condition." The camera isolates Louise Little on the porch, as the voice-over continues: "and told them my father was in Milwaukee, preaching." The screenplay then notes: "The Klan breaks all the windows in the house then rides off into the glorious D. W. Griffith *Birth of a Nation* moonlit night."[116] At the outset, Spike Lee states that he intended *Malcolm X* to be a contrast to *The Birth of a Nation*.[117] As the scene with the children and as this scene before he was even born indicate, *Malcolm X* is about the *rebirth* of a nation. If the first birth of the American nation was premised on the religious violence of slaveholding, as represented by the hooded white figures of the KKK, the nation will be reborn on a nonviolent foundation, through a religion more congenial to art than to force.

The key change in producing this new religion must be how this transcendence is constructed or imagined. The scene that clarifies this point occurs when Malcolm is in jail, where he is befriended by an older inmate, named Bembry, who introduces Malcolm to Islam. Malcolm supposes Islam to be another hustle, like the one he used to get himself out of the draft. Bembry replies: "I'm telling you God's words, not no hustle. I'm talking the words of Allah, the black man's God. I'm telling you, boy, that God is black." Malcolm replies, incredulous: "What? Everybody knows God is white." Bembry's response crystallizes centuries of displacements, reiterating the logic of Rev. Armstrong and every devotee of the religion of slaveholding, and exposing its folly:

BEMBRY: But everything the white man taught you, you learned. He told
you you were a black heathen and you believed him. He told you
how he took you out of darkness and brought you to the light. And
you believed him. He taught you to worship a blond, blue-eyed God
with white skin—and you believed him. He told you that black was
a curse, you believed him.

Bembry then takes out a dictionary and asks Malcolm to look up "black." He reads that it means: "destitute of light, devoid of color, enveloped in darkness. Hence, utterly dismal or gloomy. . . soiled with dirt, foul; sullen, hostile, forbidding—as a black day." Malcolm exclaims: "Hey, they's some shit, all right." Then they read how the dictionary defines "white:" "Of the color of pure snow; reflecting all the rays of the spectrum. The opposite of black, hence free from spot or blemish; innocent, pure, without evil intent, harmless. Honest, square-dealing, honorable." And Malcolm concludes, emphatically: "That's bullshit."[118]

This is not just reading or speaking; it's reading *race* critically and constructing a ground for transcendence other than the usual innocence of a dominating "white" God: *God* is black. That this basic premise gave rise to the *nation* of Islam is no coincidence, but Lee tells the story of Malcolm in a way that identifies him not with a separatist vision but with the legacy of Douglass. Lee imagines, through Malcolm's tragedy, a rebirth of American culture that transcends its nationalist construction on a foundation of "whiteness." Instead, viewers of the film—not all of whom are black—are encouraged by "any means necessary" to identify with Malcolm X as "American manhood." Just how important and problematic this identification can be is the subject of the next chapter. But set in the context of the story of Malcolm's senseless sacrifice, Lee's rhetorical invocation of Malcolm's aphorism to achieve freedom "by any means necessary" can hardly be taken as a counsel of physical violence or as a retreat into romantic religion. Instead, such rhetoric turns the viewer toward art and toward a religion that seeks something other than sacrifice at its center. The only means that can take down the religion of slaveholding is *religious* means. Lee's loving representation of Malcolm's lost future pushes viewers to imagine an America welcome to new discourses (such as Islam), new practices (such as filmmaking), and new communities (across nations and generations).

It will not do, however, to reinscribe the instrumental worldview of slavery into an instrumental view of African American religion, whether Christian or Muslim. Ordinarily, as historian Curtis J. Evans has shown, this approach to black religion sets up a dichotomy.[119] Black-white, resistance-accommodation, activist-escapist, oppressive-liberative forms of religion set the terms in which African American historical texts and institutions are interpreted. Instead, Evans encourages reading texts and religious practices in their contexts and recognizing the varied, complex, and multivalent voices across constructions of race in American history. At one level, this is unmistakably correct. At another level, however, Evans himself tracks a key trajectory that traverses the contingencies he describes, namely, the construction of "religion" itself in its associations with race. It is precisely that construction, and the *racial* work that "religion" has carried out in American history which we have tried to plot here, that is associated with various forms of violence important to scrutinize across contexts.

Whatever "religion" has meant in the many and varied experiences of whites or blacks, Latinos and Latinas, Germans, Italians, Japanese—and so on, in America, religion has often appeared as glorious sacrifice, with the nation or markets understood as transcendent and with individuals (or entire groups) as expendable scapegoats. Such a religious process of blessing brutality has consistently depended on a dichotomy of domination-subordination, in which a human being must be displaced to advance another's interests. No amount of complexity or variability or historicizing can wipe away those tragic legacies of religion in America. In fact, the refusal to acknowledge the enduring sway of those dichotomies probably makes their durability and usefulness that much more likely.

That said, Evans's vision of a place for African American religion(s) within an expansive, varied, complex, polyglot, and open American culture clearly builds on the kind of power in faith that African American cultural critics from Jarena Lee to Spike Lee have proclaimed. Such a power faces tragedy but seeks hope in the participation of the multitudes through art, politics, economics, and religion, in short, by any means necessary. Such a model of cultural power does not place a romantic burden on religion or dismiss its tragic limits and legacies. But neither does such a model of power dismiss the resources that people have found in religions to live lives of integrity and forge communities of compassion that helped them survive.[120] As Spike Lee wrote: If a work of art can "move us, it's because it's about the HUMAN SPIRIT."[121] Being moved by rituals and policies that promote and produce mastery, not of one human being over another, but of the proper instruments through which art and society are built into structures both just and beautiful, is only one legacy of the long critique of religious violence in America by African Americans. In sum, this critique points to a way forward with less emphasis on order and control, more improvisation, and, above all, less sacrifice, in an "interplay of individuality and unity," as Cornel West termed it.[122] Alternatively, that way forward builds on the past of "protests and struggle, on the streets and in the courts, through a civil war and civil disobedience, and always at great risk—to narrow that gap between the promise of our ideals and the reality of [our] time."[123] Perhaps those words from Barack Obama— the son of a white woman from Kansas and a black man from Kenya, as if in ironic fulfillment of D. W. Griffith's nightmare—do point the way toward an American rebirth. If so, any such renewal must surely include more than a measure of justice for those who actually give birth to all humans, that is, women. In other words, any critique of religious violence in American history must also attend to the enduring and regulating hierarchies and dichotomies between constructions of gender that have often been rooted in religious discourses, practices, and communities. In the next chapter, we turn to that challenge and to the even broader efforts to control sexuality with religious violence in the American past (and present).

---

4 —

Sacrificing Gender

From "Republican Mothers"
to Defense of Marriage Acts

I long to hear that you have declared an independency—and
by the way in the new Code of Laws, which I suppose it will
be necessary for you to make, I desire you would Remember
the Ladies, and be more generous and favourable to them than
your ancestors. Do not put such unlimited power into the
hands of the Husbands. Remember all Men would be tyrants
if they could. If peculiar care and attention is not paid to the
Ladies we are determined to foment a Rebellion, and will not
hold ourselves bound by any Laws in which we have no voice,
or Representation.
                    —Abigail Adams to her husband, John, March 1776

In slavery, masters held people in bondage using religious reasoning
that worked in tandem with ruthless economic exploitation and brutal force.[1]
European "Christians" exercised this innocent domination with unique zeal
against Africans, but they also used it with other groups, particularly the
indigenous peoples of North America.[2] But perhaps the most remarkable
and consistent feature of religious tyranny in American history, as the epigraph from Abigail Adams might suggest, is its application to constructions
of gender and sex.[3] Until 1920, women were systematically excluded from
voting in U.S. federal elections. That this exclusion was grounded in religion
is still not widely recognized. But in the nineteenth century, when women
began to agitate in earnest for suffrage during what some scholars have called
the first wave of American feminism, activists such as Elizabeth Cady Stanton, author of *The Woman's Bible*, came to recognize that earning the vote
would depend on undermining some durable religious constructions.[4] In
American history, religious violence has often been focused on displacing
sexual desire and compressing or regulating sexual relations into normalized

forms, all with a patina of transcendent innocence or moral righteousness.[5] Women have been the most frequent victims.[6]

Over the course of American history, anxiety over gender differentiation has repeatedly produced violence, in which religion has served as a "hidden hand" to protect and produce patriarchal or hierarchical privilege.[7] If religions exist to eliminate things in the interest of concentrating cultural power, they have proved to be consistent, if slippery, cultural vehicles to eliminate the voices and agency of some people. They have done so through constructs of male and female gender roles, identities, or sexual practices operating as conventions. In these constructs, which carry the weight of transcendent authority (as either natural or God's law), some people are allowed to express their desires while others must be suppressed and contained.[8] This violence that sacrifices sex—to put it bluntly—has taken many forms. But as historian Nancy F. Cott has persuasively shown, the American nation-state has consistently sought to channel sexual desire into what has come to be called a monogamous heterosexual marriage, in which male dominance is exercised over female submission and heterosexual dominance is asserted over and against gays and lesbians.[9] Even more, what literary scholar Amy Kaplan cleverly dubbed "manifest domesticities" have had imperial consequences that framed public policies through the elimination or sacrifice of some private practices.[10]

These sacrifices of sex are *religious* constructs, which again is the crucial point. Sexuality is, of course, one of the main sources of human desire, and its regulation is a regular feature of most religious traditions. In American history, however, these religious efforts have blurred or even obliterated the lines between church and state, between private acts and public policies. In recent decades, various patriarchs (and their female consorts) in the United States have tended to target their concern about some forms of sexual expression or sexual desire on efforts to contain gay and lesbian sexual practices. These efforts to channel desire have been carried out through the so-called DOMA laws, or "Defense of Marriage Acts."[11] These acts are officially constructed in "secular" terms in a nod to the First Amendment's disestablishment of religion, but in fact the language of the acts reveals how fully they borrow from and build on explicitly religious efforts to fix a stable heterosexual norm for marriage and on the efforts to eliminate public expressions of female desire that Abigail Adams regarded as a "tyranny" and against which she threatened rebellion.[12]

A remarkable text from early America in which these patterns play out is the *Memoirs of Abigail Abbot Bailey*, first published in 1815. The journal of this New England woman was edited and released in 1988 in a scholarly edition with an excellent introduction by religion scholar Ann Taves, under the title *Religion and Domestic Violence in Early New England*.[13] Abigail Abbot was born in 1746 in what is now New Hampshire. She spent most of her life in small New England towns and died in 1815. Her posthumously published memoirs do not describe the typical events of her lifetime that have attracted historical attention, like the American Revolution or the founding of the Republic, although these events are implicit in the events of her life. Instead, Abigail Abbot talks about the complicated domestic developments that took place from 1767, when she married Asa Bailey, to 1793, when she divorced him. In between, Asa committed adultery with a servant girl and attempted to rape a second, for which he was indicted (but acquitted) by a grand jury. Finally, for nearly two years, Asa Bailey sexually assaulted his and Abigail's adolescent daughter, Phebe.

Throughout her narrative, Abigail Bailey explores how her deep religious faith was connected to these events. According to Ann Taves, Abigail secured her divorce from Asa when she changed from "dependence upon Asa to dependence on God."[14] Although this assertion is not inaccurate, it hides as much as it reveals. Abigail's trust in God was perhaps the one steady factor throughout her ordeal. What changed, as she put it, was her recognition that "trusting in God implies the due use of all proper means."[15] Her *Memoirs* thus describes less a change in the object of Abigail's dependence than a change in her use of the means in relation to that object. More precisely, she moved from devotion to a projection of transcendent authority in which God exercised "power-over" her and all others, which she conventionally associated with various forms of innocent male privilege, to a conviction that God's power was "power-with" the natural and social world, including her own language, social networks, communities, and the institutions of society.[16] This shift—taking God's power into her own female hands, so to speak—allowed Abigail to gain the cultural power that conventionally supported male privilege and power-over women and allowed her to marshal her resources to protect herself and her children from an abusive, vindictive, and scheming man. She learned to trust a projection of transcendent authority in which her own agency was included, rather than just to trust the conventional locus of cultural power in male ministers and her male husband, which had caused her such trauma.

Sorting out the complex relationship between Abigail and Asa Bailey is a historical case study with many layers of significance and many potential historical trajectories related to religion and violence. In trying to clarify some of them, I have found three different discourses operating throughout Abigail's narrative. The first is Asa's tale, a tale of patriarchal privilege lost. Asa lived with an assumption of gender privilege that was produced, if not guaranteed, by the social context of Revolutionary America and the early Republic. His adultery, attempted rape, and incest—egregious as they seem to us today— were probably not enough by themselves to end his relationship with Abigail. Indeed, as legal historian Hendrik Hartog pointed out in his history of marriage in America, in a chapter devoted to Abigail's *Memoirs*, she bore Asa children after she had discovered the incest.[17] Nonetheless, Asa was exiled from New England and from Abigail's affection as the conventions governing gender dynamics began to change—revolutionarily, some would say—across the new republic.[18]

Women had been at the forefront of the "Great Awakenings" of the early eighteenth century and continued to take their place as members of churches in numbers far beyond those of men throughout the century.[19] Abigail was just one example of these changes as an articulate and passionate convert to evangelical Christianity. For whatever reasons, Asa seemed unable to accommodate himself to these changes and reacted against them. He saw Abigail, and apparently other women as well, as threats that he needed to dominate and control.[20] Accordingly, Asa's tale represents an essentially conservative or reactionary discourse of religiously inscribed gender dominance. He sought to defend the privileges that men took for granted or wrote into common law, and he acted out in his private life a larger public or cultural backlash against "noisy" women that eventually came to dominate the period of the Revolution and early Republic.[21] As historian Catherine Brekus observed, "Americans had rebelled against the king, their metaphorical father, [but] still insisted that women must submit to male authority."[22] Historian Susan Juster put it even more sharply: "Women [like] blacks suffered a debilitating ideological loss in the decades following the Revolution, a period that both created new political and legal disabilities for them and reinforced existing ones."[23] Asa Bailey exploited this backlash, seeking to (re)establish male privilege in an age in which gender roles were changing. And despite his sexual misconduct and assault, he nearly succeeded in keeping Abigail beholden to him.

Asa's tale is an extreme example of ordinary cultural processes by which the male domination of women was rendered "innocent" in early America. In the second thread of discourse running throughout Abigail's tale, we can recognize, by contrast, a victim of violence gaining some liberation from it. Here the potential of religion to eliminate violence becomes manifest.

Undoubtedly, as Ann Taves first pointed out, in her *Memoirs* Abigail drew on literary tropes popular in captivity narratives written by other women of her time.[24] But Abigail's narrative had deeper roots than American soil; she described her tale in biblical terms. She was like the patriarch Joseph, who was sold into slavery by his brothers but eventually liberated and even made a prince, by God's providence. Although Abigail would reject a direct analogy, the contours of her narrative depicted her in ways akin to the suffering Christ, albeit in a maternal guise. Abigail was deprived of her intimate partner and separated from her most profound "earthly pleasure" and "sensible delight."[25] She sacrificed sex. She felt forsaken by God as she was forced to abandon her own children. Eventually, she was saved from her evil captor and restored to good moral status in her maternal role. If this was not a "resurrection," it surely reinforced the importance of the new birth, and more conventional births as well, in the context of evangelical America.

Abigail's story does reveal how religion can liberate. Her suffering and her salvation were no mere physical events; sometimes God uses ordinary means to accomplish divine purposes. God worked through Abigail's prayers, through her writing, through her maternal desires, through her family and friends, and through police, prisons, and the law, to bring some closure to or put some bounds around her suffering sacrifice. At some level, then, Abigail demonstrated how a biblical conception of salvation could relocate divine power away from patriarchal power-over her. Instead, God worked through Abigail and ordinary means as part of his providential and morally uplifting purposes. Abigail's religious faith shifted from one in which projections of transcendent authority, that is, a masculine God, afflicted her to one in which she used projections of transcendent authority—her prayers and other means of cultural power—to eliminate the violence she had endured.

But in Abigail's worldview, nothing happened by chance. Rather, everything demonstrated the power of God's providence or the importance of moral duty.[26] If Abigail's tale thus echoes how many women in her era and since have discovered power in religion and sought to use it, her tale also finally records not primarily a protofeminist tale of liberation, attractive as it might be to cast it in this light. Instead, hers is—and this is our third thread of discourse—a handmaid's tale of continuing submission conjoined with a limited freedom. Despite all the freedom Abigail Bailey and Abigail Adams fought for and enjoyed during the period of the early Republic, this freedom still depended on a providence that was intimately bound up with projections of transcendent masculine power. Moreover, this masculine power was increasingly articulated not through laws forged by consent, as Abigail Adams desired, but through rebellions and military might in which the nation could and would in all innocence continue to demand that women offer up their bodies and the bodies of their children as sacrificial vessels. These women became "Republican Mothers," in historian Linda Kerber's excellent phrase for the ideal.[27]

In *The Handmaid's Tale*, a 1990 film directed by the award-winning Volker Schlondorff and based on the 1985 novel by Margaret Atwood, this notion of "Republican Motherhood" is given a particularly dystopian display. Indeed, this film can help clarify this third plotline of religious violence at the root of Abigail Abbot Bailey's *Memoirs* and its long trajectory down to the Defense of Marriage Acts. In the film, women serve as "handmaids;" as sexual vessels. This sacrificial sex is supported by a totalitarian religious state whose laws, practices, and military might sustain rigid hierarchies of value in which some desires are allowed outlets and others are eliminated. Some sex is sanctioned; some sacrificed. Across America in the last decade of the twentieth and the first decade of the twenty-first century, in ways eerily similar to the film *The Handmaid's Tale*, a hybrid religious-political movement emerged to consolidate cultural power and to "defend" heterosexual marriage by eliminating public expressions of gay and lesbian desire, principally by outlawing homosexual marriages. That this "defense" is a form of *religious violence* needs to be reiterated. Just as surely as Asa Bailey abused Abigail Abbot and the handmaids sacrificed their sex to a totalitarian religious-political system, so too the DOMA laws hurt gays and lesbians by scapegoating them and consolidating cultural power by eliminating public recognition of their relationships.

The Memoirs of Abigail Abbot Bailey provides a fitting means to explore the ways in which gender and sex join age and race as durable social constructions around which religious violence has originated in American history.[28] In American history, innocent domination has frequently been exercised in self-righteousness regarding sex. The historical trajectory I trace here is only one of many possible plotlines. Still, we are fortunate to have Abigail Abbot's *Memoirs* as a voice in the silence to which women and sexual minorities have often been subjected.[29] But it would be an error, given the ongoing constraints that many women and sexual minorities face, to romanticize Abigail's voice. To do so would be to misread the difficulty and struggle through which her freedom, limited and fragile as it was, was gained. To depict her tale romantically would be to bless the brutalities she and so many before and since have endured, yet again.

Asa's Tale: Patriarchy Lost

The violence enacted by Asa Bailey during his marriage to Abigail Abbot constituted a pattern that today would mark him as a criminal if not a psychopath. In the context of his time, however, even his most egregious behaviors only resulted in a brief prison term.[30] Asa had his first sexual affair with a woman hired to help on the family's farm, in 1770, three years after his marriage to Abigail. The affair apparently was known only to Asa, Abigail, and the unnamed servant. There were no public consequences. In 1773, however, another hired woman who was living with the family charged Asa with rape. This time, Bailey was brought to court, where he was acquitted by a grand jury when the testimony came down to his word against hers. Although Asa's reputation suffered some damage from this incident, forcing a move to a nearby village, his economic and military career proceeded largely unchecked. He acquired more property and was made a major in the Twenty-fifth Regiment of the New Hampshire militia in 1785. In 1788, Abigail began to suspect Asa of incest with their daughter, Phebe, then sixteen, suspicions that were later confirmed. Although many people were aware of these charges of sexual violence against Asa, they were never formalized. Finally, for a four-month period in 1792, through a series of shrewd land deals and false promises, Asa effectively kidnapped Abigail and took her to the frontier in upstate New York, leaving behind their minor children in New England. When Asa returned to New England four months later to settle his estate and claim his children, he proclaimed that Abigail was "happy" in New York, and no one apparently doubted him.[31] But Abigail surprised Asa by returning to the region herself after an arduous journey that she describes in vivid prose filled with theological interpretation. Upon her arrival back in New England, Abigail contradicted Asa's tale of her "happiness" in New York. The boldness of her solo trek across country, combined with the previous scandals that had marred Asa's character, finally convinced her family and leading public men to jail Asa and to secure for Abigail a property settlement and divorce from him.

What might startle a contemporary reader about this litany of events is, first, that it went on for so long and, second, that Abigail endured it.[32] But in the context of early America, innocence and virtue were generally ascribed to men like Asa as a cultural sign of their achieved status, for no more daunting an accomplishment than being male. As table 6 suggests, in what is also a visual outline or flowchart for this section of the chapter, Asa could conventionally

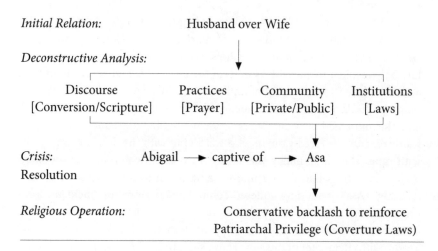

TABLE 6. *Asa's Tale*

Initial Relation: Husband over Wife

Deconstructive Analysis:

| Discourse [Conversion/Scripture] | Practices [Prayer] | Community [Private/Public] | Institutions [Laws] |

Crisis: Abigail ⟶ captive of ⟶ Asa

Resolution

Religious Operation: Conservative backlash to reinforce Patriarchal Privilege (Coverture Laws)

assume control over his wife, as well as over the four domains of religion identified by historian of religions Bruce Lincoln and also described in chapter 1.[33] Asa assumed that he could control how Abigail spoke and represented herself in public: her discourses, what practices she engaged in, which communities she joined, and how their property was held under legal institutions. So when a man like Asa contradicted the convention of patriarchal innocence in an act of blatant violence, even the victim found it astonishing. Abigail expressed it well herself in 1790, in a letter to Asa that she later included in her *Memoir*.[34] "Consider at what a dear rate," Abigail wrote to Asa,

> you have sinned. You have had great light and knowledge. You have enjoyed rich religious privileges. You once professed great love to God, and great attachment to the cause of Christ. You are the father of a great family. . . . Now, after all these things . . . that you should most barbarously conduct yourself as you have done, and seek to destroy your own family;— it is in every view most astonishing![35]

Abigail herself was astonished by Asa's behavior, not because she was particularly naïve, but because she accepted the convention of society by which a successful patriarch was also, by definition, a virtuous one.

To get to the root of Asa's tale, it is necessary to get rid of some contemporary assumptions about gender that vex understandings of early America. In early America, wives were legally considered part of a man's property, based on English common law (and religious convention), under laws collectively known as *coverture*. Sir William Blackstone was the most prominent codifier of coverture, and according to his *Commentary on the Laws of England* (1765), a wife was "covered" by her legal relationship to her husband; that is, her existence was subsumed under his.[36] To recognize that this legal arrangement prevailed throughout the American colonies and early Republic does not mean that there were no emotional attachments between husbands and wives or that gender dynamics were not matters of constant negotiation. Rather, this legal arrangement confirms that the ties of companionship between sexual partners that are conventionally assumed today were subordinated to economic and political interests in early America, in which wives were, by law, subordinated to husbands.[37] Divorce was both rare and difficult, although it became easier in some places and during some decades over the eighteenth century.[38]

For Abigail and Asa, the boundaries between public and private life were more permeable than they are today. Historian Catherine Brekus explains: "Colonists believed that the family was inextricably linked to the state: it was not a retreat from the pressures of the world, but a little commonwealth that served as a model for the hierarchical ordering of society as a whole."[39] Although the separation of church and state was cited as a principle in the First Amendment during Abigail's lifetime, it was not put into practice in many areas until well into the nineteenth century (if then). Furthermore, magical thinking about the relation of sexual virtue, "family values," and national well-being endured much longer.[40] Still, during the time that Abigail and Asa were married, the proper relations between law and economic life, religion and domesticity, and church and state were in flux as the Revolution unraveled British control of the colonies and a new nation took shape. In that process, some conservatives longed for a virtuous patriarch—George Washington is a good example—to hold together both public and private life.[41] Asa Bailey appears to have been just such a conservative individual. His wife's *Memoirs* offer abundant evidence that Asa felt responsible for controlling even the smallest details, leading him into behaviors that eventually ruined him and his family.

What ruined one man, however, could uplift another. In early America, moral strength or virtue included both restraint and the exercise of control and violence in warfare, over the land, and over enemies international, domestic, and spiritual.[42] Indeed, as the example of General (and slave-holder) Washington can attest, the Revolutionary era and the founding of the Republic also saw the rise of an assertive, calculating, dominant, and controlling American male archetype.[43]

In her groundbreaking *The Bonds of Womanhood: "Woman's Sphere" in New England, 1780–1835,* historian Nancy F. Cott was perhaps the first to argue that the chief feature of gender relations during the period of Abigail's and Asa's marriage was the emergence of different "spheres" for men and women, with men engaged in an emerging competitive market economy and women controlling the "domestic" sphere.[44] In fact, however, the relations between Asa and Abigail show how contested these matters could be.[45] Asa sought to extend a model of manly control across both public and private "spheres." His moral violations were sexual enactments that were conservative reactions to Abigail's own embrace of enlarged spheres of public activity, especially at church. That is, Asa asserted his patriarchal privilege over and against Abigail's passionate piety. According to historian Susan Juster, "Sex became an object of intense scrutiny [and increasing regulation] at the same time that the modern nation-state was arising out of the ashes of the traditional monarchy, and the two processes were intimately linked. Sexual desire was yoked to national patriotism through the fictive metaphor of marriage."[46] But the yokes between patriotism and patriarchal desire in marriage were hardly only metaphorical or fictive in early America. In the tale of Major Asa Bailey, we can recognize an early, but hardly the last, religious backlash against gender anxiety in American history.[47] Asa manifested in private a fear that many ministers and civil leaders articulated in public over the same period: women were stepping out of their place.[48]

The religious contours of this backlash become apparent across the four domains of religion: discourse, practices, community, and institution. Asa used words to mimic, and thereby attempt to undermine, Abigail's own access to spiritual power through discourse. Asa was, as Abigail put it, skilled at "confessions, entreaties, arguments and pleadings. . . . He truly had a talent at this kind of business."[49] Two episodes from the *Memoirs* reveal Asa's essentially conservative attempt to wrest the power of religious discourse from Abigail's control. The first was early in his marriage to Abigail, after she had discovered his infidelity. When Abigail confronted Asa about his repeated misconduct, Asa's initial response was anger. "He fell into a passion with me," Abigail put it. Fearing for her own life, Abigail prayed that her husband would not kill her. The next day, after Abigail refused to budge in her accusations, Asa confessed murderous impulses toward his wife (in what was also a veiled threat). But shortly thereafter, Asa turned to religion to protect himself:

> He said he had a most frightful view of himself. All his sins stared him in the face. . . . The threatenings and curses denounced against the wicked, in the whole Bible, seemed to thunder against him . . . with such power . . . that he cried to God for mercy. Upon which, the invitations and promises of the Gospel came wonderfully into his mind; and the way of salvation by Christ appeared plain and beautiful. He was now, he said, overcome with love. His soul was drawn out after Christ.[50]

For the next two days, the couple "conversed much upon religion," and Asa confessed to attempted infidelity with the hired servant, although "he gave [Abigail] to understand that he was unable to accomplish his wicked designs."[51]

Besides revealing religious discourse to be Abigail's strength, since she used it extract a confession from Asa, this episode also demonstrates that Asa assumed he could claim the power of religion for his own purposes. Absent any trial transcripts, we can only speculate that several months later, after being publicly accused of rape, Asa in all likelihood used a similar appeal to spiritual renewal in his trial before the grand jury. In any event, if such an appeal was as effective with the jury as it was with Abigail, it is no wonder that he remained free. Abigail surely questioned whether her husband had truly experienced "grace." Nevertheless, his "confession and entreaties" led her to forgive him, and her private support undoubtedly helped him overcome whatever public shame had been associated with the case. In time, he became "one of the leading men in the town," Abigail recalled, the owner of a farm with more than two hundred acres of land and a commissioned officer in the New Hampshire militia. Pushed into religion by his wife's insistent accusation and then by the scandal of a trial, Asa used the discourse of conversion to reestablish himself first with his wife and then with the community.[52]

A second incident in which Asa claimed the power of religious discourse for himself came later in their marriage, with a similar outcome. Here, Asa attempted to use scripture to demonstrate his innocence while he was in fact conspiring to kidnap Abigail. After discovering Asa's repeated incest with their daughter, Abigail eventually banned Asa from the family farm, only to have him return on several occasions to try to plead his case with Abigail, accompanied by various promises of a property settlement. It was during one of these visits that Asa claimed to have arranged to sell the family farm to a man in New York, on the condition that Abigail accompany him to sign the papers. Abigail understandably had her doubts. So Asa took out his Bible, opened it to a particular passage, and then read it aloud to Abigail as a purported testimony to his veracity. This passage, which in all likelihood was randomly selected, happened to be Isaiah 33, which read (as Abigail quoted the King James version): "'Woe to thee, that spoilest, and thou wast not spoiled; and dealest treacherously, and they dealt not treacherously with thee!' What thou shalt cease to spoil, thou shalt be spoiled."

Abigail's commentary on the incident, which again reveals her own facility as an interpreter of religious discourse, continues:

> After he had paused, I remarked to him, that I wished I could always see the path of my duty in every case, as plainly as I could see his in some things, and as I could see him marked out in the passage just read! I asked him to take particular notice of the first verse,—the woe against the spoiler, and treacherous dealer, who had commenced this cruelty and wickedness, without any just cause; none had treated him in this manner. I tenderly reminded Mr. B. that he did begin to spoil and to ruin our family, when they were at peace with him, and none were molesting him. And I added, that if he should still continue to afflict or deal treacherously with them, he might expect . . . that God, in his providence, would prepare some spoiler for him.[53]

This spoiler would be Abigail herself. At the time, however, Abigail went with Asa to New York. In this incident, it is less that Asa's rhetoric was effective; in fact, it failed miserably and with more than a touch of ironic humor. But the utterly insincere, even ridiculous, "oath" shows that he regarded religion as a "hidden hand" that could justify his duplicitous domination of his wife. Asa's desperate, reactionary appeal to religious discourse invoked nothing more substantive than his patriarchal privilege and (contrary to what one might expect, given the evidence) produced the effects he intended.

Throughout their life together, Asa displayed considerable anxiety over Abigail's religious practice, the second domain of religion in Lincoln's configuration, and this anxiety escalated as their marriage began to unravel. Prayer, for instance, was a regular feature of Abigail's daily routine: she generally prayed after awakening each morning. One day, while Asa was living with the family after returning from exile, he asked Abigail about the substance of her prayers. "Mr. B. asked me, how I prayed? Whether I felt a forgiving temper? For if I did not, God would not hear my prayers. He wished also to know whether I prayed against him?"[54] On the one hand, these questions reveal Asa's assumption that it was his right to control Abigail's prayers, for he presumed to instruct her on how God would respond. But on the other hand, they reveal his anxieties about her praying. Abigail wrote: "It was very evident that the greatest fear he had of me was from my prayers, seeking and obtaining help from God. He had discovered evident fear of this."[55] Hendrik Hartog reinforces the conclusion: "[Asa] was clearly frightened of her religious authority."[56]

Consistently, as in the case above, Asa's moral violations were *fueled* by Abigail's religious facility. As she grew more pious, he grew more base— while professing piety when convenient. The crucial case is his violation of Phebe. The violence followed a long period of intense religious activity on Abigail's part. She writes, about the year 1788, when the incest began: "This year God granted me some special blessings in the things of religion. I had opportunity to hear preaching more often than before. . . . My faith was now strengthened, and my joy in God abounded." Within the year, two separate ministerial visits were made to the Bailey home, one of which involved the baptism of several of Asa and Abigail's children. It was after one of these ministerial visits that Abigail undertook to instruct her children and husband. "I endeavored," she put it, "to impress these things on the minds of my husband, and children, with an ardent desire that they might feel their need of the Saviour, secure his salvation, and be prepared for all the will of God concerning them."[57]

All his wife's "ardent desire" had a perverse effect on Asa. By December, Abigail reported that he was acting "strangely," including long periods of silence—as if in a trance—although "he did not appear like one senseless. . . . His eyes would sparkle with the keen emotions of his mind."[58] Eventually, after several days and nights, Asa revealed what he had been pondering: he planned to move the family to "Ohio territory," thereby controlling his wife by displacing her into a new community: Lincoln's third domain of religion. Abigail immediately objected, especially expressing concern about finding a suitable church community in Ohio. But Asa again assumed the mantle of the patriarch and dictated to his wife and children the future contours of their spiritual, as well as physical, lives: "He said he had considered all those things; that he well knew what kind of minister, and what people would suit me; and he would make it his care to settle where those things would be agreeable to me." Eventually, Abigail and the children "consented, at last, to follow our head and guide, wherever he should think best; for our family had ever been in the habit of obedience: and perhaps never were more pains taken to please the head of a family, than had ever been taken in our domestic circle."[59]

Having secured a promise of obedience from his family, including control over his wife's religious life, the incest began. Abigail describes in painful detail how the violence proceeded first through flattery—"idle stories, foolish riddles, and singing songs"—and then through force:

> Sometimes he corrected her with a rod; and sometimes with a beach stick, large enough for the driving of a team; and with such sternness and anger sparkling in his eyes, that his visage seemed to resemble an infernal; declaring, that if she attempted to run from him again, she should never want but one correction more; for he would whip her to death.[60]

Abigail only gradually became aware that these brutal and vicious "corrections" were accompanied by sexual assaults on Phebe, which apparently occurred over the course of two years. Abigail was pregnant through much of the period and felt helpless to stop the violence, not only because of her physical condition, but also because she "knew not that I could make legal proof." Abigail "could not prevail upon [Phebe] to make known to me her troubles, or to testify against the author of them." In early America, a patriarch like Asa could dominate the bodies of his wife and children, innocently counting on their silence, even when there was nothing innocent about the relationship.

Phebe moved out of Asa's household immediately after turning eighteen in the spring of 1790. It was not until September 1790, however, that Abigail finally expelled Asa from the family farm and began to seek a property settlement from him. Asa returned to the farm in the spring of 1792 and communicated to Abigail the ruse of the New York sale. After getting Abigail's consent to accompany him and after traveling (by sleigh) for several days (thereby removing Abigail from her family and friends), he revealed to her that the "sale" was a fraud. In revealing his scheme, Asa appealed directly to the laws of patriarchal privilege in terms that he explicitly juxtaposed to Abigail's piety. The result, Abigail reports, was that Asa felt "strong in himself." Asa Bailey was counting on a backlash against female piety, exerted on the body of his wife and those of his servants and daughter through the laws of New York State, to (re)inforce his masculine privilege. That is, Asa counted on institutional support—Lincoln's fourth domain of religion—for his innocent domination.

It was on March 19, 1792, that the crucial conversation occurred. Asa and Abigail had just crossed into New York when Asa "threw off the mask at once," as Abigail put it. "He told me, we are now in the State of New York, and now you must be governed by the laws of this State, which are far more suitable to govern women such as you, than are the laws of New Hampshire." Significantly, Asa then qualified what he meant by "women such as Abigail." He accused her of being too "noisy." "If I would drop all that was past," he said, "and concerning which I had made so much noise, and would promise never to make any more rout about any of those things; and to be a kind and obedient wife to him, without any more ado; it was well!" It was apparently Abigail's very speaking—her voice, whether in prayer or practice—that had offended Asa.[61] Once the plot was revealed, Asa "exulted in the thought of his being 'long headed,'" Abigail recalled, "and of his having so completely outwitted me; I saw that he felt very strong in himself. He seemed to imagine that he had done all those feats by his own mighty wisdom:—That he now had me in his power, and could in all things do according to his own will." Asa then juxtaposed Abigail's piety to his own power. He "asked me, what I now thought of my former hope and confidence in God? He seemed thus to say with Joseph's brethren, 'And we will see what will become of his dreams?' and with the impious, of whom we read, 'Where is their God?'"[62] Here Abigail directly linked her plight to that of the patriarch Joseph, who had been betrayed by his brothers out of jealousy.

Was Asa Bailey jealous of his wife's piety? That question is impossible to answer, but it does seem clear that he felt compelled to control the ambivalence between his privilege, under the law, and Abigail's claim to speak with divine privilege.[63] Asa Bailey thus manifested, in brutally violent private acts, patterns of "innocent domination" similar to those by which the Revolution succeeded and the Republic was established. He was a patriarch in the civil religion, or as Susan Juster calls it, the "triumphal path of American democracy" had its shadow side. The nation was created through military victories over Great Britain, as well as a "massive cultural assault on female and black sexuality" that developed to control the women (and blacks) whose voices had proved so "noisy" in the wake of the Protestant revivals just two decades earlier.[64] Major Asa Bailey thus no doubt saw himself, and was by and large seen by his peers, as a good, even conservative and righteous, citizen. He wanted a woman's deference to demonstrate his own power in the new Republic. But what he failed to understand was that in this new nation, such deference was compatible with both motherhood and "noisy" piety. Susan Juster again puts it well, in what concludes this brief effort to reconstruct Asa Bailey's tale from the words of his wife: "The patriarchal authority republican men strove for in their domestic relations was always in danger of being undercut by the passionate feelings such relations engendered."[65] Asa did not share Abigail's piety, but he surely experienced her "ardent desire." It evidently drove him wild.[66]

Abigail's Tale: Providential Power

In the conventional understanding of gender relations during colonial America, it was women, not men, who were driven wild by lust.[67] The stories of Anne Hutchinson, the Salem witches, and various and sundry adventuresses form a template against which Abigail Abbot's carefully constructed (and probably censored) *Memoirs* must be read. Two features mark Abigail's rhetoric. First, Abigail represented herself as a devoted, dutiful, and sacrificial mother who was sorely aggrieved when she was unable to fulfill her role. Like the suffering Christ, she felt forsaken by God and unable to put into practice the love that was her duty and joy. Behind this rhetoric of duty, however, lies another, the rhetoric of desire. Throughout her narrative, Abigail reveals subtle clues to the pleasure, even ecstasy, she took in various practices, of which her relations with Asa were included as her "greatest earthly joy." During her narrative, however, the range of activities from which Abigail derived pleasure and over which she demonstrated mastery, gradually grew. Through the record she left of her "afflictions" by Asa and how she overcame them, we can see how female control over household and traditional religion, the chief domains in which women exercised power during the "separate spheres ideology" that dominated the nineteenth century, was not easily achieved but a matter of fierce domestic and public struggle (see table 7).

In contrast to Asa's conservative assumption of male privilege, Abigail apparently entered marriage with the desire of finding a true companion and partner. She described her family of origin as one in which she was "ever treated with the greatest kindness by my tender parents."[68] Consequently, she hoped "to find in my husband a true hearted and constant friend." This hope was compatible, however, with accepting subordination. "My desires and hopes were," Abigail began,

> that we might live together in peace and friendship; seeking each other's true happiness. . . . I did earnestly look to God for his blessing upon this solemn undertaking [i.e., marriage]. . . . As, while I lived with my parents, I esteemed it my happiness to be in subjection to them; so now I thought it must be a still greater benefit to be under the aid of a judicious companion, who would rule well his own house.[69]

TABLE 7. *Abigail's Tale*

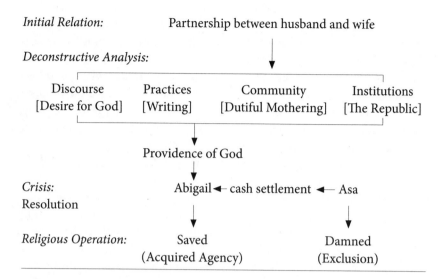

Initial Relation:	Partnership between husband and wife		
Deconstructive Analysis:			
Discourse [Desire for God]	Practices [Writing]	Community [Dutiful Mothering]	Institutions [The Republic]

Providence of God

Crisis: Resolution	Abigail ◄— cash settlement ◄— Asa	
Religious Operation:	Saved (Acquired Agency)	Damned (Exclusion)

In this passage Abigail's desire (and expectations) for Asa, her willing subordination to a "judicious companion," and her "earnest" attraction to God all come together.[70]

According to Abigail's discourse, she learned very early in her marriage that her desire for a companion would be frustrated with Asa. "Before one month, from my marriage day, had passed, I learned that I must expect hard and cruel treatment in my new habitation." Nevertheless, "my complaint was not to man." Instead, "I had learned to go, with my trials, to a better Helper than an arm of flesh." "Help" from God enabled her to comply with the subordination Asa expected.

> I think God gave me a heart to resolve never to be obstinate, or disobedient to my husband, but to be always kind, obedient, and obliging in all things not contrary to the word of God. I thought if Mr. B. were sometimes unreasonable, I would be reasonable, and would rather suffer wrong than do wrong.[71]

As Abigail continued to experience repeated "afflictions" at Asa's hand, she increasingly took refuge in the practices of her piety and in her writing, and otherwise retreated into silence.

After Asa's first affair, Abigail recalled that "my only refuge was in God my Saviour. . . . I thought it most prudent not to make my troubles known to the world."[72] When Asa was accused of attempted rape, Abigail felt that "I could do nothing but carry my cause to God."[73] And even during Asa's incest with Phebe, Abigail experienced a silencing that prevented her from making public in any way his behavior. "I did not dare to hint any thing of my fears to him, or to any creature," she wrote in one passage.[74] Filled with a "flood of sorrow," "I seemed unable to open my difficulties to any one: I must bear them all alone."[75] Finally, as Asa delayed and schemed to take the property from her, her friends counseled her that "they considered Mr. B a cunning, crafty man." But Abigail concluded that "there is a time to speak; and a time to keep silence; and that, at the present time, the latter was my duty."[76] For much of her marriage, Abigail had internalized Asa's expectations and the cultural conventions of silence. She had sacrificed her voice.

Along with submission to Asa, Abigail repeatedly stated that she subordinated her own interests to those of her children, thereby demonstrating her status as a good, sacrificial republican mother in the holy community of the family. Aside from bearing seventeen children in twenty-six years, Abigail also demonstrated her motherly duty through her prose and expressed frustration and grief when her duty could not be fulfilled. After expelling Asa from the home, she told her children that "they must no longer expect to derive the least advantage from being known as the children of Major Bailey." This indicates in one sentence how male privilege carried benefits to both wife and children and that the loss of that privilege also imposed a burden on her and them.[77] When Asa tricked her into going to New York with him, she lamented the loss of her children: "The thoughts of leaving my family of small children . . . was very grievous to me. They were eight in all" who still lived at home, ranging in age from fifteen to an infant under a year old. Upon discovering Asa's ruse, she voiced two

> things on my mind, which were far more dreadful to me than bodily tortures, or even death. 1. The miseries of my dear children. 2. The infinite dishonor my leaving them, and going off with Mr. B. would do to religion, in the view of those, who knew not the circumstances, which had led me away. . . . Oh my children, my dear, unhappy, forsaken children![78]

Abigail feared that people would presume that she had gone with Asa out of her own desire and had willingly abandoned her children. "Oh, what a monster of a mother must I appear to them!"[79] She had not, as she put it, "been very explicit" with even her closest friends and family about her design never to live with Asa again. She thus presumed (accurately, as it turns out) that many would conclude that she had left with Asa out of a desire to do so.[80]

Along with submission to Asa and to her children, however, it was submission to God—even to accepting violence—that was the near constant form of subordination that Abigail describes in the first two-thirds of her narrative. Ann Taves says it well: Abigail had internalized a "paradigm . . . of loving (and being comforted by) an authority figure who afflicts. This understanding of love was neither idiosyncratic nor culturally problematic; indeed, it lay at the core of the Calvinist understanding of how people ought to understand God."[81] According to this understanding, domination was rendered innocent, or brutalities could be blessed, through a projection of transcendent authority. Abigail was the frequent victim of this pious system of power, like the innocent Christ whose own "Father" afflicted him. For instance, as Asa began to violate Phebe, Abigail described how "In piercing trials, I felt myself . . . in the hands of Him, who is my covenant God in Christ; and hence could say, 'It is the Lord, let him do what seemeth to him good.'"[82] When Asa "turned harsh" toward Abigail, she described how "I felt myself, to be placed, by the providence of a holy God, in an iron furnace of affliction."[83] All kinds of incidents of violence could be interpreted as the will of a transcendent authority. When one of her daughters was struck in the face and badly injured by a horse's hoof, Abigail assumed: "The Lord has done it. . . . I thought the more I was chastened, the more I longed to live near to God, and could truly say, with Job, 'Though he slay me, yet will I trust in him.'"[84] Here the crucified Christ, as much as Job, is again Abigail's template to understand her experience. Finally, even Asa's deceit could fall under the sovereignty of God and its demand to submit: "I saw that I must submit to the providence of God. . . . God was laying [a] burden upon me; and I must submit."[85] As Hendrik Hartog concludes, "Human law was always secondary to God and his 'wonderful' plan' [for Abigail]. Legal power was ultimately ineffectual against the power of prayer and submission to God's will."[86]

This mentality of sacrifice and submission—Abigail as a suffering servant—constitutes the chief theme of the first two-thirds of the *Memoirs*, with the remainder tracing Abigail's gradual shift to an understanding of God's providence that worked through ordinary means, including her own desires, discourses, practices, communities, and the law. The first clue to this shift comes, ironically, when Asa gives her control over the household economy. This happened sometime between 1778 and 1788, years that she describes in the following terms:

I had been living in much peace with my companion . . . [although] he daily showed himself to be destitute of saving grace. But he had a good knowledge of the sacred scriptures; and I took great satisfaction in conversing with him upon them. I felt the tenderest affection for him as my head and husband. I ever rejoiced when he returned from abroad. Nor did I see him come in from his daily business, without sensible delight. Much pleasure I took in waiting upon him, and in doing all in my power to make him happy. And I pleased myself that I was now favored with a happy return of his kind affection. He appeared to place in me the most entire confidence; delivering into my hands his money, keys, notes, deeds, papers of every description, and all such kinds of concerns. Most sincere delight I took in taking the best care of them.[87]

Asa's trust taught Abigail skills that would prove useful to her and provided her with experiences of pleasure beyond submission.[88]

These pleasures expanded in 1790 to include her religious practices. Phebe had moved out of the household, but Abigail had still not been able to persuade her to testify against her father or even to admit that she had been raped. Abigail intentionally sought strength from religion. She asked God to "give me peculiar grace; that he would teach me what I ought to do."[89] She fasted, prayed, and studied scripture for seven consecutive Wednesdays, out of which she began

to be able to derive instruction from every thing, which I saw, heard, or met with. God was in every thing. Every thing led my mind to him. I was filled with a kind of pleasing astonishment at his infinite condescension in taking such notice of a most unworthy worm.[90]

Then one Sunday, she was able to attend services, at which she was able to relate to a minister, "without letting him know my particular trials," some of the difficulties she had been enduring. The minister "remarked upon the trials of Joseph . . . and he was led to give me a most lively view of casting my burdens on the Lord, and waiting patiently for him."

The minister thus confirmed the conventional approach Abigail had been taking to her difficulties while also identifying her struggles with those of a patriarch. When he preached three sermons that day, Abigail's response was ecstatic:

This was a joyful day to me. God did truly meet me, in the assembly of his saints. . . . I was so swallowed up in God, that I seemed to lose a view of all his creatures. I do not know that I had a thought of myself. I seemed hid from a sight of the world in an ocean of bliss.[91]

On one level, these mystical experiences confirmed Abigail's patient submission to Asa. She was still a "lowly worm," "swallowed up in God."[92] But on another level, these experiences in community encouraged her to seek remedies for her earthly plight.[93] "One result of all my examinations and prayers was," she concludes, "a settled conviction, that I ought to seek a separation from my wicked husband." It was being in the company of the saints, hearing the contours of sin confirmed and having her own righteousness reinforced, that enabled her to marshal power to her own cause. "I longed for the overthrow of Satan's kingdom," which in this case could only be Asa's violent rule, so "that the kingdom of Christ," here identified with her own agency and duties as a mother, "may be [built] up in glory." "Sin, and the conduct of the enemies of God, appeared to me inexpressibly hateful . . . [while] I was struck with wonder at the union between Christ and believers. This union, I felt a humble confidence that I did enjoy."[94] Thus mystically united with Christ, Abigail's pleasure was now located in her own choices. *She* was identified with transcendent authority, marshaled with all believers against the enemies of God who were damned sinners in league with Satan. By constructing this dualism, Abigail inverted the religious violence she was experiencing and identified herself not as a victim but as a source of cultural power.

Shortly thereafter, Abigail went to Phebe, now living with one of Abigail's brothers, from whom she learned that "none of my dreadful apprehensions concerning Mr. B's conduct had been too high."[95] She then confronted Asa and told him that "I would never live with him any more." But she gave him a way out. "If he would do what was right, relative to our property, and would go to some distant place, where we should be afflicted with him no more, it might be sufficient; and I might be spared the dreadful scene of prosecuting my husband."[96] Thus began the nearly two years of comings and goings that led to the birth of one last child, "Patience," in May 1791 and the virtual kidnapping of Abigail to New York.[97]

Abigail's resolve grew as she discovered her power through various means. After expelling Asa from the household for the first time, she tried to keep quiet, but "the birds of the air seemed to carry the news. . . . I found a melancholy relief in conversing with others upon the subject, which had so long been confined in my sorrowful breast."[98] Her writing similarly became a source of solace. When she struggled to secure a property settlement from Asa, "I resorted to my consoling pen" and there discovered a conviction that "all things shall work together for good to them that love God" (Romans 8:28).[99] But it was especially when Abigail discovered Asa's final betrayal, on the road to New York, that she realized "that I had greatly erred, in not having opened my mind more fully" to her family and friends.[100] She struggled with her faith. When Asa challenged her to answer to God, when her plight was like Joseph's, she wavered, and wondered "if I were not the worst hypocrite in the world."[101] But then her conviction settled, first on the fact that

> he had not yet deprived me of an honest and firm heart. I was yet, as much as ever, disposed to avoid wrong, and do right. And hence I could not, and would not, ever submit to his proposals, to bury past matters, and live with him as his wife.[102]

In the language of evangelical Protestantism, a clearer discourse of embodied cultural power—an "honest and firm heart"—cannot be found.[103] Then, having discovered her own sources of power, she resolved her questions of faith: "I was soon enabled to say, and feel, that I had as much confidence in the goodness and faithfulness of God, as I ever had."[104] Here, her voice, appropriate for her piety, was passive. But her sense of self, her "honest and firm heart," now became a locus for action that led to her freedom. She resolved to "take care of myself."[105]

It took four months. Asa eventually took Abigail to a homestead near the present Utica, New York, where a smallpox epidemic was raging. Abigail was inoculated against the disease, but as was frequently the case, the inoculation produced a grave illness of its own. It took her weeks to recover. During this time, she managed to trick Asa into revealing the names of each town through which they had passed on their route west. This provided her with a mental map for her journey back to her children and extended family. Her opportunity came on May 9, 1792, when Asa left New York (on foot) for New England. On May 24, still somewhat ill, she set out on her own on horseback. After riding for a few miles with her oldest son, whom Asa had taken to New York with him, she then rode for several more miles through woods until an hour before dark, when "for the first time in my life, I called for entertainment at a tavern."[106] The next morning, as she prepared to depart, the tavern owner:

presented me with refreshing things, of his own kindness . . . wished me prosperity, and directed me on my way. The weather continued fine. These things gave courage to my drooping heart; they strengthened my faith in God. I rode on through the woods alone. And yet I could say, I am not alone; but my Father is with me. His comforts delighted my soul. I saw him in every tree, and every shaking leaf. The little birds seemed to sing his praise.[107]

This theological foundation—seeing God in and through the ordinary— became the pattern that sustained Abigail throughout her two-week journey across the woods of upstate New York and across the Green Mountains.

The God who had appeared to afflict Abigail now turned benevolent toward her as she claimed her own ability to negotiate the journey. "I rejoiced that I had set out on this journey. I believed God had called me to it; and would carry me safely through; and I found it easy, as well as comfortable, to cast my burden upon him." Simple events and coincidences Abigail imagined as God's providence. A breeze blows up on a hot spring day.[108] She stops at a random house on her journey, and the family hosts her warmly.[109] Her horse's back gives out, and she trades it for a healthy one.[110] "Thus I lived on a series of mercies. . . . God smiled upon me. His providence smiled. And all his works and creatures seemed to smile."[111] Upon returning to New England, she discovers that Asa had been unable to sell the farm, so she is reunited with her children. And by enlisting the support of her brothers, other public leaders, and the justice of the peace, she secures a property settlement from Asa, after having to imprison him briefly. Even in prison, though, Asa refuses to give up his patriarchal control. Through an intermediary, "Captain White," he tries to send the children away to New York, loading them all, even the infant Patience, in a wagon and heading west. But they are caught by Abigail's brother, who persuades Captain White to turn back.

Abigail learned two lessons from these final experiences with Asa's scheming attempts to assert patriarchal power. First, "I then and ever understood that trusting in God implies the due use of all proper means."[112] Transcendent authority works through ordinary vehicles. Second, she learned that "a merciful God restored my dear children again. My soul praised and adored him for his goodness."[113] That it was, in fact, her brother and the justice of the peace who restored her children to her did not in the least matter. To identify God with the laws of the land and the institutional agents who enforced it became conventional as republican mothers, filled with virtue and piety, spread throughout the land. Ironically, from this identification of women with motherhood, virtue, and piety also came a new breed of patriarchs who would work with republican mothers to build a new nation. They would put up with some "noisy" piety in exchange for a tranquil and well-ordered household.[114]

Tempting as it is to see Abigail's story as a simple liberation from her oppressor, the story is actually more complex. Even after Abigail decided to separate from Asa, she had to endure no less than six extended negotiating sessions with him over two years, according to Hartog's accounting.[115] Abigail also endured at least one pregnancy during this period. She was kidnapped. She feared for the loss of all her children (and Asa did take the three oldest boys with him back to New York). Finally, Abigail gave up whatever status she had once enjoyed as the wife of Major Asa Bailey. As Hartog explained, "Even after all that had happened in the family, even after what Asa had done to his daughter, nothing would change the legal fact of his patriarchal authority. . . . [Abigail's] capacity to resist and to reconstruct her life depended on her submission to a patriarchal order."[116] It would take many more negotiations, over decades, by thousands of women, before the limited liberation that Abigail managed to acquire—with the help of providence—would begin to be written into law. It would be even longer before the blessed brutalities of sacrificing sex that Abigail endured, as embedded in discourses and practices and extending across the "family values" of the American civil religion, would come close to ending.

The Hidden Hand in Handmaids' Tales

In *The Wealth of Nations*, published in 1776 just as Abigail Abbot Bailey was enduring her difficulties, Adam Smith argued that free markets regulated themselves through competitive laws of supply and demand that he termed a "hidden" or "invisible" hand. This "hidden hand" operated to turn self-interest into social benefits because no one wanted rampant scarcity or unbridled rapacity. For a long time, this "hidden hand" was understood almost mechanistically, as if supply and demand were a law of nature. More recently, however, a number of commentators have noted that there might be a hidden hand behind the hidden hand, that Smith presumed something like a "theology."[117] Intriguingly, just as Abigail Bailey found a limited freedom by seeing God's hand invisibly at work in and through the natural world, so have constructions of gender norms and sexual relations been guided by various forms of religious logic that appear to mirror the hidden hand behind the hidden hand of markets. The hidden hand of religion, which in America has meant especially the practice of sacrifice, has produced both relative gender freedom and hypersensitive (at best) and hypocritical (at worst) efforts at controlling human sexual behavior, under the emerging sway of supposedly "free" markets.

The history here is, again, long and complex. The trajectory we intend to trace can be at least partially clarified by examining a novel-made-into a film, *The Handmaid's Tale*. The film, released in 1990 and based on the 1985 award-winning novel by Margaret Atwood, is a thinly veiled critique of the U.S. civil or cultural religion and the efforts of its devotees to regulate sexual desire and behavior. It depicts a dystopia in which fundamentalist Christianity has come to dominate politics. The film outlines the contours of a hidden hand behind the ordinary way of imagining Adam Smith's economic assumptions, which can help us see the continuity from Asa Bailey's backlash against his wife's passionate piety to a more recent backlash against other kinds of passion. More specifically, the film *The Handmaid's Tale* can help us see that when she called on providential discourse to prop up her own power, Abigail Abbot Bailey was not only, and not primarily, a good Christian.[118] Instead, she proved to be a better capitalist and republican mother, a true believer in the American empire of sacrifice.[119] Her story, like so many others from then until now, was indeed a handmaid's tale. Her agency was sacrificed first to her husband and then to the state and the markets, those male-dominated institutions that shaped, albeit indirectly, what it meant to see the coming of the Lord. That the same violent logic has recently been applied to gays and lesbians through the DOMA laws (and, in many and ongoing ways, against women) is the continuity from then to now that defines one strand of religious violence in American history.

The film of *The Handmaid's Tale*, directed by the Academy Award and Palm d' Or winner Volker Schlondorff from a screenplay by Harold Pinter, begins with the protagonist, whose name we learn later is Kate, accompanied by an unidentified man and a young girl, driving through a barren, snow-covered landscape in a jeep. The wintry scene is a not-too-subtle metaphor for the frigid status of sex in what we will soon learn is an imperial regime masquerading as a republic. Eventually, the two adults get out of the jeep and switch positions, passenger to driver and vice versa, suggesting a gender equality that sets up a contrast to the rigid roles soon to be enforced. A quick cut shows the three getting out of the jeep and walking through a snow-covered woods. The girl protests, "Mommy, I'm tired." Spotlights appear in the distance, and a loud male voice rings out as sirens blare: "You are approaching the border of the Republic of Gilead. Turn back." Soldiers appear on black all-terrain vehicles, the spotlights flash, sirens wail, and as the man begins to run, a machine gun is fired and he falls. Kate then runs, but the soldiers quickly surround her and capture her, leaving her daughter behind.[120] Like Abigail Abbot Bailey, Kate is separated from her desire and duty as a partner and mother, and she will learn, repeatedly, about sacrificing sex. Kate's sexual sacrifices, however, will not be made to "providence." They will be made to the state.

The film continues with another abrupt cut as the camera then looks down on a black military transport vehicle at night. The truck crosses railroad tracks and enters a barbed-wire enclosure that simultaneously evokes an industrial wasteland, a prison, and a concentration camp. The title of the film, *The Handmaid's Tale*, then appears on the screen. Kate is shown leaving the truck and being herded with dozens of other women through chainlink corridors in what appears to be a warehouse. Kate joins a single line of women, passing a table where a stern woman, dressed in gray, calls out a series of numbers, followed by the words *positive* or *negative*. Panic sets in among some of the women, who are quickly surrounded by military officers and herded into another set of trucks. On one of them a soldier crosses out an old label, *Livestock*, and writes *116 women* in its place. As the trucks pull away, the camera pans along the sides of the trucks as they pass. Women's arms reach through the slats. The image clearly evokes the transport of human cargo from another society dedicated to the sacrifice of scapegoats, that of the director's native Germany during the Shoah.[121]

Kate is not on one of these trucks. Instead, she is shown sitting outside the warehouse with a small group of women. It is now daytime. A woman in a brown dress appears and begins to speak to the group as a freight train (clearly marked with U.S. corporate logos) passes slowly in the background. "I'm Aunt Lydia," the woman intones. "You're healthy. You're free of infections. And you're the only ones whose tests are positive. You're the lucky ones. Amen." The women reply: "Amen." Aunt Lydia continues: "You are going to be handmaids. You are going to serve God. And your country." These two projections of transcendent authority are conveniently conflated. Serving God is equivalent to serving one's country. The women are then loaded onto a black bus, where Kate befriends a woman whose name we learn later is Moira. Moira asks Kate: "How'd they get you?" Kate replies: "We tried to cross the border." Moira admits they got her for "gender treachery." "I like girls," she says. "Jesus," Kate replies. "They could have sent you to the colonies for that." Moira cynically comments: "They don't send you to the

TABLE 8. *The Logic of Handmaids' Tales*

Initial Relation: Man-Woman as Procreative Partners

Crisis: Romantic Love/Ideal of Maternal Affection or Duty

Sacrifice of Sex to State Control/Providence

Deconstructive Analysis:

Discourses	Practices	Community	Institutions
Uniforms	"The Ceremony"	Patriarchy	State/Military

Religious Operation:
The Regulation of Gender Norms/Sexuality
(e.g., The "Innocent Domination" of Female Virtue or DOMA Laws)

---

colonies if your ovaries are still jumping." We have traced this opening scene in the film at length because it establishes the key conjunctions at the core of the Republic of Gilead—echoing those in Abigail Abbot Bailey's *Memoirs* and anticipating those in the DOMA laws—of religion, the state, and sexual or gender regulation.[122]

Table 8 summarizes the logic linking the film with the *Memoirs* and historical structures. The film's first scene shows men and women as procreative and companionate partners. But because of environmental degradation, 99 percent of women living in the Republic of Gilead are sterile. Children are scarce, which throws into crisis both the romantic love that binds partners and the idea of maternal affection or duty that binds mothers to children. Kate's crisis in the "fictional" Republic of Gilead, in short, is similar to the crisis that Abigail Abbot and Abigail Adams faced in the early Republic of the United States: she has to negotiate a backlash against passionate piety in which piety is used to limit or control what it means to a mother, a woman, a spouse. By vividly depicting discrete discourses and practices and an idealized community that is ruthlessly enforced by strict institutional controls, *The Handmaid's Tale* reveals through fiction decidedly real patterns in which the sacrifice of sex has been religiously produced in America, from the abuse of Major Asa Bailey in the early Republic to the backlash against women's rights and gay and lesbian rights in the recent past.

In the fictional Republic of Gilead, sexual norms and behavior are carefully, even ritualistically, regulated in ways that exaggerate actual trends in American religious history. Women in Gilead are hierarchically organized into castes, and they wear uniforms that express in a visible discourse the internalized discipline imposed by the state through its religious-political system. The most notable are the Handmaids, like Kate, those few fertile women who will serve as sexual surrogates. The Handmaids dress in red, the color of blood and sacrifice, signaling their service as substitutes for the sterile wives of military officers. This sign of their displacement, or of their sacrifice in service to the state, is reinforced through various practices. We will look at three: the "consecration" ritual through which they are initiated as Handmaidens, the "Ceremony" through which they have ritualized sex with their "owners," and a punishment ceremony, called the *particicution*, in which a woman and a man guilty of violating gender norms are publicly executed. After examining these rituals, we will understand how these exaggerated (and fictionalized) practices can be grounded in a specific historic "community" and "institution." In short, we will be able to see the religious contours of a unified patriarchal family–state system in America, whose roots go back at least as far as the experience of Abigail Abbot Bailey.

In the film, the "crisis" posed to this system appears when Kate (re)discovers authentic maternal and sexual love, in much in the same way that Abigail constantly reiterated her maternal desire (or duty) in her *Memoirs*. Kate learns from the wife of the military officer, nicely named Serena Joy and played by Faye Dunaway, that the daughter she left behind when she was captured is alive. Kate also (re)discovers sexual desire, after having sex with a gardener/chauffeur (named Nick). Serena Joy offers Nick to Kate as a surrogate for her husband (whose name is Fred and is played by Robert Duvall) because Serena Joy suspects that Fred is himself sterile (which, of course, cannot be admitted in the patriarchal system). Eventually, Kate is drawn into the "underground resistance," whose members are labeled "terrorists" by the state. When Kate becomes pregnant by Nick, she rediscovers maternal emotion along with romantic love. At the same time, she plots with the resistance to assassinate Fred and one night kills him by slitting his throat. Nick then "arrests" her, but Kate discovers that he also is a freedom fighter. As she escapes into the mountains, presumably located outside Gilead, he promises to eventually join Kate "and their child."

Needless to say, this "crisis" is a bit contrived, and the way the film resolves the story with a typical Hollywood ending undermines its cultural critique. One must either submit to the regime or flee society into the wilderness after first being willing to risk assassination in a quest for romantic bliss and maternal joy. This weakness in the film's constructive vision makes it less than satisfying as a work of art. But aside from this weakness, the film is a clear critique of a state's attempts to use religion to regulate sexuality. It is precisely that continuity—in ways that hark back to Abigail Abbot Bailey and forward to the DOMA laws—that is our point. The film is an attempt to expose the religious violence simmering throughout American history, operating as a "hidden hand" behind attempts to regulate sexuality in many and various ways.

The Handmaid's Tale depicts the uniforms organizing women into hierarchies of value in Gilead. At the top are the "wives," like Serena Joy, who wear blue. Although these women are sterile, they are married to military officers, and so they have the "privilege" of enjoying the "privileges" that officers accrue, such as comfortable suburban homes, with gardens, chauffeurs, and security. As mentioned earlier, the Handmaids wear red—the color of blood, of menstruation. This revelation compresses whatever sexual desire the handmaids might have once felt and displaces it into a public symbol in service of the transcendent state. The "Aunts," who teach sexual norms and preside over public rituals, wear brown, and the "Marthas," who work as domestic or public servants, wear gray, brown, or white. The significance of these uniforms is that all women are stigmatized. Female desire is identified as the source of Gilead's pollution and sterility, and female sex is compressed into the service of the providential state, if not eliminated altogether. Thus, during her indoctrination as a handmaid, Kate participates in a litany of accusation of a woman who reported being gang-raped in high school. "Whose fault was it?" Aunt Lydia asks. "Hers," the prospective handmaids reply. "Who led them on?" Lydia asks. "She did," the handmaids respond. "What is she? A whore." Here, discourse that scapegoats women by "blaming the victim" is evident as one of the ways that the hidden hand of religion operates in the Republic of Gilead.[123]

Gilead's rigid gender differentiations are enforced by practices that define and communicate them. Among the crucial scenes is the "Consecration Ritual" for the handmaids. The women are about to graduate and be sent on their first assignment as a sexual surrogate for the wife of a military commander. After marching to the tune of the well-known evangelical hymn "Shall We Gather at the River," a priest or pastor (a blonde male) speaks, reminding the women to "remember by what deadly steps" they came to this place. He then indicts the women for their widespread practices of "sexual promiscuity," "abortion" and "genetic engineering" in the times before sterility took over, thereby again blaming women for their own predicament and implicitly establishing the context as post–*Roe v. Wade* United States. "God in his profound compassion has seen fit to punish" Gilead with sterility, the minister continues. In contrast, "You have been given this precious gift." "Precious gift," the women ritualistically intone together. "You are fertile," the pastor goes on. "You can give birth for our country. O precious gift." "O Precious Gift," the women reply. He concludes his sermon: "May the Lord open. May the handmaids ascend." The women then ascend to a platform to receive their red veils, which they will wear while having sex with the various military officers they will serve. "We pledge allegiance to the Bible," the pastor intones, in an ironic parody of the U.S. Pledge of Allegiance.[124] In contrast to the supposedly unfettered practice of sexual gratification for pleasure in the United States, in Gilead sex is for the purpose of procreation and is regulated and ritualized by the state. Abigail Abbot Bailey, who internalized in so many ways the ideal of republican motherhood as the bearer of seventeen children, would no doubt have understood, if not concurred.

A second practice in the film that reveals the ritualized regulation of sexuality in Gilead is the "Ceremony" in which Kate has sex with the officer to whom she is assigned, Fred. As a handmaid, Kate's name becomes "Offred," literally "of Fred." The ritual is held monthly, at a time carefully calculated to take advantage of the handmaid's ovulation cycle. It begins in the living room with a Bible reading, the story of Rachel in Genesis 30, the original handmaid's tale. As the narrator, Fred reads, but Serena Joy says Rachel's lines and offers her handmaid to the patriarch in the hope of producing offspring. The scene then shifts to a bedroom, with a strong blue light filmed through a blue filter filling the room with coldness. Fred removes his jacket and approaches the bed, on which Kate is lying, wearing her red dress, which is pulled up above her knees. She is on top of Serena Joy, dressed in blue, who cradles the handmaid against her hips. Kate and Serena hold hands as Fred penetrates Kate, who cries, and then Fred thrusts away for a few minutes in the most un-erotic *ménage à trois* one could imagine. Not even titillating, the scene depicts a holy rape. Whatever spontaneous holiness one might associate with the erotic is displaced into ritualized violence. Fred reveals no emotion as he (apparently) reaches orgasm. Serena Joy simply says to Kate, "Get up and get out." After it ends, Kate is shown alone in her room. She removes her clothes and washes herself, furiously. She then throws open her window before which she stands, naked. At just this highly erotic (or at least voyeuristic) moment, the gardener/chauffeur Nick happens to walk by. This establishes the dramatic contrast between "authentic" sexual desire and the violent banality of the holy rape just observed. The point of the contrast does not take much deciphering: sex for the purpose of procreation, under the religious regulation of the state, is itself sterile, an actual practice of violence.[125] Kate, like Abigail Abbot Bailey, has done her procreative duty. Although it is impossible to know for certain, given what we do know of Asa Bailey's behavior, it is not unlikely that Abigail too endured some version of a "holy rape." Phebe surely experienced "innocent" domination at his hands.

Gilead's violent religious practices are most apparent in a third scene, of two public executions, a woman's "salvaging" and a "male particicution." Kate/Offred is shown getting off a bus along with other handmaids. Women's voices again sing "Gather at the River"(with distinctly Gileadean lyrics). All the orders of women in society are present. A gallows appears on a platform in a large, open field (in fact, the scene was filmed on the green in front of the Duke University chapel). The ceremony begins as a bass thunders on the sound track. Aunt Lydia intones: "We are here today in the name of duty. And sometimes duty is a hard taskmaster." The female is sacrificed first. She is "guilty of fornication" with a member of her medical staff. That this "crime" might occur was foreshadowed in an earlier scene. During one of Kate/Offred's regular gynecological exams, a doctor offers to "do it for her," reassuring her that "it's done all the time." Back at the "salvaging," the handmaids murmur as they hear the charges read. A plastic bag is placed over the guilty handmaid's head. A noose goes around her neck. "Why does God demand her death?" asks Aunt Lydia. "For her sins," reply the handmaids, in unison. Together, they pick up a long rope or cord lying between them and pull the cord. This collective act opens the trap floor of the gallows, and the woman is hanged. A pull-away camera shot pans back to establish the ritual context. We see the chapel steeple in the background framing the body swinging from the gallows. The handmaids applaud. The same projection of transcendent authority who afflicted Abigail has now been invoked to bless the brutal death of another handmaid.

This first act of execution is followed quickly by the "particicution." "Order! Order!" Aunt Lydia announces, and the handmaids excitedly rearrange themselves into a circle as the doctor is led into their midst. Aunt Lydia then reads from "Deuteronomy 25: 'If the man forces her, then the man that lay with her shall die.'" The handmaids then descend on the hapless physician and literally rip him to shreds with their bare hands in an unmistakable evocation of the Dionysian frenzy in *The Bacchae*. The scene is a frenzy of sacrificial ecstasy. The Aunts walk off, pleased with the success of their ritual process, and the film has reinforced how the state's regulation of sexuality has been resolved in religious violence.[126] Even the victims participate, willingly, even with pleasure, cooperating with their oppression.

Linking these discourses and practices are the communities of "families," centered on the military patriarch and the state institutions. The state seems to be perpetually involved in war, with cuts to scenes of battle and destruction repeated constantly throughout the film. Surveillance, with security apparatus—gates, guards, and weapons—is everywhere. In fact, the Republic of Gilead apparently was created by a military coup, on the basis of a Christian-based purity program, representing a backlash against and an effort to eliminate noisy, messy, forms of desire. As "Fred" explains, in a candid conversation with Kate/Offred,

> The country was in a mess. All the garbage had risen to the top. We had all these pressure groups—blacks, homos . . . women—trying to pressure us. We had to clean it up. We took a big hose, and washed the place clean. . . . Nobody felt anything. All they had was like itches. Sex itches, money itches, power itches. No common purpose, nothing to believe in, nothing to fight for. Nobody felt anything. Do they feel now? I think they do. Respect. Reverence. Values that the average person can feel right here [he touches his heart], and in your case here [he touches her womb].[127]

In short, race and gender were the constructs around which religion was used to "clean up" Gilead, in the name of family "values." Such a purity program that linked family and state in a system of transcendent discourse and practices also produced sacrifices. Early in the film, in fact, a voice-over of a television report intones: "The relocation of the children of Ham is proceeding well." The sacrifice of race blurs with the sacrifice of sex in imperial practice. And as we have already seen, one of the Handmaids in training, Moira (whose name means 'fate'), is a lesbian who eventually winds up serving as a prostitute in a state-run brothel. Her sex is sacrificed to the market, which is available, of course, only to the military officers and their consorts

It is this link between religiously produced violence and the state that connects the fictional *Handmaid's Tale* with the historical *Memoirs* of Abigail Abbot Bailey, on the one hand, and connects both these narratives to the scapegoating of gays and lesbians in the Defense of Marriage Acts, on the other hand. As in Gilead and in the experience of Abigail Abbot Bailey, the DOMA laws have a hidden hand to regulate sexuality by legislating the refusal of civil and marital rights to gays and lesbians. This effectively consolidates power and privilege in a religiously based regime based on a heterosexual, patriarchal family structure and various discourses of theological purity and practices of sacrifice.

One example is the Family Research Council (FRC)'s support for the DOMA laws. The FRC was founded in 1983 by Dr. James Dobson. Dobson made his mark in evangelical Christian circles with his 1982 book *Dare to Discipline*, which encouraged parents to use corporal punishment against "strong-willed" children. The FRC's five "core principles" form a platform that both Abigail Abbot Bailey and the patriarchs of the Republic of Gilead would like:

- God exists and is sovereign over all creation. He created human beings in His image. Human life is, therefore, sacred and the right to life is the most fundamental of political rights.
- Life and love are inextricably linked and find their natural expression in the institutions of marriage and the family.
- Government has a duty to promote and protect marriage and the family in law and public policy.
- The American system of law and justice was founded on the Judeo-Christian ethic.
- American democracy depends upon a vibrant civil society composed of families, churches, schools, and voluntary associations.[128]

The FRC's slogan is "Defending Family, Faith, and Freedom." In our terms, this means joining a compressed norm of heterosexual, patriarchal marriage with legislative efforts to displace gays and lesbians from civil rights. Gay rights are eliminated for a wildly blurred set of projections of transcendent authority. The FRC maintains that the Defense of Marriage Acts are necessary as a duty to a "sovereign" God, to honor the "Judeo-Christian ethic," and to preserve "American democracy."

Since its founding, the FRC has been remarkably effective at both the federal and state levels in gaining passage of the DOMA laws defining marriage as "the union of one man and one woman." These laws explicitly eliminate the possibility of marriage for gays and lesbians and, in some cases, also eliminate the possibility of civil unions. On September 21, 1996, President Bill Clinton signed into law the federal Defense of Marriage Act, which stipulates:

In determining the meaning of an Act of Congress, or of any ruling, regulation, or interpretation of the various administrative bureaus and agencies of the United States, the word "marriage" means only a legal union between one man and one woman as husband and wife. . . . No State, territory, or possession of the United States, or Indian tribe, shall be required to give effect to any public act, record, or judicial proceeding of any other State, territory, possession, or tribe respecting a relationship between persons of the same sex that is treated as a marriage under the laws of such other State.[129]

The House passed the bill by a vote of 342 to 67, and the Senate, by 85 to 14. Since then, thirty-seven states (as of January 2009) have passed their own Defense of Marriage Acts, many of them as an amendment to their state constitutions.[130] Two other states contain strong language in legal precedents defining marriage as "between one man and one woman."[131] Still more states have statutes that have been interpreted to prevent gays and lesbians from marrying. In only five states can gays and lesbians be legally married.[132]

The hidden hand behind the federal law—and the many state-sponsored variants of it—is a religion that does not call itself a religion. This logic was explained well by Peter Sprigg, a longtime ally of James Dobson and the FRC's senior director of research studies. According to Sprigg,

> Defining marriage as the union of male and female is not something unique to Christian theology, biblical teaching, or even a Judeo-Christian worldview. . . . Marriage is not simply a religious institution, nor is it merely a civil institution. Instead, marriage is a natural institution, whose definition as the union of a man and a woman is rooted in the order of nature itself.[133]

That this definition of "marriage" happened to accord with some versions of evangelical Christian theology was a happy coincidence; one might even call it "providential." But the "truth" of this definition does not depend on any special revelation or tradition. To do so would be to privilege a particular religious group, which, under the separation of church and state, laws cannot do.

But as Professors Ann Pellegrini and Janet Jakobsen have contended, distinctions like Sprigg's among a "religious," "civil," or "natural" matter pale when one recognizes that the sacrificial outcome is the same: some adults' consensual sexual relations or gendered identities are regulated by law into silence, obscurity, or legal disadvantages with profound economic consequences. They are, in effect, symbolically eliminated. According to Pellegrini and Jakobsen,

One of the most puzzling, yet persistent, features of public life in the United States is how quickly talking about sex turns into talking about religion and, conversely, how quickly talking about religion turns into talking about sex. It is not simply that religion is the context for public debates and policy making around sex; rather, in a fundamental sense, the secular state's regulation of the sexual life of its citizens is actually religion by other means.[134]

In short, the DOMA laws are a form of religious violence. They use a supposedly "natural" law of the civil religion to impose innocent domination on gays and lesbians. Just how brutal this blessing of normative heterosexual marriage and elimination of gay partnerships can be is evident in our second example.

The Reverend Fred Phelps's "God Hates Fags" campaign, launched in 1991, eerily echoed Fred's arguments in *The Handmaid's Tale* and revived Asa Bailey's ideal of dominant patriarchs and republican mothers. Phelps believes that because "God hates fags," America must eliminate gays and lesbians from civil society. Phelps explained his position and builds toward its conclusion with three points. "God hates fags" presumes

1. The absolute sovereignty of God in all matters whatsoever.
2. The doctrine of reprobation or God's hate involving eternal retribution or the everlasting punishment of most of mankind in Hell forever.
3. The certainty that all impenitent sodomites will inevitably go to Hell.[135]

That Phelps's first principle echoes that of the FRC is no coincidence. Phelps's conclusion also harmonizes with the FRC's drive for DOMA laws, albeit without the careful distinctions of "religious," "civil," and "natural" law. "The only lawful sexual connection is the [heterosexual] marriage bed," Phelps argued.

All other sex activity is whoremongery and adultery, which will damn the soul forever in Hell. . . . Decadent, depraved, degenerate and debauched America, having bought the lie that It's OK to be gay, has thereby changed the truth of God into a lie, and now worships and serves the creature more than the Creator, who is blessed forever.[136]

Claiming to speak for God—always an alluring temptation for any fallible human—Rev. Phelps is advocating a form of religious violence, founded on a projection of transcendent authority now made manifest. Indeed, for Phelps, the DOMA laws do not go far enough, as he also recommends capital punishment for sodomy.[137]

Rev. Phelps is an extreme case, but it shows the religious associations in the appeals to innocence behind the more moderate language of the Family Research Council's carefully crafted rhetoric. As supported by the FRC, the DOMA laws exhibit in effect the same sacrificial logic that was evident to Rev. Phelps: the elimination of gay and lesbian desire and practice from public recognition. The DOMA laws mask their religious violence as a righteous "defense" of marriage. In fact, as the language of "defense" suggests, they begin with an antagonistic (if not dualistic) mentality. To "defend" marriage, there must be an "enemy" that threatens it. That this "enemy" was gays and lesbians who desired public recognition of their mutual trust and sexual pleasure through marriage or civil unions is obvious. The DOMA laws then defined marriage explicitly to exclude gays and lesbian from civil rights that heterosexuals take for granted. Such laws thus sacrificed sex, not to mention the economic benefits that come from the legal recognition of married couples. The DOMA laws also reinforce the privilege of the powerful, since by "defending" marriage as between "one man and one woman," they legitimize the existing practices of the majority. The DOMA laws thus exemplify a third variant of American religious violence, analogous to the way that the young have been treated in the cinema of adolescent abjection and in drug laws and wars, to the ways that Africans were treated in slavery, and in direct continuity with the ways in which Abigail Abbot Bailey was treated by her husband and by the legal and cultural conventions of the early Republic.

This chapter has tried to show just how persistent this thread of the regulation of sexual or gender norms—sacrificing sex—has been in American history. It is, to be sure, a long chronological way from Abigail Abbot Bailey's eighteenth-century sacrifices in the interest of republican motherhood to the twenty-first-century sacrifices of gay and lesbian couples on the altar of "defenses" of marriage. But as *The Handmaid's Tale* suggests, imperial regimes specialize in compressing experience into normative heterosexual pathways and in displacing desire through legislative and economic privileges or exclusions. It is not that religion is necessarily the problem. Religion can both liberate and oppress. Confidence in providence by the oppressed, as in Abigail's struggle for freedom from the abusive Asa, can provide a sense of power-with others, enlisting agency in conjunction with ordinary means to accomplish collective action. But the deeper trajectory here is the recurrent pattern of religious violence associated with gender and sexuality in

American history. As the historian Hendrik Hartog concluded, "There are important continuities in our marital history, continuities revealed by gay marriage controversies."[138] Those continuities have been religious, and they have institutionalized systemic violence. In the next chapter, our final case study, we trace one origin of the innocent domination and blessed brutalities in American history back to Puritan Boston.

Sacrificing Humans

An Empire of Sacrifice from
Mary Dyer to Dead Man Walking

Eve's Apple we have shewed you,
Of that be you aware:
You have seen Jacob's Ladder too,
Upon which Angels are.
An Anchor you received have;
But let not these suffice,
Until with Abra'm you have gave,
Your best, a Sacrifice.
                    —John Bunyan, *The Pilgrim's Progress*

Nations have no clearly identifiable births, and their deaths, if they ever happen, are never natural. Because there is no Originator, the nation's biography cannot be written evangelically, "downtime," through a long procreative chain of begettings. The only alternative is to fashion it "up time." ... This fashioning, however, is marked by deaths, which, in a curious inversion of conventional genealogy, start from an originary present. ... Yet the deaths that structure the nation's biography are of a special kind. ... [The] nation's biography snatches, against the going mortality rate, exemplary suicides, poignant martyrdoms, assassinations, executions, wars, and holocausts. But, to serve the narrative purpose, these violent deaths must be remembered/forgotten as "our own."
                    —Benedict Anderson, *Imagined Communities*

American history contains recurrent patterns, I contend, of people generating and accommodating themselves to religious constructions that have produced, protected, obscured, and justified the material control or domination of land and peoples under unwarranted assertions of innocence.[1] I call this logic *innocent domination*. It has appeared in displacements of material interests onto religious constructions organized around categories of age, race, and gender (which overlap and intersect, but for the purposes of my analysis I have treated as being distinct). All these constructs communicate a peculiarly exclusive notion of "American" identity or imagine a nation— and now an empire—in which various forms of sacrifice have been acceptable or even seemed necessary. In short, what is arguably the most dominant empire in human history, or at least the political constellation with the most impressive weaponry ever assembled, has been built on a logic, psychology, and economy of sacrifice. An excellent case study of this paradox of innocent domination is the practice of capital punishment in America. Capital punishment, evident across America from 1659 to the present, eliminates a person through ritual processes that effectively function as human sacrifice.[2]

In capital punishment, the "primitive" practice of human sacrifice is rendered innocent through modern religious discourses and practices that find their roots, in American history, in the execution of four Quakers on the Boston Common between 1659 and 1661. On the one hand, the suggestion that modernity began with the Puritans might seem to be surprising, even counterintuitive. On the other hand, that religious violence characterized the Puritans would not be surprising in the least to the Puritans' victims or opponents. In the case of the Quakers, the various strands of our argument come together to show how constructions of a collective identity—call it "America"—originated in religious discourses and practices that have had a long shelf life. These constructions of transcendent authority have proved to be remarkably malleable and useful to those who have sought to control material resources and exercise power as force in the construction of an empire, albeit innocently, under the guise of sacrifice.

Sacrifice and Empire Building from the Aztecs to Puritan Boston via John Bunyan

Whatever else it is, the "modern" is what has sought to differentiate the profane from the sacred, the religious from the political, the "primitive" from "progress." Ideally, moderns tried to give religion the status of a vestige in the domain of culture, or to bury religion in the recesses of private experience.[3] Within the scope of the modern, the sacred is what has been, or should be, overcome by artists or one's own psychological strength, whereas the profane defines the horizon of action in the world by agents whose mastery is demonstrated over nature through politics, economic activity, or culture.[4] The chief institution characterizing the modern has thus been the nation-state, and its chief mythology has been the separation of religion from politics. Yet as Marcel Gauchet provocatively contended, "We have broken away from religion only by finding substitutes for it at every level."[5] In American history, the modern has been marked by various forms of sacrifice, or by what Gauchet would identify as the sacred in the form of "entrepreneurial asceticism." These noble, if not necessary, sacrifices have appeared in apparently secular guise in ways that have repeatedly produced violence.

As I sketched in chapter 1 and have alluded to throughout this book, René Girard has been perhaps the preeminent theorist of sacrifice as a logic operating in many instances of religious violence. According to Girard, literary sources from many cultures reveal that sacrifice stems from a form of desire that he variously terms "mimetic desire" or "acquisitive mimesis." In Girard's sources, a subject observes another's desire and, from this observation, learns desire. The subject's desire threatens, or actually produces, rivalry for a desired object. Girard calls this rivalry a "crisis of differentiation." Religion arises as an effort to alleviate this crisis, in Girard's sources, through sacrifice. Sacrifice resolves the crisis of differentiation, he argues, when people react to rivalry by selecting a scapegoat whose death or expulsion temporarily defuses it, uniting all against one, and thereby (re)establishing order. "Sacrifice is primarily a collective action of the entire community, which purifies itself of its own disorder through the unanimous immolation of a victim."[6] This insight into the socially unifying, though ambivalent, logic of sacrifice is hardly unique to Girard.[7] But the logic that implicates collective or mimetic desire in violence and that holds religion responsible for both containing and fueling that desire has been considered plausible since at least Augustine, and surely since Freud, both of whom Girard acknowledges as influences.[8]

If Girard believes that sacrifice has a logic that both embraces and contains violence, R. Scott Appleby, to continue our brief theoretical review, has shown us that religious violence has a psychological component. For Appleby, it is obvious that people of faith, or those affiliated with what go by the name of "religions," have produced both violence and peace, conflict and reconciliation. Appleby describes violent believers variously as "extremists," "reactionaries," and devotees of "weak" or (in another work) "strong" religions, of which he cites as the preeminent examples the global "fundamentalisms" that he traced in the five-volume project he coedited with Martin E. Marty.[9] Emerging at the core of Appleby's historical analysis of religious violence is a psychological pattern that at one point he labels "ecstatic asceticism." As we observed in chapter 1, Appleby characterizes this odd conjunction of terms as follows:

Traditional rituals and devotions that sacralize personal self-sacrifice become in extremist hands a means of preparing the devout cadres for physical warfare. . . . Such prescribed prayers and rituals, interpreted by an extremist preacher, locate the believer in a sacred cosmos that rewards martyrdom or imprisonment endured in a divine cause. . . . This ability of religion to inspire ecstasy—literally, to lift the believer psychologically out of a mundane environment—stands behind the distinctive logic of religious violence. As unpredictable and illogical as this violence may seem to outsiders, it falls within a pattern of asceticism leading to the ecstasy of self-sacrifice that runs as a continuous thread through most religions.[10]

These dense generalizations pose problems in almost every word, but the general pattern clearly emerges from Appleby's empirical studies of many instances of religious violence around the globe. That is, people find power, even ecstasy, in acts of self-sacrifice that might also involve violence against or sacrifice of others. It does not seem to dawn on Appleby that this psychological pattern might have a very peculiar cultural origin close to the home of fundamentalism, namely, in modern America.[11] Nevertheless, ecstatic asceticism—or something close to what might be encompassed in that interesting conjunction of terms—does seem evident in many instances of religious violence.

Finally, David Carrasco has written a historically specific study of the role of human sacrifice that might have surprisingly wide application for our purposes here. Carrasco's field is the Aztec empire, in which "ritual slaughter within the ceremonial precincts of Aztec life was the instrument, in part, for educating adolescents about their social future, communicating with the many gods, transmitting cosmological convictions, as well as directing social change in the form of imperial expansion."[12] Practiced repeatedly and publicly in manifold ritual forms, Aztec sacrifice was a means for the imperial city of Tenochtitlán to demonstrate control over the peripheries of its empire. Sacrifice was a tool in "the militarization of society."[13] If Girard identifies a logic of sacrifice, and Appleby a psychology, Carrasco sketches a sacrificial economy in the broadest sense of that term as a matter concerning the settling of a human community and the shaping of a cultural identity. Carrasco's work brings together three facets of historical study not often linked: attention to the material *and* symbolic processes associated with human settlement and organization; attention to the integrative *and* destructive powers of ritual and religion; and attention to the way that the history of religions itself as a discipline has developed a hermeneutic that both opens and forecloses avenues of investigation.[14]

The implications of this last feature of Carrasco's work are significant for our purposes. Carrasco finds it stunning that previous theorists of religion "*completely ignored* the most thorough record of real, historical sacrifice while favoring either distant reports of animal sacrifices *or literary sacrifices* from Western Classics!"[15] In fact, however, the scandal may be even more pronounced. The history of religions developed as a discipline, as a number of recent works have pointed out, alongside what Carrasco calls a "mass-sacrifice society," led by figures of the ilk of "'lord' Captain Cortes."[16] It may not be a coincidence that this "mass-sacrifice" society took root here in the "New World," where the discipline of the history of religions also made its most secure home in the academy.

Indeed, what should we make of the almost utter silence (with some notable exceptions) of American scholars of religion about American religious violence, over the same time span that U.S. military and economic dominance reached the point of empire?[17] In constructing a fetish of the "primitive" or foreign "other" and the sacrificial violence found there, historians of religion may have neglected some of the most powerful and significant interactions among and convergences between forms of cultural authority regarding U.S. practices of sacrifice. Blinded by what was supposed to be the "modern," Americans embraced countless "primitive" practices.

The root and branches of this process can be traced not only, as Max Weber contended, to John Calvin, Benjamin Franklin, and others who crafted what has come to be called the *Puritan ethic*, but perhaps even more vividly to one of Calvin's popularizers, John Bunyan. Before turning to how an empire of sacrifice originated in a particularly concentrated microcosm, in Puritan Boston, we will journey briefly across the Atlantic to see the sacrificial logic manifest in the work that one scholar has named "without doubt the most influential religious book ever written in the English language," *The Pilgrim's Progress*.[18]

Bunyan published his magnum opus in two parts, in 1678 and 1684, and it reflected his thinking as shaped by the formative events of the English civil war and the brief reign of Oliver Cromwell, which ended in 1658. Bunyan's work is, in effect, an antipilgrimage pilgrimage. Taking the form of a medieval morality tale embedded in an account of a spiritualized journey, the work contrasts with the bawdy, antimoralizing, antispiritualizing romp of Chaucer's *Canterbury Tales*. In its heavy-handed metaphors and literalizing analogies, *The Pilgrim's Progress* clears the way for the taking of land that became the epitome of a wide variety of European (and eventually American) empires. It does so by allegorizing pilgrimage, evacuating the experience of any actual place. More precisely, *The Pilgrim's Progress* condenses experience into an allegorical form, a series of displacements subject to the cultural mastery of the artist. Bunyan was in prison while conceiving of and writing much of the work, so by thus spiritualizing pilgrimage into a "transcendent" realm that might be anywhere, Bunyan disenchants the "real" world. He eliminates matter. Bunyan's devotion to a spiritualized "progress" thus established the primary dichotomy between profane matter to be dominated and sacred culture to be revered of the modern. This sacrifice of place might not be immediately clear as a chief instrument of modern empire and a central warrant for religious violence.[19] But it will become clearer after a quick foray into Bunyan's allegories, before a more extended examination of Puritan Boston, where the same nexus of ideas was put into political practice in the sacrifice of Mary Dyer and three other Quakers between 1659 and 1661.

The two parts of *The Pilgrim's Progress* work together. In the first, a "man," whom Bunyan eventually names Christian, appears to him in a dream. Christian is distressed by a vision of his city being "burned with fire from Heaven." He foresees that he, his wife, Christiana, and their children "shall miserably come to ruin" in this God-sent conflagration unless "some way of escape can be found." The plot of *The Pilgrim's Progress* then relates how Christian, in part 1, and Christiana and the children, in part 2, "escape" from the "City of Destruction." The "City of Destruction" is, in fact, any city in "the world," or perhaps every city. Eventually, all the pilgrims make their way to paradise; which Bunyan depicts as a place that is no place, since it is reached (or, perhaps, taken) precisely by shedding matter. Indeed, the basic plot that Bunyan develops, as the title indicates, is the classical modern notion of progress: from matter to spirit, from sin to salvation, from destruction to glory, from earth to heaven.[20] Throughout the two sections, Christian and Christiana face various perils. All of them involve some kind of material temptation, and all of them they manage (by grace and sometimes aided by a good sword) to overcome. For the sake of brevity, we will examine only one of the perils faced by Christian, one by Christiana, and their sacrificial logic. Rather than rely only on Bunyan's words, however, which may have been commented on often enough, I will refer as well to the woodcuts accompanying these two scenes, which were published during his lifetime.[21]

The first scene of sacrifice takes place at the famous (or infamous) Vanity Fair. Christian arrives at this town near the end of his journey to paradise. Vanity Fair is a notorious den of thieves, scoundrels, hypocrites, and liars, most of whom are merchants. Christian is accompanied there by "Faithful," who becomes the scapegoat whose sacrifice propels Christian's pilgrimage.

Before arriving at the town, "Evangelist," another guide, warns the pilgrims that "you must through many tribulations enter into the Kingdom of Heaven. . . . He that shall die there, although his death will be unnatural, and his pain perhaps great, he will have the better of his fellow" (86). This perverse logic of ecstatic asceticism, of glory through suffering, of course proves to be prophetic. Faithful and Christian are captured, primarily because they wear bad clothes and do not buy the wares of the city's merchants. They are then tortured, beaten, and led in chains through the streets "for an example and a terror to others" (88). After a parody of a "trial," led by "Lord Hategood," with "Envy" and "Superstition" among the witnesses, Faithful is martyred. Bunyan describes the execution step by step: "First they Scourged him, then they Buffeted him, then they Lanced his flesh with Knives; after that they Stoned him with Stones, then prickt him with their Swords, and last of all they burned him to Ashes at the Stake. Thus came Faithful to his end" (95). In fact, however, this is not Faithful's end at all, as Bunyan reports seeing him transported on a chariot "up through the Clouds, with sound of Trumpet," directly into Heaven. In the remaining scenes of part 1, "Hopeful" takes Faithful's place as Christian's pilgrim guide, playing essentially the same virtuous role. The woodcut that accompanied this scene reveals the sacrifice of Faithful (see figure 1).

Surrounded by soldiers with their spears, Faithful appears to be an ordinary human. It is hardly accidental that the unknown woodcut artist depicted Faithful anthropomorphically, since Bunyan's vivid description of Faithful's tortures and death mirrored the actual practices in seventeenth-century England. In the woodcut, as the flames lick at Faithful's feet, the smoke ascends to clouds in which a chariot appears. Faithful is thus shown literally displaced: in two places at once. He is both in the flames and transported beyond them into the clouds. That this displacement reflects the simple one-to-one analogies by which Christian's pilgrimage progresses also is no coincidence. Matter must give way to something more transcendent; being faithful means leaving matter behind. That this "truth" is realized by a reader as inscribed in material signs on a page or as carved into material lines in a woodcut, in a book that the reader is likely to have purchased from a merchant, is the vanity that Bunyan cannot, or will not, admit. Yet it is at this level—where religion, trade, and politics all come together, as we shall see—at which the Puritans in Boston attempted to put their own vision of progress into practice. The leaders of Massachusetts Bay imagined that they could sacrifice a single human being to preserve the purity, or faithfulness, that they felt it was their duty to preserve. In attempting to be faithful, they killed one who was faithful. This was a pattern repeated again and again.

Figure 1. Woodcut
of "Faithful" from
Pilgrim's Progress.

In part 2 of *The Pilgrim's Progress*, the religious violence escalates. Bunyan's
pilgrims execute their enemies with a vigor equal to, or beyond, the zeal exercised by the merchants of Vanity Fair in the sacrifice of Faithful. The crucial scene is when Christiana, guided by "Great-Heart," encounters "Giant
Despair." Christian himself encountered Giant Despair in part 1, when he and
Hopeful were captured and imprisoned in the Giant's "Doubting Castle." While
in prison, the pilgrims were beaten repeatedly and tempted by the Giant's wife,
"Diffidence," to commit suicide. Hopeful persuaded Christian to refuse this

temptation (citing the fifth commandment not to kill), and the two escaped when Christian remembered that all along he had held in his possession the key to any locked gate: the key of "Promise." In part 2, however, the pilgrims take a more preemptive approach to Giant Despair, and the fifth commandment is conveniently forgotten. By the time they arrive at Doubting Castle, Great Heart has already defeated three other Giants in battle: Giant Grim (207), Giant Maull (who "spoiled pilgrims with sophistry," 229–30), and Giant Slay-Good (248–49). Each Giant met the same end: beheading, followed by public display of his severed head on a post "for a Terror" to all who observed it (249).

The battle with Giant Despair reaches the same predictable outcome. Great Heart does not fight after being captured, imprisoned, or tortured by Giant Despair but preemptively seeks out the Giant to "fight the good Fight of Faith. [For] I pray," Great-heart explains to readers, "with whom should I fight this good Fight, if not with Gyant-dispair?" (261–62). The battle is enjoined with the Giant and with his wife, Diffidence, who dies quickly. The Giant, however, "was very loth to die. He struggled hard, and had, as they say, as many lives as a Cat, but Great-heart was his death, for he left him not till he had severed his head from his shoulders" (262). The pilgrims then demolish Doubting Castle. The vandalism takes seven days, which is a good biblical number. After the castle is dismantled, the pilgrims take "with them the Head of the Gyant," presumably carrying it by the hair. When the other pilgrims (waiting below on the King's Highway) see this spectacle, they become "very jocund and merry." The women make music, and even the lame (such as "Ready-to-Halt") dance. Then "Mr. Great-heart-took the Head of Gyant-Dispair, and set it upon a Pole by the Highway side" (264).

All this decapitation of giants and severed heads stuck on poles is obviously violent, if not downright grisly. Some readers would protest that this is all allegory referring to the internal struggle of Christians, the psychological (although the word did not exist then) conflict within the soul against despair and sin that requires a "good heart" to overcome. In fact, this allegory emerged from, and had an odd tendency to keep reappearing in, literal and profoundly material forms. For instance, when the Puritans claimed control of Great Britain in 1649, they beheaded Charles I. And after Oliver Cromwell died in 1658, he was exhumed in 1661, hanged from a gallows, and decapitated. So Bunyan drew on images well known from the spiritual lives of his people and their political experience. The woodcut in figure 2 reveals the head of Giant Despair looking very much like the head of a king, and the ruined castle behind him looks very much like any monarch's domain. The pilgrims, who look like ordinary Englishmen and women, make merry

Figure 2. Woodcut of "Gyant Dispair" from *Pilgrim's Progress*.

around the gruesome spectacle of sacrifice. The verse explains the moral of this event:

> The doubting Castle be demolished
> And the Gyant dispair hath lost his head
> Sin can rebuild the Castle, make't remaine,
> And make despair the Gyant live againe.

This was a sacrifice that also would need to be repeated.

And it was. The modern dawned in episodic spasms of religious violence: civil wars, public executions, and bloody spectacles of severed heads on posts. It progressed, if that is the correct term, to carefully ritualized, organized, systematized genocide, preemptive wars, and the massing of arsenals of weapons of mass destruction.[22] Disenchanted by nature, modern people struggled to figure out how to make progress without destruction. The ironies were ample. Fleeing destruction, pilgrims destroyed. But since they had been saved by grace, they could establish colonies in New England where they imagined instituting the purity denied them of old. On a material level, this brought Bunyan's vision of progress to fruition: the pilgrims prevailed. But on another level, the nation building that followed colonial projects ironically undermined the hope of the grace-driven Bunyan (and many like him) for spiritual progress over vanity, for spiritual freedom from imprisonment, and for spiritual maturity to resolve conflicts without violence. Within a generation of the founding of Massachusetts Bay and over and over again in the history of America ever since, such a hope in grace and faith was turned, one might say, quite directly on its head.[23]

Mimesis in Massachusetts, 1656–1657

The colony of Massachusetts Bay was settled by Christians intent on creating a holy commonwealth. Perry Miller long ago described the Puritan "errand into the wilderness" through which a public theologian like John Winthrop could, in all modesty, arrogate to himself and his followers to be a "modell of Christian charity" on whom the eyes of the world were surely trained.[24] Such a modeling process presupposed an object to be admired and mirrored, a "charity" to be imitated and realized. "When God gives a special Commission," which Winthrop could obviously assume that he had to the New England Puritans, "he lookes to have it strictly observed in every Article." Such mimesis, which could not deviate in the slightest, was all but bound to produce strife. Indeed, strife (or at least the opposite of charity) was implicit in the very injunction itself, not to mention in the wilderness that the Puritans imagined they were sent to settle.[25] Consequently, within a generation of their arrival among the Massachusetts, the English resolved more prosaically, in the Cambridge Platform of 1648, that "idolatry, blasephemy, heresie, venting corrupt and pernicious Opinions . . . are to be restrained and punished by Civil Authority."[26] This made the matter clearer than Winthrop's noble theological rhetoric had done and set the stage for the arrival of the Quakers in Boston in 1656, only four years after George Fox had seen the "inner light" and started his own controversial career as a lay preacher.[27]

The first two Quakers to arrive in New England were women, Mary Fisher and Anne Austin. Their gender did not help their cases.[28] Richard Bellingham, the deputy governor of Massachusetts Bay, had received a warning that some enthusiasts were due in Boston Harbor. He thereupon dispatched a few soldiers to detain the wayward women while still on board ship and to search their shipping trunks. The soldiers confiscated about a hundred suspect books. In what must have been a panic, Bellingham managed to convene Boston's magistrates the next day to pass a law prescribing the burning of any Quaker books and holding Fisher and Austin in the Boston jail. The language of the law is instructive. Quaker ideas were "very dangerous, heretical, and blasphemous opinions," replicating the language of the Cambridge Platform and thereby justifying through a self-fulfilling prophecy Bellingham's exercise of his civil authority to contain and punish the Quakers. Even worse, in the eyes of the law, the Quakers "do acknowledge . . . that they came here purposely to propagate their said Errors and Heresies." The letter of the law was thereby fulfilled: the Quaker books were sacrificed the next morning in a fire tended by a hangman on the Boston Common. But the spirit of the law and the contagion of these errors that might be propagated seemed to call for extraordinary measures: the women were thus strip-searched while in prison. This was done "under pretence of searching whether they were witches," explained the eighteenth-century Quaker chronicler Joseph Besse. Just to make sure the danger did not spread, the window of the jail was then boarded up in order to prevent all conversation with these blasphemous propagators of contagious ideas. After five weeks of what must have been a long silence, Austin and Fisher were put on a boat back to Barbados, from whence they had come, via England.[29]

Within days, eight more Quakers arrived in Boston, and they were imprisoned for eleven weeks. Boston's general court was feeling overwhelmed and thus passed the second anti-Quaker law in that year, 1656, mandating a fine of one hundred pounds for any ship commander who transported Quakers into Boston, along with sufficient security to pay for their removal from the colony. The Quakers themselves now not only would be subject to imprisonment and banishment but also would be officially silenced by an explicit prohibition that none could be "suffered to converse or speak with them," which would obviously make difficult any defense they might muster. As the Puritan judges saw it, Quakers were contagious and needed to be contained. Quakers dared, the law stated, to "speak and write blasphemous opinions . . . [and were] seeking to turn the People from the Faith and gain Proselytes to their pernicious ways." Ironically, this law had the effect of only increasing the flow of Quakers into Boston. Anne Burden, a widow, and Mary Dyer—well known to the Massachusetts Bay authorities as a supporter of Anne Hutchinson—were the next to reside in Boston's prison. Mary Clark followed shortly thereafter, and a precedent soon to be enshrined in law was set when she received "twenty stripes of a three-corded whip on her naked back." A crisis of differentiation was under way in the wilderness. John Winthrop's city on the hill was now beset by rival models of what Christian "charity" actually meant.[30]

Even stronger measures in defense of "charity" seemed necessary. A third law passed against the Quakers by Boston's general court clarified further what the magistrates thought was at stake. This was a crisis of language, about which words could be disseminated and which needed to be contained or sacrificed. In the characteristically magical mentality of matching a torture to fit the crime, the punishments followed suit:

> Every such Male Quaker shall for the first Offence [of coming to Boston, after having once been banished], have one of his Ears cut off . . . and for the second Offence, shall have his other Ear cut off. And every Woman Quaker that has suffered the Law here. . . . shall be severely whipt, and kept at the House of Correction at Work. . . And for every Quaker, he or she that shall a third Time herein again offend, they shall have their Tongues bored through with an hot Iron.[31]

Such threats to their abilities to hear or speak did not deter the Friends from visiting Boston; in fact, they came in droves: William Shattock, a shoemaker; Sarah Gibbons, Dorothy Waugh, and Horred Gardner all suspected of witchery; Laurence, Cassandra, and Josiah Southwick, an entire family of heretics; along with various individuals like Joshua Buffum, Thomas Harris, and William Brend. Brend was incarcerated in late 1657 and whipped nearly one hundred strokes, until "the Blood hanging as it were in Bags under his Arms, and so into one was his Flesh beaten, that the Sign of a particular Blow could not be seen."[32] The growing Puritan uncertainty about their errand into the wilderness, their undifferentiated frustration about exactly what kind of charity they were supposed to be modeling, was inscribed on the body of William Brend.

Within a few years of settling in New England, the Puritan founders faced new rivalries, and they chose to respond with force: first by keeping the Quakers in prison, then by burning their books, and finally by subjecting them to physical punishment. Eliminating a spiritual threat seemed to require eliminating concrete matter: words, skin, ears, tongues. These measures, enacted in all purity as legal defenses of an innocent and even holy order, ironically escalated the conflicts the Puritans thought they were resolving, for the mimesis in Massachusetts was not subject only to Puritan control. The Quakers had a voice in how it happened; their desires would not be so easily contained.

Ecstatic Asceticism:
The Domination of Discourse and Rhetorical Inversion, 1658–1661

The earliest Quakers were, by the standards of their day, uncivil. They were engaged in what the most colorful of their original members, James Nayler, called "The Lamb's War."[33] It was a "lamb's" war because it was fought primarily with words, with silence, or with what has come to be called "civil disobedience." Quakers interrupted the preaching of established ministers or simply refused to attend established worship services. Alternatively, when they did worship, they refused to use formal printed prayers or to recognize clerical and gender hierarchies. In public life, they declined to participate in major rituals, such as the taking of oaths, and minor ones, such as the doffing of hats, that demonstrated deference to laws and superiors or respect for equals. As the Puritan commonwealth spun out of control and veered toward the Restoration of the monarchy in 1660, Quakers were increasingly subject to persecution and repression throughout the transatlantic world. In reaction, Friends demonstrated both an annoying tendency toward self-righteous assertions of innocence and a surprising facility at crafting apocalyptically tinged curses. Along with the Puritan laws that imposed on them a rhetoric of domination, the Quakers developed corrosive rhetorics of their own that inverted the Puritan efforts at domination. Quaker curses also demonstrated a familiarity with suffering that magistrates understandably feared.[34] Finally, in 1689 in England, the Edict of Toleration ended the official persecution of Quakers, but in Boston, the matter came to a more dramatic end, with four Quaker executions between 1659 and 1661.

The first Quakers to feel the wrath of Boston's new laws were Christopher Holder, John Rouse, and John Copeland. All three were arrested for the second time in Boston in 1658. By then, Governor John Endecott had made the scapegoating of Quakers a primary feature of his administration. "The Quakers have nothing to prove their Commission by," he contended, "but the Spirit within them, and that is the Devil."[35] Endecott presided as Holder, Rouse, and Copeland all had their ears cropped in a bloody private ceremony that a historian might study more closely some day.[36] In reaction, the Quaker trio suggested that any who undertook such an act with malicious intent (as if there were any other way to cut off someone's ear): "Let our Blood be upon their Heads; and such shall know, in the Day of Account, that every Drop of our Blood shall be as heavy upon them as a Mill-stone."[37] This set the ritual pattern: official punishment (or threat of punishment) to reinforce and mark domination, followed by retaliatory imprecation that rhetorically inverted power. The conflict escalated, lasting for nearly four years.

The Puritan magistrates responded to being cursed with what in hindsight appears to be a lack of legislative restraint: they passed a fourth law against the Quakers, which imposed "banishment upon pain of death." "By Word and Writing [the Quakers] have published and maintained many dangerous and horrid Tenets," the law redundantly stated. Such tenets were "insinuating themselves into the Minds of the Simple . . . whereby diverse of our Inhabitants have been infected." Such "infection" was no illusion. According to Joseph Besse, the new law barely passed, by a vote of thirteen to twelve. Crucial to its passing was a strong argument in its favor by Boston's ministerial leadership, notably Rev. John Norton, whose stake in this case we shall discover shortly. Its passage also was helped by an amendment stipulating that any case involving the death penalty against Quakers must be "tried by a special Jury."[38]

In response to being threatened with the death penalty, the Quakers turned to even more exaggerated rhetoric, which put them in the role of judging their judges. Humphrey Norton (no relation to Rev. John Norton) had arrived in Rhode Island in 1657 and had promptly set out to preach his Quaker faith in Plymouth. There he warned the governors that if they harassed Quakers, God would punish them with pain "like gnawing worms lodging betwixt thy heart and liver."[39] His reward for such vivid anatomical detail was to be twice arrested and flogged, after which he fled Plymouth for New Haven in hopes of finding a more congenial audience. He did not, but he did leave Connecticut with a new badge of honor: an "H" branded on his right hand to permanently signify his status as a heretic.

Norton had never set foot in Boston, but after learning of the three Friends' ear cropping, he wrote to Massachusetts Bay Governor Endecott a letter that eventually was made public to a "great noise" in the city. The letter has the rhythm of an "imprecatory psalm," according to historian Frederick B. Tolles: "Accursed are thy rulers," the letter begins, "thou Town of Boston, for they are become the High Priests servants, and hath cut thy Saints right Ears." In quick succession, Norton strings together curses against Boston's teachers, people, counsel, governor, hangman, and anyone who even had sympathy for the hangman:

> Cursed be the Tongue, that takes pitty on [the hangman], for he pittied not his own Soul, neither showed he mercy to the Saints of the most High. Double give him to drink for what he hath done. . . . Let not the earth be suffered to drink up his blood, but let it rot in his breasts, as an untimely birth: Vengeance for evermore is thy reward thou Manslayer. The irresistible curse swallow thee up for evermore.

Given that he crafted such niceties for anyone who even sympathized with the Puritans, Norton naturally summoned the ultimate transcendent authority in his judgment of Governor Endecott: "The curse of God rest upon thee, Joh. Indicott, for my brethren and Companions sake, the curse of God rest upon thee, thy deeds shalt thou answer for, as sure as ever thou consentedst to that deed, thou Son of a Murtherer." Norton's letter was published by the Boston authorities, with a foreword asking its readers "to consider how consistent the Toleration of such persons is with the Subsistence of a Land."[40]

By October 1659 the Boston magistrates were ready to demonstrate just how far they would go to protect their subsistence. Quakers William Robinson, Marmaduke Stevenson, and Mary Dyer were arrested in Boston after having previously been banished. All three were summarily sentenced to death in a trial presided over by Endecott. On October 27, the three were marched to the gallows on the Boston Common, accompanied by a large band of soldiers, including some on horses. John Wilson, the pastor of First Church, Boston, was in attendance, as was Captain James Oliver and Marshal General Edward Michelson. Besse describes the scene:

> Now the procession began, and a Drummer going next before the Condemned, when any of them attempted to speak, the Drums were beaten. Glorious Signs of Heavenly Joy and Gladness were beheld in the Countenances of the three Persons, who walked Hand in Hand, Mary being in the Middle, which made the Marshal say to her. . . . "Are not you ashamed to walk thus Hand in Hand betwixt two young men." She replied, "No; this is to me an Hour of the greatest Joy I ever had in this World: No Ear can hear, no Tongue can utter, and no Heart can understand, the sweet Incomes or Influence, and the Refreshings of the Spirit of the Lord which now I feel." Thus going along, W. Robinson said, "This is your Hour, and the Power of Darkness;" but presently the Drums were beaten, yet shortly after, the

Drummers ceasing, Marmaduke Stevenson said, "This is the Day of your Visitation, wherein the Lord hath visited you." More he spake, but could not be understood, because of the Drums beating again, yet they went on with great Chearfulness, as going to an Everlasting Wedding, and rejoicing that the Lord had counted them worthy to suffer Death for his Name's Sake.[41]

Then the two men were hanged, in public spectacles of sacrifice. Dyer received a reprieve, due perhaps to an earnest letter written to Endecott by her more or less orthodox husband and to the personal intervention of her son.[42] Besse records that as the large crowd dispersed after the executions, a drawbridge gave way under the weight. "Several were hurt, especially a wicked Woman, who had reviled the said persons at their Death." It was no doubt, Besse reasoned, a sign that due to her injuries, "the Flesh rotted from her Bones, which made such a Stink, that the People could not endure to be with her." In this "miserable condition, she died." The magistrates naturally took no notice of the providential retribution.[43]

After her reprieve, Mary Dyer managed to fulfill her banishment to Rhode Island for a full four months. But in March, after sneaking away without her husband's knowledge, Dyer was arrested for the third time in the city. Now there would be no reprieve. As she was marched to the gallows, "the drums [were] beaten before and behind her, and so continued, that none might hear her speak all the Way to the Place of Execution, which was about a Mile." At the gallows, she was given an opportunity to address the crowd. "I came [back] to keep Blood-Guiltiness from you, desiring you to repeal the unrighteous and unjust Law of Banishment upon pain of death, made against innocent Servants of the Lord." This assertion of her innocence did not persuade the crowd, some of whom argued with her, including one who taunted her that she must have really loved the Boston prison to visit it so frequently. To this taunt Dyer replied: "Yea, I have been in Paradise these several Days." Yet this paradise was nothing, she continued, compared with the place she would soon inhabit. Her destination was "the Will of my Father," and the real reason she came back to Boston was so that "in Obedience to his Will, I stand even to Death." "And more," Besse concludes, "she spoke of the Eternal Happiness, into which she was now to enter. Thus Mary Dyer departed from this Life."[44] Her "progress" was perhaps not quite as smooth as Bunyan might have imagined it for more orthodox pilgrims, but she surely had given "her best, a sacrifice."

Such ecstasy through suffering awaited one other Quaker, William Leddra, who was executed by Boston's authorities in January 1661. His execution followed the ritual pattern. Leddra knew the law but defied it in an effort to remind the colony's leaders how they themselves had once been innocently accused and persecuted. "How have [you] defiled the Bed of Virginity," he accused the Puritans, "who once in a great Measure had escaped the Corruptions that are in the World through Lust!" The Puritans, however, had no trouble venting their lust on the poor Leddra, who claimed to feel, if not ecstasy, no pain or to hear no torment in "the Noise of the Whip on my Back, all the Imprisonments, Sound of an Halter, from their Mouth, who Jezabel-like, fat on the imperious Throne of Iniquity, did no more affright me, through the Strength of the Power of God, than if they had threatned [sic] to have bound a Spider's Web to my finger." Leddra felt the hangman's noose around his neck on January 14. Over the next few months, as many as twenty-eight Quakers were imprisoned at a time in Boston. Most were released. One more, Wenlock Christison, was sentenced to death. But on September 9, 1661, King Charles II intervened, in a letter sent to a Salem Quaker, who carried it to Endecott. The letter mandated that "if there be any of those People called Quakers amongst you, now already condemned to suffer Death, or other Corporal Punishment, or that are imprisoned, or obnoxious to the like Condemnation, you are to forbear to proceed any farther."[45] With that, the killing of Quakers in early America came to an end.

Much is curious about this set of events. First is the ineffectiveness of the Puritan effort at deterrence. The punitive laws passed by the Massachusetts General Court to threaten and exclude Quakers were matched by a corresponding escalation of the Quaker presence in Boston. Such a presence mirrored the Puritan effort at domination with curses whose rhetorical effect was to invert and undermine the Puritan claim to power. Behind this mimetic crisis, however, is the curious question of the early Quaker *mentalité*. What motivated and sustained these ordinary men and women to find such glory in their suffering and to express joy in the face of brutal physical punishment and death? Finally, behind both the crisis of differentiation and the ecstatic asceticism—if we may place these curiosities in these categories—is the even more curious question of the Puritans' motive. Why did Endecott, Norton, Bellingham, and the rest imagine, so obviously wrongly, that the sacrifice of a few Quakers would help establish their holy commonwealth in New England? To answer that question, we need to return to the project of empire building and the interaction between the Puritans and the Quakers in the larger context of "settling" the "New World."[46]

Sacrificial Rites and an Imagined Community, 1620–1776

In much of the prevailing historiography of American religions, the Puritans lost. Their effort to construct a holy commonwealth gave way—at one point or another, and scholars differ by centuries about exactly when that point was reached—to the flourishing of religious liberty and to the Yankee project of building a truly secular society.[47] I suspect, however, and I hope that by this time readers have come to suspect with me, that the process was somewhat more complex than this progressive narrative of secularization can encompass. On the level of institutions, on which historians for many decades earned their bread and butter, there is some truth to the shift from Puritan to Enlightenment modes of organization in America. But on the level of lived experience, or the so-called domain of culture, returning to this "founding event" in American history and tracing its trajectories can help us see that the quest for holiness and the settling of the "New World" were not well-differentiated processes.[48] In fact, the settling of the New World may have been far more consistent with the Puritan project than much recent scholarship seems willing to admit.[49]

To help understand the continuities between the Puritan project of building a holy commonwealth and the ongoing projects of nation or empire building, we shall briefly return to the Aztecs. According to David Carrasco, the Aztecs used public sacrifices to forge an economy based on military expansion. For the Aztecs, sacrifices were a means to communicate with the gods, to indoctrinate youth, and to direct "social change in the form of imperial expansion." More specifically, sacrifices were tools "in the militarization of society" and, even more particularly, ways to establish a "center" in the sacred city of Tenochtitlàn that would radiate power outward to the peripheries of the empire and thereby ensure their loyalty and patronage.[50] The Puritan effort in killing Quakers may have served similar functions and stemmed from similar motives. Although the Quakers themselves were safe after 1661, the impulse that led to the burning of their books on the Boston Common hardly vanished from American history, as I have tried to show throughout the preceding chapters. In fact, sacrifice in various forms may have become the very fuel of the economic order on which a new nation would arise.

The Puritan effort to sacrifice Quakers was obviously in the interest of controlling the peripheries of their imagined community.[51] As historians Jonathan Chu and Carla Pestana have demonstrated, the Quakers who were sacrificed came from outside Boston, yet it was only in Boston that Quakers were put to death.[52] On the peripheries of Massachusetts Bay in places such as Plymouth, Hampton, Kittery, and even nearby Salem, Quakers were, if not tolerated, at least never killed. As Chu suggests, in these localities community leaders were more concerned about establishing any English presence, even heterodox, than in regulating uniformity regarding the doffing of hats. In Boston, however, the "advancement" of the civilizing process and the centralization of power required an effort to extend the "settlement" process to the peripheries of the colony. As Rev. John Norton put it, the execution of Quakers was along the lines of "preventing of infection, and spreading contagion." "Impunity of the sinner encourageth others to do the like," the Rev. Norton went on, "but punishment speedily and seasonably inflicted, makes others more afraid of such evills."[53] Plymouth, Hampton, Kittery, and Salem—not to mention Rhode Island—were infected, and the preemptive sacrifices of a few Quakers in Boston would both demonstrate the proper medicine and deter the spread of the disease. It did not matter in the least that this deterrence was effective only in Norton's imagination. His vision of a pure commonwealth now had the force of reason behind it.

The killing of the Quakers also had a theological rationale, as the sacrifices preserved good commerce between the Puritans and their God. Rev. Norton again put it well. The execution of the Quakers "may be looked upon as an Act which the court was forced unto . . . in defence of Religion, themselves, the Church, and this poor State and People." It was not that God required a state to do his business, for he could just as easily have smote the Quakers immediately through some special providence. But "that God makes use of Civil power, consequently of man, is not from his need of him, but his favor to him. Not from defect of power, but abundance of goodness."[54] Indeed, the Puritans killed the Quakers out of goodness and in "all humility" and good "conscience," as Governor Endecott explained in a letter to the king.[55] The Puritans merely "held the point of the sword" toward the Quakers, who in their "desperate turbulency" wittingly went "rushing themselves thereupon." They were, after all, "blasphemers" who questioned the Trinity, defamed Christ's divinity, and undermined the scriptures with their dependence on an "inner light." To kill the Quakers was only to preserve "pure scripture worship" and to preserve the Puritan errand into the wilderness, for which they had foresworn the comforts of old England and had decided to settle among "the heathen." The Puritans were innocent in their domination because they were God's agents in settling the New World.

Such a claim was little different from the Quakers' own to possess God's "inner light," as Quaker apologists quickly pointed out.[56] But the two parties were obviously engaged in a contest to define which vision of the New World would prevail and which parties would participate in the economic project of settling it. Rev. Norton knew this on a personal level, as he received a generous land grant as payment for completing his apology for the Quaker killings. His apology had the sentimental title *The Heart of New-England Rent*, and we have already quoted from it at length.[57] In it, Norton contended (optimistically and in direct contravention of the facts he was supposed to be explaining) that "all orders and persons amongst us respectively, sanctifie God according to the prescript of Scripture, and that at such a time in the regular exercise whereof, we may secure ourselves of a greater blessing than the adversary threatens trouble." This was dubious Protestant theology, as sanctification was a questionable doctrine at best. To imagine that human works could "secure" any blessing from the sovereign God was to walk a narrow line indeed. But Norton's imagination was not focused on salvation, or at least not as salvation had been understood in classical Christianity. The current crisis was surely a "test" for his people, Norton admitted, but "though the Beast blasphemeth, the witnesses overcame." This was the victor's classical argument. When you kill your enemies, you are allowed to describe how just your cause was and what beasts they were. While the Quakers had been beasts filled with zeal, out of the struggle Norton fully expected to "bring forth so much the more zealous and luculent a confession of the Trueth."[58]

Finally, the "Trueth" involved was political and economic as well as theological; in brief, it was civil and cultural. The executions of the Quakers were rituals in a civil religion, accompanied by all the trappings of military technology that the Puritans could muster. Carla Pestana, a historian of early America, was the first to show that the Quaker hangings were surrounded from beginning to end by "military maneuvers" that far exceeded the normal procedures in public executions according to common law.[59] The Boston jail holding Quaker prisoners was surrounded by a night watchman, and a fence was built around the prison enclosure, both to keep out crowds and to limit communication with the prisoners. And as we have already seen, fully armed soldiers, complete with drummers, accompanied the procession of the damned through the city to the Common in a public spectacle. The martyrdom of the Quakers in Puritan Boston was thus as much a show of political as ecclesiastical strength.

As such, it was no doubt reassuring to many citizens. Consequently, Norton could end his apology on a flourish. Having lined up the provinces, God, and the military to his cause, in his final effort to explain himself and his people Norton declared that nothing less than the entire religious project of New England was at stake in quelling Quaker dissent:

> The Rule of doctrine, discipline, and order, is the Center of Christianitie. Sincere and grave Spirits are like grave bodies, they cannot rest out of their Center, ie. the Rule. Religion admits of no eccentrick motions. . . . It concerneth N.-E. always to remember, that Originally they are a Plantation Religious, not a plantation of Trade.[60]

This was a thoroughly modern, even scientific, rationale. But by thus contrasting religion and trade so starkly, Norton opened the way—as the literary historian Sacvan Bercovitch demonstrated about jeremiads—to harmonize exactly the forces he claimed to oppose. Thus he could lament while still celebrating: If New England, which "hath now shined twenty years and more, like a light upon a Hill, it should at last go out in the snuff of . . . Corn-fields, Orchards, Streets inhabited, and a place of Merchandize," then people will say, "New England is not to be found in New England."[61] New England was not, emphatically, to be a place like Vanity Fair.

But this was much easier for Rev. Norton to say now that he had his land grant. In the end, there was no contradiction between the Puritan sacrificial spirit and Yankee ingenuity, at least in this original episode. In fact, the two depended on each other to produce domination that might look innocent. As Max Weber intuited, it was an inner-worldly but still ecstatic asceticism of commerce, backed by a zealous militia and a ready hangman, that led to the founding of this new nation.[62] Fortunately, a recent flurry of scholarship has revealed how the Revolutionary generation mobilized itself to engage in violence against the British, precisely through rhetorical appeals to and economic practices of "sacrifice."[63] To be sure, these sacrifices were conditioned by desires for glory, consumer baubles, and creature comforts like land, shelter, and even tea. But it was the willingness of Yankees to sacrifice these comforts in various rituals, such as hurling tea into Boston Harbor or burning it in bonfires on the Boston Common, that may have motivated and united them in willingness to risk sacrificing themselves and the British in the battles that led to independence. These sacrifices, of both tea and people, were enshrined in public memory as the heroic deeds of "patriots" and "founding fathers," if not the "freedom fighters" against whom future generations would be measured and whose sacrifices they would have to meet or exceed. Over time, the object to be sacrificed shifted from Quakers to youth or Quakers to slaves or Quakers to women or Quakers to Redcoats or even Quakers to tea. But that did not change the basic economic logic. By creating a scapegoat and then executing what they could call a "sacrifice," Americans would secure the "blessing" of a free flow of commerce between God and humanity. Amid the burning of Quaker books, the hanging of four Quakers, and the bonfires of tea that all took place on the Boston Common, the American nation was set on its trajectory as an empire of sacrifice, an imagined community built on blessed brutalities.

Dead Man Walking *and an American Empire of Sacrifice*

Early American history has often had an antiquarian tone that, when not overtly patriotic, makes it susceptible to nostalgic and anachronistic distortion. Such is the legacy of Mary Dyer, who sits enshrined in a marble monument erected in 1959 at the Boston State House, across from her friend and companion Anne Hutchinson. Dyer is a witness, so the statue's inscription states, to "religious freedom."[64] The quotation from Dyer memorialized on the shrine, however, remembers her more accurately not as a partisan for some right preserved by the state but as a zealous devotee of religious truth: "My life not availeth me," it reads, "in comparison to the liberty of the truth." Ironically, this statue makes a person executed by the state into a witness to the state, or at least to the power the state must recognize or take away, a right that Dyer herself would probably not have recognized as "religious freedom." But that is the way public memory often works and why it is necessary to dredge up once more the state's role, in an episode much closer to our time, in presiding over rituals that have little to do with freedom.[65]

Dead Man Walking is a two-hour cinematic meditation on the death penalty, released in 1996. It concludes with a vivid depiction of the execution by lethal injection of Matthew Poncelet, a Louisiana man convicted of rape and murder, who is played in the film by Sean Penn. The movie is adapted from the memoirs of a nun, Sister Helen Prejean, who ministered to a number of death-row prisoners in Louisiana, of whom Poncelet is a composite.[66] Prejean is played in the film by Susan Sarandon, who earned an Academy Award for her portrayal. Directed by Sarandon's husband, Tim Robbins, the film was nearly universally praised by critics for its "balance," evenhandedness, and absence of "preaching." Robbins himself acknowledged that he wanted to make a movie "about love and compassion, and also about violence and our own capacity for violence and our own capacity for revenge. And . . . in dealing with this, I just felt it was really important . . . to not make judgments."[67]

The film's dramatic tension comes from the way in which viewers are invited to identify with the dilemma that an individual like Poncelet poses to a civil society. On the one hand, the character played by Sean Penn is no innocent. The film gradually reveals that he was, contrary to his own protestations, guilty of both rape and murder. The families of Poncelet's victims play prominent roles in the film, inviting viewers to identify with the agony of grief and the desire for vengeance that society enacts and protects against in the criminal justice system. On the other hand, the film gradually reveals that Poncelet was a fragile and lonely, dirt-poor human being. Poncelet's own friends and family, principally his mother and younger brother, are introduced to viewers to elicit the irreplaceable loss that even the execution of a racist murderer and rapist entails. The film's dramatic tension centers on these oscillating identifications that the screenplay, visual images, and soundtrack of the film evoke. It is a rare viewer who is not moved by this film.

Mediating and extending the tension of the film is the presence of Sister Prejean who represents (in her own words) a "face of love" to Poncelet. Robbins juxtaposes this "holy" presence to various representatives of the state, from ineffective or callous lawyers and politicians to the all-too-efficient prison guards and nurse who kill Poncelet. In the final scene, the principal parties come together as the prisoner is removed from his cell and taken to the execution chamber. "Dead Man Walking!" shouts a guard, in a ritual invocation that starts the chain of events that take up the last twenty minutes of the film. For our purposes, what is significant about this extraordinary depiction of a ritual sacrifice is how the church and state, prayer and politics, work together in the process. A prison chaplain—the nun's supervisor—stands watch and makes the sign of the cross over the prisoner, an ironic gesture, since the audience learned earlier that he is an ardent supporter of capital punishment and an authoritarian prig who dismisses Prejean's attempt to love even an enemy. Lest we have any question about the significance of this convergence of forms of authority, Robbins creates a tableau, just before the button is pushed to release the poison, in which Sean Penn is strapped to a hospital gurney, with his arms spread to his sides. The camera looks directly down on the young man, and viewers are unmistakably implicated in a crucifixion. The sterile, technological brutality of the process is juxtaposed to the killer's humanity. He utters his last words to the family of one of his victims, who watch the procedure from behind a glass wall, which is the same vantage most often shared by the camera. "I hope my death brings some peace to you," he utters, but then he continues to issue a judgment: "But I think killing is wrong, whether done by me, or by the government."

Despite a very shrewd series of cinematic maneuvers that do bring "balance" to the film, such a judgment is, finally, the one shared by the nun whose memoirs inspired the film. Sister Helen Prejean has been a frequent advocate for abolition of the death penalty ever since observing her first execution in 1984. As she put it in one interview:

> Execution is the opposite of baptism into a community. Baptism into a community means "We are all connected, we are all one family and you are part of us." And execution is removing a person from the human family, step by step, saying, "You are no longer part of us. You are not human, like we are, and so we can terminate you." When you hear of the terrible things people have done, you can say they deserve to die, but the key moral question is "Do we deserve to kill?"[68]

One can quibble with the comparison of execution and baptism, which justifies an ecclesiastical ritual at the expense of one by the state, in historically indefensible ways. Baptism, too, has produced more than its share of exclusion and killing.[69]

But in her effort to embrace people across boundaries and to question the innocence of the state to execute justice through force, Prejean's argument is consistent with the clearest voice in the film. The scene in the killing chamber is a vivid depiction of a technology of sacrifice, set in an American empire of sacrifice, in which the asymmetries at the foundation of this ritual process are made plain. The state, a murderer, and each viewer are implicated in killing as bureaucrats and hirelings perform their "duties" dispassionately. Poncelet has no illusions about the economic forces at work behind his execution. "Ain't no rich people on death row," he remarks early in the film.[70] The church seems powerless to change this economy, because the protest of Sister Prejean reacts to the process only when it is well under way. Indeed, while the nun offers a counterweight "face of love" to bring solace to the suffering, the church is also complicit in the execution and plays a role in normalizing the sacrifice through banal rituals and pious discourse. All Sister Prejean can do, and we with her, is witness yet another sacrifice to state power, with which we perhaps concur and for which no one will ever be held accountable. It is as if Rev. Norton had come back from the dead to assert once more to an unquestioning audience as he accepted the generous land grant the magistrates offered him for executing his duty: The United States is a "Plantation Religious," not a "Plantation of Trade." Or as a Quaker might have pointed out: the trade on this plantation is primarily religious:

the recurrent practice of sacrifice to produce and normalize the power of the state and its markets.[71]

In sum, the historical trajectory from Mary Dyer to Matthew Poncelet in *Dead Man Walking* may not be quite direct, but it does reveal that capital punishment from the seventeenth century to the present has been surrounded with discourses and rituals that mark it as human sacrifice.[72] Such sacrifices serve to condense and display the power of a regime, to indoctrinate youth, and to prepare for the broader militarization of society. When dressed up in civil ritual and theological rhetoric, capital punishment also serves to cast a halo of innocence and purity over the brutal act of killing. But capital punishment is only a microcosm of the way that religions produce violent power. The macrocosm is warfare. Accordingly, we can find a fitting way to conclude our studies of innocent domination across American history with a brief examination of the "Global War on Terror" and especially the call for sacrifices in the buildup to the invasion of Iraq.

Epilogue

Innocent Domination in
the "Global War on Terror"

Freedom is on the march.
        —President George W. Bush, 2004

After September 11, 2001, citizens of the United States had an opportunity to shape a remarkable global consensus against religious violence. The "blessed brutalities" of suicide bombers might have mobilized Americans to lead a global and interfaith movement to renounce such a use of religion for nefarious ends. Instead, policies and practices emerged that mirrored the terrorists' religious violence, now with the weight of American military might and economic power. As it developed, the "global war on terror" was framed in unmistakable ways as a religious war, albeit in ways that many citizens failed to recognize as religious. These religious justifications, which did not appear to be religious, might help explain why nearly three out of four U.S. citizens supported the U.S. invasions of Afghanistan and Iraq.[1] These wars were not explicitly crusades of Christians against Muslims, or so countless advocates for the invasion insisted. Instead, the "war on terror" fused traditional Christian symbols with elements of the civil religion and cultural religion. Such a hybrid religion extended the sacrificial logic that we have argued led to the execution of Mary Dyer, that caused so much suffering in the life of Abigail Abbot Bailey, that cost the lives of six million or more Africans in the slave trade, and that has had tragic consequences in the lives of young people victimized by the "war" on drugs in the late twentieth century and by the nearly perpetual foreign wars on the part of America during the last four decades.

The attacks of September 11 were chilling examples of the conjunction of violence and religion. But they were attacks whose scope was limited and whose damage was calculated to have a maximum symbolic impact. Their religious grounds were obvious, but the opposite was the case with the U.S. retaliatory war.[2] When U.S. forces invaded first Afghanistan and then Iraq, the justifications came with massive militaries amassed by a "secular" government. But very quickly into the war religious questions began to crop up, and more overt justifications appeared.[3] On one level, these justifications came from representatives of discrete traditions, especially conservative Christian and Jewish ideologues who argued that the war met the criteria of a "just" war.[4] More substantively, however, the justifications for violence appealed to elements of the American civil religion.[5]

Preeminent among these symbols was innocence itself.[6] For instance, the first name for the "war on terror" was "Operation Infinite Justice." When Muslims complained that this name was an arrogant affront to Allah, who alone could dispense infinite justice, the Pentagon changed it to "Operation Enduring Freedom."[7] But both titles bore a patina of innocence. "Justice," of course, is an effort to right a wrong, and "freedom" is among the most durable, if not transcendent, ideals of American discourse. But it was the qualifiers of both terms, "infinite" and "enduring," that masked U.S. exercises of force in assertions of transcendent innocence. What galls many foreign observers about such rhetoric, aside from the fact that dropping bombs on people is rarely innocent, is that in neither Afghanistan nor Iraq was U.S. involvement without a long history of anything-but-innocent precedent. At some level, this war was being waged against the United States' own prior policies. As Arundhati Roy put it, less than a week after the September 11 attacks,

> In America there has been rough talk of "bombing Afghanistan back to the stone age." Someone please break the news that Afghanistan is already there. And if it's any consolation, America played no small part in helping it on its way. The American people may be a little fuzzy about where exactly Afghanistan is . . . but the US government and Afghanistan are old friends.[8]

U.S. policies funded the Afghan "holy warriors" against the Soviets, and U.S. policies provided Iraq with weapons in its war against Iran. By calling its military adventures "Operation *Infinite* Justice" or "Operation *Enduring Freedom*," the Bush administration sought through euphemism to cloak in religious innocence a history of U.S. complicity in creating the very enemies that it now intended to destroy.

But discourses like "infinite justice" and "enduring freedom" are not the only ways that efforts at domination were rendered innocent in this conflict.

War strategy also acquired symbolic significance. For instance, the media routinely reported on the mobilization of troops by showing the tearful good-byes of those being sent overseas. These touching video and audio bites on the nightly news reinforced the impression that U.S. warriors were innocent family members, not trained killers.[9] Another example is that shortly before the invasion of Iraq, the United States tested a nine-and-one-half-ton bomb known as a massive ordinance air blast, or MOAB. The name, of course, is from the Bible, referring first to the son of Lot, born from an incestuous relationship, and then to the people ostensibly descended from him, who were neighbors of the people of Israel. The test of the MOAB bomb actually brought a smile to the face of then Secretary of Defense Donald Rumsfeld, when he deadpanned in an interview afterward that the bomb was "not small."[10] He then confirmed implicitly that the test was timed to serve as a threat to the Iraqis. As he noted, "There is a psychological component to all aspects of warfare."[11] Given the bomb's name, it is fair to suggest that this practice also had religious significance. It was an example of what Mark Juergensmeyer has called "performative violence" in the "theater of terror."[12] The bomb test was conducted as if perfectly "innocent," accompanied with a smile, when in fact MOAB has a "lethal range" of up to nine hundred feet, or three football fields in diameter. That is not small. It also makes one wonder what kind of mentality might be behind a *smile* when considering unleashing such a weapon of mass destruction.

More directly, Americans wrapped this war in prayer, in congregations all over the United States. The Reverend Pat Robertson, founder of the Christian Broadcasting Network, undertook a particularly notable effort in this regard by calling his effort "Operation Prayer Shield." "At this very moment," read the official news release, "America's armed forces—men and women, ready to lay down their lives for you and me—are standing strong in the face of the enemy. They are our brothers, our sons and daughters, our fathers, our mothers, and our friends." Once again, this rhetoric identified warriors with the intimacy of family ties in an attempt to render them innocent. The press release went on to recommend that "as never before we need to invoke the help of Almighty God in protecting and guiding our nation. . . . We urge you to join with us in praying a shield of protection and righteousness across our beloved America for our troops and their families." Needless to say, Jesus' recommendation to "pray for those who persecute you" or to "love your enemies" did not make an appearance here. Two other practices did receive Robertson's recommendation, however. The first was to fast. "Let God know that you mean business as you forgo a meal, a TV show, an activity . . . in order to pray for our nation." The second was to make a financial pledge to Robertson's CBN. "Pledge your prayer and receive a bumper sticker. Enter the name of a loved one in the military and receive special resources to help you triumph in these difficult days."[13]

These practices are clearly "religious"; they are, even, sacrifices, of food and money. But they are not specifically Christian. They are "national" in intent, and they clearly have a general aura of innocence. Who can argue with praying for our "boys and girls?" Just such a patina of innocence, however, created the conditions in which the campaign in Iraq could be justified, even though the primary reason given was that Saddam Hussein was *suspected* of having weapons of "mass destruction," when the U.S. already had MOAB and many more. The ironies, again, are ample. Every assault in the "war on terrorism" did not differ in kind from the violence of terrorist attacks. Buildings crumbled and people died in both practices. The usual distinction—that terrorists kill "innocent" people, whereas militaries follow rules of engagement—takes us directly into the problem we have identified. Setting aside the question of whether a modern war has ever been conducted without civilian casualties, we need to ask again why this assumption of American "innocence" is so durable. Suffice it to say that the qualifications for innocence may not be so simple to determine when we remember that the targets attacked by the September 11 terrorists were architectural symbols of global markets and military dominance: the World Trade Center and the Pentagon. Moreover, for many people around the world, globalizing markets and the American military have been anything but innocent. I am not trying to justify the terrorist attacks, which were cowardly acts of resentment dressed up as courageous martyrdom and which killed thousands of people. Instead, I am trying to demonstrate that the attacks might have promoted a degree of national self-criticism rather than simple assertions of innocence that have since justified violence far beyond anything the terrorists could possibly marshal. In a war, innocence is usually the first casualty, or as Pascal Bruckner put it: "What is obscene about war is the inevitable complicity that it ends up weaving between enemies who think they have nothing in common but who end up resembling each other more and more."[14] As reports surfaced of U.S. involvement in the torture of captives—at Abu Ghraib prison, at Guantánamo Bay, and in various CIA facilities around the globe— the resemblances grew too stark to ignore.[15]

Similarly, coinciding with the way that the Islamist martyrs sacrificed themselves in suicide bombings around the globe was the way that President George W. Bush, and a veritable army of cultural commentators, consistently invoked religious language, and especially "sacrifice," to justify military activity in Iraq.[16] During his remarks at Washington, D.C.'s National Cathedral during the National Day of Prayer on September 14, 2001, the president claimed that his response to the terrorist attacks would be to "rid the world of evil." What it would take to accomplish this modest goal became clearer later in the address when he linked "our national character" to "eloquent acts of sacrifice."[17] At the time, the "sacrifices" he meant were those of firefighters and police. Soon, however, they would include soldiers. Thus, in an address on Monday, October 7, 2002, in Cincinnati shortly before the invasion of Iraq, the president first demonized or scapegoated Saddam Hussein and then claimed repeatedly that Hussein both possessed chemical and biological weapons and sought nuclear weapons. Bush then asserted that Americans would sacrifice, in war if necessary, but ideally such "sacrifices" would be made "for peace":

> I hope this will not require military action, but it may. . . . If we have to act, we will take every precaution possible. We will plan carefully. We will act with the full power of the United States military. We will act with allies at our side, and we will prevail.
>
> As Americans, we want peace. We work and sacrifice for peace. But there can be no peace if our security depends on the will and whims of a ruthless and aggressive dictator. I'm not willing to stake one American life on trusting Saddam Hussein.[18]

Instead, he would sacrifice thousands.

Even the president himself called these deaths in Iraq "sacrifices." In a speech on September 7, 2003, Bush noted that "these months have been a time of new responsibilities, and sacrifice, and national resolve and great progress," now attaching Bunyan's spiritual ideal to warfare. Later in the same speech, he reiterated that the war "will take time and require sacrifice."[19] Then in a speech at the U.S. Naval Academy on November 30, 2005, Bush asserted more generally that "a time of war is a time of sacrifice," thus baptizing war yet again in the religious language of sacrifice. Invoking the Revolutionary legacy, the president declared further that "advancing the ideal of democracy and self-government is the mission that created our nation." Here, too, the religious language of "mission" could not be a coincidence. Indeed, this mission entailed a "calling," yet another significant religious term, "of a new generation of Americans," thus implicating the young men and women in a future of "sacrifice." Throughout the buildup to and the waging of war in Iraq, President Bush cloaked the deaths-by-policy in the innocence of religious discourse. He could thereby assert a future of American dominance: "We will answer history's call with confidence—because we know that freedom is the destiny of every man, woman and child on this earth."[20] The naval cadets applauded. As theologian Kelly Denton-Borhaug concluded, for George W. Bush, "the rhetoric of sacrifice was shaped in a purposefully strategic fashion so as to coincide with perceived American cultural values and expectations. . . . Spotlighting sacralized military sacrifice has had the intended consequence of veiling, discouraging or mystifying hard questions."[21]

We have traced the roots and trajectories of these "cultural values and expectations" across a wide range of sources. How distinctly "American" are they? I do not need to argue that these patterns are unique to the United States. Nor is it necessary for me to show that such patterns are not found in justifications for religious violence elsewhere. It is enough, for me at least, to show that they *have* been found in American history, that religious violence has been a recurrent feature in the formation and development of the United States. To counter that discourses and practices of "sacrifice" for the nation or markets is a conventional euphemism found in other cultures does not mitigate the problem. Indeed, that such patterns are euphemisms largely unrecognized in America and perhaps elsewhere *is* the problem. Presidents have hardly been alone in appealing to "sacrifice" in conjunction with national policies. Thus the "progressive" journalist Jim Lehrer, in what was supposed to be a hard-hitting January 16, 2007, interview, challenged the president to explain his policies by asking him why *more* sacrifices were not demanded. "Why have you not, as President of the United States," Lehrer pushed, "asked more Americans and more American interests to sacrifice something? The people who are now sacrificing are, you know, the volunteer military—the Army and the U.S. Marines and their families. They are the only people who are actually sacrificing anything at this point."[22]

President Bush's response was revealing and also completely consistent with the logic of John Bunyan and Rev. John Norton centuries ago. Bush first insisted that Americans were sacrificing "peace of mind when they see the terrible images of violence on TV every night." This conveniently did not mention that the most horrific images had been carefully censored out of most TV news broadcasts. Yet, the president continued, "the psychology of the country . . . is somewhat down because of this war." This was not exactly "Giant Dispair," but it was as close as this president could get. Bush also made it clear that the way to slay this Giant was, basically, to grow the American economy, to make American into a "Plantation religious" in which the religion was all about trade:

Now, here in Washington . . . they say, "Well, why don't you raise their taxes, that'll cause there to be a sacrifice," I strongly oppose that if that's the kind of sacrifice people are talking about, I'm not for it, because raising taxes will hurt this growing economy. And one thing we want during this war on terror is for people to feel like their life's moving on, that they're able to make a living and send their kids to college and put more money on the table.[23]

Here, then, was the motive requiring the "sacrifices" of soldiers in Iraq, the lives of Iraqi civilians, prisons in Cuba, and torture, if necessary: to enable American citizens to "put more money on the table."

National self-criticism is difficult, and during the "war on terror," it appears to have been nearly impossible. The contradictions between assertions of American innocence and American behavior were not enough to stop the shift from attacks in Afghanistan against al Qaeda—which the vast majority of the world would have seen as just—to attacks against Saddam Hussein in Iraq. This fundamentally irrational policy had religious roots. Saddam Hussein became a scapegoat. This Iraqi tyrant became an icon whose sacrifice would condense the loyalty of a nation and displace aggression into a victim whose violation would not, because he could not, trigger proportionate retaliation. Yet as with the sacrifice of Mary Dyer, the crisis of differentiation in Iraq was not satisfied by this one sacrifice. It would require repetition.

The ultimate contradiction in the "war on terror" has been the contradiction inherent in President Bush's favorite sound bite, which is the epigraph to this epilogue. "Freedom," he often asserted, "is on the march." The innocence of "freedom," which would seem to involve almost anything other than the lock-step uniformity of marching, is expressed here through the dominating policies of military intervention.[24] Ironically, the "global war on terror" articulated what I have argued is the basic religious function: eliminating violence. Terror, the psychological response to violence, or terrorism, the physical cause of violence, was what needed to be eliminated. But the means used as U.S. policy developed, namely, war, ironically mirrored and even embraced precisely what the policy sought to eliminate. This contradiction is, in short, the paradox of innocent domination that we have seen time and time again wreaking havoc in the lives of the young and those who are marked as racially and sexually different in American history.

As theologian and ethicist Miroslav Volf stated, assertions of innocence tend to implicate the subject in ironic forms of guilt:

The tendency to set the morally pure over against the morally corrupt is understandable. We need morally clear narratives to underwrite morally responsible engagement. Yet the very act of mapping the world of noninnocence into the exclusive categories of "pure" vs. "corrupt" entails corruption; "pure" and "corrupt" are constructs that often misconstrue the other. The reason is not simply the lack of adequate information about the parties in conflict. The deeper reason is that every construction of innocence and guilt partakes in the corruption of the one undertaking the construction because every attempt to escape noninnocence is already ensnared by noninnocence. Just as there is no absolute standpoint from which relative human beings can make absolute judgments, so also there is no "pure" space from which corrupt human beings can make pure judgments about purity and corruption.[25]

A "contrived innocence" has often, in American history, proceeded hand in hand with practices of brutal violence.

The problem is hardly intractable, however, and is not inevitable. I have tried to point out some of the ways that blessed brutalities have occurred in relation to specific contexts of age, race, gender, and religion in discrete moments and across discrete trajectories of American history. I have tried to show how various forms of sacrifice have been mandated in relation to first the emergence of a new nation-state and its civil religion and now in relation to an empire of markets closely allied with American policies and practices: a cultural religion. Such efforts to spread "freedom" have been associated with assertions of innocence that in fact arise from various forms of privilege and various efforts to consolidate cultural and material power. Such constructions are increasingly open to scrutiny and criticism.

In the final analysis, beyond critique, innocence does exist, and when it does, it is to be admired. Even more, "freedom" and "self-government" are surely preferable to tyranny and oppression. But tyrants can easily quote sacred scriptures when it serves their purposes or put halos of discourse around systems of practice that do not produce what they promise. Such failures to join rhetoric to reality are more likely when citizens, or scholars, isolate religions in institutional boxes and fail to recognize that religions arise from specific social and political contexts and metamorphose into complex constructions of authority cutting across domains. An American empire of sacrifice has emerged from Puritan Boston to the "global war on terror" in ways that have depended on innocent domination, on efforts to put a halo of blessing on brutalities. But that is hardly the only side of the historical story, and again, nothing in it is inevitable.

In a future work, I will examine the historical emergence of a public presence for religion in American history that points in a different direction, neither innocent nor dominant but actually stronger for the absence of both. That prospect, which I call "a coming religious peace," depends on recognizing that under the conditions of religious liberty and of the rule of law, religions are disestablished of their historic responsibility to prop up systems of force.[26] Under such conditions, people of faith can join with other citizens in mobilizing to eliminate the systemic forms of violence that threaten the free exercise of our most profound collective commitments. Under such conditions, people of faith can join with other advocates of justice and peace to hold nations accountable to be as just and peaceful as possible. After all, nonviolence is already the prevailing practice of human beings everywhere on the globe in our day-by-day relations. Ordinarily, we trust one another and trust in the power of language to build bridges between us through our abilities to persuade one another to follow laws, honor contracts, and so forth. Nonviolence also is the normative life path that follows from the deepest truths in otherwise very different faith traditions.[27] Again, religions exist in order to end violence.

Might it be that religious liberty offers us an opportunity to realize that people of faith can help form societies not predicated on force or domination or blessed brutalities but on something as fragile (yet powerful) as, say, grace or mercy or compassion or collective goodwill?[28] To be sure, the flourishing of such grounds for authority not based in force is a lively and perhaps even holy experiment, with roots nearly as deep as those that gave rise to an empire of sacrifice. It cannot be only an American accomplishment. But from this vantage point, the American empire of sacrifice, perhaps along with other forms of religious violence in other contexts, may be dismantled by the very disestablishment of religion and flourishing of religious liberty that allows religions to communicate effectively those deepest truths and purest practices aimed at eliminating violence. Holy hatreds might finally give way to sheer blessing, and even mercy, in which all can share. At that time, only the brutal will be left out, unblessed.

In the words of Immanuel Kant, in his 1795 essay "Perpetual Peace: A Philosophical Sketch,"

The concept of a law of nations as a right to make war does not really mean anything, because it is then a law of deciding what is right by unilateral maxims through force and not by universally valid public laws which restrict the freedom of each one. The only conceivable meaning of such a law of nations [to wage war] might be that it serves men right who are so inclined that they should destroy each other and thus find perpetual peace in the vast grave that swallows both the atrocities and their perpetrators.[29]

When we stop blessing our brutalities and when people of faith are actually engaged in the ethical practices we preach, then perhaps we will find our ways to write the laws that Kant imagined, which might actually bring peace. Such a precarious path has been foreshadowed, if hardly foreordained, in American history, right along with the religious violence. The very possibility of such a religious peace, however, is a fragile last word of hope in the otherwise long history of the American innocent domination, of blessed brutalities, that built an empire of sacrifice.

Notes

INTRODUCTION

1. The epigraph from Freud is from *The Future of an Illusion*, trans. W. D. Robson-Scott and ed. James Strachey (New York: Anchor Books, 1964), 67. For the Asad quotation, see Talal Asad, *On Suicide Bombing* (New York: Columbia University Press, 2007).

2. See Lydia Saad, "Iraq War Triggers Major Rally Effect," Gallup News Service, March 25, 2003, available at http://www.gallup.com/poll/8074/Iraq-War-Triggers-Major-Rally-Effect.aspx (accessed January 22, 2009).

3. See Bruce Lincoln, *Religion, Empire and Torture: The Case of Achaemenian Persia, with a Postscript on Abu Ghraib* (Chicago: University of Chicago Press, 2007).

4. See R. Scott Appleby, *The Ambivalence of the Sacred: Religion, Violence and Reconciliation* (Lanham, MD: Rowman & Littlefield, 2000); Mark Juergensmeyer, *Terror in the Mind of God: The Global Rise of Religious Violence* (Berkeley: University of California Press, 2000); Charles Kimball, *When Religion Becomes Evil* (San Francisco: Harper, 2002); and Jessica Stern, *Terror in the Name of God: Why Religious Militants Kill* (New York: Harper-Collins, 2004). The list could go on; many more titles are cited in subsequent notes.

5. The alarmism is positively alarming. See, for instance, Kevin Phillips, *American Theocracy: The Peril and Politics of Radical Religion, Oil, and Borrowed Money in the 21st Century* (New York: Viking, 2006); and Chris Hedges, *American Fascists: The Christian Right and the War on America* (New York: Free Press, 2007).

6. This emphasis on millennialism is evident in the otherwise helpful and somewhat balanced Robert Jewett, *Mission and Menace: Four Centuries of American Religious Zeal* (Minneapolis: Fortress Press, 2008).

7. Less balanced but developing the same theme is Rosemary Radford Ruether, *America, Amerikkka: Elect Nation and Imperial Violence* (Oakville, CT: Equinox, 2007). For an uncritical embrace of the nexus of American innocent domination, see, among many others, Ted Widmer, *Ark of the Liberties: America and the World* (New York: Hill & Wang, 2008). For some classics in the long history of religious involvement in American public life, see Robert T. Handy, *A Christian America: Protestant Hopes and Historical Realities* (New York: Oxford University Press, 1971); and John F. Wilson, *Public Religion in American Culture* (Philadelphia: Temple University Press, 1979); along with Marjorie Garber and Rebecca L. Walkowitz, eds., *One Nation under God: Religion and American Culture* (New York: Routledge, 1999). A recent monograph restores our focus on the interaction between Puritan (or Protestant more generally) and secular histories. See Tracy Fessenden, *Culture and Redemption: Religion, the Secular, and American Literature* (Princeton, NJ: Princeton University Press, 2007).

8. See, for instance, the occasionally alarmist but generally reasonable Randall Balmer, *Thy Kingdom Come: How the Religious Right Distorts the Faith and Threatens America; An Evangelical's Lament* (New York: Basic Books, 2006); Michael Lerner, *The Left Hand of God: Taking Back Our Country from the Religious Right* (San Francisco: Harper San Francisco, 2006); Jonathan Sacks, *The Dignity of Difference: How to Avoid the Clash of Civilizations* (London: Continuum, 2002); Jim Wallis, *God's Politics: Why the Right Gets It Wrong and the Left Doesn't Get It* (San Francisco: Harper San Francisco, 2005); and, from the political side, Madeleine Albright, *The Mighty and the Almighty: Reflections on America, God, and World Affairs* (New York: HarperCollins, 2006).

9. See especially Talal Asad, *Formations of the Secular: Christianity, Islam, Modernity* (Stanford, CA: Stanford University Press, 2003); Jon Butler, *Awash in a Sea of Faith: Christianizing the American People* (Cambridge, MA: Harvard University Press, 1990); and Fessenden, *Culture and Redemption*.

10. On empire, see Michael Hardt and Antonio Negri, *Empire* (Cambridge, MA: Harvard University Press, 2000); along with Philip Pomper, "The History and Theory of Empires," *History and Theory* 44 (December 2005):1–27; and Amy Kaplan, "Violent Belongings and the Question of Empire Today, Presidential Address to the American Studies Association, October 17, 2003," *American Quarterly* 56 (January 2004):1–18.

11. Catherine L. Albanese, *America: Religions and Religion*, 3rd ed. (Belmont, CA: Wadsworth, 1999), 498.

12. See Drew Gilpin Faust, *This Republic of Suffering: Death and the American Civil War* (New York: Knopf, 2007).

13. Richard T. Hughes, *Myths America Lives By* (Urbana: University of Illinois Press, 2003), 153.

14. Ibid., 158.

15. Albert I Baumgarten, ed., *Sacrifice in Religious Experience*. NUMEN Books Series: Studies in the History of Religions, no. 93 (Leiden: Brill, 2002); and Jeffrey Carter, ed., *Understanding Religious Sacrifice: A Reader*, Controversies in the Study of Religion (London: Continuum, 2003); Kathryn McClymond, "The Nature and Elements of Sacrificial Ritual," *Method and Theory in the Study of Religion* 16 (2004):337–66.

16. For some of the positive side of the sacrifice ledger, see Bruce Chilton, "Sacrificial Mimesis," *Religion* 27(1997):225–30; and his *The Temple of Jesus: His Sacrificial Program within a Cultural History of Sacrifice* (University Park: Pennsylvania State University Press, 1992).

17. For an early statement of the basically dualistic mindset, see Samuel Huntington, *The Clash of Civilizations and the Remaking of World Order* (New York: Free Press, 2002), based on a 1996 article; and for a more recent version of the assertion of American innocence, see Norman Podhoretz, *World War IV: The Long Struggle against Islamofascism* (New York: Doubleday, 2007). For different perspectives on similar dynamics, see the collection of essays edited by Wes Avram, *Anxious about Empire: Theological Essays on the New Global Realities* (Grand Rapids, MI: Brazos Press, 2004); and Andrew J. Bacevich, *American Empire: The Realities and Consequences of U.S. Diplomacy* (Cambridge, MA: Harvard University Press, 2002). While strong on the military and foreign policy dimensions of U.S. history, Bacevich's book misses the internal religious logic, grounded in history, through which these policies have been found persuasive.

18. See especially Appleby, *The Ambivalence of the Sacred*.

19. Robert A. Orsi, *Between Heaven and Earth: The Religious Worlds People Make and the Scholars Who Study Them* (Princeton, NJ: Princeton University Press, 2004), 177.

20. For one statement of the question, see Christopher Layne and Bradley A. Thayer, *American Empire: A Debate* (London: Routledge, 2007).

21. Advocates of the former term include E. J. Hobsbawn, *On Empire: America, War, and Global Supremacy* (New York: Pantheon Books, 2008); John A. Agnew, *Hegemony: The New Shape of Global Power* (Philadelphia: Temple University Press, 2005); and Donald Nuechterlein, *Defiant Superpower: The New American Hegemony* (Washington, DC: Potomac Books, 2004). I am largely in agreement with the argument of Andrew Bacevich, who contends that America has been under the sway of a "myth of the reluctant superpower," or, as Gary Dorrien puts it, that the United States has been "an empire in denial." It is this dynamic of religious obfuscation, if not the production of power, that I find interesting. Whether one calls it myth making, denial, hegemony, or empire actually matters less than the relations between constructions of dominance and innocence. See Bacevich, *American Empire*; and Gary Dorrien, *Imperial Designs: Neoconservatism and the New Pax Americana* (London: Routledge, 2004).

22. On the history of anti-imperialism, see Frank Ninkovich, *The United States and Imperialism* (Oxford: Blackwell, 2001). For a different view of the same period, see Mona Domosh, *American Commodities in an Age of Empire* (New York: Routledge, 2006). See also the groundbreaking synthesis by V. G. Kiernan that nicely bridges the two disputed terms, *America: The New Imperialism. From White Settlement to World Hegemony* (London: Verso, 2005).

23. See, for cases contra, John Bellamy Foster and Robert W. McChesney, eds., *Pox Americana: Exposing the American Empire* (New York: Monthly Review Press, 2004). For cases pro, see Demetrios James Caraley, ed., *American Hegemony: Preventive War, Iraq, and Imposing Democracy* (New York: Academy of Political Science, 2004). For works with direct bearing on questions of religion, see Michael Northcott, *An Angel Directs the Storm: Apocalyptic Religion and American Empire* (London: I. B. Tauris, 2004); and Matthew Fraser, *Weapons of Mass Distraction: Soft Power and American Empire* (Toronto: Key Porter Books, 2003). A third genre, of lament, has recently begun to appear. See Charles W. Kegley Jr. and Gregory A. Raymond, *After Iraq: The Imperiled American Imperium* (Oxford: Oxford University Press, 2007); and Chalmers Johnson, "Empire vs. Democracy," TomPaine.com, January 31, 2007, available at http://www.tompaine.com/articles/2007/01/31/empire_vs_democracy.php (accessed January 19, 2009).

24. See Hardt and Negri, *Empire*.

25. In this sense, my argument is akin to that of Amy Kaplan, *The Anarchy of Empire in the Making of U.S. Culture* (Cambridge, MA: Harvard University Press, 2002), who roots empire not only in foreign policy (though, of course, also there) but also across domains of "culture."

CHAPTER 1

1. The epigraphs can be located as follows: Kierkegaard's *The Present Moment* is available online at *Selections from the Writings of Kierkegaard,*, trans. L. M. Hollander, via Christian Classics Ethereal Library, at http://www.ccel.org/k/kierkegaard/selections/moment.htm (accessed January 19, 2009); Louise Erdrich, *Tracks* (New York: Harper & Row, 1988), 225; and Benedict Anderson, *Imagined Communities: Reflections on the Origins and Spread of Nationalism*, rev. and expanded ed. (London: Verso, 1991), 198.

2. The traditions I know best in this regard are the Lenape, Menominee, and Lakota. I was raised near Menominee lands in Wisconsin, now live on lands traversed by the Lenape, and have frequently visited South Dakota and the lands of the Lakota. The scholarship on the contours of these traditions and how violence marked so many European misapprehensions of them and led to genocidal efforts to end them continues to grow. For general overviews of the diverse traditions, see Suzanne J. Crawford, *Native American Religious Traditions* (New York: Prentice-Hall, 2007); Suzanne J. Crawford and Dennis Kelley, eds., *American Indian Religious Traditions: An Encyclopedia*, 3 vols. (New York: ABC-Clio, 2005); and Joel Martin, *The Land Looks after Us: A History of Native American Religion* (Oxford: Oxford University Press, 1999). On the Lakota, see the remarkable webpage, Martin Broken Leg and Raymond Bucko, eds., *Lakota na Dakota* Wowapi Oti Kin, The Lakota Dakota Information Home Page, available at http://puffin.creighton.edu/lakota/ (accessed January 19, 2009). On the Lenape, see Carla Messenger, *Native American Heritage Programs*, available at http://www.lenapeprograms.info/ (accessed January 19, 2009). On the early history of violence, see Peter Rhoads Silver, *Our Savage Neighbors: How Indian War Transformed Early America* (New York: Norton, 2008). For an overview of the history of conflict, see Michael L. Nunnally, *American Indian Wars: A Chronology of Confrontations between Native People and Settlers and the United States Military, 1500s–1901* (Jefferson, NC: McFarland, 2007). For one important interpretation of the religious dimensions of conflict, see George E. Tinker, *Missionary Conquest: The Gospel and Native American Cultural Genocide* (Minneapolis: Fortress Press, 1993).

3. This definition agrees, to a point, with those of Marjorie Hewitt Suchocki, *The Fall to Violence: Original Sin in Relational Theology* (New York: Continuum, 1994); and Robert McAfee Brown, *Religion and Violence: A Primer for White Americans* (Philadelphia: Fortress Press, 1987).

4. For a "minimalist" approach, see Gerald Runkle, "Is Violence Always Wrong?" *Journal of Politics* 38 (1976):367–89.

5. For a more recent "minimalist" study, see Mark Cooney, *Warriors and Peacemakers: How Third Parties Shape Violence* (New York: New York University Press, 1998), 12.

6. I adapted this metaphor from a video produced by Ted Yaple, *Christian Faith in a Violent World: Study Guide* (Cincinnati: Friendship Press, 1997), 5. Yaple credits Vera K. White, *A Call to Hope: Living as Christians in a Violent Society* (New York: Friendship Press, 1997), for originating the metaphor.

7. On this, see Michel Foucault, *Discipline and Punish: The Birth of the Prison*, trans. Alan Sheridan (New York: Vintage Books, 1979); and Norbert Elias, *Power and Civility: The Civilizing Process*, vol. 2, trans. Edmund Jephcott (New York: Pantheon Books, 1982).

8. See Talal Asad, *Genealogies of Religion: Discipline and Reasons of Power in Christianity and Islam* (Baltimore: Johns Hopkins University Press, 1993); and for a response, see Bruce Lincoln, *Holy Terrors: Thinking about Religion after September 11* (Chicago: University of Chicago Press, 2003), 1–3.

9. See Russell McCutcheon, *Manufacturing Religion: The Discourse on Sui Generis Religion and the Politics of Nostalgia* (New York: Oxford University Press, 1997); and Tomoko Masuzawa, *The Invention of World Religions: Or, How European Universalism Was Preserved in the Language of Pluralism* (Chicago: University of Chicago Press, 2005).

10. The language of "relational networks" comes from Robert A. Orsi, *Between Heaven and Earth: The Religious Worlds People Make and the Scholars Who Study Them* (Princeton,

NJ: Princeton University Press, 2004). The language of "authority" is, in fact, also Bruce Lincoln's and points to the difference between religious power and political power that I want to emphasize. See Bruce Lincoln, *Authority: Construction and Corrosion* (Chicago: University of Chicago Press, 1994).

11. The language of "desire" here is crucial to understanding the particular passions found in religion and seems a notable omission from Lincoln's elements. This element in the history of religions is most helpfully explored and applied by René Girard, *Violence and the Sacred*, trans. Patrick Gregory (Baltimore: Johns Hopkins University Press, 1977).

12. My sources range well beyond Lincoln to include Sigmund Freud, *The Interpretation of Dreams*, trans. and ed. James Strachey (New York: Basic Books, 1960); Mary Douglass, *Purity and Danger: An Analysis of the Concept of Purity and Taboo* (New York: Routledge Classics, 2002); Ludwig Feuerbach, *The Essence of Christianity*, trans. George Eliot (New York: Harper, 1957); Elaine Scarry, *The Body in Pain: The Making and Unmaking of the World* (New York: Oxford University Press, 1985); Regina Schwartz, *The Curse of Cain: The Violent Legacy of Monotheism* (Chicago: University of Chicago Press, 1999); and Jonathan Z. Smith, *To Take Place: Toward Theory in Ritual* (Chicago: University of Chicago Press, 1987).

13. This is not to say that transcendence does not "exist," only that it is empirically unverifiable, or not susceptible to historical investigation. What is available to critical reason are the historical, social, and cultural roots of any claims to transcendence.

14. On this theme, see Hector Avalos, *Fighting Words: The Origins of Religious Violence* (New York: Prometheus Books, 2005).

15. See Jonathan Z. Smith, *Map Is Not Territory: Studies in the History of Religions* (Chicago: University of Chicago Press, 1993); and Jonathan Z. Smith, *Imagining Religion: From Babylon to Jonestown* (Chicago: University of Chicago Press, 1988).

16. See Mircea Eliade, *The Sacred and the Profane: The Nature of Religion,* trans. Willard Trask (New York: Harcourt, Brace and World, 1959); and Mircea Eliade, *Patterns in Comparative Religion*, trans. Rosemary Sheed (Lincoln: University of Nebraska Press, 1996).

17. Clifford Geertz, *The Interpretation of Cultures* (New York: Basic Books, 2000).

18. Thomas A. Tweed, *Crossing and Dwelling: A Theory of Religion* (Cambridge, MA: Harvard University Press, 2006), 54.

19. Finally, the inspiration for this approach to religion is Freud's *The Interpretation of Dreams*, trans. A. A. Brill (New York: Modern Library, 1950), esp. chap. 6. I cannot explore here the similarities and differences between religion and dreaming, but I hope to do so in a future work. My thanks to Jason Josephson for this helpful analogy.

20. See, for instance, Eric D. Weitz, *A Century of Genocide: Utopias of Race and Nation* (Princeton, NJ: Princeton University Press, 2003).

21. See Michael Hardt and Antonio Negri, *Empire* (Cambridge, MA: Harvard University Press, 2000); my *Shopping Malls and Other Sacred Spaces: Putting God in Place* (Grand Rapids, MI: Brazos Press, 2003); and the feature documentary, *Malls R Us*, for one study of the global spread of commodity capitalism in the particular spatial configuration of the mall as at least a quasi-religious process. The film was directed by Helene Klodawsky and produced by Ina Fichman and Luc Martin-Gousset for Instinct Films and the CBC, among others. A brief description is available at http://icarusfilms.com/new2009/mall.html (accessed February 28, 2009).

22. The flip side of this story is the subordination of traditional religious power to duly warranted political authority, on the one hand, and the critical application of religious

power to political power when it turns violent, on the other. This subplot is the result of living into pluralism, as many observers have noticed and as I hope to develop in a future volume. For some of the trajectories on the U.S. scene, see Diana Eck, *A New Religious America: How a "Christian Country" Has Now Become the World's Most Religiously Pluralistic Nation* (San Francisco: Harper San Francisco, 2001); and for the ethical horizons appearing on a global stage, see Hans Küng, *A Global Ethic: The Declaration of the World's Parliament of Religions* (New York: Continuum, 1993).

23. In the epilogue, I explore the question of whether this American dynamic might be unique.

24. An entire scholarly society, the Colloquium on Violence and Religion, has existed since 1990 to explore Girardian thought. See the group's webpage at http://theol.uibk. ac.at/cover/ (accessed January 19, 2009).

25. Girard, *Violence and the Sacred*, 145 (italics in original).

26. Ibid., 51.

27. Ibid., 55.

28. Ibid., 24.

29. Ibid., 144.

30. Girard's theory has its weaknesses, especially a tendency evident in his followers to speak in exclusivist language about the "Christ-event" as the unique and sole solution to the problem of violence and to cast global aspersions on "religions" that seem unwarranted by evidence or argument. Suffice it to say for this forum that I agree with most of Girard's diagnosis and apply it not only to "pagan" religions as well as to the interactions between Christianity and the civil and cultural religions in the United States. Of these, Girard has said little or nothing.

31. See also the five volumes edited by Appleby with our mutual mentor, Martin E. Marty, and sponsored by the American Academy of Arts and Sciences, which are cited in the bibliography. As with Girard, we tried to extend Appleby's analysis of "religious violence" to the hybrid forms of religion that have emerged in the modern world in civil and cultural religions and especially in the United States.

32. Juergensmeyer's best-known work is *Terror in the Mind of God: The Global Rise of Religious Violence* (Berkeley: University of California Press, 2000). But Juergensmeyer's earlier works were more wide-ranging. See, for instance, Mark Juergensmeyer, "The Global Rise of Religious Nationalism," in *Religions/Globalizations: Theories and Cases*, ed. Dwight N. Hopkins et al. (Durham, NC: Duke University Press, 2001); and a fuller version of the same argument, in Mark Juergensmeyer, *The New Cold War? Religious Nationalism Confronts the Secular State* (Berkeley: University of California Press, 1993). I have applied Juergensmeyer's insights to American culture, a move he did not, for whatever reason, make himself.

33. Regina Schwartz, *The Curse of Cain: The Violent Legacy of Monotheism* (Chicago: University of Chicago Press, 1997).

34. Ibid., xi.

35. Ibid., 6. The quotation is from Carl Schmitt, *Political Theology*, trans. George Schwab (Cambridge, MA: MIT Press, 1988), originally published as *Politische Theologie: Vier Kapital zur Lehre von der Souveränitat* (Munich: Duncker und Humblot, 1922), 36.

36. Schwartz, *The Curse of Cain*, 11.

37. Ibid., 12.

38. Schmitt, *Political Theology*, 39, as cited in Schwartz, *The Curse of Cain*, 12–13.

39. Schwartz, *The Curse of Cain*, 13, who here cites Peter Alter, *Nationalism*, trans. Stuart McKinnin-Evans (London: E. Arnold, 1989), 10.

40. See Max Weber, *The Protestant Ethic and the Spirit of Capitalism*, trans. Talcott Parsons (New York: Scribner, 1976); and David Loy, "The Religion of the Market," *Journal of the American Academy of Religion* 65 (summer 1997):275.

41. Jon Goss, "Once-upon-a-Time in the Commodity World: An Unofficial Guide to the Mall of America," *Annals of the Association of American Geographers* 89 (March 1999):18.

42. I explore the conjunction of malls and religious violence more thoroughly in "The Desire to Acquire: Or, Why Shopping Malls Are Sites of Religious Violence," in *The Religion and Culture Web Forum*, May 2007, available at http://divinity.uchicago.edu/martycenter/publications/webforum/052007/ (accessed January 14, 2009).

43. The most fruitful works have been at the intersection of religions and popular culture. See, for instance, Leigh Eric Schmidt, *Consumer Rites: The Buying and Selling of American Holidays* (Princeton, NJ: Princeton University Press, 1995); R. Laurence Moore, *Selling God: American Religion in the Marketplace of Culture* (New York: Oxford University Press, 1994); Colleen McDannell, *Material Christianity: Religion and Popular Culture in America* (New Haven, CT: Yale University Press, 1995).

CHAPTER 2

1. The Derrida epigraph is from *The Gift of Death*, trans. David Wills (Chicago: University of Chicago Press, 1995), 85–86. The Graff quotation is from Harvey Graff, *Conflicting Paths: Growing Up in America* (Cambridge, MA: Harvard University Press, 1995), 332. An earlier, more general version of this essay was published as "Spectacles of Sacrifice: The Cinema of Adolescence and Youth Violence in American Culture," in *Visible Violence: Sichtbare und verschleierte Gewalt im Film*, ed. Gerhard Larcher (Münster: Lit Verlag, 1998), 169–86.

2. See David R. Loy, "The Religion of the Market," *Journal of the American Academy of Religion* (spring 1996):275.

3. See Edward Shils, *Tradition* (Chicago: University of Chicago Press, 1981). For the most helpful and succinct overview of "civil religion" and "cultural religion" as understood in American religious history, see Catherine L. Albanese, *America: Religions and Religion*, 3rd ed. (Belmont, CA: Wadsworth, 1999), 432–500.

4. On this theme, see my *Youth Ministry in Modern America: 1930 to the Present* (Peabody, MA: Hendrickson, 2000).

5. For these statistics, see Andrew J. Bacevich, *The New American Militarism: How Americans Are Seduced by* War (New York: Oxford University Press, 2005), 19. On war and its symbolic justifications, see, among others, George L. Mosse, *Fallen Soldiers: Reshaping the Memory of the World Wars* (New York: Oxford University Press, 1990); Daniel Pick, *War Machine: The Rationalization of Slaughter in the Modern Age* (New Haven, CT: Yale University Press, 1993); and Chris Hedges, *War Is a Force That Gives Us Meaning* (New York: Public Affairs, 2001).

6. Joseph F. Kett, *Rites of Passage: Adolescence in America, 1790 to the Present* (New York: Basic Books, 1977). This is not to imply that some youth are not, in fact, "at risk,"

only that there is considerable interest and power, institutional and otherwise, in the use of this label.

7. Some fine work has been done on the Ys. See Nina Mjagkij, *Light in the Darkness: African Americans and the YMCA, 1852–1946* (Lexington: University of Kentucky Press, 1994); Judith Weisenfeld, *African American Women and Christian Activism: New York's Black YWCA, 1905–1945* (Cambridge, MA: Harvard University Press, 1997); Nina Mjagkij and Margaret Spratt, eds., *Men and Women Adrift: The YMCA and the YWCA in the City* (New York: New York University Press, 1997); John Thares Davidann, *A World of Crisis and Progress: The American YMCA in Japan, 1890–1930* (Allentown, PA: Lehigh University Press, 1998); Thomas Winter, *Making Men, Making Class: The YMCA and Workingmen, 1877–1920* (Chicago: University of Chicago Press, 2002); and Nancy Marie Robertson, *Christian Sisterhood, Race Relations, and the YWCA, 1906–1946* (Urbana: University of Illinois Press, 2007).

8. For a contrast, see some profiles of effective youth-serving institutions in urban America, notable for their exception to the rule of irrelevance or worse, as found in Milbrey W. McLaughlin et al., eds., *Urban Sanctuaries: Neighborhood Organizations in the Lives and Futures of Inner-City Youth* (San Francisco: Jossey-Bass, 1994).

9. See especially the works of sociologist Mike A. Males, *The Scapegoat Generation: America's War on Adolescents* (Monroe, ME: Common Courage Press, 1996), and *Framing Youth: Ten Myths about the Next Generation* (Monroe, ME: Common Courage Press, 1999).

10. On this theme, see John C. Lyden, *Film as Religion: Myths, Morals, and Rituals* (New York: New York University Press, 2003).

11. David M. Considine, *The Cinema of Adolescence* (Jefferson, NC: McFarland, 1985). A fuller study of this genre would have to include more than the violent films that I am working on, which are marketed primarily to white middle-class male youth and represent violence as titillating spectacles of sacrifice. The genre of "the cinema of adolescence," properly speaking, would also include "coming of age" films, or movies that depict alternative routes to adulthood that do not implicate youth in violence, for instance, *Stand by Me*, *Hoop Dreams*, and *Bend It like Beckham*. Another way to divide the genre would be to compare films that represent the experience of groups defined by class, race, or gender. A film like *Boyz 'n' the Hood*, for instance, includes a critique of the effects of violence on young black males that differs dramatically from the titillating depiction in the films studied here, although that film is not without its own sacrificial elements. The difference, perhaps, is that the latter film does not manifest (or encourage) the callous distance from the disposability and erasure of youth that characterizes the subgenre whose trajectory I am tracing here. On gender, see Georganne Scheiner, *Signifying Female Adolescence: Film Representations and Fans, 1920–1950* (Westport, CT: Praeger, 2000). On race, see Ed Guerrero, *Framing Blackness: The African American Image in Film* (Philadelphia: Temple University Press, 1993); S. Craig Watkins, *Representing: Hip Hop Culture and the Production of Black Cinema* (Chicago: University of Chicago Press, 1998); and Daniel Bernardi, ed., *Classic Hollywood, Classic Whiteness* (Minneapolis: University of Minnesota Press, 2001). On sexual orientation, particularly provocative is Wheeler Winston Dixon, *Straight: Constructions of Heterosexuality in the Cinema* (Albany: State University of New York Press, 2003).

12. On the general problem, see Nick Brown, ed., *Refiguring American Film Genres: History and Theory* (Berkeley: University of California Press, 1998); and Steve Neale, *Genre*

and Hollywood (London: Routledge, 2000). Several works have helped me shape my boldness about genre. See most generally James Monaco, *How to Read a Film: Movies, Media, and Multimedia*, 3rd ed. (New York: Oxford University Press, 2000). For a more focused analysis of the critic's task, see Graeme Turner, ed., *The Film Cultures Reader* (London: Routledge, 2002). On the specific genre of horror films, see Jason Colavito, *Knowing Fear: Science, Knowledge and the Development of the Horror* Genre (Jefferson, NC: McFarland, 2008); Rick Worland, *The Horror Film: An Introduction* (Malden, MA: Blackwell, 2007); John Kenneth Muir, *Horror Films of the 1980s* (Jefferson, NC: McFarland, 2007); Peter Hutchings, *The Horror Film* (New York: Pearson Longman, 2004); Mark Jancovich, ed., *Horror, the Film Reader* (New York: Routledge, 2002); Barry Keith, ed., *The Dread of Difference: Gender and the Horror Film* (Austin: University of Texas Press, 1996); Carol Clover, *Men, Women, and Chain Saws: Gender in the Modern Horror Film* (Princeton, NJ: Princeton University Press, 1992); Vera Dika, *Games of Terror:* Halloween, Friday the 13th, *and the Films of the Stalker Cycle* (Rutherford, NJ: Fairleigh Dickinson University Press, 1990). On the exploitation roots of the cinema of adolescence, see Lea Jacobs, *The Wages of Sin: Censorship and the Fallen Woman Film, 1928–1942* (Madison: University of Wisconsin Press, 1991); and Randall Clark, *At a Theater or Drive-in Near You: The History, Culture, and Politics of the American Exploitation Film* (New York: Garland, 1995); Brian Albright, *Wild Beyond Belief! Interviews with Exploitation Filmmakers of the 1960s and 1970s* (Jefferson, NC: McFarland, 2008).

13. See John Stephens, "I'll Never Be the Same after That Summer: From Abjection to Subjective Agency in Teen Films," in *Youth Cultures: Texts, Images, and Identities*, ed. Kerry Mallan and Sharyn Pearce (New York: Praeger, 2003), 123–37.

14. For a definition of "violence," see the introduction and my "Violence from Religious Groups," in *An International Handbook of Violence Research*, ed. W. Heitmeyer and J. Hagan (Dordrecht: Kluwer Academic, 2003), 323–38. The existence of this "message," however, does not determine how it is received by youth, whose agency in reading film has been a considerable retrieval in the current generation of criticism. On this matter, see Hors Schaefer and Dieter Baacke, *Leben wie im Kino: Jugendkulturen und Film* (Frankfurt: Fischer Taschenbuch Verlag, 1994). The more recent approach contrasts with an earlier paradigm that emphasized the propagandistic or mechanistic "manipulation" of viewers by cinematic spectacle. On this topic, see John Fiske, *Power Plays, Power Works* (London: Verso, 1993).

15. See Mark Janovich et al., eds., *Defining Cult Movies: The Cultural Politics of Oppositional Taste* (Manchester: Manchester University Press, 2003).

16. Isabel Cristina Pinedo points out that the "temporally and spatially finite nature of film" makes viewing horror films both possible and enjoyable, in her "Postmodern Elements of the Contemporary Horror Film," in *The Horror Film*, ed. Stephen Prince (New Brunswick, NJ: Rutgers University Press, 2004), 85–117. See also her *Recreational Terror: Women and the Pleasures of Horror Film Viewing* (Albany: State University of New York Press, 1997).

17. See Richard Maltby, *Harmless Entertainment: Hollywood and the Ideology of Consensus* (Metuchen, NJ: Scarecrow Press, 1983). More pointedly, see Adam Lowenstein, *Shocking Representation: Historical Trauma, National Cinema, and the Modern Horror Film* (New York: Columbia University Press, 2005), 111–43, who connects filmic horror to the Vietnam conflict.

18. Religious efforts to censor films or control believers' access to particular imagery are legendary and ongoing. See, for instance, William Bruce Johnson, *Miracles and Sacrilege: Roberto Rossellini, the Church, and Film Censorship in Hollywood* (Toronto: University of Toronto Press, 2008); Thomas Patrick Doherty, *Hollywood's Censor: Joseph I. Breen and the Production Code* (New York: Columbia University Press, 2007); Gregory D. Black, *The Catholic Crusade against the Movies, 1940–1975* (Cambridge: Cambridge University Press, 1997); and Charles Lyons, *The New Censors: Movies and the Culture Wars* (Philadelphia: Temple University Press, 1997).

19. The history of children and youth is a growth area in recent years, as evident in the Society for the History of Children and Youth (available at http://www.h-net.org/~child/SHCY/, accessed January 20, 2009), which publishes the *Journal of the History of Childhood and Youth* (available at http://www.umass.edu/jhcy/, accessed January 20, 2009). Two recent works give a good overview of this emerging field. Steven Mintz, *Huck's Raft: A History of American Childhood* (Cambridge, MA: Harvard University Press, 2004), is the finest general monograph; and Paula S. Fass and Mary Ann Mason, *Childhood in America* (New York: New York University Press, 2000), is a fine collection of source materials and secondary essays. See also Paula S. Fass's three-volume *Encyclopedia of Children and Childhood in History and Culture* (New York: Macmillan, 2004).

20. See Kett, *Rites of Passage*.

21. For this elision of religion, see the otherwise excellent collection of essays by Joe Austin and Michael Nevin Willard, eds., *Generations of Youth: Youth Cultures and History in Twentieth-Century America* (New York: New York University Press, 1998). For an argument tracing the influence of modern patterns from the perspective of the history of parents, see Peter N. Stearns, *Anxious Parents: A History of Modern Childrearing in America* (New York: New York University Press, 2003).

22. On this connection between film and national politics, see Sabine Hake, *Popular Cinema of the Third Reich* (Austin: University of Texas Press, 2001), who complicates the tendency to locate German cinema between 1933 and 1945 in an exceptional category of "aberration" and instead sees it as "an integral part of the aesthetic and ideological legacies of the twentieth century" (viii).

23. Thomas Doherty, *Teenagers and Teenpics: The Juvenilization of American Movies in the 1950s*, rev. and expanded ed. (Philadelphia: Temple University Press, 2002), 2.

24. In fact, the re-release of the film stemmed from its purchase in 1971, by Keith Stroup, founder of the National Organization for Reform of Marijuana Laws, who bought a print of *Reefer Madness* for less than $300. He began showing the film at pro-pot rallies around the United States, and it caught on. On this point, see Kevin Murphy and Dan Studney, "A Brief History of Reefer Madness," available at http://www.reefermadness.org/writers/authors.html (accessed July 9, 2008). On marijuana use in films more generally, see Dennis Grady, "From *Reefer Madness* to *Freddy's Dead*: The Portrayal of Marijuana Use in Motion Pictures," in *Beyond the Stars III: The Material World in the American Popular Film*, ed Paul Loukides and Linda K. Fuller (Bowling Green, OH: Bowling Green State University Press, 1993).

25. Mark Thomas McGee, and R. J. Robertson, *The J. D. Films: Juvenile Delinquency in the Movies* (Jefferson, NC: McFarland, 1982).

26. J. R. Young, "Dr. Terror Stalks Hollywood," *Chic Magazine*, August 1979, available at http://www.theofficialjohncarpenter.com/pages/press/chic0879.html (accessed July 9, 2008).

27. *Scream* led to two sequels, which together made the trilogy the highest-grossing teen horror films of all time, earning nearly $300 million, according to Timothy Shary, *Generation Multiplex: The Image of Youth in Contemporary American Cinema* (Austin: University of Texas Press, 2002), 296.

28. For the trailer of *Hostel*, also released in a sequel, *Hostel II*, in 2007, see http://www.hostelfilm.com/ (accessed July 9, 2008).

29. Jon Lewis, *The Road to Romance and Ruin: Teen Films and Youth Culture* (New York: Routledge, 1992), designates this "absent presence" with the phrase "nostalgia for authority," leading to a logic of "self-sacrifice" (32).

30. Barbara Creed, "Horror and the Monstrous-Feminine: An Imaginary Abjection," in *The Dread of Difference: Gender and the Horror Film*, ed. Barry Keith Grant (Austin: University of Texas Press, 1996), 41. See also Julia Kristeva, *Powers of Horror: An Essay on Abjection*, trans. Leon S. Roudiez (New York: Columbia University Press, 1982).

31. Timothy Shary, *Generation Multiplex: The Image of Youth in Contemporary American Cinema* (Austin: University of Texas Press, 2002), 178.

32. Stephen Prince, "Dread, Taboo, and *The Thing*," in *The Horror Film*, ed. Stephen Prince (New Brunswick, NJ: Rutgers University Press, 2004), 129.

33. The film is available in a number of DVD editions; see in particular the cutely titled *Reefer Madness: Special Addiction* (Twentieth-Century Fox, 2004), which contains both the original B/W and a colorized version.

34. The DVD was released as *Rebel without a Cause* (Burbank, CA: Warner Brothers Home Video, 1999).

35. The scene takes nearly ten minutes of screen time. See *Rebel*, 45:33–54:54.

36. *Rebel*, 1:34:44–41:50:51.

37. William Baer, "On *Rebel without a Cause*: A Conversation with Stewart Stern," *Michigan Quarterly Review* 38 (fall 1999):581.

38. Doherty, *Hollywood's Censor*, 84.

39. See Richard Barrios, *Screened Out: Playing Gay in Hollywood from Edison to Stonewall* (New York: Routledge, 2003), 237.

40. On this link between masculinity and violence, see, among others, Myriam Miedzian, *Boys Will Be Boys: Breaking the Link between Masculinity and Violence* (New York: Anchor Books, 1991).

41. The DVD was released in 2000. See *John Carpenter's Halloween* (Troy, MI: Anchor Bay Entertainment, 2000).

42. *Halloween*, 00:00–6:55.

43. On this role, see Carol Clover, *Men, Women, and Chain Saws: Gender in the Modern Horror Film* (Princeton, NJ: Princeton University Press, 1992), 35.

44. *Halloween*, 1:15–1:16.

45. See Dika, *Games of Terror*.

46. See John Modell, *Into One's Own: From Youth to Adulthood in the United States, 1920–1975* (Berkeley: University of California Press, 1989).

47. *Scream* (Walt Disney Video, 1997), 1:13:05–1:14:00.

48. In a fascinating monograph, Kirsten Moana Thompson distinguishes three kinds of "dread" evident in recent American cinema, two of which, "scopic dread" and "specular dread," are particularly relevant here. See her *Apocalyptic Dread: American Film at the Turn of the Millennium* (Albany: State University of New York Press, 2008), 25.

49. Bill Stamets, "Bloody Deconstruction," *Chicago Reader,* January 1997, available at http://www.chireader.com/movies/archives/0197/01177a.html (accessed July 9, 2008).

50. Paul R. La Monica, "'Torture Porn' Helps Lionsgate Roar," *CNNMoney.com,* June 8, 2007, available at http://money.cnn.com/2007/06/08/news/companies/lionsgate/index. htm (accessed July 8, 2008).

51. Peter Hutchings, *The Horror Film* (Harlow: Pearson/Longman, 2004), 72.

52. For the USCCB review, see http://www.usccb.org/movies/h/hostel.shtml (accessed July 8, 2008.

53. On this theme, see Shary, *Generation Multiplex,* who distinguishes four (and perhaps) five subgenres of "youth" films between 1980 and 2000: "Youth in School," "Delinquent Youth," "The Youth Horror Film," "Youth and Science," and "Youth in Love and Having Sex."

54. Mary Beth Oliver and Meghan Sanders, "The Appeal of Horror and Suspense," in *The Horror Film,* ed. Stephen Prince (New Brunswick, NJ: Rutgers University Press, 2004), 243–59.

55. On this topic, see Mary Ann Mason, *From Father's Property to Children's Rights: The History of Child Custody in the United States* (New York: Columbia University Press, 1994), who coins the term *superparent* to describe the functioning of the state in relation to children. See also Michel Foucault, *Discipline and Punish: The Birth of the Prison,* trans. Alan Sheridan (New York: Vintage Books, 1977).

56. For an interpretation of how these films might function as tools of resistance, see Stuart Hall and Tony Jefferson, eds., *Resistance through Rituals: Youth Subcultures in Postwar Britain* (London: Hutchinson, 1976).

57. See Oliver and Sanders, "The Appeal of Horror and Suspense." On rites of passage, see, among many others, Ronald Grimes, *Deeply into the Bone: Reinventing Rites of Passage* (Berkeley: University of California Press, 2000); and my *Youth Ministry in Modern America.*

58. For a stunning and provocative argument about the origins of these patterns in American culture, see James R. Kincaid, *Child-Loving: The Erotic Child and Victorian Culture* (New York: Routledge, 1992).

59. While sharing affinities with what is called "ideological" criticism of films, this conclusion suggests that the patterns of discourse and image go beyond ideology into the structure of "religion" itself. For the former approach, see Michael A. Oliker and Walter P. Krolikowski, S.J., eds., *Images of Youth: Popular Culture as Educational Ideology* (New York: Peter Lang, 2001); and, more generally, Joel W. Martin and Conrad E. Ostwalt Jr., eds., *Screening the Sacred: Religion, Myth, and Ideology in Popular American Film* (Boulder, CO: Westview Press, 1995).

60. Creed, "Horror and the Monstrous-Feminine," 46, 40.

61. Ibid., 38.

62. See Richard Slotkin's many works cited in the bibliography, and Martin E. Marty, *Righteous Empire: The Protestant Experience in America* (New York: Harper & Row, 1970).

63. Horror is not only an American phenomenon, although I believe it is fair to say that it originated and has had its most profitable career here. See Steven Jay Schneider and Tony Williams, eds., *Horror International* (Detroit: Wayne State University Press, 2005). On the role of American religions and markets, see, among many others, R. Laurence Moore, *Selling God: American Religion in the Marketplace of Culture* (New York: Oxford

University Press, 1994); and Richard T. Hughes, *Myths America Lives By* (Urbana: University of Illinois Press, 2003).

64. See my "Sacrifice in American Film," in *The Routledge Companion to Religion and Film*, ed. John Lyden (New York: Routledge, 2009).

65. See Prince, "Dread, Taboo, and *The Thing*," 32, who cites a number of other historians to this effect.

66. *Rebel*, 38:15–39:53.

67. The conversation between Annie and Laurie is in *Halloween*, 33:56–34:26; the "knitting" scene, after the children have gone to sleep, is brief, 1:07:25–30, but the knitting needles later help "protect" Laurie against Michael, when she stabs him with one of them.

68. See especially René Girard, *The Scapegoat*, trans. Yvonne Freccero (Baltimore: Johns Hopkins University Press, 1986).

69. Linda Williams thus contends that while it would appear that these films have "matured" in their approach toward women's sexuality, in fact the opposite is the case:

The sexual "freedom" of [recent horror] films, the titillating attention given to the expression of women's desires, is directly proportional to the violence perpetrated against women. The horror film may be a rare example of a genre that permits the expression of women's sexual potency and desire and that associates this desire with the autonomous act of looking, but it does so in these more recent examples only to punish her for this very act, only to demonstrate how monstrous female desire can be. (Linda Williams, "When the Woman Looks," in *The Dread of Difference: Gender and the Horror Film*, ed. Barry Keith Grant [Austin: University of Texas Press, 1996], 32–33)

70. Mark Juergensmeyer, *Terror in the Mind of God: The Global Rise of Religious Violence* (Berkeley: University of California Press, 2001), 122.

71. *Scream*, "Director's Commentary," 00:07:01–00:09:09. Cynthia A. Freeland, *The Naked and the Undead: Evil and the Appeal of Horror* (Boulder, CO: Westview Press, 2000), takes a point of view sympathetic to Craven's. Horror films engage desires and fears and also trigger people's thinking about "evil." This might be true, at some level, but both the reduction of many of these films to the category of "entertainment" and the limitation of public debate over them to the "scandalized" character of their depictions of bodily destruction indicate that the "thinking" has not proceeded to very substantive levels of analysis. The "evils" involved are at the tip of the violence iceberg (see chapter 1) and are not the kinds of systemic, policy "evils" that do the most harm to youth, as the epigraph from Derrida suggests.

72. Juergensmeyer, *Terror in the Mind of God*, 123.

73. Ibid., 123–24.

74. Ibid., 132. See also Bruce Lincoln, *Holy Terrors: Thinking about Religion after September 11* (Chicago: University of Chicago Press, 2003), 16, who points out the symbolic significance of the 9/11 targets of the World Trade Center and the Pentagon.

75. The possibility also remains that marginality is itself constructed as a mask for privilege. The white male audiences who make up the largest consumers of these films, and the white male directors and producers who made them, may have good reason to obscure the role of privilege in access to material resources and to represent themselves as victims. This process of victim-identity-construction operates beyond the categories

of age, gender, and race, but those three constructions have surely been crucial markers within it.

76. R. Scott Appleby, *The Ambivalence of the Sacred: Religion, Violence, and Reconciliation* (Lanham, MD: Rowman & Littlefield, 2000), 91.

77. See the provocative argument of Hedges, *War Is a Force That Gives Us Meaning*.

78. The literature on the contours of American empire is growing rapidly. See Michael Hardt and Antonio Negri, *Empire* (Cambridge, MA: Harvard University Press, 2000); and David Ray Griffin et al., eds., *The American Empire and the Commonwealth of God: A Political, Economic, Religious Statement* (Louisville: Westminster Press, 2006).

79. This extends somewhat the argument of Mona Domosh, *American Commodities in an Age of Empire* (London: Routledge, 2006).

80. See Tracy Fessenden, *Culture and Redemption: Religion, the Secular, and American Literature* (Princeton, NJ: Princeton University Press, 2007). This is also the problem with the works of authors such as Sam Harris, *The End of Faith: Religion, Terror, and the Future of Reason* (New York: Norton, 2004), who fail to realize the irrational (or perhaps prerational) commitments to the nation and other constructs that undergird their own limited views of "reason."

81. Harvey Roy Greenberg, "King Kong: The Beast in the Boudoir—Or, "You Can't Marry That Girl, You're a Gorilla!" in *The Dread of Difference: Gender and the Horror Film*, ed. Barry Keith Grant (Austin: University of Texas Press, 1996), 338. The phrase "monstrous penetration of the bedroom" is from Grant's introduction, 5.

82. The literature on the reception of these films is growing. See especially Cynthia Freeland, *The Naked and the Undead: Evil and the Appeal of Horror* (Boulder, CO: Westview Press, 2000); and Andrew Tudor, "Why Horror? The Peculiar Pleasures of a Popular Genre," in *Horror, the Film Reader*, ed. Mark Jancovich (New York: Routledge, 2002), 47–56.

83. John Dewey, *A Common Faith* (New Haven, CT: Yale University Press, 1934).

84. Mark Jancovich, *Rational Fears: American Horror in the 1950s* (Manchester: Manchester University Press, 1996); Cyndy Hendershot, *I Was a Cold War Monster: Horror Films, Eroticism, and the Cold War Imagination* (Bowling Green, OH: Bowling Green State University Popular Press, 2001).

85. Males, *Framing Youth*.

86. For this phenomenon and drug use, see Marvin Zuckerman, *Behavioral Expressions and Biosocial Bases of Sensation Seeking* (Cambridge: Cambridge University Press, 1994); and for the link with film, see James B. Weaver III and Ron Tamborini, eds., *Horror Films: Current Research on Audience Preferences and Reactions* (Mahwah, NJ: Erlbaum, 1996).

87. See Males, *Framing Youth*, who claims that especially through marijuana policies, "the drug war increasingly targets kids, the least of the drug problem" (115). For instance, drug deaths among teenagers have fallen steadily since 1970, whereas among adults older than twenty, they have risen. See Males, *The Scapegoat Generation*, 162. Of course, age is not the only factor in this "war," which specifically targets young black males.

88. Academic critiques of the policy—nearly universal in their condemnation—seem to have little impact on its sway, largely (I believe) because they fail to reckon with the religious functions of this "war" and because they address critiques only to the level of rational policy analysis. See, for instance, Jeffrey A. Miron, *Drug War Crimes: The Costs and Consequences of Prohibition* (Oakland, CA: Independent Institute, 2004); and Eva Ber-

tram, et al., eds., *Drug War Politics: The Price of Denial* (Berkeley: University of California Press, 1996).

89. For these figures, see Roy Walmsley, "World Prison Population List," 7th ed., available at http://www.apcca.org/stats/7th%20Edition%20(2007).pdf (accessed January 19, 2008). For a wide range of statistics on U.S. drug policy, see http://www.drugwarfacts.org (accessed July 9, 2008).

90. In fact, the prison boom is also a global phenomenon. See Zygmunt Bauman, *Globalization: The Human Consequences* (New York: Columbia University Press, 1998), who details how prison operates to "immobilize," rather than "correct," populations.

91. See especially chapter 2, "Theatrics and Sacrifice," of Mark Lewis Taylor, *The Executed God: The Way of the Cross in Lockdown America* (Minneapolis: Fortress Press, 2001), 48–67.

92. My interest in religion and the memory of Vietnam was initially triggered by Walter Capps, ed., *The Vietnam Reader* (London: Routledge, 1991). On memory, see Thomas A. Tweed, *Crossing and Dwelling: A Theory of Religion* (Cambridge, MA: Harvard University Press, 2006).

93. At one time this rhetoric was evident on the official Vietnam Veterans Memorial website and also was included in a brochure distributed to visitors, sponsored by the National Park Service. Hart's language endures with the help of Wikipedia. See "The Three Soldiers," available at http://en.wikipedia.org/wiki/The_Three_Soldiers (accessed July 9, 2008).

94. Robert S. McNamara, *In Retrospect: The Tragedy and Lessons of Vietnam* (New York: Vintage Books, 1996).

95. The official National Park Service suggests that the memorial can "deliberately set aside the controversies of the war," available at http://www.nps.gov/vive/ (accessed July 9, 2008).

96. Jon Pahl, "A National Shrine to Scapegoating? The Vietnam Veterans Memorial, Washington, D.C.," *Contagion: Journal of Violence, Mimesis, and Culture* 2 (spring 1995):165.

97. As Jeffrey F. Meyer noted, the Vietnam Memorial is, in its earthy simplicity, "like no other in Washington, its statement the opposite of every other architectural statement made in this city of dominant white memorials." See Jeffrey F. Meyer, *Myths in Stone: Religious Dimensions of Washington, D.C.* (Berkeley: University of California Press, 2001), 191. Meyer documents in vivid detail that this imperial city is "a fusion of the secular and sacred, a uniquely modern blend of politics and religion that is nevertheless grounded in the archaic past" (8).

98. "Gibbons Statement on Introduction of Vietnam Veterans Memorial Visitor Center Legislation," available at http://www.vietnamwar.com/vietnamveteransmemorial-legishouse.htm (accessed July 9, 2008). As of late 2008, the plans for the new "center" had proceeded to site evaluation, with the most likely location being directly north and west of the memorial, near the street, which means that visitors are likely to go through the center visiting the memorial. This suggests that many visitors' experience of the wall, with its somber reminder of the cost of war for the lives of individuals, is likely to be preempted by an "official" interpretation of the wall that is, in all probability, likely to reinforce the rhetoric of "sacrifice" so prominent in the legislation promoting it.

99. "Gibbons Statement." It is not my concern to develop an alternative to the euphemism of "sacrifice" for death in war, but I find helpful the commentary of Daniel Pick, *War Machine: The Rationalisation of Slaughter in the Modern Age* (New Haven, CT: Yale University Press, 1993), who contends that "the most productive accounts of war . . . are those which recognise, precisely, the unavoidable roughness of the outcome, the lacunae, the inconsistencies of the execution, the questionable nature of the very enterprise" and that instead "call into question some of the clichés of our current discourse, the platitudes which still have their purchase today, their numbing and exonerating effect" (10–11).

100. On the problems that this link between sacrifice and the nation can bring, see Allen J. Frantzen, *Bloody Good: Chivalry, Sacrifice, and the Great War* (Chicago: University of Chicago Press, 2003); Ivan Strenski, *Contesting Sacrifice: Religion, Nationalism, and Social Thought in France* (Chicago: University of Chicago Press, 2002); and Carolyn Marvin and David W. Engle, *Blood Sacrifice and the Nation: Totem Rituals and the American Flag* (Cambridge: Cambridge University Press, 1999).

101. Hannah Arendt, *Eichmann in Jerusalem: A Report on the Banality of Evil* (New York: Penguin, 1994).

102. See Kevin P. Phillips, *Wealth and Democracy: A Political History of the American Rich* (New York: Broadway Books, 2002).

103. This is especially evident in *Hostel*. The plot follows the formula: of young people seeking thrills, and especially promiscuous sex, in a European youth hostel (a paradigmatic youth-serving institution). But as the accompaniment of their sexual pleasure, they encounter torture, murder, and mayhem, all inflicted by adults.

104. John Lyden, *Film as Religion: Myths, Morals, and Rituals* (New York: New York University Press, 2003), 4.

105. Ibid., 98.

106. Jeffrey Stout, *The Flight from Authority: Religion, Morality, and the Quest for Autonomy* (Notre Dame, IN: University of Notre Dame Press, 1981).

107. This basic confusion between force and power was accurately mapped, to my mind, by Hannah Arendt, in *On Violence* (New York: Harvest Books, 1970).

108. Margaret Miles, *Seeing and Believing: Religion and Values in the Movies* (Boston: Beacon Press, 1996), 23.

109. Ibid., 183.

CHAPTER 3

1. The epigraph from James Baldwin is from *The Fire Next Time* (New York: Dell, 1962), 15–16; for the other epigraph, see Toni Morrison, *Playing in the Dark: Whiteness and the Literary Imagination* (New York: Vintage Books, 1993), 56–59. On Nietzsche, see *Genealogy of Morals*, trans. Walter Kaufmann (New York: Random House, 1989).

2. Undoubtedly the most comprehensive attempt to describe the relations between religion and slaveholding in American history is Eugene Genovese and Elizabeth Fox-Genovese, *The Mind of the Master Class: History and Faith in the Southern Slaveholders' Worldview* (Cambridge: Cambridge University Press, 2005). Other works focus more narrowly but still have value. See especially Douglas Ambrose, *Henry Hughes and Proslavery Thought in the Old South* (Baton Rouge: Louisiana State University Press, 1996); Mitchell Snay, *Gospel of Disunion: Religion and Separatism in the Antebellum South* (Cambridge:

Cambridge University Press, 1993); and John R. McKivigan and Mitchell Snay, eds., *Religion and the Antebellum Debate over Slavery* (Athens: University of Georgia Press, 1998).

3. This is true even of the finest single study of slavery yet published, that by David Brion Davis, *Inhuman Bondage: The Rise and Fall of Slavery in the New World* (Oxford: Oxford University Press, 2006). See also his *In the Image of God: Religion, Moral Values, and Our Heritage of Slavery* (New Haven, CT: Yale University Press, 2001).

4. See, from among many, Barbara L. Solow, ed., *Slavery and the Rise of the Atlantic System* (Cambridge: Cambridge University Press, 1991); Hugh Thomas, *The Slave Trade: The Story of the Atlantic Slave Trade, 1440–1870* (New York: Simon & Schuster, 1997); John Kelly Thornton, *Africa and Africans in the Making of the Atlantic World, 1400–1800*, 2nd ed. (Cambridge: Cambridge University Press, 1998); and for a work that draws out some of the rationale behind this change and its historiographical significance, Thomas Bender, ed., *Rethinking American History in a Global Age* (Berkeley: University of California Press, 2002).

5. The African American church is a critical case here. For the problem, see Peter J. Paris, *The Social Teaching of the Black Churches* (Philadelphia: Fortress Press, 1985). For a still useful historical overview, see E. Franklin Frazier and C. Eric Lincoln, *The Negro Church in America / The Black Church since Frazier* (New York: Schocken Books, 1974). More sociologically sophisticated is C. Eric Lincoln and Lawrence H. Mamiya, *The Black Church in the African American Experience* (Durham, NC: Duke University Press, 1990). The best narrative history is Vincent Harding, *There Is a River: The Black Struggle for Freedom in America* (New York: Harcourt Brace Jovanovich, 1981). The history of African American Islam also is important. See C. Eric Lincoln, *Black Muslims in America*, 3rd ed. (Grand Rapids, MI: Eerdmans, 1994).

6. Jon Butler, *Awash in a Sea of Faith: Christianizing the American People* (Cambridge, MA: Harvard University Press, 1990); Orlando Patterson, *Slavery and Social Death: A Comparative Study* (Cambridge, MA: Harvard University Press, 1982). See also Patterson's more recent *Rituals of Blood: Consequences of Slavery in Two American Centuries* (Washington, DC: Civitas/Counterpoint, 1998).

7. Curtis J. Evans, *The Burden of Black Religion* (New York: Oxford University Press, 2008), x.

8. Davis, *Inhuman Bondage*, 87, observes that "the Atlantic Slave System foreshadowed certain features of our modern global economy." On scapegoating, see René Girard's many works, listed in the bibliography.

9. See Cheryl I. Harris, "Whiteness as Property," *Harvard Law Review* 106 (1993):1709–37.

10. See Harry S. Stout, *Upon the Altar of the Nation: A Moral History of the Civil War* (New York: Viking, 2006); and Drew Gilpin Faust, *This Republic of Suffering: Death and the American Civil War* (New York: Knopf, 2008).

11. Faust, *This Republic of Suffering*, xiii–xiv.

12. On this theme, see Colin Kidd, *The Forging of Races: Race and Scripture in the Protestant Atlantic World, 1600–2000* (Cambridge: Cambridge University Press, 2006).

13. Here see Cornel West, *Race Matters*, 2nd ed. (Boston: Beacon Press, 2001).

14. On antislavery, see, among many others, John R. McKivigan, ed., *Abolitionism and American Religion* (New York: Garland, 1999); Deborah Bingham Van Broekhoeven, *Devotion of These Women: Rhode Island in the Antislavery Network* (Amherst: University

of Massachusetts Press, 2002); Anna Speicher, *The Religious World of Antislavery Women: Spirituality in the Lives of Five Abolitionist Lecturers* (Syracuse, NY: Syracuse University Press, 2000); and John R. McKivigan, *The War against Proslavery Religion: Abolitionism and the Northern Churches, 1830–1865* (Ithaca, NY: Cornell University Press, 1984).

15. See, for example, Peter Garnsey, *Ideas of Slavery from Aristotle to Augustine* (Cambridge: Cambridge University Press, 1996); and Jennifer A. Glancy, *Slavery in Early Christianity* (New York: Oxford University Press, 2002).

16. I am not saying that people are as familiar with the Bible as in the past, only that the authority ascribed to the Bible, through the various "inerrancy" and "inspiration" debates of the twentieth century, has actually increased, whereas use of the text has decreased. See Joseph T. Lienhard, *The Bible, the Church, and Authority: The Canon of the Christian Bible in History and Theology* (Collegeville, MN: Liturgical Press, 1995).

17. Here see Alain Badiou, *Saint Paul: The Foundation of Universalism*, trans. Ray Brassier (Stanford, CA: Stanford University Press, 2003).

18. This process took many forms, often sexualized. For a provocative argument, see Uta Ranke-Heinemann, *Eunuchs for the Kingdom of Heaven: Women, Sexuality, and the Catholic Church*, trans. Peter Heinegg (New York: Doubleday, 1990).

19. On black-white constructions, David Brion Davis traces the negative valence associated over time with "blackness" and how this came to be inscribed along the lines of skin color and ethnicity, in *Inhuman Bondage*, 79. He fails to attend to the converse construction. Fortunately, other scholars have examined the complex constructions of "whiteness," although the vast majority of monographs come from cultural studies or literature rather than history. See, from among many examples, James W. Perkinson, *White Theology: Outing Supremacy in Modernity* (New York: Palgrave Macmillan, 2004). More historically oriented (if problematic at points) is Theodore W. Allen, *The Invention of the White Race*, 2 vols. (New York: Verso, 1994 and 1997), who traces the congealing of American identity around "whiteness" to at least the eighteenth century, if not earlier. A definitive study linking the nation and whiteness remains to be written. For an initial foray, see Gary Taylor, *Buying Whiteness: Race, Culture, and Identity from Columbus to Hip-Hop* (New York: Palgrave Macmillan, 2005). Connecting race and gender oppression is Ruth Frankenberg, *White Women, Race Matters: The Social Construction of Whiteness* (Minneapolis: University of Minnesota Press, 1993).

20. Max Weber, *The Protestant Ethic and the Spirit of Capitalism*, trans. Talcott Parsons (New York: Scribner, 1958). I explore a contemporary application of this logic in my *Shopping Malls and Other Sacred Spaces: Putting God in Place* (Grand Rapids, MI: Brazos Press, 2003).

21. For a reinterpretation of Weber's venerable thesis, see Margaret C. Jacob and Matthew Kadane, "Missing, Now Found in the Eighteenth Century: Weber's Protestant Capitalist," *American Historical Review* 108 (February 2003), available at http://www.historycooperative.org/journals/ahr/108.1/ah0103000020.html (accessed January 21, 2009).

22. My interpretation accords well with Eva Cherniavsky's argument in her *Incorporations: Race, Nation, and the Body Politics of Capital* (Minneapolis: University of Minnesota Press, 2006); and, in a very different vein, Mark Noll, *The Civil War as a Theological Crisis* (Chapel Hill: University of North Carolina Press, 2006).

23. See Stout, *Upon the Altar of the Nation*.

24. William L. Andrews and William S. McFeely, eds., *Narrative of the Life of Frederick Douglass, an American Slave, Written by Himself* (New York: Norton, 1997 [1845]). See also Frederick Douglass, *My Bondage and My Freedom* (New York: Orton and Mulligan, 1855); and Frederick Douglass, *Life and Times of Frederick Douglass, Written by Himself* (Hartford, CT: Park Publishing, 1881).

25. For this way to identify the "domains" of religion, see Bruce Lincoln, *Holy Terrors: Thinking about Religion after September 11* (Chicago: University of Chicago Press, 2003).

26. See Frederick Douglass, "American Slavery, American Religion, and the Free Church of Scotland: An Address Delivered in London, England, on 22 May 1846," in *The Frederick Douglass Papers*, series 1: *Speeches, Debates, and Interviews*, vol. 1, *1841–1846*, ed. John W. Blassingame (New Haven, CT: Yale University Press, 1979), 269–99.

27. See "Douglass to Theophilus Gould Steward," July 27, 1886 (1921), in *The Oxford Frederick Douglass Reader*, ed. William L. Andrews (New York: Oxford University Press, 1996), 313.

28. See Patterson, *Rituals of Blood*, 192.

29. See Paul Harvey, *Freedom's Coming: Religious Culture and the Shaping of the South from the Civil War through the Civil Rights Era* (Chapel Hill: University of North Carolina Press, 2007).

30. See Derrick Bell, *Faces at the Bottom of the Well: The Permanence of Racism* (New York: Basic Books, 1992); Michael Barkun, *Religion and the Racist Right: The Origins of the Christian Identity Movement*, rev. ed. (Chapel Hill: University of North Carolina Press, 1997); Ann Burlein, *Lift High the Cross: Where White Supremacy and the Christian Right Converge* (Durham, NC: Duke University Press, 2002); and T. Richard Snyder, *The Protestant Ethic and the Spirit of Punishment* (Grand Rapids, MI: Eerdmans, 2001).

31. "Transcript: Sen. Barack Obama Addresses Race at the Constitution Center in Philadelphia," [aka "'A More Perfect Union' Speech,"], *Washington Post*, March 18, 2008, available at http://www.washingtonpost.com/wp-dyn/content/article/2008/03/18/AR2008031801081.html (accessed January 21, 2008). See also Linda Frost, *Never One Nation: Freaks, Savages, and Whiteness in U.S. Popular Culture, 1850–1877* (Minneapolis: University of Minnesota Press, 2005).

32. See my "The Inaugural Speech: Religion's Role in the New Era of Responsibility," *Religion in American History*, January 20, 2009, available at http://usreligion.blogspot.com/2009/01/inaugural-speech-religions-role-in-new.html (accessed January 21, 2009).

33. Most notably, the King James version.

34. Glancy, *Slavery in Early Christianity*, 153.

35. Ibid., 154.

36. See Badiou, *Saint Paul and the Foundations of Universalism*.

37. Galatians is the text in which Paul most severely criticizes slavery, but even here he uses it as a metaphor to describe how Christians should be "slaves to one another" (5:13). Paul's use of the metaphor of slavery also extends to himself, a "slave to all" (I Cor 9:19). In deutero-Pauline and other epistolary literature, the ongoing existence of the institution of slavery in Christianity is clearest. Ephesians proclaims that slaves must "obey [their] earthly masters" (6:5), as does Colossians (3:22), I Timothy (6:1), Titus (2:9), I Peter (2:18), and, ambiguously, in Philemon, where Paul may plead for the manumission of the slave Onesimus.

38. Glancy, *Slavery in Early Christianity*, 103.

39. Ibid., 119.

40. See Walter Wink, *Jesus and Nonviolence: A Third Way* (Minneapolis: Fortress Press, 2003).

41. Glancy, *Slavery in Early Christianity*, 120.

42. Ibid., 129.

43. Martin Luther, *Christian Liberty*, ed. Harold J. Grimm (Philadelphia: Fortress Press, 1957 [1520]).

44. For the broader evidence, see J. Albert Harrill, "The Use of the New Testament in the American Slave Controversy: A Case History in the Hermeneutical Tension between Biblical Criticism and Christian Moral Debate," *Religion and American Culture* 10 (summer 2000):149–86; and Genovese and Fox-Genovese, *The Mind of the Master Race.*

45. George D. Armstrong, *The Christian Doctrine of Slavery* (New York: Scribner, 1857), 7.

46. Ibid.

47. Ibid., 9 (italics in original).

48. Ibid., 92.

49. Ibid., 129–30.

50. Ibid., iii.

51. Ibid., 72–73.

52. Ibid., 74.

53. Ibid., 113.

54. Ibid., 131.

55. Ibid., 94.

56. Ibid., 114.

57. Ibid.

58. See also Frederick Douglass, "Slavery in the Pulpit of the Evangelical Alliance: An Address Delivered in London, England, on 14 September 1846," in *Douglass Papers*, series 1, vol. 1, 407–16, in which Douglass directly plays on this blurring of boundaries: "I have heard sermon after sermon, when a slave, intended to make me satisfied with my condition, telling me that it is the position God intended me to occupy; that if I offend against my master, I offend against God" (409).

59. The following quotations are from the Norton edition and are cited in parentheses.

60. There has been some reluctance to acknowledge Douglass's career as a preacher, which he recounts in only one oblique sentence in the *Narrative* (75), but in more detail in *My Bondage and My Freedom*. I follow William L. Andrews in concluding that there need be little doubt that Douglass did in fact serve as a preacher for the African Methodist Episcopal Zion congregation in New Bedford, Massachusetts, beginning in 1839. See William L. Andrews, "Frederick Douglass, Preacher," *American Literature* 54 (December 1982):592–97.

61. On Douglass's religion, see Scott C. Williamson, *The Narrative Life: The Moral and Religious Thought of Frederick Douglass* (Macon, GA: Mercer University Press, 2002); James B. Hunt, "The Faith Journey of Frederick Douglass," *Christian Scholar's Review* 14 (1986):228–46; and Waldo E. Martin Jr., *The Mind of Frederick Douglass* (Chapel Hill: University of North Carolina Press, 1985).

62. Douglass himself used the language of "idolatry," in his speeches but not in the *Narrative*. See, for example, "Too Much Religion, Too Little Humanity: An Address Delivered in New York . . . on 9 May 1849," in *The Frederick Douglass Papers*, series 1, *Speeches,*

Debates, and Interviews, vol. 2, *1847–54*, ed. John W. Blassingame (New Haven, CT: Yale University Press, 1979), where it is recorded that his use of the word *idol* brought "hisses" from the crowd. See also "Frederick Douglass and the American Jeremiad," in *To Tell a Free Story: The First Century of Afro-American Autobiography, 1760–1865*, by William L. Andrews (Urbana: University of Illinois Press, 1986), 123–132, as excerpted in *Narrative*, 157–66.

63. On this theme, see Ann Kibbey, "Language in Slavery," in *Frederick Douglass's Narrative of the Life of Frederick Douglass*, ed. Harold Bloom (New York: Chelsea House, 1988), 131–52; and Dwight A. McBride, *Impossible Witnesses: Truth, Abolitionism, and Slave Testimony* (New York: New York University Press, 2001).

64. See William L. Van Deburg, "Frederick Douglass and the Institutional Church," *Journal of the American Academy of Religion* 14 (June 1977):515–37, who concludes that Douglass was "selective in his attendance," yet "those religious bodies which had attempted to remove both spiritual and physical fetters received his approbation" (515).

65. See David M. Goldenberg, *The Curse of Ham: Race and Slavery in Early Christianity, Judaism, and Islam* (Princeton, NJ: Princeton University Press, 2003); and Sylvester Johnson, *The Myth of Ham in Nineteenth-Century American Christianity: Race, Heathens, and the People of God* (New York: Palgrave Macmillan, 2004).

66. Armstrong, *The Christian Doctrine of Slavery*, 110–13.

67. The relationship between this kind of corrupted or exclamatory discourse and "curses" proper, or oaths, is a largely unexplored area of analysis by historians of religions. See, for one specific example, John G. Gager, ed., *Curse Tablets and Binding Spells from the Ancient World* (New York: Oxford University Press, 1992).

68. In addition to the examples cited later, see the *Narrative*, 24, 61, 63.

69. The political significance of this high value placed on the fragile power of language is what Tracy Fessenden misses in her otherwise splendid and provocative *Culture and Redemption: Religion, the Secular, and American Literature* (Princeton, NJ: Princeton University Press, 2007).

70. "American Slavery, American Religion," in *Douglass Papers*, series 1, vol. 1, 273.

71. Kibbey, "Language in Slavery," 151.

72. Much attention has recently been paid to the ways Douglass promotes a particularly "masculine" understanding of freedom, or at least has been constructed to do so by his many interpreters. See Deborah E. McDowell, "In the First Place: Making Frederick Douglass and the Afro-American Narrative Tradition," in *Critical Essays on Frederick Douglass*, ed. William L. Andrews (Boston: G. K. Hall, 1991), 195–99, 201–8, as excerpted in the *Narrative*, 172–79, who argues that any construction of a "heroic" Douglass depends on an elision of "the black woman's body" which renders Douglass narratives "erotic" and "sexualized," in which the "spectator becomes voyeur" in ways that "imitate and articulate the pornographic scene." There is much to consider in this "gendered" reading of Douglass, but any such reading must balance the scenes of violence against women's bodies in the *Narrative* with the spectacles of violence against male bodies in the text, including against Douglass's own, which are also rendered in vivid detail. See, for instance, the murder of Demby, p. 24, the violation of Douglass's brother on p. 36, Douglass's description of his own unwilling nakedness while being whipped by Mr. Covey on p. 43, and the depiction of Douglass's beating by a group of thugs in anatomical detail on p. 63. Much of the confusion here has centered on the interpretation of Douglass's famous confrontation

with Mr. Covey, in which he turned to "violence" to defend himself and thereby "became a man," p. 47. On this theme, see Darryl Dickson-Carr, "Now You Shall See How a Slave Was Made a Man: Gendering Frederick Douglass' Struggles with Christianity," in *The Puritan Origins of American Sex*, ed. Tracy Fessenden, Nicholas F. Radel, and Magdalena J. Zaborowska (New York: Routledge, 2001), 127–44. Suffice it to say that it would be remarkable if Douglass did not equate manhood with violence, given the prevalence of this convention in American culture, which continues today. At the same time, however, Douglass is less advocating violence as essential to manhood in this story than narrating the story of how he risked his physical well-being in an effort to defend himself from persistent violation. It is ambiguous, furthermore, whether Douglass truly believed that he became a man by means of his own physical power or whether it was the conjuring "root" (and the African religion implicit in such a practice) that he was given by Sandy Jenkins that protected him. In any case, Douglass cites several means by which he escaped from slavery into a fuller humanity, so to reduce his narration to only its gendered or racial or literary components is to impose on the text a simplicity I do not find in it.

73. For a profound meditation on the relationship of bodies, torture, pain, and performance in framing "civilization," see Elaine Scarry, *The Body in Pain: The Making and Unmaking of the World* (New York: Oxford University Press, 1985). For more recent reflections, see Mark Franko, ed., *Ritual and Event: Interdisciplinary Perspectives* (New York: Routledge, 2007); and especially Catherine M. Soussloff, "Post-Colonial Torture: Rituals of Viewing at Abu Ghraib," in *Ritual and Event: Interdisciplinary Perspectives*, ed. Mark Franko (New York: Routledge, 2007), 159–89.

74. The same link between the practice of prayer and the practice of physical cruelty is evident, though less directly, in Douglass's description of the character of Mr. Covey, *Narrative*, 44ff.

75. I do not develop here how the Auld's child, Thomas, and his young friends, wittingly or unwittingly, became Douglass's accomplices in his quest for freedom, but this way in which the patriarchal family failed to control effectively its youngest members is an interesting subtheme in Douglass's narrative, with special implications for the history of children. See pp. 34 and 38, where Douglass describes how the "little Baltimore boys" aided his "lessons."

76. Andrews, "Frederick Douglass and the American Jeremiad," 157.

77. Douglass, "American Slavery, American Religion," 271.

78. "Love of God, Love of Man, Love of Country: An Address Delivered in Syracuse, New York, on 24 September, 1847," in *Douglass Papers*, series 1, vol. 2, 101.

79. "What to the Slave Is the Fourth of July?: An Address Delivered in Rochester, New York, on 5 July 1852, in *Douglass Papers*, series 1, vol. 2, 385 (italics and caps in original). On this famous address, see James Colaicio, *Frederick Douglass and the Fourth of July* (New York: Palgrave Macmillan, 2006).

80. Douglass's ambivalence about the nation endured. See "Love of God, Love of Man, Love of Country," 189.

81. See, for instance, the significantly entitled "I Am a Radical Woman Suffrage Man: An Address Delivered in Boston, Massachusetts, on 28 May 1888," in *Douglass Papers*, series 1, vol. 5, 379.

82. Lee's life and writing have received some serious attention, usually in works devoted to larger themes. See Frances Foster Smith, *Written by Herself: Literary Production*

by *African American Women, 1746–1892* (Bloomington: Indiana University Press, 1993); Carla L. Peterson, *Doers of the Word: African American Women Speakers and Writers in the North (1830–1880)* (New York: Oxford University Press, 1995); and Jocelyn Moody, *Sentimental Confessions: Spiritual Narratives of Nineteenth-Century African American Women* (Athens: University of Georgia Press, 2001). Both Moody's emphasis on the theological significance of Lee's work and Peterson's emphasis on the role of embodiment in Lee's narrative are crucial insights that I seek to develop here.

83. *The Life and Religious Experiences of Jarena Lee, A Coloured Lady, Giving an Account of Her Call to Preach the Gospel. Revised and Corrected from the Original Manuscript, Written by Herself*, in *Sisters of the Spirit: Three Black Women's Autobiographies of the Nineteenth Century*, ed. William L. Andrews (Bloomington: Indiana University Press, 1986 [1836]), 28 (italics in original).

84. Ibid., 29 (italics in original). For an astute commentary on Lee's work, see Katherine Clay Bassard, *Spiritual Interrogations: Culture, Gender, and Community in Early American Women's Writing* (Princeton, NJ: Princeton University Press, 1999).

85. Bassard, *Spiritual Interrogations*, 103.

86. Truth's narration was recorded by a white woman, Olive Gilbert, who served as Truth's amanuensis and occasionally inserted her own commentary into the text.

87. Jeffrey C. Stewart, ed., *Narrative of Sojourner Truth; A Bondswoman of Olden Time, with a History of Her Labors and Correspondence Draw from Her "Book of Life,"* Schomburg Library of Nineteenth-Century Black Women Writers, gen. ed. Henry Louis Gates (New York: Oxford University Press, 1991), 137–39.

88. This interpretation closely follows Wink, *Jesus and Nonviolence*.

89. Nell Irvin Painter, "Representing Truth: Sojourner Truth's Knowing and Becoming Known," in *This Far by Faith: Readings in African-American Women's Religious Biography*, ed. Judith Weisenfeld and Richard Newman (New York: Routledge, 1996), 287–88.

90. Melvyn Stokes, *D. W. Griffith's THE BIRTH OF A NATION: A History of "The Most Controversial Motion Picture of All Time"* (Oxford: Oxford University Press, 2007).

91. "Prelude to *The Birth of a Nation*" [interview of D. W. Griffith with John Huston, 1930], in *Special Features DVD, D. W. Griffith's* The Birth of a Nation (New York: Kino Video, 2002), 5:00–5:18.

92. The shooting script is conveniently included in Robert Lang, ed., *The Birth of a Nation: D. W. Griffith, Director* (New Brunswick, NJ: Rutgers University Press, 1992). The scene with Flora's death is on pp. 120–23.

93. Richard C. Salter, "The Birth of a Nation as American Myth," *Journal of Religion and Film* 8 (October 2004), available at http://www.unomaha.edu/jrf/Vol8No2/Salter-Birth.htm (accessed January 22, 2009).

94. "Reply by Griffith's Lawyer, Albert H. T. Banzhaf, to the Motion Picture Commission of the State of New York," December 1922, in *Special Features DVD, D. W. Griffith's* The Birth of a Nation.

95. See American Film Institute Catalog, "The Birth of a Race," available at http://gateway.proquest.com/openurl?ctx_ver=Z39.88-2003&xri:pqil:res_ver=0.2&res_id=xri:afius&rft_id=xri:afi:film:2099 (accessed January 22, 2009).

96. Judith Weisenfeld, "'For the Cause of Mankind': The Bible, Racial Uplift, and Early Race Movies," in *African Americans and the Bible: Sacred Texts and Social Textures*, ed. Vincent L. Wimbush (New York: Continuum, 2000), 734.   .

97. Ibid., 739.

98. Amy Kaplan, *The Anarchy of Empire in the Making of U.S. Culture* (Cambridge, MA: Harvard University Press, 2002), 163.

99. See my *Youth Ministries in Modern America: 1930–The present* (Peabody, MA: Hendrickson, 2000).

100. See here again Evans, *The Burden of Black Religion*, who links a particular interpretation of King to "a sacrificial Uncle Tom figure, representative of Blacks in general, [who] could through a nonviolent and deeply grounded biblical faith absorb the racial and other evils of American society" (275).

101. See Edward J. Blum, *Reforging the White Republic: Race, Religion, and American Nationalism, 1865–1898* (Baton Rouge: Louisiana State University Press, 2005).

102. The literature on the civil rights movement is, of course, vast. Taylor Branch's two books, *Parting the Waters: America in the King Years, 1954–63* (New York: Simon & Schuster, 1998), and *Pillar of Fire: America in the King Years, 1963–65* (New York: Simon & Schuster, 199) are highly recommended. Excellent on King's religious thinking and context is Adam Fairclough, *To Redeem the Soul of America: The Southern Christian Leadership Conference and Martin Luther King, Jr.* (Athens: University of Georgia Press, 1987). Aldon D. Morris, *The Origins of the Civil Rights Movement: Black Communities Organizing for Change* (New York: Free Press, 1984), is a classic. For teaching, I find valuable Juan Williams and Quinton Dixie, *This Far by Faith: Stories from the African American Religious Experience* (New York: Amistad (HarperCollins), 2003), the accompaniment to the PBS series of the same title, available at http://www.pbs.org/thisfarbyfaith/ (accessed January 22, 2009).

103. Howard Thurman, *Jesus and the Disinherited*, with a foreword by Vincent Harding (Nashville: Abingdon-Cokesbury, 1949), 100.

104. Evans, *The Burden of Black Religion*, 275.

105. This is, of course, what gives film (and theater) its power: viewers are invited to identify with, or to be repelled by, the roles being enacted and thereby to experience emotions that transcend the mundane. An intriguing, if theoretically flawed, argument for the religious function of film is John Lyden, *Film as Religion: Myths, Morals, and Rituals* (New York: New York University Press, 2003).

106. The "conk" scene takes up nearly the first seven minutes of the film, 00:00–7:00, *Malcolm X* (Burbank, CA: Warner Home Video, 2005).

107. "Dignity of difference" is Rabbi Jonathan Sacks's phrase, in his *The Dignity of Difference: How to Avoid the Clash of Civilizations* (New York: Continuum, 2003).

108. This despite bell hooks, "Consumed by Images," *Artforum*, February 1993, 5–6. See also Gerald Horne, "'Myth' and the Making of 'Malcolm X,'" *American Historical Review* 98 (April 1993):440–50. Perhaps most accurate is Nell Irvin Painter, "Malcolm X across the Genres," *American Historical Review* 98 (April 1993):432–39.

109. See here Orlando Patterson, *The Ordeal of Integration: Progress and Resentment in America's "Racial" Crisis* (Washington, DC: Counterpoint, 1997), who sees "remarkable progress" but brutal and lasting legacies of slavery as well.

110. On the significance of the flag as icon, see Carolyn Marvin and David W. Ingle, *Blood Sacrifice and the Nation: Totem Rituals and the American Flag* (Cambridge: Cambridge University Press, 1999).

111. See Benedict R. Anderson, *Imagined Communities: Reflections on the Origin and Spread of Nationalism*, rev. ed. (London: Verso, 1991).

112. John Simon, "Malcolm X," *National Review*, December 28, 1992, available at http://www.findarticles.com/p/articles/mi_m1282/is_n25_v44/ai_13367203 (accessed January 22, 2009).

113. On this theme, see James H. Cone, *Martin and Malcolm and America: A Dream or a Nightmare* (New York: Orbis Books, 1992).

114. I am persuaded to see history in this way by Cornel West, most notably in his *Prophesy Deliverance! An Afro-American Revolutionary Christianity*, 20th anniversary ed. (Louisville: Westminster / John Knox, 2002).

115. My argument here follows Jonathan Scott Lee, "Spike Lee's *Malcolm X* as Transformational Object," *American Imago* 52 (1995):155–67.

116. The script is found in Spike Lee, with Ralph Wiley, *By Any Means Necessary: The Trials and Tribulations of the Making of Malcolm X* (New York: Hyperion, 1992), 174.

117. Lee continued this effort even more directly in *Bamboozled*. See Michael H. Epp, "Raising Minstrelsy: Humor, Satire and the Stereotype in *The Birth of a Nation* and *Bamboozled*," *Canadian Review of American Studies* 33 (January 2003):17–35.

118. Lee, *By Any Means Necessary*, 231–33. The scene occupies roughly six minutes, 1:06:10–1:12.

119. Evans, *The Burden of Black Religion*.

120. I have in mind here Hannah Arendt's distinction between force and power, with the latter being "the ability of people to act in concert" and the former being an essentially superficial (if at times necessary) act of physical strength or violence. See Hannah Arendt, *On Violence* (New York: Harvest, 1969), esp. 39–56.

121. Lee, *By Any Means Necessary*, xiii (caps in original).

122. Cornel West, "Malcolm X and Black Rage," in *Race Matters*, 1st ed. (New York: Vintage, 1993), 150.

123. "Transcript: Sen. Barack Obama Addresses Race at the Constitution Center in Philadelphia," *Washington Post*, March 18, 2008, available at http://www.washingtonpost.com/wp-dyn/content/article/2008/03/18/AR2008031801081.html (accessed January 22, 2009).

CHAPTER 4

1. The epigraph is from "Letters between Abigail Adams and Her Husband John Adams," March 31, 1776, available at http://www.thelizlibrary.org/suffrage/abigail.htm (accessed January 22, 2009).

2. The literature on Native–Christian interaction is vast. An excellent monograph on an early, and pivotal, event is Jill Lepore, *The Name of War: King Philip's War and the Origins of American Identity* (New York: Knopf, 1998).

3. Throughout this chapter, I intentionally link gender, sex, and sexuality as related constructions. Suffice it to say that I concur with theorists like Michael L. Wilson who suggest that "the sex/gender distinction has been increasingly eroded. . . . Biological knowledge of sex differences cannot be considered reliable, transparent, or innocent." I realize there might be much to be gained politically from disentangling gender from sex and from distinguishing sexual practice from sexual identity. Yet the emphasis that modern individuals put on a discrete realm of sex or sexuality was largely not familiar to early Americans, who blurred realms of desire, discourse, enchantment, ecstasy, and

more. I am persuaded, in short, by Judith Butler to see "performativity" all the way down. See Michael L. Wilson, "Thoughts on the History of Sexuality, Forum: Reconsidering Early American Sexuality," and Anne G. Myles, "Queering the Study of Early American Sexuality," both in *William and Mary Quarterly* 60 (January 2003), available at http://www. historycooperative.org/journals/wm/60/1/forum_wilson.html (accessed July 16, 2008). On Butler's extensive influence, I have found helpful Moya Lloyd, *Judith Butler: From Norms to Politics* (Cambridge, MA: Polity Press, 2007); Vicki Kirby, *Judith Butler: Live Theory* (London: Continuum, 2006); and Sara Salih, *Judith Butler* (New York: Routledge, 2002). My thanks to Anthony Petro for his help on these topics.

4. For a general history of the women's suffrage movement in the United States, see Robert Cooney, *Winning the Vote: The Triumph of the American Woman Suffrage Movement* (Santa Cruz, CA: National Women's History Project / American Graphic Press, 2005). On Stanton, see Ellen Carol DuBois and Richard Candida Smith, eds., *Elizabeth Cady Stanton, Feminist as Thinker: A Reader in Documents and Essays* (New York: New York University Press, 2007); and Kathi Kern, *Mrs. Stanton's Bible* (Ithaca, NY: Cornell University Press, 2001).

5. The language of "regulating" sexuality is found in Janet R. Jakobsen and Ann Pellegrini, *Love the Sin: Sexual Regulation and the Limits of Religious Tolerance* (New York: New York University Press, 2003), whose contention that sexual freedom is a form of religious freedom frames the outer limits of both the contexts of this essay and the normative trajectory toward which it argues.

6. For a classic examination of a well-known episode, see Carol F. Karlsen, *The Devil in the Shape of a Woman: Witchcraft in Colonial New England* (New York: Norton, 1987). Building on this approach to the history of women in early America is Elisabeth Reis, *Damned Women: Sinners and Witches in Puritan New England* (Ithaca, NY: Cornell University Press, 1997). For another well-known episode in early America and its implications regarding constructions of gender (the Antinomian controversy), see Jane Kamensky, *Governing the Tongue: The Politics of Speech in Early New England* (Cambridge: Cambridge University Press, 1997). The best overview of the relationship between women and religion in early America is Marilyn J. Westerkamp, *Women and Religion in Early America, 1600–1850* (New York: Routledge, 1999). Helpful are recent essays collected in Catherine A. Brekus, ed., *The Religious History of American Women: Reimagining the Past* (Chapel Hill: University of North Carolina Press, 2007).

7. For a provocative study of how this pattern appeared in a later period of American history, see Betty A. DeBerg, *Ungodly Women: Gender and the First Wave of American Fundamentalism, 1875–1925* (Philadelphia: Fortress Press, 1987).

8. I realize that the language of "agency" is itself contested. As I use it, "agency" is never single but always the result of complex contingencies, including embodiment, social context, region, class, and race. The ideal, however, has no doubt been formative in American culture, as evident in the massive work of political philosophy with a historical patina. See James E. Block, *A Nation of Agents: The American Path to a Modern Self and Society* (Cambridge, MA: Harvard University Press, 2002). My own thinking has been informed by a range of feminist theologians and philosophers, many of whom are profiled in Diana Meyers, "Feminist Perspectives on the Self," *Stanford Encyclopedia of Philosophy*, available at http://plato.stanford.edu/entries/feminism-self/ (accessed January 22, 2009), but the most profound influence on me has been Sallie McFague, *Models of God: Theol-*

ogy for an Ecological, Nuclear Age (Minneapolis: Fortress Press, 1987), whose work I have taught nearly every year of my nearly twenty years of teaching to an audience.

9. See Nancy F. Cott, *Public Vows: A History of Marriage and the Nation* (Cambridge, MA: Harvard University Press, 2000). The relationship of constructions of marriage, heterosexuality, and the nation-state are fascinating and complex across eras of American history. For one provocative argument about the mid-twentieth-century relationships, see Margot Canaday, "Building a Straight State: Sexuality and Social Citizenship under the 1944 G.I. Bill," *Journal of American History* 90, no. 3 (2003):935–57.

10. Kaplan's phrase nicely highlights the intersection of foreign policy with domestic practice. See Amy Kaplan, *The Anarchy of Empire in the Making of U.S. Culture* (Cambridge, MA: Harvard University Press, 2002). The most prominent agencies active in targeting gay and lesbian practice are the Family Research Council, www.frc.org, and Focus on the Family, www.family.org and www.focusonthefamily.com (accessed January 22, 2009). Both are informed by an evangelical or fundamentalist form of Christianity and were influential in the presidential administration of George W. Bush. For one account of some consequences of this current form of backlash against the sexual revolution, see Chesire Calhoun, *Feminism, the Family, and the Politics of the Closet: Lesbianism and Gay Displacement* (New York: Oxford University Press, 2000). The term *homosexual* was coined in 1869; for one history, see Francis Mark Mondimore, *A Natural History of Homosexuality* (Baltimore: Johns Hopkins University Press, 1996).

11. This is not to say that women do not continue to suffer disabilities and injustice. See Laura Flanders, ed., with Phoebe St. John and Livia Tenzer, *The W Effect: Bush's War on Women* (New York: Feminist Press at the City University of New York, 2004).

12. See Laura Briggs, *Reproducing Empire: Race, Sex, Science, and U.S. Imperialism in Puerto Rico* (Berkeley: University of California Press, 2002).

13. Ann Taves, ed., *Religion and Domestic Violence in Early New England: The Memoirs of Abigail Abbot Bailey* (Bloomington: Indiana University Press, 1988).

14. Taves appeals to this change twice, initially writing that for Abigail, "God began to replace her husband as the one on whom she depended, for whom she longed and with whom she shared intimate fellowship" (19). To put it so starkly is to surface exactly the issue that needs causal clarification: did Abigail turn increasingly to God as Asa proved unreliable, or did Asa begin to prove increasingly unreliable as Abigail turned toward God? I believe that the process probably worked both ways, in a mutually reinforcing cycle of misunderstanding (on Abigail's part) and abusive efforts to control Abigail (by Asa). Taves also claims that religion helped Abigail "shift her feelings of dependence from Asa to God" (20). I see little evidence of this from Abigail's own words. Rather, Abigail came to trust in other men and in her own agency, of which "God" was, on the level open to historical analysis, an imaginative projection.

15. Taves, *Religion and Domestic Violence*, 174.

16. In theological terms, this suggests that Abigail participated in a much larger shift in American culture from a strict Calvinist, predestinarian view of God's agency to one making more room for human participation, often described as "Arminian." On this theme, see my *Paradox Lost: Free Will and Political Liberty in American Culture, 1630–1760* (Baltimore: Johns Hopkins University Press, 1992); and Allen C. Guelzo, *Edwards on the Will: A Century of American Theological Debate* (Middletown, CT: Wesleyan University Press, 1989).

17. Hendrik Hartog, *Man and Wife in America: A History* (Cambridge, MA: Harvard University Press, 2000), 49.

18. See Richard Godbeer, *Sexual Revolution in Early America* (Baltimore: Johns Hopkins University Press, 2002).

19. See Catherine A. Brekus, *Strangers and Pilgrims: Female Preaching in America, 1740–1845* (Chapel Hill: University of North Carolina Press, 1998), who builds on the earlier conclusions of Ann Douglas, *The Feminization of American Culture* (New York: Knopf, 1977); Mary P. Ryan, "A Women's Awakening: Evangelical Religion and the Families of Utica, New York, 1800–1840," *American Quarterly* 30 (winter 1978):602–23; and Richard Shiels, "The Feminization of American Congregationalism, 1730–1835," *American Quarterly* 33 (1981):46–62.

20. I thus align myself with feminist theorists who agree with what Elizabeth Hackett and Sally Haslanger call "the dominance approach." See Elizabeth Hackett and Sally Haslanger, *Theorizing Feminisms: A Reader* (New York: Oxford University Press, 2006). This is also why I take the risky step of reading into Abigail's prose the story of her abusive husband and beginning with it rather than (as one reader suggested) beginning with Abigail's own story, in her own words, and then turning to Asa's tale. In fact, Asa's dominance was the legal and cultural foundation of their relationship, as Abigail's words repeatedly confirm.

21. Two monographs that are foundational to understanding the following argument are Jon Butler, *Awash in a Sea of Faith: Christianizing the American People* (Cambridge, MA: Harvard University Press, 2000); and Christine Leigh Heyrman, *Southern Cross: The Beginnings of the Bible Belt* (Chapel Hill: University of North Carolina Press, 1997). Following Butler, I read Bailey's story as a microcosm of the "Christianizing" influence in American culture, in ways that produced both democratizing effects and violence. See Nathan Hatch, *The Democratization of American Christianity* (New Haven, CT: Yale University Press, 1989). Following Heyrman, I read Bailey's story as a tale of how religion both accommodated and resisted "family values," or patriarchal structures that eventually became the ideology of the "separate spheres."

22. Brekus, *Strangers and Pilgrims*, 72.

23. Susan Juster, "To Slay the Beast: Visionary Women in the Early Republic," in *A Mighty Baptism: Race, Gender, and the Creation of American Protestantism*, ed. Susan Juster and Lisa McFarlane (Ithaca, NY: Cornell University Press, 1996), 23.

24. The most famous, no doubt, is Mary Rowlandson, *The Sovereignty and Goodness of God: Together with the Faithfulness of His Promises Displayed: Being a Narrative of the Captivity and Restoration of Mrs. Mary Rowlandson and Related Documents*, ed. Neal Salisbury (Boston: Bedford Books, 1997 [1682]). A helpful collection is Alden T. Vaughan and Edward W. Clark, eds., *Puritans among the Indians: Accounts of Captivity and Redemption, 1676–1724* (Cambridge, MA: Harvard University Press, 1981). An influential interpretation is Gary L. Ebersole, *Captured by Texts: Puritan to Postmodern Images of Indian Captivity* (Charlottesville: University Press of Virginia, 1995). A recent spate of works have deepened our awareness of the complex interactions among the variables in these narratives. See especially Teresa Toulouse, *The Captive's Position: Female Narrative, Male Identity, and Royal Authority in Colonial New England* (Philadelphia: University of Pennsylvania Press, 2007); and, on "captivity" in a very different (but related) sense, Jason Haslam and Julia M. Wright, eds., *Captivating Subjects: Writing Confinement, Citizenship, and Nationhood in the Nineteenth Century* (Toronto: University of Toronto Press, 2005).

25. Taves, *Religion and Domestic Violence*, 66.

26. This conjunction of providence with moralism is the crucial dynamic I see, in my *Paradox Lost*, in place during this period of American history. Providential thinking is a kinder, gentler version of the paranoid style in American politics, first unearthed by Richard Hofstadter in "The Paranoid Style in American Politics," *Harper's Magazine* (November 1964):77–86 (and later extended into a book of essays bearing the same title), which was nuanced and put in conjunction with early American moralism by Gordon S. Wood, in "Conspiracy and the Paranoid Style: Causality and Deceit in the Eighteenth Century," *William and Mary Quarterly*, 3rd ser., 39 (1982):401–41.

27. See Linda K. Kerber, *Women of the Republic: Intellect and Ideology in Revolutionary America* (Chapel Hill: University of North Carolina Press, 1980).

28. As an activist, I serve on the board of directors of Lutheran Settlement House, which runs a domestic violence hotline and shelter for women and children who have suffered from domestic abuse and violence. For these women, Abigail's story is anything but an antiquarian account. See the LSH webpage at http://www.lutheransettlement.org/ (accessed January 22, 2009).

29. On this theme of silencing, see Jon Pahl, ed., *An American Teacher: Coming of Age, and Coming Out—The Memoirs of Loretta Coller* (Conshohocken, PA: Infinity Publishing, 2009).

30. For a good survey of how rape and sexual violence were handled legally and culturally in early America, see Sharon Block, *Rape and Sexual Power in Early America* (Chapel Hill: University of North Carolina Press, 2006).

31. Interestingly, however, Asa could not find anyone willing to purchase his land, suggesting that there was resistance,, even if passive, to his efforts to control his own affairs.

32. I have taught this text to both undergraduates and graduate students and in almost every case have had to turn conversation away from how Abigail "put up with" Asa for so long in order to engage students in serious consideration of Asa's motivations and behaviors. Such blaming of the victim is a recurrent feature of gender dynamics in many cultures, as historical studies of rape demonstrate. See Merril D. Smith, ed., *The Encyclopedia of Rape* (Westport, CT: Greenwood Press, 2004). For a broader study of contemporary relations between religion and violence against women, including some explanations for "why women stay," see the work of my former colleague, Pamela Cooper-White, *The Cry of Tamar: Violence against Women and the Church's Response* (Minneapolis: Fortress Press, 1995).

33. Bruce Lincoln, *Holy Terrors: Thinking about Religion after September 11* (Chicago: University of Chicago Press, 2003).

34. Abigail included the letter in effects she packed for Asa to take with him when he was first exiled from the family home, at Abigail's insistence, on September 8, 1790. How the letter survived to be transcribed in the *Memoirs* is unclear.

35. Taves, *Religion and Domestic Violence*, 94.

36. See *Commentaries on the Laws of England* , 4 vols. (Chicago: University of Chicago Press, 1979). Monographs on the topic include Marylynn Salmon, *Women and the Law of Property in Early America* (Chapel Hill: University of North Carolina Press, 1986); and Kathleen L. Sullivan, *Constitutional Context: Women and Rights Discourse in Nineteenth-Century America* (Baltimore: Johns Hopkins University Press, 2007).

37. Hendrik Hartog, *Man and Wife in America: A History* (Cambridge, MA: Harvard University Press, 2000), includes a chapter on the legal issues surrounding Abigail Bailey's case (40–63).

38. See Cott, *Public Vows*, 55.

39. Brekus, *Strangers and Pilgrims*, 27.

40. The history of American family life is gradually being written. See the excellent collection Susan M. Ross, ed., *American Families Past and Present: Social Perspectives on Transformations* (New Brunswick, NJ: Rutgers University Press, 2006).

41. See François Furstenberg, *In the Name of the Father: Washington's Legacy, Slavery, and the Making of a Nation* (New York: Penguin Press, 2006).

42. Tangentially relevant here is the provocative classic by J. G. A. Pocock, *The Machiavellian Moment: Florentine Political Thought and the Atlantic Republican Tradition* (Princeton, NJ: Princeton University Press, 1975), which posited a hypermasculine *virtu* at the root of Republican arisings.

43. The literature on constructions of manhood in American history is flourishing. See the groundbreaking Gail Bederman, *Manliness and Civilization: A Cultural History of Gender and Race in the United States, 1880–1917* (Chicago: University of Chicago Press, 1995); and Susan Juster, *Disorderly Women: Sexual Politics and Evangelicalism in Revolutionary New England* (Ithaca, NY: Cornell University Press, 1994), esp. chap. 4, "To Grow Up into a State of Manhood: The Sexual Politics of Evangelicalism in Revolutionary America." On an earlier period, see Lisa Wilson, *Ye Heart of a Man: The Domestic Life of Men in Colonial New England* (New Haven, CT: Yale University Press, 1999); and Ann M. Little, *Abraham in Arms: War and Gender in Colonial New England* (Philadelphia: University of Pennsylvania Press, 2007). For a nicely nuanced study in a later period, see John Pettegrew, *Brutes in Suits: Male Sensibility in America, 1890–1920* (Baltimore: Johns Hopkins University Press, 2007). A delightful general history is Michael S. Kimmel, *Manhood in America: A Cultural History*, 2nd ed. (New York: Oxford University Press, 2006).

44. Nancy F. Cott, *The Bonds of Womanhood: "Woman's Sphere" in New England, 1780–1835*, 2nd ed. (New Haven, CT: Yale University Press, 1997).

45. For another example, see Anya Jabour, *Marriage in the Early Republic: Elizabeth and William Wirt and the Companionate Ideal* (Baltimore: Johns Hopkins University Press, 1998).

46. Susan Juster, "The Spirit and the Flesh: Gender, Language, and Sexuality in American Protestantism," in *New Directions in American Religious History*, ed. Harry S. Stout and D. G. Hart (New York: Oxford University Press, 1997), 350.

47. For the origins of this notion of "backlash," see Susan Faludi, *Backlash: The Undeclared War Against American Women* (New York: Crown, 1991).

48. See Susan Hall Lindley, *"You have Stept out of your Place": A History of Women and Religion in America* (Louisville: Westminster John Knox Press, 1996).

49. Taves, *Religion and Domestic Violence*, 99.

50. Ibid., 60–61.

51. Ibid., 61.

52. This could also work in reverse, as historian Leslie J. Lindenauer has shown about an earlier period in American history:

A married woman could juxtapose her own piety against her husband's impurity in ways that convinced the court to undermine laws of coverture. When a wife could prove that by his impious behavior a husband had violated the terms of the marriage contract, she could wrest control of property in the name of protecting and supporting herself and her children. (*Piety and Power: Gender and Religious Culture in the American Colonies, 1630–1700* [New York: Routledge, 2002], 58)

More recently, both pious women and men have used religious rhetoric to claim power or recover privilege. See R. Marie Griffith, *God's Daughters: Evangelical Women and the Power of Submission* (Berkeley: University of California Press, 1997).

53. Taves, *Religion and Domestic Violence*, 118.

54. Ibid., 104–5.

55. Ibid., 105.

56. Hartog, *Man and Wife in America*, 49.

57. Taves, *Religion and Domestic Violence*, 63, 67.

58. Ibid., 69.

59. Ibid.

60. Ibid., 75.

61. Words like *noise, rout,* and so forth were also characteristic terms by which opponents of evangelical revivals described them. See especially the debates between Jonathan Edwards and Charles Chauncy, excerpted in Alan Heimert and Perry Miller, eds., *The Great Awakening: Documents Illustrating the Crisis and Its Consequences* (Indianapolis: Bobbs-Merrill, 1967).

62. Taves, *Religion and Domestic Violence*, 122–32. Abigail's recollection of their conversation for this day is by far the longest description of any single incident in the *Memoirs*. We can surmise that the crucial dynamic between Asa and Abigail can be located here, in the contrast he draws between his "power" and her "piety."

63. The place of the patriarch in early American family life has been described by Philip J. Greven in several groundbreaking books, particularly *The Protestant Temperament: Patterns of Child-Rearing, Religious Experience, and the Self in Early America* (New York: Knopf, 1977).

64. Juster, "The Spirit and the Flesh," 350.

65. Ibid.

66. For a provocative interpretation that at certain points accords with my argument here, see Thomas A. Foster, *Sex and the Eighteenth-Century Man: Massachusetts and the History of Sexuality in America* (Boston: Beacon Press, 2006).

67. See Marilyn J. Westerkamp, *Women and Religion in Early America, 1600–1850* (New York: Routledge, 1999).

68. Taves, *Religion and Domestic Violence*, 56.

69. Ibid.

70. In his careful treatment of Abigail's *Memoirs*, Hendrik Hartog explains Abigail's subordination under the laws of coverture did not produce a loss of self so much as the emergence of a "submissive self" (*Man and Wife*, 41).

71. Taves, *Religion and Domestic Violence*, 57.

72. Ibid., 58.

73. Ibid., 62.

74. Ibid., 71.

75. Ibid., 74.

76. Ibid., 116. On the journey to New York with Asa, Abigail described the mentality in particularly vivid metaphors: 'I was shut up, and could do nothing" (132).

77. Taves, *Religion and Domestic Violence*, 95.

78. Ibid., 125.

79. Ibid., 126.

80. Ibid.

81. Ibid., 32.

82. Ibid., 74.

83. Ibid., 103.

84. Ibid., 109.

85. Ibid., 116–17.

86. Hartog, *Man and Wife in America*, 41.

87. Taves, *Religion and Domestic Violence*, 65–66.

88. This level of participation in economic life was not uncommon among women in early New England. See Laurel Thatcher Ulrich, *Good Wives: Image and Reality in the Lives of Women in Northern New England, 1650–1750* (New York: Knopf, 1982); and the more recent, focused study by Lisa Norling, *Captain Ahab Had a Wife: New England Women and the Whalefishery, 1720–1870* (Chapel Hill: University of North Carolina Press, 2000).

89. Taves, *Religion and Domestic Violence*, 83.

90. Ibid., 84.

91. Ibid., 86.

92. On Protestant mysticism in early America, see, among others, Janice Knight, *Orthodoxies in Massachusetts: Rereading American Puritanism* (Cambridge, MA: Harvard University Press, 1994).

93. See the emerging literature on the complex functions of this sort of language: Griffith, *God's Daughters*; and Margaret Bendroth, *Fundamentalism and Gender, 1875 to the Present* (New Haven, CT: Yale University Press, 1993), who builds on Nancy Hardesty's description of an apparent paradox of "evangelical feminism" in a way that could be read back into Bailey's discourse. See Nancy Hardesty, *Women Called to Witness: Evangelical Feminism in the 19th Century* (Nashville: Abingdon, 1984).

94. Taves, *Religion and Domestic Violence*, 86. This language of "union with Christ" is, of course, a classic in Christian mysticism, and its erotic elements are worth noting. See Bernard McGinn, ed., *The Essential Writings of Christian Mysticism* (New York: Modern Library, 2006).

95. Taves, *Religion and Domestic Violence*, 87.

96. Ibid., 88.

97. Abigail describes how Asa, on his first return to the farm after being exiled, seduced her with alternating flattery and fear tactics. At one point, tellingly, Asa offers to give up his patriarchal privilege and live in submission to Abigail: "He knew his conduct had been so abominable, that he did not ask the honor of his usual place in the family; but I should have the preeminence, and he would willingly take the place of an assistant." This essentially hierarchical thinking confirms the sense that Asa struggled to understand the new dynamic between men and women that was emerging and clung to a unified model of one "on top" of the other, rather than sharing discrete "spheres" of power and control. Such appeals were, needless to say, difficult for Abigail to endure. She struggled to hold onto her resolve never to live with him again. "Judge, ye tender partners in life, what

must have been my scenes of woe" (99). The experience of abduction has, more often, been the lot of children in America. For her coverage of children kidnapped from the late nineteenth century on, see Paula S. Fass, *Kidnapped: Child Abduction in America* (New York: Oxford University Press, 1997).

98. Taves, *Religion and Domestic Violence*, 95.

99. Ibid., 106–7.

100. Ibid., 126. The narrative from pp. 122 to 132 covers a single day, Monday, March 19, 1792, and is a remarkable record of the "internal dialogue" that Abigail experienced after discovering Asa's betrayal and a telling window into the changes occurring in her theology. It is the longest single narrative account in the *Memoirs*, constantly turning back on itself and filled with self-recrimination, self-awareness, and shifting emotions.

101. Ibid., 131.

102. Ibid., 129.

103. For an examination of this rhetoric in a later period and its compatibility with market processes, see John Corrigan, *Business of the Heart: Religion and Emotion in the 19th Century* (Berkeley: University of California Press, 2001).

104. Taves, *Religion and Domestic Violence*, 131.

105. Ibid., 135.

106. Ibid., 158.

107. Ibid., 159.

108. Ibid., 160.

109. Ibid., 161.

110. Ibid., 165.

111. Ibid., 166–67.

112. Ibid., 174.

113. Ibid., 175.

114. On this point, see Jay Fliegelman, *Prodigals and Pilgrims: The American Revolution against Patriarchal Authority, 1750–1800* (Cambridge: Cambridge University Press, 1982), who traces the rise of the "national" family to replace the older form of patriarchy based explicitly on religion.

115. Hartog, *Man and Wife in America*, 54.

116. Ibid., 60–61.

117. See especially Lisa Hill, "The Hidden Theology of Adam Smith," *European Journal of the History of Economic Thought* 8 (March 2001):1–29.

118. On the theme of providence in the civil religion, for one side, see Steven Waldman, *Founding Faith: Providence, Politics, and Religious Freedom in America* (New York: Random House, 2008). For another side of the story, see Nicholas Guyatt, *Providence and the Invention of the United States, 1607–1876* (Cambridge: Cambridge University Press, 2007).

119. On the relations between Protestant theology and markets, see Mark Valeri, "Religious Discipline and the Market: Puritans and the Issue of Usury," *William and Mary Quarterly*, 3rd ser., 54 (October 1997):747–68. Valeri contends that ideas of "Providence" among Protestants actually constrained entrepreneurial energy. Suffice it to say that while this was, moralistically, the ideal, the practices of those guided by Providence suggest, in fact, less self-discipline and more willingness to discipline others than Valeri seems willing to acknowledge. For a more critical, albeit less historically nuanced, reading of the

Protestant legacy, see Mark C. Taylor, *Confidence Games: Money and Markets in a World without Redemption* (Chicago: University of Chicago Press, 2004). For a dated, overly sanguine but still valuable tracking of the role of Arminian theology underlying the American civil religion, see William G. McLoughlin, *Revivals, Awakenings, and Reform: An Essay on Religion and Social Change in America, 1607–1977*, Chicago History of American Religion (Chicago: University of Chicago Press, 1978).

120. *The Handmaid's Tale* (MGM Home Entertainment, 1990), 00:00–00:27.

121. Ibid., 00:28–5:05.

122. Ibid., 5:05–7:45.

123. Ibid., 16:00–17:45.

124. Ibid., 21:10–23:15.

125. Ibid., 26:40–32:05.

126. Ibid., 1:13:25–1:18:25.

127. Ibid., 1:11:45–1:13:25.

128. "Core Principles," Family Research Council Webpage, available at http://www.frc.org/get.cfm?c=ABOUT_FRC (accessed July 18, 2008). The site changed in late 2008, but the current "Mission Statement," at http://www.frc.org/mission-statement (accessed January 22, 2009), reiterates the crucial language.

129. The full text can be found, along with many other helpful documents, at DOMAwatch.org, http://www.domawatch.org/about/federaldoma.html (accessed January 22, 2009). For a print collection of documents and arguments related to the same-sex marriage debate, see Andrew Sullivan and Joseph Landau, eds., *Same-Sex Marriage, Pro and Con: A Reader* (New York: Vintage, 2004).

130. See *DOMA Watch: Your Legal Source for Defense of Marriage Acts Information*, available at http://www.domawatch.org/index.php (accessed January 22, 2009).

131. For a helpful summary of the debate, see also Ontario Consultants on Religious Tolerance, "Prohibiting Same-Sex Marriages in the U.S.: Federal and State 'DOMA' Legislation," available at http://www.religioustolerance.org/hom_mar6.htm (accessed January 22, 2009).

132. See "Status of Same Sex Relationships Nationwide," available at http://www.lambdalegal.org/publications/articles/nationwide-status-same-sex-relationships.html (accessed January 22, 2009).

133. Peter Sprigg, "Same-Sex Marriage Is Not a Civil Right," remarks at a "Defend Maryland Marriage" rally, January 27, 2005, available at Family Research Council, http://www.frc.org/get.cfm?i=PD05B01 (accessed January 22, 2009). For a more extended version, with language evocative of the purity programs of the Republic of Gilead, see Peter Sprigg, *Outrage: How Gay Activists and Liberal Judges Are Trashing Democracy to Redefine Marriage* (Washington, DC: Regnery, 2004).

134. Pellegrini and Jakobsen, *Love the Sin*, 19.

135. "The Meaning of God Hates Fags," available at http://www.godhatesfags.com/written/wbcinfo/godhatesfags.html (accessed January 22, 2009).

136. Ibid.

137. "All Nations Must Immediately Outlaw Sodomy (Homosexuality) and Impose the Death Penalty," available at http://www.godhatesfags.com/written/fliers/archive/20021203_outlaw-sodomy.pdf (accessed January 22, 2009).

138. Hendrik Hartog, "What Gay Marriage Teaches about the History of Marriage," in History News Network (April 5, 2004), available at http://hnn.us/articles/4400.html (accessed January 22, 2009).

CHAPTER 5

1. The epigraph from Bunyan is from John Bunyan, *The Pilgrim's Progress*, ed. W. R. Owens Oxford World Classics (New York: Oxford University Press, 2003), 220. For the Anderson quotation, see Benedict Anderson, *Imagined Communities: Reflections on the Origins and Spread of Nationalism*, rev. and expanded ed. (London: Verso, 1991), 205–6. For provocative interpretations of some of these dynamics that we cannot explore here, see Richard Hofstadter, *Anti-Intellectualism in American Life* (New York: Knopf, 1963); and Mark Noll, *The Scandal of the Evangelical Mind* (Grand Rapids, MI: Eerdmans, 1994). On innocence, see Richard T. Hughes, *Myths America Lives By* (Urbana: University of Illinois Press, 2003).

2. For one narrative history, see Eliza Steelwater, *The Hangman's Knot: Lynching, Legal Execution, and America's Struggle with the Death Penalty* (Boulder, CO: Westview Press, 2003).

3. On the category of the "modern," see Martin E. Marty, *Modern American Religion*, vol. 1, *The Irony of It All, 1893–1919* (Chicago: University of Chicago Press, 1986). Marty defines the "modern" as a category of time, which surely is accurate, but I date its onset somewhat earlier than he, although with the same sense, I hope, of irony about how the modern has enveloped and incorporated the "religious" under other guises.

4. See Harvey Cox, *The Secular City: Secularization and Urbanization in Theological Perspective* (New York: Macmillan, 1965); Talal Asad, *Formations of the Secular: Christianity, Islam, Modernity* (Stanford, CA: Stanford University Press, 2003); and Gustavo Benavides, "Modernity," in *Critical Terms for Religious Studies*, ed. Mark C. Taylor (Chicago: University of Chicago Press, 1998), 186–204.

5. See Marcel Gauchet, *The Disenchantment of the World: A Political History of Religion*, trans. Oscar Burge (Princeton, NJ: Princeton University Press, 1997).

6. René Girard, "Mimesis and Violence: Perspectives in Cultural Criticism," *Berkshire Review* 14 (1979):9–19, cited in James W. Williams, ed., *The Girard Reader* (New York: Crossroad, 2000), 11. See also the many monographs by René Girard, particularly *Violence and the Sacred* , trans. Patrick Gregory (Baltimore: Johns Hopkins University Press, 1974).

7. In lesser hands, Girard's theory can have the ironic outcome of scapegoating religious traditions other than Christianity. See, for example, Robert G. Hamerton-Kelly, *Sacred Violence: Paul's Hermeneutic of the Cross* (Minneapolis: Fortress Press, 1992). Girardian thought has fostered an academic society, the Colloquium on Violence and Religion, which meets biannually and has a home on the web at http://theol.uibk.ac.at/cover/ (accessed January 22, 2009).

8. Bruce Lincoln presents, to my mind, a helpful corrective in understanding the logic of sacrifice:

Sacrifice is most fundamentally a logic, language, and practice of transformative negation, in which one entity . . . is given up for the benefit of some other. . . . There are many distinguished scholars who take a rather benevolent view of sacrifice, stressing the way in which it furthers the construction of community or assists in the canalization of violence. . . . Yet I continue to be troubled by the radical asymmetry that exists between the sacrificer and the sacrificed. . . . More often than not, the calls to sacrifice which prove effective strike me as offensive and the performances that are actually staged seem little short of criminal. (*Death, War, and Sacrifice: Studies in Ideology and Practice* [Chicago: University of Chicago Press, 1991], 204)

This becomes problematic, of course, when the sacrificer *is* the sacrificed, although even then the cultural systems that warrant the sacrifice may be riddled with asymmetries that border on or cross into the criminal, albeit in forms that are rarely susceptible to accountability.

9. In *The Ambivalence of the Sacred: Religion, Violence and Reconciliation* (Lanham, MD: Rowman & Littlefield, 2000), Appleby offers the notion of "weak religions" to describe extremisms. In a later work, he develops the opposite (and more conventional metaphor). See Gabriel A. Almond, R. Scott Appleby, and Emmanuel Sivan, *Strong Religion: The Rise of Fundamentalisms around the World* (Chicago: University of Chicago Press, 2003). For the five volumes, see Martin E. Marty and R. Scott Appleby, eds., *Fundamentalisms Observed*; *Fundamentalisms and the State: Remaking Polities, Economies, and Militance*; *Fundamentalisms and Society: Reclaiming the Sciences, the Family, and Education*; *Accounting for Fundamentalisms: The Dynamic Character of Movements*; and *Fundamentalisms Comprehended* (Chicago: University of Chicago, 1991, 1993, 1994, and 1995).

10. Appleby, *The Ambivalence of the Sacred*, 91.

11. I admire Appleby's work immensely, but as I stated in chapter 1, I think he dismisses too glibly the role of the nation-state in fostering religious extremism and violence. For contrast, see Noam Chomsky, *Power and Terror: Post-9/11 Talks and Interviews* (New York: Seven Stories Press, 2003).

12. David Carrasco, *City of Sacrifice: The Aztec Empire and the Role of Violence in Civilization* (Boston: Beacon Press, 1999), 3.

13. Ibid., 195.

14. Ibid., 5.

15. Ibid., 8 (italics in original).

16. See especially the works of Russell T. McCutcheon, *The Discipline of Religion: Structure, Meaning, Rhetoric* (New York: Routledge, 2003), and *Manufacturing Religion: The Discourse on Sui Generis Religion and the Politics of Nostalgia* (New York: Oxford University Press, 1997).

17. I have found illuminating the recent work of Michael Hardt and Antonio Negri, *Empire* (Cambridge, MA: Harvard University Press, 2000), although I think they overestimate the decline of nationalism in a globalizing, capitalist empire. For examples of scholars who have studied sacrifice in the history of rising American political power, see Robert Jewett and John Shelton Lawrence, *Captain America and the Crusade against Evil: The Dilemma of Zealous Nationalism* (Grand Rapids, MI: Eerdmans, 2003); and Robert Jewett, *Mission and Menace: Four Centuries of American Religious Zeal* (Minneapolis: Fortress Press, 2008); Edward Tabor Linenthal, *Sacred Ground: Americans and Their Battlefields* (Urbana: University of Illinois Press, 1993); Ira Chernus, *Dr. Strangegod: On the Symbolic Meaning of Nuclear Weapons* (Columbia: University of South Carolina Press, 1986); and Catherine L. Albanese, *Sons of the Fathers: The Civil Religion of the American Revolution*

(Philadelphia: Temple University Press, 1976). See also Bruce Lincoln, *Holy Terrors: Thinking about Religion after September 11* (Chicago: University of Chicago Press, 2003).

18. Alexander M. Witherspoon, preface to *The Pilgrim's Progress*, by John Bunyan (New York: Pocket Books, 1957), vi.

19. I cannot explore this provocative hypothesis more fully here, but consider linkages between various constructions of transcendence and both environmental degradation and genocide. For the former, see from a theological point of view the arguments of Sallie McFague, *Models of God: Theology for an Ecological, Nuclear Age* (Philadelphia: Fortress Press, 1987); and Mark I. Wallace, *Finding God in the Singing River: Christianity, Spirit, Nature* (Minneapolis: Fortress Press, 2006). From a historian of religion's approach, see Jonathan Z. Smith, *To Take Place: Toward Theory in Ritual* (Chicago: University of Chicago Press, 1987); and from a historian of culture, see Eric D. Weitz, *A Century of Genocide: Utopias of Race and Nation* (Princeton, NJ: Princeton University Press, 2003), and *In God's Name: Genocide and Religion in the 20th Century* (New York: Berghahn Books, 2001).

20. This notion is often located first in the Enlightenment, but its roots start much earlier. See Carl Becker, *The Heavenly City of the 18th Century Philosophers* (New Haven, CT: Yale University Press, 1932).

21. Despite his great popularity (the book has never been out of print), Bunyan's works have not received the attention from historians of religion they deserve. The last bibliography of scholarly studies dates from 1987. See Beatrice E. Batson, *John Bunyan's* Grace Abounding *and* The Pilgrim's Progress: *An Overview of Literary Studies, 1960–1987* (New York: Garland, 1988). For a fine study of the work in its contexts, see Kathleen M. Swain, *Pilgrim's Progress, Puritan Progress: Discourses and Contexts* (Urbana: University of Illinois Press, 1993). For some of the profound influence of the work (including as an agent of empire), see Isabel Hofmyer, *The Portable Bunyan: A Transnational History of* The Pilgrim's Progress (Princeton, NJ: Princeton University Press, 2004).

22. On preemptive war, see Matthew Flynn, *First Strike: Preemptive War in Modern History* (New York: Routledge, 2008).

23. For an updated version of what Bunyan imagined, see Jimmy Carter, *Our Endangered Values: America's Moral Crisis* (New York: Simon & Schuster, 2005).

24. Perry Miller, *Errand into the Wilderness* (New York: Harper & Row, 1956).

25. The 1838 edition of Winthrop's document is available through the Hanover College History Department Historical Documents Project, at http://history.hanover.edu/texts/winthmod.html (accessed January 22, 2009). Perhaps the most astute student of the paradoxical character of Puritan rhetoric remains Sacvan Bercovitch, *The American Jeremiad* (Madison: University of Wisconsin Press, 1978).

26. The entire document is available at http://www.pragmatism.org/american/cambridge_platform.htm (accessed January 22, 2009). Attention to the embrace of "discipline" by Puritans is perhaps the central insight of the most recent scholarship on the movement, along with its indelibly transatlantic character. See especially Theodore Dwight Bozeman, *The Precisianist Strain: Disciplinary Religion & Antinomian Backlash in Puritanism to 1638* (Chapel Hill: University of North Carolina Press, 2004); Laura Lunger Knoppers, ed., *Puritanism and Its Discontents* (Newark: University of Delaware Press, 2003); Philip H. Round, *By Nature and by Custom Cursed: Transatlantic Civil Discourse and New England Cultural Production, 1620–1660* (Hanover, NH: University Press of New England,

1999); and Jane Kamensky, *Governing the Tongue: The Politics of Speech in Early New England* (New York: Oxford University Press, 1997).

27. On early Quakerism, see Hugh Barbour and Arthur O. Roberts, eds., *Early Quaker Writings 1650–1700* (Grand Rapids, MI: Eerdmans, 1973); and Hugh Barbour and J. William Frost, *The Quakers. Denominations in America, Number 3* (New York: Greenwood Press, 1988). Still useful, and typical in its subtle anti-Quaker bias is the survey by Arthur J. Worrall, *Quakers in the Colonial Northeast* (Hanover, NH: University Press of New England, 1980).

28. See Elizabeth Reis, *Damned Women: Sinners and Witches in Puritan New England* (Ithaca, NY: Cornell University Press, 1997), who traces how sin and evil were constructed in heavily gendered terms in early America.

29. I follow Besse's account throughout. See Joseph Besse, *A Collection of the Sufferings of the People Called Quakers, For the Testimony of a Good Conscience, from the Time of their being first distinguished by that NAME, to the time of the act, commonly called the Act of Toleration, granted to Protestant Dissenters in the first Year of the Reign of King William the Third and Queen Mary, in the Year 1689. Taken from Original Records and other Authentic Accounts*, 2 vols. (London: Luke Hinde, 1753), vol. 2, 177–78, available at Swarthmore College, Friends Historical Library. My gratitude to Christopher Densmore, curator of the collection, for his expert assistance in my research.

30. Besse, *A Collection of the Sufferings*, 179–81.

31. Ibid., 183.

32. Ibid., 183–86.

33. On Nayler, see Leo Damrosch, *The Sorrows of the Quaker Jesus: James Nayler and the Puritan Crackdown on the Free Spirit* (Cambridge, MA: Harvard University Press, 1996).

34. Bruce Lincoln, *Authority: Construction and Corrosion* (Chicago: University of Chicago Press, 1994).

35. Besse, *A Collection of the Sufferings*, 189. See the only extant biography of Endecott, written by an heir, Lawrence Shaw Mayo, *John Endecott: A Biography* (Cambridge, MA: Harvard University Press, 1936). My thanks to Haverford College, and especially Ann Upton and Joelle Bertolet of the Quaker Collection, for their assistance in my research.

36. It is easy enough to dismiss these practices as mere "magic," but I suspect their significance goes much further. In an oral-aural culture such as that the Puritans created, ears assumed the status not only as vehicles of grace but also (when damaged) as public signs of reprobation. On the importance of orality or aurality in early New England, by way of its transformation during the Enlightenment, see Leigh Eric Schmidt, *Hearing Things: Religion, Illusion, and the American Enlightenment* (Cambridge, MA: Harvard University Press, 2000).

37. The image of the millstone was well known to the Puritans. Jesus invoked this curse in the gospel of Luke: "Woe to anyone by whom occasions for stumbling come! It would be better for you if a millstone were hung around your neck and you were thrown into the sea than for you to cause one of these little ones to stumble" (17:1–2).

38. Besse, *A Collection of the Sufferings*, 190.

39. Frederick B. Tolles, *A Quaker's Curse—Humphrey Norton to John Endecott, 1658*, reprinted from *Huntington Library Quarterly* 14 (August 1951):416; available at Swarthmore College, Friends Historical Library.

40. Tolles, *A Quaker's Curse*, 420.

41. On the significance of the drumming, and the importance of sound more generally in early America, see Richard Cullen Rath, *How Early America Sounded* (Ithaca, NY: Cornell University Press, 2003).

42. The letter can be found in *Mary Dyer, Quaker: Two Letters of William Dyer of Rhode Island, 1659–60* (Cambridge: Cambridge University Press, printed for Charles Dyer Norton and Daniel B. Dyer, [1927?]), available at Swarthmore College, Friends Historical Library.

43. Besse, *A Collection of the Sufferings*, 204–5.

44. Ibid., 206–7.

45. Ibid., 215–19.

46. See the provocative argument of Mark A. Petersen, *The Price of Redemption: The Spiritual Economy of Puritan New England* (Stanford, CA: Stanford University Press, 1997), who links Puritanism from the earliest settlement to the revivals of 1730 to 1740 to the flourishing of market-based religion, without, however, grounding this economy in its sacrificial or violent implications.

47. This calls for an essay in its own right some day, tracing the wildly varying (and, to my mind, altogether premature) accounts of the "demise" of Puritan or Protestant influence in American culture, which historians have placed everywhere from 1661 to 1776 to 1860 to 1970. Two influential works that put dates on when the Puritan "epoch" in America ended are Sydney E. Ahlstrom, *A Religious History of the American People* (New Haven, CT: Yale University Press, 1972); and Robert T. Handy, *A Christian America: Protestant Hopes and Historical Realities* (New York: Oxford University Press, 1971). Handy actually describes two "disestablishments." Suffice it to say that I think a third is needed. In an understandable (and absolutely necessary) effort to "unseat" the Puritan master narrative, by means of which only dead white Protestant men received attention as agents in history, historians have obscured some of the complex violence committed in the name of privilege and power by white men (and perpetuated by their historical investigatees or their representatives).

48. See Amy Kaplan, *The Anarchy of Empire in the Making of U.S. Culture* (Cambridge, MA: Harvard University Press, 2002).

49. Despite a generation of excellent scholarship on religion in America, there still is misunderstanding and deep-rooted suspicion between secular historians and those working in religious studies. The unfortunate result is that when treated by scholars housed in history or American studies departments, theoretically sophisticated and critically rigorous ways to understand religion are not often translated into or applied to historical works on religious subjects.

50. See Carrasco, *City of Sacrifice*, esp. chaps. 2 and 3: "Templo Mayor: The Aztec Vision of Place," and "The New Fire Ceremony and the Binding of the Years: Tenochtitlán's Fearful Symmetry," 49–114.

51. Throughout this chapter, I depend on the construction of nationalism first identified by Anderson, *Imagined Communities*.

52. See Jonathan M. Chu, *Neighbors, Friends, or Madmen: The Puritan Adjustment to Quakerism in Seventeenth-Century Massachusetts Bay* (Westport, CT: Greenwood Press, 1985); and Carla Gardina Pestana, *Quakers and Baptists in Colonial Massachusetts* (Cambridge: Cambridge University Press, 1991).

53. John Norton, *The Heart of N-England Rent at the Blasphemies of the Present Generation. Or a Brief Tractate concerning the Doctrine of the Quakers. . . .* ([Cambridge, MA]): Samuel Green, 1659), available at Swarthmore College, Friends Historical Library.

54. Ibid., 56.

55. The letter is reprinted in its entirety in Mayo, *John Endecott*, 252–53.

56. Endecott's petition is quoted verbatim and answered point by point by Quaker apologist Edward Burrough, in *A Declaration of the Sad and Great Persecution and Martyrdom of the People of God, Called Quakers, in New England for the Worshipping of God* (London: Robert Wilson, [1660]), in *Three Quaker Writings by Edward Burrough*, Occasional Papers, Reprint Series no. 6 (San Francisco: California State Library, 1939), 3, available at Swarthmore College, Friends Historical Library.

57. The terms of the commission are recorded in a *Resolution of the Massachusetts General Court*, November 4, 1659, Massachusetts Archives, 10:260A, State House, Boston, as cited by Chu, *Neighbors, Friends, or Madmen*, 31.

58. Norton, *The Heart of N-England*, 57.

59. Pestana, *Quakers and Baptists in Colonial Massachusetts*, 34. David D. Hall, *Worlds of Wonder, Days of Judgment: Popular Religious Belief in Early New England* (New York: Knopf, 1989), describes the usual procedures.

60. Norton, *The Heart of N-England*, 58.

61. Ibid.

62. Max Weber, *The Protestant Ethic and the Spirit of Capitalism*, trans. Talcott Parsons (New York: Scribner, 1958).

63. See Sarah J. Purcell, *Sealed with Blood: War, Sacrifice, and Memory in Revolutionary America* (Philadelphia: University of Pennsylvania Press, 2002); and T. H. Breen, *The Marketplace of Revolution: How Consumer Politics Shaped American Independence* (New York: Oxford University Press, 2004).

64. A picture of the statue and an excellent biography of Dyer in relationship to Hutchinson, along with a number of primary sources online, can be found at "Notable Women of America," available at http://www.rootsweb.com/~nwa/dyer.html (accessed January 22, 2009).

65. Along these lines, see Mark L. Taylor, *The Executed God: The Way of the Cross in Lockdown America* (Minneapolis: Fortress Press, 2001).

66. See Sister Helen Prejean, *Dead Man Walking* (New York: Vintage Books, 1993). I am not an unbiased reporter of Prejean's life and work. For an account of my one meeting with her, see my "America's Sister," *Journal of Lutheran Ethics* 6 (December 2006), available at http://archive.elca.org/jle/article.asp?k=679 (accessed January 22, 2009).

67. "Tim Robbins Interview," *Frontline*: "Angel on Death Row," February 8, 1996, transcript available at http://www.pbs.org/wgbh/pages/frontline/angel/walking/timrobbins.html (accessed January 22, 2009).

68. "Helen Prejean Interview," *Frontline*: "Angel on Death Row," April 9, 1996, transcript available at http://www.pbs.org/wgbh/pages/frontline/angel/angelscript.html (accessed January 22, 2009).

69. For example, see James Carroll, *Constantine's Sword: The Church and the Jews—A History* (Boston: Houghton Mifflin, 2001).

70. See Dead Man Walking: *The Shooting Script* (New York: Newmarket Press, 1997), 38.

71. For these processes, see Michel Foucault, *Discipline and Punish: The Birth of the Prison*, trans. Alan Sheridan (New York: Vintage Books, 1995).

72. See Brian K. Smith, "Capital Punishment and Human Sacrifice," *Journal of the American Academy of Religion* 68 (March 2000):3–25. Smith is not quite as emphatic as I am about this association; but his evidence clearly leans in this direction.

1. See Lydia Saad, "Iraq War Triggers Major Rally Effect," Gallup News Service, March 25, 2003, available at http://www.gallup.com/poll/8074/Iraq-War-Triggers-Major-Rally-Effect.aspx (accessed January 22, 2009).

2. Hence the subtitle of David Keen, *Endless War: Hidden Functions of the "War on Terror"* (London: Pluto Press, 2006).

3. Among the more elevated of the debates of the matter, see Paul Griffiths and George Weigel, "Just War: An Exchange," *First Things* 122 (April 2002):31–36. For the typical attitude of the "Christian right" toward the war, see Chuck Colson, "Just War in Iraq," *Christianity Today* 46 (December 9, 2002), available at http://www.christianitytoday.com/ct/2002/december9/41.72.html (accessed January 22, 2009). The article notes that Colson met twice with Secretary of Defense Rumsfeld to "explain" to him the meaning of the "just war theory," in what can only be imagined as a very cordial conversation.

4. I find uncompelling the arguments that drew on the "just war" theory in relationship to Iraq; Afghanistan strikes me as a different case. See Gary M. Simpson, *War, Peace, and God: Rethinking the Just War Tradition* (Minneapolis: Augsburg Fortress Press, 2007); and for an argument for the "realistic" character of militant nonviolence, see Walter Wink, *Jesus and Nonviolence: A Third Way* (Minneapolis: Fortress Press, 2003).

5. As indicated, I use this label heuristically, aware that the contours of this construct have been stretched. See the original, Robert N. Bellah, "Civil Religion in America," *Daedalus* 96 (winter 1967):1–21, which is largely sympathetic, since it locates the system primarily in John F. Kennedy's inaugural. For a more critical viewpoint, largely in tune with my central hypothesis and giving it some historic specificity, see Garry Wills, *Reagan's America: Innocents at Home* (Garden City, NY: Doubleday, 1987).

6. See also John F. Wilson, *Public Religion in American Culture* (Philadelphia: Temple University Press, 1979), who argues that a "major element" in American civic faith has been the belief that "American society [is] perfected and pure, unalloyed and uncompromised," in a word, innocent (96).

7. Of course, "enduring freedom" can also be construed as a religious claim. President Bush himself has affirmed as much. In his 2002 State of the Union address, he insisted that "the liberty we prize is not America's gift to the world, it is God's gift to humanity." See the full transcript at "Bush State of the Union Address," available at http://archives.cnn.com/2002/ALLPOLITICS/01/29/bush.speech.txt/ (accessed January 22, 2009).

8. See Arundhati Roy, "The Algebra of Infinite Justice," *The Guardian*, September 29, 2001, available at http://www.guardian.co.uk/Archive/Article/0,4273,4266289,00.html (accessed January 22, 2009).

9. For example, see "Warships Depart Virginia, as Deployment Grows," Monday, January 13, 2003, available at http://www.foxnews.com/story/0,2933,75324,00.html (accessed January 22, 2009).

10. See Tom Infield, Diego Ibarguen, and Martin Merzer, "In Sign to Iraq, U.S. Tests Huge Bomb," *Philadelphia Inquirer*, March 12, 2003, A01.

11. "Air Force Tests Monster MOAB Bomb," United Press International, available at http://www.upi.com/view.cfm?StoryID=20030311-040832-2415r (accessed March 15, 2003;

link broken as of December 20, 2007). For a related story, see "U.S. Tests Super Bomb in Florida," available at http://www.cbsnews.com/stories/2003/03/11/iraq/main543611.shtml (accessed January 22, 2009).

12. Mark Juergensmeyer, *Terror in the Mind of God*, 119–41.

13. "Praying A Shield of Protection," available at http://cbn.org/special/PrayerShield/index.asp (accessed January 22, 2009).

14. Pascal Bruckner, *The Temptation of Innocence: Living in the Age of Entitlement* (New York: Algora Publications, 2000), 244.

15. In this context, see Bruce Lincoln, *Religion, Empire and Torture: The Case of Achaemenia Persia, with a Postscript on Abu Ghraib* (Chicago: University of Chicago Press, 2007).

16. For a provocative argument about how Bush's language of sacrifice accomplished "symbolic hijacking" to mobilize public support for war, see Paul Christopher Johnson, "Savage Civil Religion," *Numen* 52 (2005):289–324.

17. "Transcript of President Bush's Prayer Service Remarks," available at http://www.opm.gov/guidance/09-14-01gwb.htm (accessed January 22, 2009).

18. "President Bush Outlines Iraqi Threat," available at http://www.cfr.org/publication/8352/president_bush_outlines_iraqi_threat.html (accessed January 22, 2009).

19. "President Addresses the Nation, September 7, 2003," available at http://transcripts.cnn.com/TRANSCRIPTS/0309/07/se.04.html (accessed January 22, 2009).

20. "Transcript: President Bush's Speech on the War on Terrorism. Delivered at the U.S. Naval Academy in Annapolis, Maryland," available at http://www.washingtonpost.com/wp-dyn/content/article/2005/11/30/AR2005113000667.html (accessed January 22, 2009).

21. Kelly Denton-Borhaug, "The Language of 'Sacrifice' in the Buildup to War: A Feminist Rhetorical and Theological Analysis," *Journal of Religion and Popular Culture* 15 (spring 2007), available at http://www.usask.ca/relst/jrpc/art15-langsacrifice.html (accessed January 22, 2009).

22. "President Bush Defends Decision to Send Additional Troops to Iraq," interview with Jim Lehrer, *Online News Hour with Jim Lehrer*, January 16, 2007, available at http://www.pbs.org/newshour/bb/white_house/jan-june07/bush_01-16.html, (accessed January 22, 2009).

23. Ibid.

24. "Text: President Bush's Acceptance Speech to the Republican National Convention," available at http://www.washingtonpost.com/wp-dyn/articles/A57466-2004Sep2.html (accessed January 22, 2009).

25. Miroslav Volf, *Exclusion and Embrace: A Theological Exploration of Identity, Otherness, and Reconciliation* (Nashville: Abingdon Press, 1996), 83.

26. I have been talking about a "coming religious peace" for at least four years since delivering a lecture with that title at Central Baptist Church, Wayne, PA, on January 18, 2004, so I was pleased to see the phrase developed by Alan Wolfe, "A Coming Religious Peace," *Atlantic Monthly*, March 2008, available at http://www.theatlantic.com/doc/200803/secularism (accessed January 22, 2009).

27. See, for instance, the "Universal Declaration of a Global Ethic," one version of which was written by Leonard Swidler, available at http://astro.temple.edu/~dialogue/Center/declarel.htm (accessed January 22, 2009). A complementary version, by Tubingen's

Hans Küng, can be found in *A Global Ethic for Global Politics and Economics*, trans. John Bowden (New York: Oxford University Press, 1998). The six principles in Küng's formulation have the wisdom of brevity. They are (1) Treat others as you would like to be treated (i.e., the so-called Golden Rule); (2) Every human being must be treated humanely; (3) Have respect for life; (4) Deal honestly and fairly; (5) Speak and act truthfully; and (6) Respect and love one another, and be responsible for your partner's happiness. See also Hans Küng, ed., *Yes to a Global Ethic* (New York: Continuum, 1996). Both efforts are based on the United Nations Universal Declaration of Human Rights, available at http://www.un.org/Overview/rights.html (accessed January 22, 2009). Finally, on the difficulty of translating parochial traditions into global ethics, see Thomas Axworthy, ed., *Bridging the Divide: Religious Dialogue and Universal Ethics* (Kingston, ON: School of Policy Studies, Queen's University, 2008).

28. See my argument in *Shopping Malls and Other Sacred Spaces: Putting God in Place* (Grand Rapids, MI: Brazos Press, 2003).

29. Immanuel Kant, "Perpetual Peace: A Philosophical Sketch," trans. Kevin Paul Geiman, available at http://www.mtholyoke.edu/acad/intrel/kant/kant1.htm (accessed January 22, 2009).

Bibliography

Agnew, John A. *Hegemony: The New Shape of Global Power*. Philadelphia: Temple University Press, 2005.

Ahlstrom, Sydney E. *A Religious History of the American People*. New Haven, CT: Yale University Press, 1972.

Albanese, Catherine L. *America: Religions and Religion*. 3rd ed. Belmont, CA: Wadsworth, 1999.

———. *Sons of the Fathers: The Civil Religion of the American Revolution*. Philadelphia: Temple University Press, 1976.

Albright, Brian. *Wild beyond Belief! Interviews with Exploitation Filmmakers of the 1960s and 1970s*. Jefferson, NC: McFarland, 2008.

Albright, Madeleine. *The Mighty and the Almighty: Reflections on America, God, and World Affairs*. New York: HarperCollins, 2006.

Allen, Theodore W. *The Invention of the White Race*. 2 vols. New York: Verso, 1997.

Alliance Defense Fund. "Federal Defense of Marriage Act (DOMA)." *DOMA Watch*. Available at http://www.domawatch.org/about/federaldoma.html (accessed July 18, 2008).

Almond, Gabriel A., R. Scott Appleby, and Emmanuel Sivan. *Strong Religion: The Rise of Fundamentalisms around the World*. Chicago: University of Chicago Press, 2003.

Alter, Peter. *Nationalism*. Trans. Stuart McKinnin-Evans. London: E. Arnold, 1989.

Ambrose, Douglas. *Henry Hughes and Proslavery Thought in the Old South*. Baton Rouge: Louisiana State University Press, 1996.

American File Institute. "The Birth of a Race." *American Film Institute Catalog*. Available at http://gateway.proquest.com/openurl?ctx_ver=Z39.88-2003&xri:pqil:res_ver=0.2&res_id=xri:afi-us&rft_id=xri:afi:film:2099.

Anderson, Benedict. *Imagined Communities: Reflections on the Origin and Spread of Nationalism*. Rev. ed. London: Verso, 1991.

Andrews, William L. "Frederick Douglass and the American Jeremiad." In *To Tell a Free Story: The First Century of Afro-American Autobiography, 1760–1865*, ed. William L. Andrews, 123–32. Urbana: University of Illinois Press, 1986.

———. "Frederick Douglass, Preacher." *American Literature* 54 (December 1982):592–97.

———, and William S. McFeely, eds. *Narrative of the Life of Frederick Douglass, an American Slave, Written by Himself*. New York: Norton, 1997 (orig. pub. 1845).

Appleby, R. Scott. *The Ambivalence of the Sacred: Religion, Violence and Reconciliation*. Lanham, MD: Rowman & Littlefield, 2000.

———, and Martin E. Marty, eds. *Accounting for Fundamentalisms: The Dynamic Character of Movements*. Chicago: University of Chicago Press, 1994.

———, and Martin E. Marty, eds. *Fundamentalisms and Society: Reclaiming the Sciences, the Family, and Education.* Chicago: University of Chicago Press, 1993.

———, and Martin E. Marty, eds. *Fundamentalisms and the State: Remaking Polities, Economies, and Militance.* Chicago: University of Chicago Press, 1993.

———, and Martin E. Marty, eds. *Fundamentalisms Comprehended.* Chicago: University of Chicago Press, 1995.

———, and Martin E. Marty, eds. *Fundamentalisms Observed.* Chicago: University of Chicago Press, 1991.

Arendt, Hannah. *Eichmann in Jerusalem: A Report on the Banality of Evil.* New York: Penguin, 1994.

———. *On Violence.* New York: Harvest Books, 1970.

Armstrong, George D. *The Christian Doctrine of Slavery.* New York: Scribner, 1857.

Asad, Talal. *Formations of the Secular: Christianity, Islam, Modernity.* Stanford, CA: Stanford University Press, 2003.

———. *Genealogies of Religion: Discipline and Reasons of Power in Christianity and Islam.* Baltimore: Johns Hopkins University Press, 1993.

———. *On Suicide Bombing.* New York: Columbia University Press, 2007.

Associated Press. "Warships Depart VA as Deployment Grows." *Fox News,* January 13, 2003. Available at http://www.foxnews.com/story/0,2933,75324,00.html (accessed July 23, 2008).

Austin, Joe, and Michael Nevin Willard, eds. *Generations of Youth: Youth Cultures and History in Twentieth-Century America.* New York: New York University Press, 2003.

Avalos, Hector. *Fighting Words: The Origins of Religious Violence.* New York: Prometheus Books, 2005.

Avram, Wes, ed. *Anxious about Empire: Theological Essays on the New Global Realities.* Grand Rapids, MI: Brazos Press, 2004.

Axworthy, Thomas, ed. *Bridging the Divide: Religious Dialogue and Universal Ethics.* Kingston, ON: School of Policy Studies, Queen's University, 2008.

Bacevich, Andrew J. *American Empire: The Realities and Consequences of U.S. Diplomacy.* Cambridge, MA: Harvard University Press, 2002.

———. *The New American Militarism: How Americans Are Seduced by War.* New York: Oxford University Press, 2005.

Badiou, Alain. *Saint Paul: The Foundation of Universalism.* Trans. Ray Brassier. Stanford, CA: Stanford University Press, 2003.

Baer, William. "On *Rebel without a Cause*: A Conversation with Stewart Stern." *Michigan Quarterly Review* 38 (fall 1999):580–83.

Bainton, Roland H. *Christian Attitudes toward War and Peace: A Historical Survey and Critical Revaluation.* New York: Abingdon Press, 1960.

Bajaj, Monisha. *Encyclopedia of Peace Education.* Charlotte, NC: Information Age Publishers, 2008.

Baldwin, James. *The Fire Next Time.* New York: Dell, 1962.

Balmer, Randall. *Thy Kingdom Come: How the Religious Right Distorts the Faith and Threatens America: An Evangelical's Lament.* New York: Basic Books, 2006.

Banzhalf, Albert H. T. "Reply by Griffith's Lawyer, Albert H. T. Banzhaf, to the Motion Picture Commission of the State of New York," December 1922. *Special Features DVD, D. W. Griffith's The Birth of a Nation.* Directed by D. W. Griffith. New York: Kino Video, 2002.

Barbour, Hugh, and J. William Frost. *The Quakers. Denominations in America, Number 3.* New York: Greenwood Press, 1988.

———, and Arthur O. Roberts, eds. *Early Quaker Writings 1650–1700.* Grand Rapids, MI: Eerdmans, 1973.

Barker, Chris. *Making Sense of Cultural Studies: Central Problems and Critical Debates.* London: Sage, 2002.

Barkun, Michael. *Religion and the Racist Right: The Origins of the Christian Identity Movement.* Rev. ed. Chapel Hill: University of North Carolina Press, 1997.

Barrios, Richard. *Screened Out: Playing Gay in Hollywood from Edison to Stonewall.* New York: Routledge, 2003.

Bassard, Katherine Clay. *Spiritual Interrogations: Culture, Gender, and Community in Early American Women's Writing.* Princeton, NJ: Princeton University Press, 1999.

Batson, Beatrice E. *John Bunyan's* Grace Abounding *and* The Pilgrim's Progress: *An Overview of Literary Studies, 1960–1987.* New York: Garland, 1988.

Bauman, Zygmunt. *Globalization: The Human Consequences.* New York: Columbia University Press, 1998.

Baumgarten, Albert I., ed. *Sacrifice in Religious Experience.* NUMEN Book Series: Studies in the History of Religions no. 93. Leiden: Brill, 2002.

Becker, Carl. *The Heavenly City of the 18th Century Philosophers.* New Haven, CT: Yale University Press, 1932.

Bederman, Gail. *Manliness and Civilization: A Cultural History of Gender and Race in the United States, 1880–1917.* Chicago: University of Chicago Press, 1995.

Bell, Derrick. *Faces at the Bottom of the Well: The Permanence of Racism.* New York: Basic Books, 1992.

Bellah, Robert N. "Civil Religion in American." *Daedalus* 96 (1967):1–21.

———, and Phillip E. Hammond, eds. *Varieties of Civil Religion.* San Francisco: Harper, 1980.

Benavides, Gustavo. "Modernity." In *Critical Terms for Religious Studies,* ed. Mark C. Taylor, 186–204. Chicago: University of Chicago Press, 1998.

Bender, Thomas, ed. *Rethinking American History in a Global Age.* Berkeley: University of California Press, 2002.

Bendroth, Margaret. *Fundamentalism and Gender, 1875 to the Present.* New Haven, CT: Yale University Press, 1993.

Bercovitch, Sacvan. *The American Jeremiad.* Madison: University of Wisconsin Press, 1978.

Bernardi, Daniel, ed. *Classic Hollywood, Classic Whiteness.* Minneapolis: University of Minnesota Press, 2001.

Bertram, Eva, et al., eds. *Drug War Politics: The Price of Denial.* Berkeley: University of California Press, 1996.

Besse, Joseph. *A Collection of the Sufferings of the People Called Quakers, For the Testimony of a Good Conscience, from the Time of their being first distinguished by that NAME, to the time of the act, commonly called the Act of Toleration, granted to Protestant Dissenters in the first Year of the Reign of King William the Third and Queen Mary, in the Year 1689. Taken from Original Records and other Authentic Accounts.* 2 vols., vol. 2, 177–78. London: Luke Hinde, 1753. Swarthmore College, Friends Historical Library.

Birkel, Michael L., and John W. Newman, eds. *The Lamb's War: Quaker Essays to Honor Hugh Barbour.* Richmond, IN: Earlham College Press, 1992.

Bittle, William G. *James Nayler, 1618–1660: The Quaker Indicted by Parliament.* York: Friends United Press, 1986.

Black, Gregory D. *The Catholic Crusade against the Movies, 1940–1975.* Cambridge: Cambridge University Press, 1997.

Block, James E. *A Nation of Agents: The American Path to a Modern Self and Society.* Cambridge, MA: Harvard University Press, 2002.

Block, Sharon. *Rape and Sexual Power in Early America.* Chapel Hill: University of North Carolina Press, 2006.

Blum, Edward J. *Reforging the White Republic: Race, Religion, and American Nationalism, 1865–1898.* Baton Rouge: Louisiana State University Press, 2005.

Blumhofer, Edith L., and Randall Balmer, eds. *Modern Christian Revivals.* Urbana: University of Illinois Press, 1993.

Bodnar, John. *Remaking America: Public Memory, Commemoration, and Patriotism in the Twentieth Century.* Princeton, NJ: Princeton University Press, 1992.

Boime, Albert. *The Unveiling of the National Icons: A Plea for Patriotic Iconoclasm in a Nationalist Era.* Cambridge: Cambridge University Press, 1998.

Bozeman, Theodore D. *The Precisionist Strain: Disciplinary Religion and Antinomian Backlash in Puritanism to 1638.* Chapel Hill: University of North Carolina Press, 2004.

Branch, Taylor. *Parting the Waters: America in the King Years, 1954–63.* New York: Simon & Schuster, 1998.

———. *Pillar of Fire: America in the King Years, 1963–65.* New York: Simon & Schuster, 1998.

Breen, T. H. *The Marketplace of Revolution: How Consumer Politics Shaped American Independence.* New York: Oxford University Press, 2004.

Brekus, Catherine A., ed. *The Religious History of American Women: Reimaging the Past.* Chapel Hill: University of North Carolina Press, 2007.

———. *Strangers and Pilgrims: Female Preaching in America, 1740–1845.* Chapel Hill: University of North Carolina Press, 1998.

Briggs, Laura. *Reproducing Empire: Race, Sex, Science, and U.S. Imperialism in Puerto Rico.* Berkeley: University of California Press, 2002.

Brown, Nick, ed. *Refiguring American Film Genres: History and Theory.* Berkeley: University of California Press, 1998.

Brown, Robert McAfee. *Religion and Violence: A Primer for White Americans.* Philadelphia: Fortress Press, 1987.

Bruckner, Pascal. *The Temptation of Innocence: Living in the Age of Entitlement.* New York: Algora Publications, 2000.

Burlein, Ann. *Life High the Cross: Where White Supremacy and the Christian Right Converge.* Durham, NC: Duke University Press, 2002.

Burrough, Edward. *A Declaration of the Sad and Great Persecution and Martyrdom of the People of God, Called Quakers, in New England for the Worshipping of God* (London: Robert Wilson, 1660), in *Three Quaker Writings by Edward Burrough.* Occasional Papers, Reprint Series no. 6. San Francisco: California State Library, 1939. Swarthmore College, Friends Historical Library.

Bush, George W. "Bush State of the Union Address [January 29, 2002]." Available at http://archives.cnn.com/2002/ALLPOLITICS/01/29/bush.speech.txt/ (accessed January 22, 2009).

———. "President Addresses the Nation, September 7, 2003." Available at http://transcripts.cnn.com/TRANSCRIPTS/0309/07/se.04.html (accessed January 22, 2009).

———. "President Bush Outlines Iraqi Threat, October 7, 2002." Available at http://www.cfr.org/publication/8352/president_bush_outlines_iraqi_threat.html (accessed January 22, 2009)

———. "President Bush's Acceptance Speech to the Republican National Convention," September 2, 2004. Available at http://www.washingtonpost.com/wp-dyn/articles/A57466-2004Sep2.html (accessed July 7, 2008).

———. "Transcript of President Bush's Prayer Service Remarks [September 14, 2001]." Available at http://www.opm.gov/guidance/09-14-01gwb.htm (accessed January 22, 2009)..

———. "Transcript: President Bush's Speech on the War on Terrorism. Delivered at the U.S. Naval Academy in Annapolis, Maryland [November 30, 2005]." Available at http://www.washingtonpost.com/wp-dyn/content/article/2005/11/30/AR2005113000667.html (accessed January 22, 2009).

Butler, Jon. *Awash in a Sea of Faith: Christianizing the American People.* Cambridge, MA: Harvard University Press, 1990.

———. "Jack-in-the-Box Faith: The Religion Problem in Modern American History." *Journal of American History* 90 (2004). Available at http://www.historycooperative.org/journals/jah/90.4/butler.html (accessed September 7, 2008).

Butler, Judith. *Precarious Life: Violence, Mourning, Politics.* New York: Verso, 2004.

Calhoun, Chesire. *Feminism, the Family, and the Politics of the Closet: Lesbianism and Gay Displacement.* New York: Oxford University Press, 2000.

Canaday, Margot. "Building a Straight State: Sexuality and Social Citizenship under the 1944 G.I. Bill." *Journal of American History* 90, no. 3 (2003):935–57.

Capps, Walter. ed. *The Vietnam Reader.* London: Routledge, 1991.

Caraley, Demetrios James, ed. *American Hegemony: Preventive War, Iraq, and Imposing Democracy.* New York: Academy of Political Science, 2004.

Carrasco, Davìd. *City of Sacrifice: The Aztec Empire and the Role of Violence in Civilization.* Boston: Beacon Press, 1999.

Carroll, James. *Constantine's Sword: The Church and the Jews—A History.* Boston: Houghton Mifflin, 2001.

Carter, Jeffrey, ed. *Understanding Religious Sacrifice: A Reader.* Controversies in the Study of Religion Series. London: Continuum, 2003.

Carter, Jimmy. *Our Endangered Values: America's Moral Crisis.* New York: Simon & Schuster, 2005.

Casanova, Jose. *Public Religion in the Modern World.* Chicago: University of Chicago Press, 1994.

CBS Broadcasting Inc. "U.S. Tests Super Bomb in Florida," March 11, 2003. Available at http://www.cbsnews.com/stories/2003/03/11/iraq/main543611.shtml (accessed July 23, 2008).

Cherniavsky, Eva. *Incorporations: Race, Nation, and the Body Politics of Capital.* Minneapolis: University of Minnesota Press, 2006.

Chernus, Ira. *Dr. Strangegod: On the Symbolic Meaning of Nuclear Weapons.* Columbia: University of South Carolina Press, 1986.

Chilton, Bruce. "Sacrificial Mimesis." *Religion* 27 (1997):225–30.

———. *The Temple of Jesus: His Sacrificial Program within a Cultural History of Sacrifice.* University Park: Pennsylvania State University Press, 1992.

Chomsky, Noam. *Power and Terror: Post-9/11 Talks and Interview.* New York: Seven Stories Press, 2003.

Christian Broadcasting Network. "Praying a Shield of Protection." Available at http://cbn. org/special/PrayerShield/index.aspx (accessed July 23, 2008).

Christian Faith in a Violent World: Study Guide. VHS. Produced by Ted Yaple. Cincinnati: Friendship Press, 1997.

Chu, Jonathan M. *Neighbors, Friends, or Madmen: The Puritan Adjustment to Quakerism in Seventeenth-Century Massachusetts Bay.* Westport, CT: Greenwood Press, 1985.

Clark, Randall. *At a Theater or Drive-in Near You: The History, Culture, and Politics of the American Exploitation Film.* New York: Garland, 1995.

Clover, Carol. *Men, Women, and Chain Saws: Gender in the Modern Horror Film.* Princeton, NJ: Princeton University Press, 1992.

Colaicio, James. *Frederick Douglass and the Fourth of July.* New York: Palgrave Macmillan, 2006.

Colavito, Jason. *Knowing Fear: Science, Knowledge and the Development of the Horror Genre.* Jefferson, NC: McFarland, 2008.

Colloquium on Violence and Religion. *Homepage.* Available at http://www.uibk.ac.at/theol/cover/ (accessed July 23, 2008).

Colson, Charles W. "Just War in Iraq." *Christianity Today*, December 9, 2002. Available at http://www.christianitytoday.com/ct/2002/december9/41.72.html (accessed December 20, 2007).

Cone, James H. *Martin and Malcolm and America: A Dream or a Nightmare.* New York: Orbis Books, 1992.

Considine, David M. *The Cinema of Adolescence.* Jefferson, NC: McFarland, 1985.

Cooney, Mark. *Warriors and Peacemakers: How Third Parties Shape Violence.* New York: New York University Press, 1998.

Cooper-White, Pamela. *The Cry of Tamar: Violence against Women and the Church's Response.* Minneapolis: Fortress Press, 1995.

Corrigan, John. *Business of the Heart: Religion and Emotion in the 19th Century.* Berkeley: University of California Press, 2002.

Cortright, David. *Peace: A History of Movements and Ideas.* Cambridge: Cambridge University Press, 2008.

Cott, Nancy F. *The Bonds of Womanhood: "Woman's Sphere" in New England, 1780–1835.* 2nd ed. New Haven, CT: Yale University Press, 1997.

———. *Public Vows: A History of Marriage and the Nation.* Cambridge, MA: Harvard University Press, 2000.

Cox, Harvey. *The Secular City: Secularization and Urbanization in Theological Perspective.* New York: Macmillan, 1965.

Creed, Barbara. "Horror and Monstrous-Feminine: An Imaginary Abjection." In *The Dread of Difference: Gender and the Horror Film,* ed. Barry Keith Grant, 35–65. Austin: University of Texas Press, 1996.

Cristi, Marcela. *From Civil to Political Religion: the Intersection of Culture, Religion, and Politics.* Waterloo, ON: Wilfried Laurier Press, 2001.

Damrosch, Leo. *The Sorrows of the Quaker Jesus: James Nayler and the Puritan Crackdown on the Free Spirit*. Cambridge, MA: Harvard University Press, 1996.

Davidann, John T. *A World of Crisis and Progress: The American YMCA in Japan, 1890–1930*. Allentown, PA: Lehigh University Press, 1998.

Davis, David Brion. *Inhuman Bondage: The Rise and Fall of Slavery in the New World*. Oxford: Oxford University Press, 2006.

———. *In the Image of God: Religion, Moral Values, and Our Heritage of Slavery*. New Haven, CT: Yale University Press, 2001.

Dayton, Donald W. *Discovering an Evangelical Heritage*. New York: Harper & Row, 1976.

Dead Man Walking: The Shooting Script. New York: Newmarket Press, 1997.

DeBeneditti, Charles. *The Peace Reform in American History*. Bloomington: Indiana University Press, 1980.

DeBerg, Betty A. *Ungodly Women: Gender and the First Wave of American Fundamentalism, 1875–1925*. Philadelphia: Fortress Press, 1987.

Dennett, Daniel C. *Breaking the Spell: Religion as a Natural Phenomenon*. New York: Viking, 2006.

Denton-Borhaug, Kelly. "'The Language of 'Sacrifice' in the Buildup to War: A Feminist Rhetorical and Theological Analysis." *Journal of Religion and Popular Culture* 15 (spring 2007). Available at http://www.usask.ca/relst/jrpc/art15-langsacrifice.html (accessed July 23, 2008).

Derrida, Jacques. *The Gift of Death*. Trans. David Wills. Chicago: University of Chicago Press, 1995.

Dewey, John. *A Common Faith*. New Haven, CT: Yale University Press, 1934.

Dickson-Carr, Darryl. "Now You Shall See How a Slave Was Made a Man: Gendering Frederick Douglass' Struggles with Christianity." In *The Puritan Origins of American Sex*, ed. Tracy Fessenden, Nicholas F. Radel, and Magdalena J. Zaborowska, 127–44. New York: Routledge 2001.

Dika, Vera. *Games of Terror: Halloween, Friday the 13th and the Films of the Stalker Cycle*. Rutherford, NJ: Farleigh Dickinson University Press, 1990.

Dixon, Wheeler W. *Straight: Constructions of Heterosexuality in the Cinema*. Albany: State University of New York Press, 2003.

Doherty, Thomas. *Hollywood's Censor: Joseph I. Breen and the Production Code*. New York: Columbia University Press, 2007.

———. *Teenagers and Teenpics: The Juvenilization of American Movies in the 1950s*. Rev. ed. Philadelphia: Temple University Press, 2002.

Dolan, Jay. *Catholic Revivalism: The American Experience, 1830–1900*. Notre Dame, IN: University of Notre Dame Press, 1978.

Domosh, Mona. *American Commodities in an Age of Empire*. New York: Routledge, 2006.

Dorrien, Gary. *Imperial Designs: Neoconservatism and the New Pax Americana*. New York: Routledge, 2004.

Douglas, Ann. *The Feminization of American Culture*. New York: Knopf, 1977.

Douglass, Frederick. "American Slavery, American Religion, and the Free Church of Scotland: An Address Delivered in London, England, on 22 May 1846." In *The Frederick Douglass Papers*. Series 1: Speeches, Debates, and Interviews. Vol. 1: *1841–1846*, ed. John W. Blassingame, 268–99. New Haven, CT: Yale University Press, 1979.

———. "Douglass to Theophilus Gould Steward," July 27, 1886 (1921). In *The Oxford Frederick Douglass Reader*, ed. William L. Andrews. New York: Oxford University Press, 1996.

———. "I Am a Radical Woman Suffrage Man: An Address Delivered in Boston, Massachusetts, on 28 May 1888." In *The Frederick Douglass Papers*. Series 1: Speeches, Debates, and Interviews, Vol. 5, *1881–95*, ed. John W. Blassingame and John R. McKivigan, 378–405. New Haven, CT: Yale University Press, 1979.

———. *Life and Times of Frederick Douglass, Written by Himself.* Hartford, CT: Park Publishing, 1881.

———. "Love of God, Love of Man, Love of Country: An Address Delivered in Syracuse, New York, on 24 September, 1847." In *The Frederick Douglass Papers. Series 1: Speeches, Debates, and Interviews. Vol. 2, 1847–54*, ed. John W. Blassingame, 93–105. New Haven, CT: Yale University Press, 1979.

———. *My Bondage and My Freedom.* New York: Orton and Mulligan, 1855.

———. *Narrative of the Life of Frederick Douglass, An American Slave, Written by Himself.* Ed. William L. Andrews and William S. McFeely. New York: Norton, 1997.

———. "Slavery in the Pulpit of the Evangelical Alliance: An Address Delivered in London, England on 14 September 1846." In *The Frederick Douglass Papers*. Series 1: *Speeches, Debates, and Interviews. Vol. 2, 1847–54*, ed. John W. Blassingame, 407–16. New Haven, CT: Yale University Press, 1979.

———. "Too Much Religion, Too Little Humanity: An Address Delivered in New York on 9 May 1849." In *The Frederick Douglass Papers*. Series 1: Speeches, Debates, and Interviews. Vol. 2, *1847–54*, ed. John W. Blassingame, 176–95. New Haven, CT: Yale University Press, 1979.

———. "What to the Slave Is the Fourth of July? An Address Delivered in Rochester, New York, on 5 July 1852." In *The Frederick Douglass Papers*. Series 1: Speeches, Debates, and Interviews. Vol. 2, *1847–54*, ed. John W. Blassingame, 359–88. New Haven, CT: Yale University Press, 1979.

Douglass, Mary. *Purity and Danger: An Analysis of the Concepts of Purity and Taboo.* New York: Routledge Classics, 2002.

DuBois, Ellen Carol, and Richard Candida Smith, eds. *Feminist as Thinker: A Reader in Documents and Essays.* New York: New York University Press, 2007.

Dyer, William. *Mary Dyer, Quaker: Two Letters of William Dyer of Rhode Island 1659–60.* Cambridge: Cambridge University Press. Printed for Charles Dyer Norton and Daniel B. Dyer, 1927(?). Swarthmore College, Friends Historical Library.

Ebserole, Gary L. *Captured by Texts: Puritan to Postmodern Images of Indian Captivity.* Charlottesville: University Press of Virginia, 1995.

Eck, Diana L. *A New Religious America: How a "Christian Country" Has Become the World's Most Religiously Diverse Nation.* San Francisco: Harper, 2001.

Eliade, Mircea. *Patterns in Comparative Religion.* Trans. Rosemary Sheed. Lincoln: University of Nebraska Press, 1996.

———. *The Sacred and the Profane: The Nature of Religion.* Trans. Willard Trask. New York: Harcourt, Brace and World, 1959.

Elias, Norbert. *Power and Civility: The Civilizing Process.* Vol. 2. Trans. Edmund Jephcott. New York: Pantheon Books, 1982.

Ellens, J. Harold. *The Destructive Power of Religion: Violence in Judaism, Christianity, and Islam.* 4 vols. Westport, CT: Praeger, 2004.

Epp, Michael H. "Raising Minstrelsy: Humor, Satire and the Stereotype in The Birth of a Nation and Bamboozled." *Canadian Review of American Studies* 33 (January 2003):17–35.

Evans, Curtis J. *The Burden of Black Religion.* New York: Oxford University Press, 2008.

Fairclough, Adam. *To Redeem the Soul of America: The Southern Christian Leadership Conference and Martin Luther King Jr.* Athens: University of George Press, 1987.

The Faith Project, Inc. *This Fair Far by Faith Website.* Ed. June Cross. Site executive producer Jessica Orkin. Available at http://www.pbs.org/thisfarbyfaith/ (accessed July 18, 2008).

Fallows, James. "What Did You Do in the Class War, Daddy?" In *The Vietnam Reader,* ed. Walter Capps, 213–21. New York: Routledge, 1991.

Faludi, Susan. *Backlash: The Undeclared War against American Women.* New York: Crown, 1991.

Family Research Council. "Core Principles." Available at http://www.frc.org/get.cfm?c=ABOUT_FRC (accessed July 18, 2008).

Fass, Paula S. *The Damned and the Beautiful: American Youth in the 1920s.* New York: Oxford University Press, 1977.

———, ed. *Encyclopedia of Children and Childhood: In History and Society.* 3 vols. New York: Macmillan Reference USA, 2004.

———. *Kidnapped: Child Abduction in America.* New York: Oxford University Press, 1997.

———, and Mary Ann Mason, eds. *Childhood in America.* New York: New York University Press, 2000.

Faust, Drew Gilpin. *The Republic of Suffering: Death and the American Civil War.* New York: Knopf, 2008.

Fenn, Richard. *Beyond Idols: The Shape of a Secular Society.* New York: Oxford University Press, 2001.

Fessenden, Tracy. *Culture and Redemption: Religion, the Secular, and American Literature.* Princeton, NJ: Princeton University Press, 2007.

Feuerbach, Ludwig. *The Essence of Christianity.* Trans. George Eliot. New York: Harper, 1957.

Fiske, John. *Power Plays, Power Works.* London: Verso, 1993.

Flanders, Laura, ed., with Phoebe St. John and Livia Tenzor. *The W Effect: Bush's War on Women.* New York: Feminist Press at the City University of New York, 2004.

Fliegelman, Jay. *Prodigals and Pilgrims: The American Revolution against Patriarchal Authority, 1750–1800.* Cambridge: Cambridge University Press, 1982.

Flynn, Matthew. *First Strike: Preemptive War in Modern History.* New York: Routledge, 2008.

Focus on the Family. Homepage. Available at www.focusonthefamily.com (accessed July 18, 2008).

Foster, John Bellamy, and Robert W. McChesney, eds. *Pox Americana: Exposing the America Empire.* New York: Monthly Review Press, 2004.

Foster, Thomas A. *Sex and the Eighteenth-Century Man: Massachusetts and the History of Sexuality in America.* Boston: Beacon Press, 2006.

Foucault, Michel. *Discipline and Punish: The Birth of the Prison.* Translated by Alan Sheridan. 2nd ed. New York: Vintage Books, 1995.

Frankenberg, Ruth. *White Women, Race Matters: The Social Construction of Whiteness.* Minneapolis: University of Minnesota Press, 1993.

Franko, Mark, ed. *Ritual and Event: Interdisciplinary Perspectives.* New York: Routledge, 2007.

Frantzen, Allen J. *Bloody Good: Chivalry, Sacrifice, and the Great War.* Chicago: University of Chicago Press, 2003.

Franzier, E. Franklin, and C. Eric Lincoln. *The Negro Church in America / The Black Church since Frazier.* New York: Schocken Books, 1974.

Fraser, Matthew. *Weapons of Mass Distraction: Soft Power and American Empire.* Toronto: Key Porter Books, 2003.

Freeland, Cynthia A. *The Naked and the Undead: Evil and the Appeal of Horror.* Boulder, CO: Westview Press, 2000.

Freud, Sigmund. *The Future of an Illusion.* Trans. W. D. Robson-Scott and ed. James W. Strachey. New York: Doubleday, 1964.

——. *The Interpretation of Dreams.* Trans. A. A. Brill. New York: Modern Library, 1950.

——. *The Interpretation of Dreams.* Trans. and ed. James Strachey. New York: Basic Books, 1960.

Frost, Linda. *Never One Nation: Freaks, Savages, and Whiteness in U.S. Popular Culture, 1850–1877.* Minneapolis: University of Minnesota Press, 2005.

Furstenberg, Francois. *In the Name of the Father: Washington's Legacy, Slavery, and the Making of a Nation.* New York: Penguin, 2006.

Gabriel, Mark A. *Islam and Terrorism: What the Qu'ran Really Teaches about Christianity, Violence, and the Goals of Islamic Jihad.* New York: Charisma House, 2002.

Gager, John G., ed. *Curse Tablets and Binding Spells from the Ancient World.* New York: Oxford University Press, 1992.

Garber, Marjorie, and Rebecca L. Walkowitz, eds. *One Nation under God: Religion and American Culture.* New York: Routledge, 1999.

Gardella, Peter. *American Domestic Religion: Work, Food, Sex and Other Commitments.* Cleveland: Pilgrim Press, 1999.

Garnsey, Peter. *Idea of Slavery from Aristotle to Augustine.* Cambridge: Cambridge University Press, 1996.

Gauchet, Marcel. *The Disenchantment of the World: A Political History of Religion.* Trans. Oscar Burge. Princeton, NJ: Princeton University Press, 1997.

Gaustad, Edwin S. *Proclaim Liberty throughout All the Land: A History of Church and State in America.* New York: Oxford University Press, 2003.

Geertz, Clifford. *The Interpretation of Cultures.* New York: Basic Books, 2000.

Genovese, Eugene, and Elizabeth Fox-Genovese. "The Divine Sanction of Social Order: Religious Foundations of Southern Slaveholders World View." *Journal of the American Academy of Religion* 55 (summer 1987):211–33.

——. *The Mind of the Master Class: History and Faith in the Southern Slaveholders' Worldview.* Cambridge: Cambridge University Press, 2005.

Gill, Gerald. "Black Soldier's Perspectives on the War." In *The Vietnam Reader,* ed. Walter Capps, 173–85. New York: Routledge, 1991.

Girard, René. *I See Satan Fall like Lightning.* Trans. James G. Williams. New York: Orbis Books, 2001.

——. *The Scapegoat.* Trans. Yvonne Freccero. Baltimore: John Hopkins University Press, 1986.

——. *Violence and the Sacred.* Trans. Patrick Gregory. Baltimore: John Hopkins University Press, 1977.

Glancy, Jennifer A. *Slavery in Early Christianity*. New York: Oxford University Press, 2002.

Godbeer, Richard. *Sexual Revolution in Early America*. Baltimore: John Hopkins University Press, 2002.

Goldenberg, David M. *The Curse of Ham: Race and Slavery in Early Christianity, Judaism, and Islam*. Princeton, NJ: Princeton University Press, 2003.

Goss, Jon. "Once-upon-a-Time in the Commodity World: An Unofficial Guide to the Mall of America." *Annals of the Association of American Geographers* 89 (March 1999):45–75.

Gottlieb, Roger S., ed. *Liberating Faith: Religious Voices for Justice, Peace, and Ecological Wisdom*. Lanham, MD: Rowman & Littlefield, 2003.

Grady, Dennis. "From *Reefer Madness* to *Freddy's Dead*: The Portrayal of Marijuana Use in Motion Pictures." In *Beyond the Stars III: The Material World in the American Popular Film*, ed. Paul Loukides and Linda K. Fuller, 51–64. Bowling Green, OH: Bowling Green State University Press, 1993.

Graff, Harvey J. *Conflicting Paths: Growing Up in America*. Cambridge, MA: Harvard University Press, 1995.

Grant, Barry Keith. "Introduction" In *The Dread of Difference: Gender and the Horror Film*, ed. Barry K. Grant, 1–14. Austin: University of Texas Press, 1996.

Greenberg, Harvey R. "King Kong: The Beast in the Boudoir—Or 'You Can't Marry That Girl, You're a Gorilla!'" In *The Dread of Difference: Gender and the Horror Film*, ed. Barry K. Grant, 338–52. Austin: University of Texas Press, 1996.

Greven, Philip J. *The Protestant Temperament: Patterns of Child-Rearing, Religious Experience, and the Self in Early America*. New York: Knopf, 1977.

Griffin, David Ray, et al., eds. *The American Empire and the Commonwealth of God: A Political, Economic, Religious Statement*. Louisville: Westminster Press, 2006.

Griffith, D. W. "Prelude to The Birth of a Nation." [Interview of D. W. Griffith with John Huston, 1930.] In *Special Features DVD, D. W. Griffith's The Birth of a Nation*. New York, Kino Video, 2002.

Griffith, R. Marie. *American Religions: A Documentary History*. New York: Oxford University Press, 2008.

———. *God's Daughters: Evangelical Women and the Power of Submission*. Berkeley: University of California Press, 1997.

Griffiths, Paul, and George Weigel. "Just War: An Exchange." *First Things* 122 (April 2002):31–36.

Grimes, Ronald. *Deeply into the Bone: Reinventing Rites of Passage*. Berkeley: University of California Press, 2000.

Guelzo, Allen C. *Edwards on the Will: A Century of American Theological Debate*. Middletown, CT: Wesleyan University Press, 1989.

Guerrero, Ed. *Framing Blackness: The African American Image in Film*. Philadelphia: Temple University Press, 1993.

Guyatt, Nicholas. *Providence and the Invention of the United States, 1607–1876*. Cambridge: Cambridge University Press, 2007.

Hackett, Elizabeth, and Sally Haslanger, eds. *Theorizing Feminisms: A Reader*. New York: Oxford University Press, 2006.

Hagedorn, Ann. *Savage Peace: Hope and Fear in America*. New York: Simon & Schuster, 2007.

The Handmaid's Tale. DVD. Directed by Volker Schlondorff. MGM Home Entertainment, 1990.

Hall, David D. *Worlds of Wonder, Days of Judgment: Popular Religious Belief in Early New England.* New York: Knopf, 1989.

Hall, Stuart, and Tony Jefferson, eds. *Resistance through Rituals: Youth Subcultures in Post-War Britain.* London: Hutchinson, 1976.

Halloween. DVD. Directed by John Carpenter. 1978; Troy, MI: Anchor Bay Entertainment, 2000.

Hamerton-Kelly, Robert G. *Sacred Violence: Paul's Hermeneutic of the Cross.* Minneapolis: Fortress Press, 1992.

Handlin, Oscar, and Lilian Handlin. *Liberty in America, 1600 to the Present.* Vols. 1–4. New York: Harper & Row, 1986–96.

Handy, Robert T. *A Christian America: Protestant Hopes and Historical Realities.* New York: Oxford University Press, 1971.

Hardesty, Nancy. *Women Called to Witness: Evangelical Feminism in the 19th Century.* Nashville: Abingdon Press, 1984.

Harding, Vincent. *There Is a River: The Black Struggle for Freedom in America.* New York: Harcourt Brace Jovanovich, 1981.

Hardt, Michael, and Antonio Negri. *Empire.* Cambridge, MA: Harvard University Press, 2000.

Harrill, J. Albert. "The Use of the New Testament in the American Slave Controversy: A Case History in the Hermeneutical Tension between Biblical Criticism and Christian Moral Debate." *Religion and American Culture* 10 (summer 2000):149–86.

Harris, Cheryl I. "Whiteness as Property." *Harvard Law Review* 106 (1993):1709–37.

Harris, Sam. *The End of Faith: Religion, Terror, and the Future of Reason.* New York: Norton, 2004.

Hart, Frederick. "Description—The Three Soldiers." *Wikipedia.* Available at http://en.wikipedia.org/wiki/The_Three_Soldiers (accessed July 9, 2008)..

Hartog, Hendrik. *Man and Wife in America: A History.* Cambridge, MA: Harvard University Press, 2000.

———. "What Gay Marriage Teaches about the History of Marriage." History News Network, April 5, 2004, Available at http://hnn.us/articles/4400.html (accessed January 22, 2009).

Harvey, Paul. *Freedom's Coming: Religious Culture and the Shaping of the South from the Civil War through the Civil Rights Era.* Chapel Hill: University of North Carolina Press, 2007.

Haslam, Jason, and Julia M. Wright, eds. *Captivating Subjects: Writing Confinement, Citizenship, and Nationhood in the Nineteenth Century.* Toronto: University of Toronto Press, 2005.

Hatch, Nathan. *The Democratization of American Christianity.* New Haven, CT: Yale University Press, 1989.

Heclo, Hugh, and Wilfred M. McClay, eds. *Religion Returns to the Public Square: Faith and Policy in America.* Washington, DC: Woodrow Wilson Center Press / Baltimore: Johns Hopkins University Press, 2003.

Hedges, Chris. *American Fascists: The Christian Right and the War on America.* New York: Free Press, 2007.

———. *War Is a Force That Gives Us Meaning*. New York: Public Affairs, 2002.

Heimert, Alan, and Perry Miller, eds. *The Great Awakening: Documents Illustrating the Crisis and Its Consequences*. Indianapolis: Bobbs-Merrill, 1967.

Heyrman, Christine Leigh. *Southern Cross: The Beginnings of the Bible Belt*. Chapel Hill: University of North Carolina Press, 1997.

Higgs, Robert. *God in the Stadium: Sports and Religion in America*. Lexington: University of Kentucky Press, 1995.

Hill, Lisa. "The Hidden Theology of Adam Smith." *European Journal of the History of Economic Thought* 8 (March 2001):1–29.

Hofmyer, Isabel. *The Portable Bunyan: A Transitional History of* The Pilgrim's Progress. Princeton, NJ: Princeton University Press, 2004.

Hofstadter, Richard. *Anti-Intellectualism in American Life*. New York: Knopf, 1963.

———. "The Paranoid Style in American Politics." *Harper's Magazine*, November 1964, 77–86.

hooks, bell. 1993. "Consumed by Images." *Artforum*, February 1993, 5–6.

Horne, Gerald. "'Myth' and the Making of 'Malcolm X.'" *American Historical Review* 98 (April 1993):440–50.

Hostel. DVD. Directed by Eli Roth. Hollywood: Lions Gate Films, 2006.

"Hostel Trailer." *Hostel*. Available at http://www.hostelfilm.com (accessed July 9, 2008).

Hughes, Richard T. *Myths America Lives By*. Urbana: University of Illinois Press, 2003.

Hunt, James B. "The Faith Journey of Frederick Douglass." *Christian Scholar's Review* 14 (1986):228–46.

Huntington, Samuel. "The Clash of Civilizations." In *The Globalization Reader*, ed. Frank J. Lechner and John Boli, 27–34. Malden, MA: Blackwell, 2000.

———. *The Clash of Civilizations and the Remaking of World Order*. New York: Free Press, 2002.

Hutchings, Peter. *The Horror Film*. Harlow: Pearson/Longman, 2004.

Hypocrites. VHS Video. Directed by Lois Weber. 1915. New York: Kino Video, 2000.

Infield, Tom, Diego Ibarguen, and Martin Merzer. "In Sign to Iraq, U.S. Tests Huge Bomb." *Philadelphia Inquirer*, March 12, 2003, A1.

Ingle, H. Larry. *First among Friends: George Fox and the Creation of Quakerism*. New York: Oxford University Press, 1994.

International Pragmatism Society. "The Cambridge Platform." 1648. Available at http://www.pragmatism.org/american/cambridge_platform.htm (accessed July 23, 2008).

Internet Movie Database. "Lois Weber." Available at http://www.imdb.com/name/nm0916665/ (accessed September 7, 2008).

Jabour, Anya. *Marriage in the Early Republic: Elizabeth and William Wirt and the Companionate Ideal*. Baltimore: John Hopkins University Press, 1998.

Jacob, Margaret C. and Matthew Kadane. "Missing, Now Found in the Eighteenth Century: Weber's Protestant Capitalist." *American Historical Review* 108 (February 2003). Available at http://www.historycooperative.org/journals/ahr/108.1/ah0103000020.html. (accessed July 16, 2008).

Jacobs, Lea. *The Wages of Sin: Censorship and the Fallen Woman Film, 1928–1942*. Madison: University of Wisconsin Press, 1991.

Jakobsen, Janet R., and Ann Pellegrini. *Love the Sin: Sexual Regulation and the Limits of Religious Tolerance*. New York: New York University Press, 2003.

Jancovich, Mark, ed. *Horror, the Film Reader*. New York: Routledge, 2002.

———, et al., eds. *Defining Cult Movies: The Cultural Politics of Oppositional Taste*. Manchester: Manchester University Press, 2003.

Jewett, Robert. *The American Monomyth*. 2nd ed. Lanham, MD: University Press of America, 1988.

———. *Mission and Menace: Four Centuries of American Religious Zeal*. Minneapolis: Fortress Press, 2008.

———, and John Shelton Lawrence. *Captain America and the Crusade against Evil: The Dilemma of Zealous Nationalism*. Grand Rapids, MI: Eerdmans, 2003.

John Paul II. "Messages of His Holiness Pope John Paul II for the Celebration of the World Day of Peace." *Vatican: The Holy See*. Available at http://www.vatican.va/holy_father/john_paul_ii/messages/peace/ (accessed September 8, 2008).

Johnson, Chalmers. "Empire vs. Democracy." January 31. *TomPaine.com*. Institute for America's Future. Available at http://www.tompaine.com/articles/2007/01/31/empire_vs_democracy.php (accessed January 31, 2007).

Johnson, Paul Christopher. "Savage Civil Religion." *Numen* 52 (2005):289–324.

Johnson, Sylvester. *The Myth of Ham in Nineteenth-Century American Christianity: Race, Heathens, and the People of God*. New York: Palgrave Macmillan, 2004.

Johnson, William Bruce. *Miracles and Sacrilege: Roberto Rossellini, the Church, and Film Censorship in Hollywood*. Toronto: University of Toronto Press, 2008.

Juergensmeyer, Mark. *Global Rebellion: Religious Challenges to the Secular State, from Christian Militias to al Qaeda*. Berkeley: University of California Press, 2008.

———. "The Global Rise of Religious Nationalism." In *Religions/Globalizations: Theories and Cases*, ed. Dwight N. Hopkins et al., 66–83. Durham, NC: Duke University Press, 2001.

———. *The New Cold War? Religious Nationalism Confronts the Secular State*. Berkeley: University of California Press, 1993.

———. *Terror in the Mind of God: The Global Rise of Religious Violence*. Berkeley: University of California Press, 2000.

Juster, Susan. *Disorderly Women: Sexual Politics and Evangelicalism in Revolutionary New England*. Ithaca, NY: Cornell University Press, 1994.

———. "The Spirit and the Flesh: Gender, Language, and Sexuality in American Protestantism." In *New Directions in American Religious History*, ed. Harry S. Stout and D. G. Hart, 334–61. New York: Oxford University Press, 1997.

———. "To Slay the Beast: Visionary Women in the Early Republic." In *A Mighty Baptism: Race, Gender, and the Creation of American Protestantism*, ed. Susan Juster and Lisa McFarlane, 19–38. Ithaca, NY: Cornell University Press, 1996.

Kamensky, Jane. *Governing the Tongue: The Politics of Speech in Early New England*. New York: Oxford University Press, 1997.

Kant, Immanuel. "Perpetual Peace: A Philosophical Sketch." Trans. Kevin Paul Geiman. Available at http://www.mtholyoke.edu/acad/intrel/kant/kant1.htm (accessed September 10, 2008).

Kaplan, Amy. *The Anarchy of Empire in the Making of U.S. Culture*. Cambridge, MA: Harvard University Press, 2002.

Karlsen, Carol F. *The Devil in the Shape of a Woman: Witchcraft in Colonial New England*. New York: Norton, 1987.

Kaufmann, Eric P. *The Rise and Fall of Anglo-America.* Cambridge, MA: Harvard University Press, 2004.

Keen, David. *Endless War: Hidden Functions of the "War on Terror."* London: Pluto Press, 2006.

Kegley, Charles W., Jr., and Gregory A. Raymond. *After Iraq: The Imperiled American Imperium.* Oxford: Oxford University Press, 2007.

Keith, Barry. *The Dread of Difference: Gender and the Horror Film.* Austin: University of Texas Press, 1996.

Kerber, Linda K. *Women of the Republic: Intellect and Ideology in Revolutionary America.* Chapel Hill: University of North Carolina Press, 1980.

———, and Jane Sherron De Hart. *Women's America: Refocusing the Past.* 6th ed. New York: Oxford University Press, 2004.

Kett, Joseph F. *Rites of Passage: Adolescence in America, 1790 to the Present.* New York: Basic Books, 1977.

Kibbey, Ann. "Language in Slavery." In *Frederick Douglass's Narrative of the Life of Frederick Douglass,* ed. Harold Bloom, 131–52. New York: Chelsea House, 1988.

Kidd, Colin. *The Forging of Races: Race and Scripture in the Protestant Atlantic World, 1600–2000.* Cambridge: Cambridge University Press, 2006.

Kiernan, V. G. *America: The New Imperialism. From White Settlement to World Hegemony.* London: Verso, 2005.

Kirby, Vicki. *Judith Butler: Live Theory.* London: Continuum, 2006.

Kimball, Charles. *When Religion Becomes Evil.* San Francisco: Harper, 2002.

Kimmel, Michael S. *Manhood in America: A Cultural History.* 2nd ed. New York: Oxford University Press, 2006.

Kincaid, James R. *Child-Loving: The Erotic Child and Victorian Culture.* New York: Routledge, 1992.

King, Martin Luther, Jr. "Nonviolence and Racial Justice." In *A Testament of Hope: The Essential Writings and Speeches of Martin Luther King, Jr.,* ed. James M. Washington, 5–9. San Francisco: Harper San Francisco, 1986.

Knight, Janice. *Orthodoxies in Massachusetts: Rereading American Puritanism.* Cambridge, MA: Harvard University Press, 1994.

Kristeva, Julia. *Powers of Horror: An Essay on Abjection.* Trans. Leon S. Roudiez. New York: Columbia University Press, 1982.

Küng, Hans. *A Global Ethic for Global Politics and Economics.* Trans. John Bowden. New York: Oxford University Press, 1998.

———. *A Global Ethic: The Declaration of the World's Parliament of Religions.* New York: Continuum, 1993.

———, ed. *Yes to a Global Ethic.* New York: Continuum, 1996.

LaCapra, Dominick. *Rethinking Intellectual History: Texts, Contexts, Language.* Ithaca, NY: Cornell University Press, 1983.

Lambert, Frank. *Pedlar in Divinity: George Whitefield and the Transatlantic Revivals, 1737–1770.* Princeton, NJ: Princeton University Press, 1994.

La Monica, Paul R. "'Torture Porn' Helps Lionsgate Roar." *CNNMoney.com.* CNN. Available at http://money.cnn.com/2007/06/08/news/companies/lionsgate/index.htm (accessed July 8, 2008).

Lang, Robert, ed. *The Birth of Nation: D. W. Griffith, Director*. New Brunswick, NJ: Rutgers University Press, 1992.

LaPlante, Eve. *American Jezebel: The Uncommon Life of Anne Hutchinson, the Woman Who Defied the Puritans*. San Francisco: Harper San Francisco, 2004.

Larcher, Gerhard, ed. *Visible Violence: Sichtbare und Verschleierte Gewalt im Film*. Munster: Lit Verlag, 1998.

Layne, Christopher, and Bradley A. Thayer. *American Empire: A Debate*. London: Routledge, 2007.

Lee, Jarena. *The Life and Religious Experiences of Jarena Lee, a Coloured Lady, Giving an Account of Her Call to Preach the Gospel. Revised and Corrected from the Original Manuscript, Written by Herself*. In *Sisters of the Spirit: Three Black Women's Autobiographies of the Nineteenth Century*, ed. William L. Andrews. Bloomington: Indiana University Press, 1986 (orig. pub. 1836).

Lee, Jonathan Scott. "Spike Lee's *Malcolm X* as Transformational Object." *American Imago* 52 (1995):155–67.

Lee, Spike. *By Any Means Necessary: The Trials and Tribulations of the Making of Malcolm X*. With Ralph Wiley. New York: Hyperion, 1992.

———. *Malcolm X*. DVD. Burbank, CA: Warner Home Video, 2005.

Lepore, Jill. *The Name of War: King Philip's War and the Origins of American Identity*. New York: Knopf, 1998.

Lerner, Rabbi Michael. *The Left Hand of God: Taking Back Our Country from the Religious Right*. San Francisco: Harper San Francisco, 2006.

Lewis, Jon. *The Road to Romance and Ruin: Teen Films and Youth Culture*. New York: Routledge, 1992.

Lienhard, Joseph T. *The Bible, the Church, and Authority: The Canon of the Christian Bible in History and Theology*. Collegeville, MN: Liturgical Press, 1995.

Limbaugh, David. *Persecution: How Liberals Are Waging War against Christianity*. Washington, DC: Regnery, 2003.

Lincoln, Bruce. *Authority: Construction and Corrosion*. Chicago: University of Chicago Press, 1994.

———. *Death, War, and Sacrifice: Studies in Ideology and Practice*. Chicago: University of Chicago Press, 1991.

———. *Holy Terrors: Thinking about Religion after September 11*. Chicago: University of Chicago Press, 2003.

———. *Religion, Empire and Torture: The Case of Achaemenia Persia, with a Postscript on Abu Ghraib*. Chicago: University of Chicago Press, 2007.

———. "The Theology of George W. Bush." In *The Martin Marty Center Religion and Culture Web Forum*. Available at http://marty-center.uchicago.edu/webforum/102004/index.shtml (accessed July 7, 2008).

Lincoln, C. Eric. *The Black Church in the African American Experience*. Durham, NC: Duke University Press, 1990.

———. *Black Muslims in America*. 3rd ed. Grand Rapids, MI: Eerdmans, 1994.

Lindenauer, Leslie. *Piety and Power: Gender and Religious Culture in the American Colonies, 1630–1700*. New York: Routledge, 2002.

Lindley, Susan Hall. *"You have Stept out of your Place:" A History of Women and Religion in America*. Louisville: Westminster John Knox Press, 1996.

Linenthal, Edward Tabor. *Sacred Ground: Americans and Their Battlefields*. Urbana: University of Illinois Press, 1993.

Lipset, Seymour Martin. *American Exceptionalism: A Double-Edged Sword*. New York: Norton, 1996.

Little, Ann M. *Abraham in Arms: War and Gender in Colonial New England*. Philadelphia: University of Pennsylvania Press, 2007.

Lloyd, Mona. *Judith Butler: From Norms to Politics*. Cambridge, MA: Polity Press, 2007.

Lockhart, Charles. *The Roots of American Exceptionalism: Institutions, Cultures, and Policies*. New York: Palgrave Macmillan, 2003.

Long, Kathryn Teresa. *The Revival of 1857–58: Interpreting an American Religious Awakening*. New York: Oxford University Press, 1998.

Lowenstein, Adam. *Shocking Representation: Historical Trauma, National Cinema, and the Modern Horror Film*. New York: Columbia University Press, 2005.

Loy, David. "The Religion of the Market." *Journal of the American Academy of Religion* 65 (summer 1997):275–90.

Lunger Knoppers, Laura, ed. *Puritanism and Its Discontents*. Newark: University of Delaware Press, 2003.

Luther, Martin. *Christian Liberty*. Ed. Harold J. Grimm. Philadelphia: Fortress Press, 1957 (orig. pub. 1520).

Lutheran Settlement House. Homepage. Available at www.lutheransettlement.org (accessed July 19, 2008).

Lyden, John C. *Film as Religion: Myths, Morals, and Rituals*. New York: New York University Press, 2003.

Lyons, Charles. *The New Censors: Movies and the Culture Wars*. Philadelphia: Temple University Press, 1997.

Malcolm X. DVD. Directed by Spike Lee. 1993.; Burbank, CA: Warner Home Video, 2005.

Males, Mike A. *Framing Youth: Ten Myths about the Next Generation*. Monroe, ME: Common Courage Press, 1999.

———. *The Scapegoat Generation: American's War on Adolescents*. Monroe, ME: Common Courage Press, 1996.

Mali, Joseph. *Mythistory: The Making of a Modern Mythistory*. Chicago: University of Chicago Press, 2003.

Mallick, Krishna, and Doris Hunter, eds. *An Anthology of Nonviolence: Historical and Contemporary Voices*. Foreword by Elise Boulding. Westport, CT: Greenwood Press, 2002.

Maltby, Richard. *Harmless Entertainment: Hollywood and the Ideology of Consensus*. Metuchen, NJ: Scarecrow Press, 1983.

Mansfield, Stephen P. *The Faith of George W. Bush*. New York: Jeremy P. Tarcher (Penguin), 2003.

Marsden, George. *The Soul of the American University: From Protestant Establishment to Established Nonbelief*. New York: Oxford University Press, 1994.

Martin, Joel W., and Conrad E. Ostwalt Jr., eds. *Screening the Sacred: Religion, Myth, and Ideology in Popular American Film*. Boulder, CO: Westview Press, 1995.

Martin, Waldo E. *The Mind of Frederick Douglas*. Chapel Hill: University of North Carolina Press, 1985.

Marty, Martin E. *Modern American Religion*. Vol. 1, *The Irony of It All, 1893–1919*. Chicago: University of Chicago Press, 1986.

———. *Modern American Religion.* Vol. 2, *The Noise of Conflict, 1919–1941.* Chicago: University of Chicago Press, 1991.

———. *The One and the Many: America's Struggle for the Common Good.* Cambridge, MA: Harvard University Press, 1997.

———. *Righteous Empire: The Protestant Experience in America.* New York: Dial Press, 1970.

Marvin, Carolyn, and David W. Engle. *Blood Sacrifice and the Nation: Totem Rituals and the American Flag.* Cambridge: Cambridge University Press, 1999.

Mason, Mary Ann. *From Father's Property to Children's Rights: The History of Child Custody in the United States.* New York: Columbia University Press, 1994.

Massey, Vera. *The Clouded Quaker Star: James Nayler, 1618–1660.* York: Friends United Press, 1999.

Masuzawa, Tomoko. *The Invention of World Religions: Or, How European Universalism Was Preserved in the Language of Pluralism.* Chicago: University of Chicago Press, 2005.

Mayer, William G., ed. *The Making of the Presidential Candidates, 2004.* Lanham, MD: Rowman & Littlefield, 2004.

Mcbride, Dwight A. *Impossible Witnesses: Truth, Abolitionism, and Slave Testimony.* New York: New York University Press, 2001.

McClymond, Kathryn. "The Nature and Elements of Sacrificial Ritual." *Method and Theory in the Study of Religion* 16 (2004):337–66.

McClymond, Michael, ed. *Embodying the Spirit: New Perspectives on North American Revivalism.* Baltimore: John Hopkins University Press, 2004.

McCutcheon, Russell T. *The Discipline of Religion: Structure, Meaning, Rhetoric.* New York: Routledge, 2003.

———. "The Imperial Dynamic in the Study of Religion: Neocolonial Practices in an American Discipline." In *Postcolonial America,* ed. C. Richard King, 275–302. Urbana: University of Illinois Press, 2000.

———. *Manufacturing Religion: The Discourse on Sui Generis Religion and the Politics of Nostalgia.* New York: Oxford University Press, 1997.

McDannell, Colleen. *Material Christianity: Religion and Popular Culture in America.* New Haven, CT: Yale University Press, 1995.

McDowell, Deborah E. "In the First Place: Making Frederick Douglass and the Afro-American Narrative Tradition." In *Critical Essays on Frederick Douglass,* ed. William L. Andrews, 195–208. Boston: G. K. Hall, 1991.

McFague, Sallie. *Models of God: Theology for an Ecological, Nuclear Age.* Minneapolis: Fortress Press, 1987.

McGee, Mark Thomas, and R. J. Robertson. *The J. D. Films: Juvenile Delinquency in the Movies.* Jefferson, NC: McFarland, 1982.

McGinn, Bernard, ed. *The Essential Writings of Christian Mysticism.* New York: Modern Library, 2006.

McKivigan, John R., ed. *Abolitionism and American Religion.* New York: Garland, 1999.

———. *The War against Proslavery Religion: Abolitionism and the Northern Churches, 1830–1865.* Ithaca, NY: Cornell University Press, 1984.

———, and Mitchell Snay, eds. *Religion and the Antebellum Debate over Slavery.* Athens: University of Georgia Press, 1998.

McLaughlin, Milbrey W., et al., eds. *Urban Sanctuaries: Neighborhood Organizations in the Lives and Futures of Inner-City Youth.* San Francisco: Jossey-Bass, 1994.

McLoughlin, William G. *Modern Revivalism: Charles Grandison Finney to Billy Graham.* New York: Ronald Press, 1959.

———. *Revivals, Awakenings, and Reform: An Essay on Religion and Social Change, 1607–1977.* Chicago History of American Religion. Chicago: University of Chicago Press, 1978.

McNamara, Robert S. *In Retrospect: The Tragedy and Lessons of Vietnam.* New York: Vintage Books, 1996.

McNeill, William H. *Mythistory and Other Essays.* Chicago: University of Chicago Press, 1986.

McVoy, Douglas A. "Drug War Facts." Common Sense for Drug Policy. Available at http://www.drugwarfacts.org/ (accessed July 9, 2008).

Meyer, Jeffrey F. *Myths in Stone: Religious Dimensions of Washington, D.C.* Berkeley: University of California Press, 2001.

Meyers, Diana. "Feminist Perspectives on the Self." *Stanford Encyclopedia of Philosophy.* Stanford University. Available at http://plato.stanford.edu/entries/feminism-self/ (accessed July 18, 2008).

Miedzian, Myriam. *Boys Will Be Boys: Breaking the Link between Masculinity and Violence.* New York: Anchor Books, 1991.

Miles, Margaret. *Seeing and Believing: Religion and Values in the Movies.* Boston: Beacon Press, 1996.

Miller, Perry. *Errand into the Wilderness.* New York: Harper & Row, 1956.

———. *Nature's Nation.* Cambridge, MA: Harvard University Press, 1967.

Miller, William L. *Dorothy Day: A Biography.* San Francisco: Harper & Row, 1982.

Mintz, Steven. *Huck's Raft: A History of American Childhood.* Cambridge, MA: Harvard University Press, 2004.

Miron, Jeffrey A. *Drug War Crimes: The Costs and Consequences of Prohibition.* Oakland, CA: Independent Institute, 2004.

Mjagkij, Nina. *Light in the Darkness: African Americans and the YMCA, 1852–1946.* Lexington: University of Kentucky Press, 1994.

———, and Margaret Spratt, eds. *Men and Women Adrift: The YMCA and the YWCA in the City.* New York: New York University Press, 1997.

Modell, John. *Into One's Own: From Youth to Adulthood in the United States, 1920–1975.* Berkeley: University of California Press, 1989.

Monaco, James. *How to Read a Film: Movies, Media, and Multimedia.* 3rd ed. New York: Oxford University Press, 2000.

Mondimore, Francis Mark. *A Natural History of Homosexuality.* Baltimore: Johns Hopkins University Press, 1996.

Moody, Jocelyn. *Sentimental Confessions: Spiritual Narratives of Nineteenth-Century African American Women.* Athens: University of Georgia Press, 2001.

Moore, R. Laurence. *Selling God: American Religion in the Marketplace of Culture.* New York: Oxford University Press, 1994.

Morris, Aldon D. *The Origins of the Civil Rights Movement: Black Communities Organizing for Change.* New York: Free Press, 1984.

Morrison, Toni. *Playing in the Dark: Whiteness and the Literary Imagination.* New York: Vintage Books, 1993.

Mosse, George L. *Fallen Soldiers: Reshaping the Memory of the World Wars.* New York: Oxford University Press, 1990.

Muir, John Kenneth. *Horror Films of the 1980's*. Jefferson, NC: McFarland, 2007.

Murphy, Kevin, and Dan Studney. "A Brief History of *Reefer Madness*." *Reefer Madness!* Available at http://www.reefermadness.org/writers/authors.html (accessed July 9, 2008).

Myles, Anna G. "Queering the Study of Early American Sexuality." Forum: Reconsidering Early American Sexuality. *William and Mary Quarterly* 60 (January 2003). Available at http://www.historycooperative.org/journals/wm/60/1/forum_wilson.html (accessed July 16, 2008).

Neale, Steve. *Genre and Hollywood*. London: Routledge, 2000.

Nietzsche, Friedrich. *Genealogy of Morals*. Trans. Walter Kaufmann. New York: Random House, 1989.

Ninkovich, Frank. *The United States and Imperialism*. Oxford: Blackwell, 2001.

Noll, Mark. "American Lutherans Yesterday and Today." In *Lutherans Today: American Lutheran Identity in the Twenty-first Century*, ed. Richard Cimino, 3–25. Grand Rapids, MI: Eerdmans, 2003.

——. *The Civil War as a Theological Crisis*. Chapel Hill: University of North Carolina Press, 2006.

——. *The Scandal of the Evangelical Mind*. Grand Rapids, MI: Eerdmans, 1994.

Norling, Lisa. *Captain Ahab Had a Wife: New England Women and the Whalefishery, 1720–1870*. Chapel Hill: University of North Carolina Press, 2000.

Northcott, Michael. *An Angel Directs the Storm: Apocalyptic Religion and American Empire*. London: I. B. Tauris, 2004.

Norton, John. *The Heart of N-England Rent at the Blasphemies of the Present Generation. Or a Brief Tractate Concerning the Doctrine of the Quakers*. Cambridge, MA: Samuel Green, 1659. Swarthmore College, Friends Historical Library.

"Notable Women of America—Mary Barrett Dyer." *Rootsweb*. Available at http://www.rootsweb.ancestry.com/~nwa/dyer.html (accessed December 20, 2007).

Nuechterlein, Donald. *Defiant Superpower: The New American Hegemony*. Washington, DC: Potomac Books, 2004.

Obama, Barack. "Transcript: Sen. Barack Obama Addresses Race at the Constitution Center in Philadelphia." *Washington Post*, March 18, 2008. Available at http://www.washingtonpost.com/wp-dyn/content/article/2008/03/18/AR2008031801081.html.

Oliker, Michael A., and Walter P. Krolikowski, eds. *Images of Youth: Popular Culture as Educational Ideology*. New York: Peter Lang, 2001.

Oliver, Mary Beth, and Meghan Sanders. "The Appeal of Horror and Suspense." In *The Horror Film*, ed. Stephen Prince, 243–59. New Brunswick, NJ: Rutgers University Press, 2004.

Ontario Consultants on Religious Tolerance. "Definitions of the Word 'Religion.'" ReligiousTolerance.org. Available at http://www.religioustolerance.org/rel_defn.htm (accessed June 16, 2007).

——. "Prohibiting Same-Sex Marriages in the U.S.: Federal and State 'DOMA' Legislation." *ReligiousTolerance.org*. Available at http://www.religioustolerance.org/hom_mar6.htm (accessed July 18, 2008).

Orsi, Robert A. *Between Heaven and Earth: The Religious World People Make and the Scholars Who Study Them*. Princeton, NJ: Princeton University Press, 2004.

Pahl, Jon. "America's Sister." *Journal of Lutheran Ethics* 6 (December 2006). Available at http://archive.elca.org/jle/article.asp?k=679 (accessed July 7, 2008).

———, ed. *An American Teacher: Coming-of-Age and Coming-Out, the Memoirs of Loretta Coller*. Conshohocken, PA: Infinity Publishing, 2009.

———. "Converging Paths, Conflicting Destinies: Youth, Christianities, and Nationalism, 1930–the Present." In *A Cultural History of Childhood and the Family in the Modern Age (1900–2000)*, ed. N. Ray Hiner and Joseph M. Hawes. New York: Routledge, forthcoming.

———. "A National Shrine to Scapegoating? The Vietnam Veterans Memorial, Washington, D.C." *Contagion: Journal of Violence, Mimesis, and Culture* 2 (spring 1995):165–88.

———. *Paradox Lost: Free Will and Political Liberty in American Culture, 1630–1760*. Baltimore: John Hopkins University Press, 1992.

———. "Sacrifice." In *The Routledge Companion to Religion and Film*, ed. John Lyden, 465–81. New York: Routledge, 2009.

———. *Shopping Malls and Other Sacred Spaces: Putting God in Place*. Grand Rapids, MI: Brazos Press, 2003.

———. "Violence from Religious Groups." In *An International Handbook of Violence Research*, ed. W. Heitmeyer and J. Hagan, 323–38. Dordecht: Kluwer Academic, 2003.

———. *Youth Ministry in Modern America: 1930 to the Present*. Peabody, MA: Hendrickson Publishers, 2000.

Painter, Nell Irvin. "Malcolm X across the Genres." *American Historical Review* 98 (April 1993):432–39.

———. "Representing Truth: Sojourner Truth's Knowing and Becoming Known." In *This Far by Faith: Readings in African-American Women's Religious Biography*, ed. Judith Weisenfeld and Richard Newman, 287–88. New York: Routledge, 1996.

Parchesky, Jennifer. "Lois Weber's *The Blot*: Rewriting Melodrama, Reproducing the Middle Class." *Cinema Journal* 39 (1999):23.

Paris, Peter J. *The Social Teaching of the Black Churches*. Philadelphia: Fortress Press, 1985.

Patel, Eboo, and Patrice Brodeur, eds. *Building the Interfaith Youth Movement*. Lanham, MD: Rowman & Littlefield, 2006.

Patterson, Orlando. *The Ordeal of Integration: Progress and Resentment in America's "Racial" Crisis*. Washington, DC: Counterpoint, 1997.

———. *Rituals of Blood: Consequences of Slavery in Two American Centuries*. Washington, DC: Civitas/Counterpoint, 1998.

———. *Slavery and Social Death: A Comparative Study*. Cambridge, MA: Harvard University Press, 1982.

PBS. "Helen Prejean Interview." Transcript, April 9, 1996. *Frontline*: "Angel on Death Row." Available at http://www.pbs.org/wgbh/pages/frontline/angel/angelscript.html, (accessed July 23, 2008).

PBS. "Interview: James Lawson." Available at http://www.pbs.org/weta/forcemorepowerful/nashville/interview.html (accessed September 1, 2004).

PBS. "President Bush Defends Decision to Send Additional Troops to Iraq." President George W. Bush interview with Jim Lehrer, January 16, 2007. *The Online News Hour*. Available at http://www.pbs.org/newshour/bb/white_house/jan-june07/bush_01-16.html. (accessed December 15, 2007).

PBS. "Tim Robbins Interview." Transcript, February 8, 1996. *Frontline*: "Angel on Death Row." Available at http://www.pbs.org/wgbh/pages/frontline/angel/walking/timrobbins. html (accessed July 23, 2008).

Perkinson, James W. *White Theology: Outing Supremacy in Modernity*. New York: Palgrave Macmillan, 2004.

Pestana, Carla Gardina. *Quakers and Baptists in Colonial Massachusetts*. Cambridge: Cambridge University Press, 1991.

Petersen, Mark A. *The Price of Redemption: The Spiritual Economy of Puritan New England*. Stanford, CA: Stanford University Press, 1997.

Peterson, Carla L. *Doers of the Word: African American Women Speakers and Writers in the North (1830–1880)*. New York: Oxford University Press, 1995.

Pettegrew, John. *Brutes in Suits: Male Sensibility in America, 1890–1920*. Baltimore: Johns Hopkins University Press, 2007.

Phillips, Kevin P. *American Theocracy: The Peril and Politics of Radical Religion, Oil, and Borrowed Money in the 21st Century*. New York: Viking, 2006.

———. *Wealth and Democracy: A Political History of the American Rich*. New York: Broadway Books, 2002.

Pick, Daniel. *War Machine: The Rationalization of Slaughter in the Modern Age*. New Haven, CT: Yale University Press, 1993.

Pinedo, Isabel Cristina. "Postmodern Elements of the Contemporary Horror Film." In *The Horror Film*, ed. Stephen Prince, 85–117. New Brunswick, NJ: Rutgers University Press, 2004.

———. *Recreational Terror: Women and the Pleasures of Horror Film Viewing*. Albany: State University of New York Press, 1997.

Plimpton, Ruth Talbot. *Mary Dyer: A Biography of a Rebel Quaker*. Boston: Branden, 1994.

Pocock, J. G. A. *The Machiavellian Moment: Florentine Political Thought and the Atlantic Republican Tradition*. Princeton, NJ: Princeton University Press, 1975.

Podhoretz, Norman. *World War IV: The Long Struggle against Islamofascism*. New York: Doubleday, 2007.

Prejean, Sister Helen. *Dead Man Walking*. New York: Vintage Books, 1993.

Prince, Stephen. "Dread, Taboo, and *The Thing*." In *The Horror Film*, ed. Stephen Prince, 118–31. New Brunswick, NJ: Rutgers University Press, 2004.

Purcell, Sarah J. *Sealed with Blood: War, Sacrifice, and Memory in Revolutionary America*. Philadelphia: University of Pennsylvania Press, 2002.

Ranke-Heinemann, Uta. *Eunuchs for the Kingdom of Heaven: Women, Sexuality, and the Catholic Church*. Trans. Peter Heinegg. New York: Doubleday, 1990.

Rath, Richard Cullen. *How Early America Sounded*. Ithaca, NY: Cornell University Press, 2003.

Rauch, Jonathan. "McGod Bless America." *National Journal*, June 26, 1999. Available at http://reason.com/rauch/99_06_26.shtml (accessed July 7, 2008).

Rebel without a Cause. DVD. Directed by Nicholas Ray. 1955; Burbank, CA: Warner Brothers Home Video, 1999.

Reefer Madness: Special Addiction. DVD. Directed by Louis Gasnier. 1936; Beverly Hills, CA: 20th Century Fox Home Entertainment, 2004.

Reis, Elizabeth. *Damned Women: Sinners and Witches in Puritan New England*. Ithaca, NY: Cornell University Press, 1997.

Robertson, Nancy Marie. *Christian Sisterhood, Race Relations, and the YWCA, 1906–1946.* Urbana: University of Illinois Press, 2007.

Ross, Andrew, and Kristin Ross, eds. *Anti-Americanism.* New York: New York University Press, 2004.

Ross, Susan M., ed. *American Families Past and Present: Social Perspectives on Transformations.* New Brunswick, NJ: Rutgers University Press, 2006.

Roth, Eli. *Hostel.* DVD. Hollywood: Lions Gate Films, 2006.

Round, Philip H. *By Nature and by Custom Cursed: Transatlantic Civil Discourse and New England Cultural Production, 1620–1660.* Hanover, NH: University Press of New England, 1999.

Routt, William D. "Lois Weber, or the Exigency of Writing." Part 5, "Lois Weber and the Mirror of Cinema." *Screening the Past.* March 1, 2001. Available at http://www.latrobe.edu.au/screeningthepast/firstrelease/fr0301/wr1fr12a.htm (accessed September 7, 2008).

Rowlandson, Mary. *The Sovereignty and Goodness of God: Together with the Faithfulness of His Promises Displayed: Being a Narrative of the Captivity and Restoration of Mrs. Mary Rowlandson and Related Documents.* Ed. Neal Salisbury. Boston: Bedford Books, 1997 (orig. pub. 1682).

Roy, Arundhati. "The Algebra of Infinite Justice." *The Guardian,* September 29, 2001. Available at http://www.guardian.co.uk/Archive/Article/0,4273,4266289,00.html (accessed July 23, 2008).

———. *War Talk.* Cambridge, MA: South End Press, 2003.

Ruether, Rosemary Radford. *America, Amerikkka: Elect Nation and Imperial Violence.* Oakville, CT: Equinox, 2007.

Runkle, Gerald. "Is Violence Always Wrong?" *Journal of Politics* 38 (1976):367–89.

Ryan, Mary P. "A Women's Awakening: Evangelical Religion and the Families of Utica, New York, 1800–1840." *American Quarterly* 30 (winter 1978):602–23.

Sacks, Jonathan. *The Dignity of Difference: How to Avoid the Clash of Civilizations.* New York: Continuum, 2003.

Salih, Sara. *Judith Butler.* New York: Routledge, 2002.

Salmon, Marylynn. *Women and the Law of Property in Early America.* Chapel Hill: University of North Carolina Press, 1986.

Salter, Richard. "The Birth of a Nation as American Myth." *Journal of Religion and Film* 8 (October 2004), available at http://www.unomaha.edu/jrf/Vol8No2/SalterBirth.htm (accessed June 4, 2009).

Sampson, Cynthia, and John Pahl Lederach, eds. *From the Ground Up: Mennonite Contributions to International Peacebuilding.* New York: Oxford University Press, 2000.

Scarry, Elaine. *The Body in Pain: The Making and Unmaking of the World.* New York: Oxford University Press, 1985.

Schaefer, Hors, and Dieter Baacke. *Leben wie im Kino: Jugendkulturen und Film.* Frankfurt: Fischer Taschenbuch Verlag, 1994.

Scheiner, Georganne. *Signifying Female Adolescence: Film Representations and Fans, 1920–1950.* Westport, CT: Praeger, 2000.

Schell, Jonathan. *The Unconquerable World: Power, Nonviolence, and the Will of the People.* New York: Metropolitan Books, 2003.

Schmidt, Leigh Eric. *Hearing Things: Religion, Illusion, and the American Enlightenment.* Cambridge, MA: Harvard University Press, 2000.

Schmitt, Carl. *Political Theology*. Trans. George Schwab. Cambridge, MA: MIT Press, 1988. Originally published as *Politische Theololgie: Vier Kapital zur Lehre von der Souveranität* (Munich: Duncker und Humblot, 1922).

Schneider, Steven Jay, and Tony Williams, eds. *Horror International*. Detroit: Wayne State University Press, 2005.

Schwartz, Regina. *The Curse of Cain: The Violent Legacy of Monotheism*. Chicago: University of Chicago Press, 1997.

Scream. DVD. Directed by Wes Craven. 1996; Burbank, CA: Walt Disney Video, 1997.

Selengut, Charles. *Sacred Fury: Understanding Religious Violence*. Walnut Creek, CA: Altamira Press, 2003.

Shary, Timothy. *Generation Multiplex: The Image of Youth in Contemporary American Cinema*. Austin: University of Texas Press, 2002.

Shaw Mayo, Lawrence. *John Endecott: A Biography*. Cambridge, MA: Harvard University Press, 1936.

Shiels, Richard. "The Feminization of American Congregationalism, 1730–1835." *American Quarterly* 33 (1981):46–62.

Shils, Edward. *Tradition*. Chicago: University of Chicago Press, 1981.

Simon, John. "Malcolm X." *National Review*, December 18, 1992. Available at http://findarticles.com/p/articles/mi_m1282/is_n25_v44/ai_13367203 (accessed June 4, 2009).

Simpson, Gary M. *War, Peace, and God: Rethinking the Just War Tradition*. Minneapolis: Augsburg Fortress Press, 2007.

Slattery, W. Michael. *Jesus the Warrior? Historical Christian Perspectives and Problems on the Morality of War and the Waging of Peace*. Milwaukee: Marquette University Press, 2007.

Slide, Anthony. *Lois Weber: The Director Who Lost Her Way in History*. New York: Greenwood Press, 1996.

Sloan, Kay. "The Hand That Rocks the Cradle: An Introduction." *Film History* 1 (1987):341.

Slotkin, Richard. *The Fatal Environment: The Myth of the Frontier in the Age of Industrialization, 1800–1890*. New York: Atheneum, 1985.

———. *Gunfighter Nation: The Myth of the Frontier in Twentieth-Century America*. New York: Atheneum, 1992.

———. *Regeneration through Violence: The Mythology of the American Frontier, 1600–1860*. Norman: University of Oklahoma Press, 2000.

Smith, Brian K. "Capital Punishment and Human Sacrifice." *Journal of the American Academy of Religion* 68 (March 2000):3–25.

Smith, Christian L., ed. *The Secular Revolution: Power, Interests, and Conflict in the Secularization of American Public Life*. Berkeley: University of California Press, 2003.

Smith, Frances Foster. *Written by Herself: Literary Production by African American Women, 1746–1892*. Bloomington: Indiana University Press, 1993.

Smith, Jonathan Z. *Imagining Religion: From Babylon to Jonestown*. Chicago: University of Chicago Press, 1988.

———. *Map Is Not Territory: Studies in the History of Religions*. Chicago: University of Chicago Press, 1993.

———. *To Take Place: Toward Theory in Ritual*. Chicago: University of Chicago Press, 1987.

Smith, Merril D., ed. *The Encyclopedia of Rape*. Westport, CT: Greenwood Press, 2004.

Smith, Timothy L. *Revivalism and Social Reform in the Mid-Nineteenth Century*. 2nd ed. Baltimore: Johns Hopkins University Press, 1980.

Smock, David R. "Religious Contributions to Peacemaking: When Religion Brings Peace, Not War." *Peaceworks* 55 (January 2006). Available at http://www.usip.org/pubs/peace-works/pwks55.html (accessed September 10, 2008).

Snay, Mitchell. *Gospel of Disunion: Religion and Separatism in the Antebellum South.* Cambridge: Cambridge University Press, 1993.

Snyder, T. Richard. *The Protestant Ethic and the Spirit of Punishment.* Grand Rapids, MI: Eerdmans, 2001.

Society for the History of Children and Youth. *Journal of the History of Childhood and Youth.* Available at http://www.umass.edu/jhcy/ (accessed July 10, 2008).

Solow, Barbara L., ed. *Slavery and the Rise of the Atlantic System.* Cambridge: Cambridge University Press, 1991.

Sommer, Doris. *Foundational Fictions: The National Romances of Latin America.* Berkeley: University of California Press, 1991.

Soussloff, Catherine M. "Post-Colonial Torture: Rituals of Viewing at Abu Ghraib." In *Ritual and Event: Interdisciplinary Perspectives,* ed. Mark Franko, 159–75. New York: Routledge, 2007.

Speicher, Anna. *The Religious World of Antislavery Women: Spirituality in the Lives of Five Abolitionist Lecturers.* Syracuse, NY: Syracuse University Press, 2000.

Spencer, Robert. *Religion of Peace? Why Christianity Is and Islam Isn't.* Washington, DC: Regnery, 2007.

Sprigg, Peter. *Outrage: How Gay Activists and Liberal Judges are Trashing Democracy to Redefine Marriage.* Washington, DC: Regnery, 2004.

———. "Same-Sex Marriage Is Not a Civil Right." Remarks at a Defend Maryland Marriage rally, January 27, 2005. Family Research Council. Available at http://www.frc.org/get.cfm?i=PD05B01 (accessed June 20, 2007).

Stamets, Bill. "Bloody Deconstruction." *Chicago Reader* (January 1997). Available at http://www.chicagoreader.com/movies/archives/0197/01177a.html (accessed July 9, 2008).

Stearns, Peter N. *Anxious Parents: A History of Modern Childrearing in America.* New York: New York University Press, 2003.

Steelwater, Eliza. *The Hangman's Knot: Lynching, Legal Execution, and America's Struggle with the Death Penalty.* Boulder, CO: Westview Press, 2003.

Stephens, John. "'I'll Never Be the Same after That Summer: From Abjection to Subjective Agency in Teen Films." In *Youth Cultures: Texts, Images, and Identities,* ed. Kerry Mallan and Sharyn Pearce, 123–37. New York: Praeger, 2003.

Stern, Jessica. *Terror in the Name of God: Why Religious Militants Kill.* New York: HarperCollins, 2004.

Stewart, Jeffrey C., ed. *Narrative of Sojourner Truth: A Bondswoman of Olden Time, With a History of Her Labors and Correspondence Drawn from Her "Book of Life."* Schomburg Library of Nineteenth-Century Black Women Writers, gen. ed. Henry Louis Gates. New York: Oxford University Press, 1991.

Stokes, Melvyn . *D. W. Griffith's "The Birth of a Nation": A History of the Most Controversial Motion Picture of All Time.* Oxford: Oxford University Press, 2007.

Stone, Bryan P. "Religion and Violence in Popular Film." *Journal of Religion and Film* 3 (April 1999):1–11. Available at http://www.unomaha.edu/jrf/Violence.htm (accessed September 8, 2008).

Stout, Harry S. *The Divine Dramatist: George Whitefield and the Rise of Modern Evangelism.* Grand Rapids, MI: Eerdmans, 1991.

———. *Upon the Altar of the Nation: A Moral History of the Civil War.* New York: Viking, 2006.

Stout, Jeffrey. *Democracy and Tradition.* Princeton, NJ: Princeton University Press, 2004.

———. *The Flight from Authority: Religion, Morality, and the Quest for Autonomy.* Notre Dame, IN: University of Notre Dame Press, 1981.

Strenski, Ivan. *Contesting Sacrifice: Religion, Nationalism, and Social Thought in France.* Chicago: University of Chicago Press, 2002.

Suchocki, Marjorie Hewitt. *The Fall to Violence: Original Sin in Relational Theology.* New York: Continuum, 1994.

Sullivan, Andrew, and Joseph Landau, eds. *Same-Sex Marriage, Pro and Con: A Reader.* New York: Vintage Books, 2004.

Sullivan, Kathleen L. *Constitutional Context: Women and Rights Discourse in Nineteenth-Century America.* Baltimore: Johns Hopkins University Press, 2007.

Swain, Kathleen M. *Pilgrim's Progress, Puritan Progress: Discourses and Contexts.* Urbana: University of Illinois Press, 1993.

Swidler, Leonard. "Universal Declaration of a Global Ethics." Philadelphia: *Temple University,* Institute for Interreligious, Intercultural Dialogue. Available at http://astro.temple.edu/~dialogue/Center/declarel.htm (accessed September 8, 2008).

Taves, Ann, ed. *Religion and Domestic Violence in Early New England: The Memoirs of Abigail Abbot Bailey.* Bloomington: Indiana University Press, 1988.

Taylor, Gary. *Buying Whiteness: Race, Culture, and Identity from Columbus to Hip-Hop.* New York: Palgrave Macmillan, 2005.

Taylor, Mark C. *Confidence Games: Money and Markets in a World without Redemption.* Chicago: University of Chicago Press, 2004.

Taylor, Mark Lewis. *The Executed God: The Way of the Cross in Lockdown America.* Minneapolis: Fortress Press, 2001.

Thatcher Ulrich, Laurel. *Good Wives: Image and Reality in the Lives of Women in Northern New England, 1650–1750.* New York: Knopf, 1982.

Thomas, George M. *Revivalism and Cultural Change: Christianity, Nation Building, and the Market in the Nineteenth-Century United States.* Chicago: University of Chicago Press, 1989.

Thomas, Hugh. *The Slave Trade: The Story of the Atlantic Slave Trade, 1440–1870.* New York: Simon & Schuster, 1997.

Thompson, Kirsten Moana. *Apocalyptic Dread: American Film at the Turn of the Millennium.* Albany: State University of New York Press, 2008.

Thornton, John Kelly. *Africa and Africans in the Making of the Atlantic World, 1400–1800.* 2nd ed. Cambridge: Cambridge University Press, 1998.

Thurman, Howard. *Jesus and the Disinherited.* Forward by Vincent Harding. Boston: Beacon Press, 1996.

Tolles, Frederick B. *A Quaker's Curse—Humphrey Norton to John Endecott, 1658.* Reprinted from *Huntingdon Library Quarterly* 14, August 1951. San Marino, CA: Henry E. Huntington Library and Art Gallery. Swarthmore College, Friends Historical Library.

Toulouse, Teresa. *The Captive's Position: Female Narrative, Male Identity, and Royal Authority in Colonial New England.* Philadelphia: University of Pennsylvania Press, 2007.

Tudor, Andrew. "Why Horror? The Peculiar Pleasures of a Popular Genre." In *Horror, the Film Reader*, ed. Mark Jancovich, 47–56. New York: Routledge, 2002.

Turner, Graeme, ed. *The Film Cultures Reader*. London: Routledge, 2002.

Tutu, Desmond. *The Rainbow People of God: The Making of a Peaceful Revolution*. New York: Doubleday, 1994.

Tweed, Thomas A. *Crossing and Dwelling: A Theory of Religion*. Cambridge, MA: Harvard University Press, 2006.

Underwood, T. L. *Primitivism, Radicalism, and the Lamb's War: The Baptist-Quaker Conflict in Seventeenth-Century England*. New York: Oxford University Press, 1997.

United Nations. "Universal Declaration of Human Rights." Available at http://www.un.org/Overview/rights.html (accessed January 23, 2008).

United Press International. "Air Force Tests Monster MOAB Bomb." Available at http://www.upi.com/view.cfm?StoryID=20030311-040832-2415r (accessed March 15, 2003).

United States Conference of Catholic Bishops. *Hostel*. Office of Film and Broadcasting. Available at http://www.usccb.org/movies/h/hostel.shtml (accessed July 8, 2008).

———. "Statement on Iraq." November 13, 2002. Available at http://www.usccb.org/bishops/iraq.shtml (accessed September 8, 2008).

Valeri, Mark. "Religious Discipline and the Market: Puritans and the Issue of Usury." *William and Mary Quarterly*, 3rd ser. 54 (October 1997):747–68.

Van Broekhoeven, Deborah Bingham. *Devotion of These Women: Rhode Island in the Antislavery Network*. Amherst: University of Massachusetts Press, 2002.

Van Deburg, William L. "Frederick Douglass and the Institutional Church." *Journal of the American Academy of Religion* 14 (June 1977):515–37.

Vaughan, Alden T., and Edward W. Clark, eds. *Puritans among the Indians: Accounts of Captivity and Redemption, 1676–1724*. Cambridge, MA: Harvard University Press, 1981.

Voegelin, Eric. *Die Politischen Religionen*. Stockholm: Berman-Fischer Verlag, 1939.

Volf, Miroslav. *Exclusion and Embrace: A Theological Exploration of Identity, Otherness, and Reconciliation*. Nashville: Abingdon Press, 1996.

Waldman, Steven. *Founding Faith: Providence, Politics, and Religious Freedom in America*. New York: Random House, 2008.

Wallace, Mark I. *Finding God in the Singing River: Christianity, Spirit, Nature*. Minneapolis: Fortress Press, 2006.

Wallis, Jim. *God's Politics: Why the Right Gets It Wrong and the Left Doesn't Get It*. San Francisco: Harper San Francisco, 2005.

———. *The Soul of Politics: A Practical and Prophetic Vision for Change*. New York: Orbis Books, 1994.

———. *Valiant for Peace: A History of the Fellowship of Reconciliation, 1914–1989*. London: Fellowship of Reconciliation, 1991.

Walmsley, Roy. "World Prison Population List." Asian & Pacific Conference of Correctional Admin. Available at http://www.apcca.org/stats/7th%20Edition%20(2007).pdf (accessed July 9, 2008).

Watkins, S. Craig. *Representing: Hip Hop Culture and the Production of Black Cinema*. Chicago: University of Chicago Press, 1998.

Weaver, James B., III, and Ron Tamborini, eds. *Horror Films: Current Research on Audience Preferences and Reactions*. Mahwah, NJ: Erlbaum, 1996.

Webel, Charles, and Johan Galtung, eds. *Handbook of Peace and Conflict Studies*. London: Routledge, 2007.

Weber, Max. *The Protestant Ethic and the Spirit of Capitalism*. Trans. Talcott Parsons. New York: Scribner, 1958.

Weisenfeld, Judith. *African American Women and Christian Activism: New York's Black YWCA, 1905–1945*. Cambridge, MA: Harvard University Press, 1997.

———. "'For the Cause of Mankind': The Bible, Racial Uplift, and Early Race Moves." In *African Americans and the Bible: Sacred Texts and Social Textures*, ed. Vincent L. Wimbush, 728–42. New York: Continuum, 2000.

Weitz, Eric D. *A Century of Genocide: Utopias of Race and Nation*. Princeton, NJ: Princeton University Press, 2003.

———. *In God's Name: Genocide and Religion in the 20th Century*. New York: Berghahn Books, 2001.

Wellman, James, Jr. *Belief and Bloodshed: Religion and Violence across Time and Tradition*. Lanham, MD: Rowman & Littlefield, 2007.

Wentz, Richard E. *American Religious Traditions: The Shaping of Religion in the United States*. Minneapolis: Fortress Press, 2003.

West, Cornel. *Prophesy Deliverance! An Afro-American Revolutionary Christianity*. 20th Anniversary ed. Louisville: Westminster/John Knox, 2002.

———. *Race Matters*. 1st ed. New York: Vintage Books, 1993.

———. *Race Matters*. 2nd ed. Boston: Beacon Press, 2001.

Westboro Baptist Church. "All Nations Must Immediately Outlaw Sodomy (Homosexuality) and Impose the Death Penalty." Available at http://www.godhatesfags.com/written/fliers/archive/20021203_outlaw-sodomy.pdf (accessed July 18, 2008).

———. "The Meaning of God Hates Fags." Available at http://www.godhatesfags.com/written/wbcinfo/godhatesfags.html (accessed April 6, 2008).

Westerkamp, Marilyn J. *Women and Religion in Early America, 1600–1850*. New York: Routledge, 1999.

Widmer, Ted. *Ark of the Liberties: America and the World*. New York: Hill & Wang, 2008.

Williams, Juan, and Quinton Dixie. *This Far by Faith: Stories from the African American Religious Experience*. New York: Amistad (HarperCollins), 2003.

Williams, Linda. "When the Woman Looks" In *The Dread of Difference: Gender and the Horror Film*, ed. Barry K. Grant, 15–34. Austin: University of Texas Press, 1996.

Williams, Peter. *Popular Religion in America: Symbolic Change and the Modernization Process*. Rev. ed. Urbana: University of Illinois Press, 1989.

Williamson, Scott C. *The Narrative Life: The Moral and Religious Thought of Frederick Douglass*. Macon, GA: Mercer University Press, 2002.

Wills, Garry. *Reagan's America: Innocents at Home*. Garden City, NY: Doubleday, 1987.

Wilson, John F. *Public Religion in American Culture*. Philadelphia: Temple University Press, 1979.

———, and Donald L. Drakeman, eds. *Church and State in American History: Key Documents, Decisions, and Community from the Past Three Centuries*. Boulder, CO: Westview Press, 2003.

Wilson, Lisa. *Ye Heart of a Man: The Domestic Life of Men in Colonial New England*. New Haven, CT: Yale University Press, 1999.

Wilson, Michael L. "Thoughts on the History of Sexuality." Forum: Reconsidering Early American Sexuality. *William and Mary Quarterly* 60 (January 2003). Available at http://www.historycooperative.org/journals/wm/60/1/forum_wilson.html (accessed July 16, 2008).

Wink, Walter. *Engaging the Powers: Discernment and Resistance in a World of Domination.* Minneapolis: Fortress Press, 1992.

———. *Jesus and Nonviolence: A Third Way.* Minneapolis: Fortress Press, 2003.

———, ed. *Peace Is the Way: Writings on Nonviolence from the Fellowship of Reconciliation.* Maryknoll, NY: Orbis Books, 2000.

Winter, Thomas. *Making Men, Making Class: The YMCA and Workingmen, 1877–1920.* Chicago: University of Chicago Press, 2002.

Winthrop, John. "A Modell of Christian Charity." 1630. Hanover College Historical Texts Project. Available at http://history.hanover.edu/texts/winthmod.html (accessed July 23, 2008).

Witherspoon, Alexander M. Preface to *The Pilgrim's Progress*, by John Bunyan. New York: Pocket Books, 1957.

Wolfe, Alan. "A Coming Religious Peace." *Atlantic Monthly*, March 2008. Available at http://www.theatlantic.com/doc/200803/secularism (accessed September 7, 2008).

Wood, Gordon S. "Conspiracy and the Paranoid Style: Causality and Deceit in the Eighteenth Century." *William and Mary Quarterly,* 3rd ser., 39 (1982):401–41.

Worland, Rick. *The Horror Film: An Introduction.* Malden, MA: Blackwell, 2007.

Worral, Arthur J. *Quakers in the Colonial Northeast.* Hanover, NH: University Press of New England, 1980.

Wuthnow, Robert. "Between the State and Market: Voluntarism and the Difference It Makes." In *Rights and the Common Good: The Communitarian Perspective*, ed. Amitai Etzioni, 209–24. New York: St. Martin's Press, 1995.

———. *The Restructuring of American Religion: Society and Faith since World War II.* Princeton, NJ: Princeton University Press, 1988.

Yarple, Ted. *Christian Faith in a Violent World: Study Guide.* Cincinnati: Friendship Press, 1997.

Young, J. R. "Dr. Terror Stalks Hollywood." *Chic Magazine*, August 1979. Available at http://www.theofficialjohncarpenter.com/pages/press/chico879.html (accessed July 7, 2008).

Zuckerman, Marvin. *Behavioral Expressions and Biosocial Bases of Sensation Seeking.* Cambridge: Cambridge University Press, 1994.

Index

Abjection, 10, 37; in film, 39; of youth, 46-47, 61
Abu Ghraib, 2, 170
Adams, Abigail, 103, 107
Adolescence. *See* Youth
Afghanistan, 2, 168
African Americans, 74, 134, 167. *See also* Race; Slavery; Whiteness
African Methodist Episcopal Zion Church, 76
Age: as category of historical analysis, 10, 47, 186n19; and religion, 38
Agency, 138, 202n8; and African Americans, 65, 96; for Frederick Douglass, 79-80; and gender, 104-5, 119, 121-22, 124; of youth, 45
Albanese, Catherine, 4
Allen, Richard, 87
America: as empire, 9, 55, 142, 162-63, 174, 178n17, 179n21; and exceptionalism, 172; and hybrid religions in, 4, 91, 108, 167; as inclusive, 93, 98, 101; and innocence, 5-6, 170; and slavery, 83-84. *See also* Empire; Nationalism; Religion(s), civil; State
Americans, Native, 13-15, 65, 103, 180n2
Anderson, Benedict, 13, 141
Andrews, William L., 83
Appleby, R. Scott, 9, 29-30, 48, 143-44
Arendt, Hannah, 59
Armstrong, Rev. George D., 72-75, 77, 99
Asad, Talal, 1-2, 18
Asceticism, ecstatic, 3, 11, 48, 52, 71, 133-34, 143-44, 158, 162; in Abigail Abbot Bailey, 123; in Bunyan, 147; defined, 29-30; and drug use, 56; worldly, 66. *See also* Violence, religious
Atwood, Margaret, 11, 108

Augustine, Saint, 28, 143
Austin, Anne, 152
Authority, 9, 21, 48, 125; across sectors of society, 28, 54, 64, 142, 145, 164, 174; and gender, 106; and innocence, 55, 175; secular, 36; and transcendence, 19, 74-75, 82, 91, 104-5, 138. *See also* Transcendence

Bacchae, The, 133
Bailey, Abigail Abbot, 11, 104-8, 167
Baldwin, James, 63
Baptism, 91, 115, 165
Bassard, Katherine Clay, 87-88
Bataille, Georges, 47
Besse, Joseph, 152, 156
Bercovitch, Sacvan, 162
Bible, Holy, 72, 113-14, 132. *See also* Discourses, religious
Birth of a Nation, The (film), 68, 90-93
Birth of a Race, The (film), 92-93
Blackstone Sir William, 111
Body, human, 66, 69, 84-85, 88, 116; integrity of, 96
Brekus, Catherine, 106, 111
Bruckner, Pascal, 170
Bunyan, John, 145-50, 172
Bush, George W., 44, 58, 167, 170-73
Butler, Jon, 3, 64

Catharsis, 6, 60
Capitalism, 1
Carrasco, Davìd, 144-45, 159
Chicago, University of, 13
Children. *See* Youth
Christ. *See* Jesus

Christianity, 8, 14-15, 162, 168; and slavery, 65, 68-75, 88-89. *See also* Tradition(s), religious

Chu, Jonathan, 159-60

Church and State, 28, 32, 72-73; blurring of, 35, 104, 136-37, 165; separation of, 111, 142-43, 175. *See also* Nationalism; Religion(s), civil; State

Civil Rights Movement, 68, 94-96

Clinton, Bill, 135

Compression (religious process). *See* Condensation

Condensation, 54, 146; and age, 37-8; and empire, 138, 166; in *Handmaid's Tale*, 131; in *Hostel*, 44-45; in *Rebel without a Cause*, 41; and race, 68, 77-85 as religious process, 6, 19-22; 25,135. *See also* Displacement; Religion(s)

Conflict. *See* Violence.

Considine, David, 36

Constitution, U.S., 84

Conversion: and Abigail Abbot Bailey, 106, 110, 113; of Jarena Lee, 86-87; and Sojourner Truth, 88

Cott, Nancy F., 104, 112

Craven, Wes, 42-43, 47, 50

Creed, Barbara, 39

Crime, 16, 97, 109. *See also* Violence

Curse(s). *See* Discourses, religious

Dead Man Walking (film), 163-66

Death, 63, 133, 141, 157, 164; in Bunyan, 147-49. *See also* Punishment, capital; Sacrifice

Defense of Marriage Acts (DOMA), 10-11, 104, 108, 127, 134-38

Democracy, 68, 94.

Denton-Borhaug, Kelly, 172

Desire, 6, 10, 19-22, 128; and displacement, 40, 88, 138; and drug use, 56; and gender, 131; for God, 119; mimetic, 28-29, 143, 151-54, 158; in Quakers, 154; as rhetoric, 118; for self-determination, 96-97; sexual, 42, 103-4, 108, 112, 132; and vengeance, 156; among youth, 37-46, 53-54, 57. *See also* Girard, René; Pleasure

Destiny, manifest. *See* Manifest destiny; Millennialism

Differentiation, crisis of, 11, 28, 48-50, 104, 130, 143, 151-54, 158. *See also* Girard, René

Discourses, religious, 3, 16, 129, 166; related to violence, 66, 77-79, 82, 154-56, 174, 197n67; and Scripture, 110; and silence, 119-120, 152; and transcendence, 19. *See also* Bible, Holy; Metaphor; Prayer(s); Symbols

Displacement, 6, 19-22, 143; and age, 37-38; and art, 146; in Bunyan, 147; in film, 40, 45, 48-49, 52; and race, 66, 68; as religious process, 32, 60, 130, 141-42; and slavery, 77-85, 99. *See also* Condensation; Religion(s); Sacrifice

Dobson, James, 135

Doherty, Thomas, 38

DOMA laws. *See* Defense of Marriage Acts

Domination, innocent: in Calvinism, 121, 153-54, 160; definition of, 2-4, 173; and gender, 106, 117, 204n20; and race, 63, 94, 96; and religion, 166, 172, 175-76; scholarly identity in, 14; and youth, 37-38, 52, 61. *See also* Innocence; Violence

Douglass, Frederick, 10, 64, 66-67, 75-85

Drugs, War on: 10, 56-57, 167, 190n88

Dualism, 3, 5; for Appleby, 29-30; in Abigail Abbot Bailey, 123; and innocent domination, 68, 100; in slavery, 72, 74, 93

Dyer, Mary, 11, 153, 156-57, 163, 167

Economics. *See* Market(s)

Ecstatic Asceticism. *See* Asceticism, ecstatic

Eliade, Mircea, 23-24

Elimination: as religious function, 20-23. *See also* Condensation; Displacement; Sacrifice

Empire: Aztec, 144-45; defined, 8-9; and film, 53; and gender, 127; and innocent domination, 47, 145-46; and race, 94, 134. *See also* America, as empire; Nationalism; Religion(s), civil

Endecott, John, 154

About the Author

JON PAHL is a professor of the history of Christianity in North America at the Lutheran Theological Seminary at Philadelphia. He is the cochair of the Religions, Social Conflict, and Peace Group of the American Academy of Religion and the author of several books, including *Shopping Malls and Other Sacred Spaces: Putting God in Place* and *Youth Ministry in Modern America: 1930–the Present.*